The Saturated Self

THE
SATURATED
SELF

*Dilemmas of Identity in
Contemporary Life*

KENNETH J. GERGEN

BasicBooks
A Division of HarperCollins*Publishers*

Library of Congress Cataloging-in-Publication Data
Gergen, Kenneth J.
    The saturated self : dilemmas of identity in contemporary life
/ Kenneth J. Gergen.
        p.   cm.
    Includes bibliographical references (p. 260) and index.
    ISBN 0-465-07186-4
    1. Self.   2. Identity (Psychology).   3. Self—Social as-
pects.   4. Identity (Psychology)—Social aspects.   5. Civiliza-
tion—20th century—Psychological aspects.   6. Pluralism
(Social sciences)—Psychological aspects.   7. Postmodernism—
Psychological aspects.
I. Title.
BF697.G39   1991
155.2—dc20   90-55597
                                                         CIP

TO

Mone Albareda · Barcelona
Judy and Larry Anastasi · Swarthmore
Patti and David Auerbach · Swarthmore
Ellen Barry and Mike Florio · San Francisco
Uschi and Peter Becker · Kirchheim-Bolanden
Fatima Cavalcante and Annibal Amorim · Rio de Janeiro
Peter Burch · Paris
Pru Churchill and Larry Plummer · Rose Valley
Lynne and Merrell Clark · Scarsdale
John Clement · Wallingford
Deborah Curtiss · Philadelphia
Gregory Fullerton · Bloomington
Harry Galifianakis · Wilkesboro
Michael Gebhart · Chester
Stephanie Goddard · Atlanta
Donna and Don Gorton · Yardley
Jane and Alan Grove · Minneapolis
Justine Gudenas · Philadelphia
Barbara and Gus Kellogg · Wilton
Marie Colette Kerstens van Spaendonck · Poppel
Sally and Steve Lisle · Minneapolis
Erika and Joe Littera · Santa Barbara
Hilde and Hans Luijten · Alphen
Brigitte, Ulrike, and Gunter Mayer · Pforzheim
Renate and David Mitchell · Sydney
Nancy Nichols · Seattle
Margit Oswald · Vienna
Bernie Reilly · Wallingford
Jan and John Reker · Winter Park
Zachary Sacks · Los Angeles
Mary and Arthur Schneider · Paris
Nadine Servais · Toulon
Franca and Carlo Severati · Rome
Margret Skitarelic · Ardmore
Sally and Norman Smith · Swarthmore
Julia Welbon · Wallingford

AND OTHERS WHO HAVE BECKONED FROM BEYOND THE TOWER

Contents

Preface

Each time the query is put forward, I pause and ponder. The question is simple enough, asked by neighbors, relatives, friends, my children, and even passing strangers—"What are you working on?" They rightly expect a clearly phrased reply. Yet invariably I falter: How can I extract from the argot of my academic guild a stunning bit of news or an insight of rippling profundity? How can I introduce into a casual conversation those lengthy lines of argument that inject the adrenaline into a given idea? And how is my sense of fascination to be transported to the disparate worlds of the attorney, the hairdresser, the surgeon, the sales manager, the engineer, the artist, the rock music enthusiast?

I began this book in an attempt to bridge these many domains. My hope was to offer insight into current academic debates to those outside the tower. There are good reasons for doing so. The academic world is now in a state of immense and far-reaching ferment. Virtually all the assumptions guiding both reason and research over the past century are coming under sharp question. Many nonacademic readers are aware of the debates over the canons of Western literature now engulfing the academic community, and the increasing currency of such terms as *deconstruction, poststructuralism,* and *postmodern.* Yet these are meager indications of the radical reconsideration of our longstanding traditions of truth and knowledge. As beliefs in objective knowledge fall into disrepute, the entire face of education, science, and "knowledge-making" in general stands to be altered. The issues are far too important, and too much fun, to be contained within the walls of academia.

One aspect of this ferment is of special concern to me. For many years one of my central interests has been the concept of self, our ways of understanding who we are and what we are about. Beliefs about the self seem pivotal to all our undertakings. We believe that as normal human beings we possess reasoning powers, emotions, conscience, intentions; these beliefs are critical to the way we relate to others. What could marriage mean if we did not feel ourselves capable of love? What would be the purpose of education if we had no concept of reason or memory? How could we trust others if we didn't believe in the power of conscience?

It is apparent that the general upheaval within the academic sphere contains profound implications for conceptions of the self. Traditional assumptions about the nature of identity are now in jeopardy. It is not simply that the present turn of events has altered the emphasis placed on rationality, the emotions, and the like, or that it adds new concepts to the traditional vernacular. Rather, like the concepts of truth, objectivity, and knowledge, the very idea of individual selves—in possession of mental qualities—is now threatened with eradication. The implications of this outcome for our lives together are both unsettling and stimulating, and deserve broad discussion.

Yet as I began the process of "speaking outward," my work began to shift direction. To bridge the gap between the academic world and the broader public requires some sensitivity to the experiences and conditions relevant to this audience. As I began to focus on the more general state of affairs, I was struck by the realization that the contemporary upheaval in the academic world is paralleled by major shifts in contemporary ways of acting and relating. Increasingly, people are living through the "dissolution of self" discussed within the academy—and experiencing directly the shocks of dislocation, the dilemmas of identity, and the thrills of newly opened vistas. I began to realize that what was needed was not a monologue—my voice making contemporary academic debates intelligible to a broader audience—but a dialogue. Those in the hurly-burly of daily life required voice, for an articulation of their experiences could enrich and edify academic debate. I hope, then, to provide some common ground for mutual exploration and enlightenment.

If the turmoil of the academic sphere coincides with a transformation in our daily experiences with self and others, a further question presents itself: Why is this so? To be sure, the fierce debate in the academic sphere is a "social indicator," pointing out the more general conditions of social life. But what explains the simultaneous upheaval within the two spheres? Why here, and why now? As I examined my own life, the experiences of those close to me, and commentaries on recent social history, one answer stood out: technological change. The technological achievements of the past century have produced a radical shift in our exposure to each other. As a result of advances in radio, telephone, transportation, television, satellite transmission, computers, and more, we are exposed to an enormous barrage of social stimulation. Small and enduring communities, with a limited cast of significant others, are being replaced by a vast and ever-expanding array of relationships.

As I hope to demonstrate, this massive increment in social stimulation—moving toward a state of saturation—sets the stage both for radical changes in our daily experiences of self and others and for an unbridled relativism within the academic sphere. Beliefs in the true and the good depend on a reliable and homogeneous group of supporters, who define what is reliably "there," plain and simple. With social saturation, the coherent circles of accord are demolished, and all beliefs thrown into question by one's exposure to multiple points of view. This is no less true in academic matters of truth and objectivity than in our daily experiences of self.

I make extensive use of the term *postmodern* in this book, as a way of defining the current conditions both within and outside the academic sphere. However, I'm not altogether happy with the term, which is also in broad currency within literary, architectural, artistic, political, and philosophical circles, and which has recently been carried over into pop culture. In part because the term fails to specify an essence (defining itself merely as "post"), its use has been multiplicitous and highly variable. And as a colleague has warned, the term is becoming so faddish that the "lounge lizards will soon move on." Still, there seems to be a corpus of coherently related ideas and images surrounding the use of the term in many of these contexts, and it would be a mistake to let the term slip away before examining its fuller significance. In effect, I argue that what is generally characterized as the postmodern condition within the culture is largely a by-product of the century's technologies of social saturation.

I am also uneasy speaking of "periods" or "phases" of history, or of cultural conditions in general. It is customary to write in these terms, but there is nothing that is written about periods, places, or cultures that cannot be discredited. One can always find strong emanations of the past in what is "new." In modern literature or art, for example, one can locate evidence of romanticism or medievalism. And within every stasis, one may discern evidence of the new and novel. For the author of Ecclesiastes, "there is nothing new under the sun"; in the eyes of a Zen priest, one may find infinite novelty in a single petal. Further, there are always individuals or events that don't fit the proposed patterns. By present standards of interpretation, Vico, Nietzsche, Bakhtin, or the dadaists seem peculiarly out of place for their times. And for each individual who does fit the patterns of a period, we can always locate evidence to contradict the placement. For every rational personality there are seasons of indiscretion, and for every profligate, periods of caution.

Such inconsistencies in period and personal lives militate against any possibility of making "accurate generalizations" about our past or present. Thus, it is most appropriate to view this book not as a picture of the world, but as a form of lens, a way of seeing things. Its value will thus depend on its intelligibility, what its particular juxtapositions and jostlings provoke in the way of insight into self and social life, and how it resonates with or challenges the imagination.

The size of this book could have been tripled with ease. Examples, elaborations, extensions, and caveats all cry out for additional space. (Once the lens is in place the entire world seems clarified and elucidated.) Yet it is one of the unfortunate implications of my thesis that indeed, the population of those willing to read at length is rapidly dwindling; to go on too long would thus be to lose the very readers with whom the volume is most centrally concerned. My hope is thus that many readers will find delight in letting the thesis ramify across the range of their own experience, and in locating personalized particulars of relevance. For those wishing to follow out various lines of argument in greater detail, numerous references will be found in the notes.

In structuring the material for this book, three different ideas have played a central role. First, I have tried to construct each chapter more or less as an essay unto itself, hoping to give the reader a sense of coherent completion at each chapter's end. Thus, someone interested in critical aspects of personal and social life today could fasten on certain chapters, while readers curious about intellectual ferment in the universities, or the historical background of these issues, might focus on others. At the same time, each chapter should stand in a resonant relationship with the others. The major thesis of each chapter should ideally gain in intelligibility, dimension, and implications when read in light of its companions.

Finally, there is the story of the whole, an unfolding logic such that the early chapters set the stage for those that follow. There is a mounting tension in the mix. To many readers I fear my story will seem like a journey into hell, as succeeding chapters cast one aspect of the Western sensibility after another into the void. However, the careful reader will also locate a more optimistic subtext, and thus, the concluding arguments can press beyond the abyss of despair. The final view is one of guarded, but excited, optimism. To be sure, there are justifiable moments of lament. As an author I do not approach these materials with but one sentiment (which is indeed a focal topic within the volume itself). As I hope to demonstrate, however, there is little hope that the past can be recovered. Our best option, then, is to play out the positive potentials of this postmodern erasure of the self.

I dedicate this book to a number of friends, playmates, and longtime associates who are part of much that I do, but whose presence there is seldom acknowledged in my professional life. Without their curiosity the book would not have been written. In many respects this is an "authorless text." My arguments grow from the soil of longstanding debates and inquiries, volumes stretching across centuries, and exchanges with many students and colleagues over the years. Credit for authorship must also extend to the numerous friends and acquaintances who have shared aspects of their postmodern life styles with me, most especially Diana Whitney, of Taos and Philadelphia, and Susan Huber, from the European Community. Without this generative context, these pages would have been filled with much less life. I also owe a special debt to my old friend, colleague, and sometime mentor, David Riesman, for he more than anyone else has demonstrated the possibility of provoking dialogue beyond the academic sphere. Certain individuals have also been of enormous help in furnishing detailed criticisms of the work. Margaret Stroebe and Barnett Pearce deserve my deepest gratitude. Richard Eldridge, Emil Walter, and Efrat Tseelon have graciously enriched particular sections of the book. Stimulating commentary and useful information have also been provided by Jerome Bruner, Esther Cohen-Doran, Laura and Stan Gergen, Jeffrey Goldstein, Justine Gudenas, Aubeigne Gergen Hickson, Bill Hollis, Gudmund Iversen, Sheila McNamee, and John Shotter. Regine Walter has invited a useful dialogue between the volume and the visual media. For their much-needed support at various stages of the book's development I am grateful to Didi Beebe, Stephanie Dudek, Anne and David Gergen, Gunhild Hagestad, Linda Harris, T. George Harris, Roberta Iversen, Hanna and Arie Kruglanski, Anne Marie and John Rijsman, Wojciech Sadurski, Alan Siegler, and Wolfgang Stroebe. I am much indebted as well to Dirk van de Kaa and the Netherlands Institute for Advanced Study, to James England and the Eugene Lang Fellowship Committee at Swarthmore College, and to Carl Graumann and Norbert Groeben at the University of Heidelberg for furnishing time and circumstance to write without teaching duties. For their valuable input into the manuscript, from initial conception to final editing, I owe much to the

Basic Books crew, especially Judy Greissman, JoAnn Miller, David Frederickson, and Jen Fleissner. Lisa Gebhart, Ann Simpson, and Joanne Bromley have devoted many patient hours to producing the manuscript, and Bill Martin and Joe Gangemi have also furnished invaluable assistance. Throughout, Mary Gergen has been a continuous source of inspiration and support, more than anyone else foreshadowing the shift from self to relatedness.

ONE

The Self Under Siege

I had just returned to Swarthmore from a two-day conference in Washington, which had brought together fifty scholars from around the country. An urgent fax from Spain lay on the desk, asking about a paper I was months late in contributing to a conference in Barcelona. Before I could think about answering, the office hours I had postponed began. One of my favorite students arrived and began to quiz me about the ethnic biases in my course syllabus. My secretary came in holding a sheaf of telephone messages, and some accumulated mail, including an IRS notice of a tax audit and a cancellation notice from the telephone company. My conversations with my students were later interrupted by phone calls from a London publisher, a colleague in Connecticut on her way to Oslo for the weekend, and an old California friend wondering if we might meet during his summer travels to Holland. By the morning's end I was drained. The hours had been wholly consumed by the process of relating—face to face, electronically, and by letter. The relations were scattered across Europe and America, and scattered points in my personal past. And so keen was the competition for "relational time" that virtually none of the interchanges seemed effective in the ways I wished.

I turned my attention optimistically to the afternoon. Perhaps here I would find moments of seclusion, restoration, and recentering. No such luck. There were not only two afternoon classes, one rescheduled from the time spent in D.C., but more calls, an electronic-mail dispatch, more students, and a colleague visiting the campus from Chicago. At day's end, should I by chance feel understimulated, my car radio and the cassette deck awaited the homeward drive. Arriving at home I noticed that the grass was overgrown and the house trim badly needed painting. No time for such matters, as there was also the day's mail, newspapers, and my family eagerly waiting to talk about what they had been doing. There would be messages on the answering machine, additional calls from friends, and the television beckoning with twenty-six channels of escape. But how could I afford to escape with so many unfilled obligations for research papers, letters, and course preparations? In effect, I was immersed in and consumed by social connection, and the results were numbing.

Perhaps teachers are more socially engaged than most people; communication is, after all, central to teaching and research. However, my state of social immersion is hardly unique; in fact, compared to many business and professional people, scholars are fairly insulated. The signs of global immersion are everywhere:

- A call to a Philadelphia lawyer is answered by a message recorded in three languages.
- A business acquaintance complains that his weekly tennis group expanded several years ago from four to six persons because everyone in the group was so often traveling. This year they are adding a seventh.
- I gave a short speech at a birthday party in Heidelberg last year. When I returned to the United States three days later, a friend on the opposite coast called to tell me about the guests' reactions to the talk. He had gotten the gossip two days earlier via electronic mail.
- A newsstand near me offers no less than twenty-five different magazines on computers, word processing, and desktop publishing.
- Over 20 million vacationers from around the globe now visit Disney World each year. (London's *Independent* predicts that by the year 2000 tourism will be the largest industry in the world.)[1]
- A *USA Today* headline, "If you wonder where in the world to eat . . .", is followed by detailed descriptions of top restaurants in seven countries from Europe to Asia.

Lest we forget, not one of these observations could have been made even ten years ago.

I grew up in a small North Carolina town. Except for the junior-class trip to Washington in 1952, most of my high-school classmates had never set foot across the state line. Even Chapel Hill seemed mysterious and exotic if you lived fifteen long miles away in Durham. Letters were special events in most families I knew; family members might be drawn together for a reading of the precious lines. Long-distance phone calls were so rare that people would talk about them for weeks. Visitors from outside the state acquired the status of virtual royalty; visitors from abroad were almost nonexistent. The local newspaper and the three available radio stations concentrated heavily on local events—farm prices, state politics, the joys and sorrows of the Durham Bulls. If we had one important tie beyond the community, it was to Dixie, land of the proud rebellion, aristocratic gentility, and human letters, our cultural past. The problem was not how to keep up with an incessant parade of passing voices, but rather how to sustain a valued heritage.

Yet even this tranquil existence seems chaotic if we turn the calendar back a few more decades. Recently I spoke with a neighbor who had just celebrated her hundredth birthday. She talked about her childhood, and the joys of a life based on a limited and unchanging set of relationships. As a child she knew virtually everyone she saw each day. Most relationships were carried out face to face, with visits to friends made on foot or by carriage. Calling cards were essential to signal one's intention for connection. She remembered her thrill when her father announced to the family that an apparatus called the telephone would soon be installed—now they would be able to talk to neighbors three blocks away without leaving the house.

The contrast to my typical day at work makes clear that I am the victim (or benefactor) of profound changes that have been taking place throughout the twentieth century. New technologies make it possible to sustain relationships—either directly or indirectly—with an ever-expanding range of other persons. In many respects we are reaching what may be viewed as a state of social saturation.

Changes of this magnitude are seldom self-contained. They reverberate throughout the culture, slowly accumulating until one day we are shocked to realize that we've been dislocated—and can't recover what has been lost. Although some of these effects are directly disruptive, my chief quarry in this book is more subtle and elusive. Specifically, I wish to explore the impact of social saturation on our ways of conceptualizing the human self and related patterns of social life. Our vocabulary of self-understanding has changed markedly over the past century, and with it the character of social interchange. With the intensifying saturation of the culture, however, all our previous assumptions about the self are jeopardized; traditional patterns of relationship turn strange. A new culture is in the making.

CHANGING CONCEPTS OF THE SELF

[Concepts of the self] operate in the individual and in the society as functional realities *which play a key part in helping to fix the bounds of that very human nature of which they are supposed to be a model.*
—David Bohm, *Human Nature as the Product of Our Mental Models*

What is it about our characterizations of self—the ways in which we make ourselves intelligible to each other—that is so critical to our lives? What makes changes in these characterizations important subjects of concern? Consider:

It is a pivotal moment in their relationship. They have enjoyed each other's company for months, but have never spoken of their emotions. She now feels a strong need for self-expression and for clarification of his feelings. But what is she to say? Her vocabulary of self-expression is large enough. For example, she might demurely admit that she is "attracted," "stimulated," "fascinated," or "intrigued." More boldly, she could say she is "infatuated" or "falling in love," or, more riskily, that she is "intoxicated" or "madly passionate." Such terms as "soul," "need," "want," and "lust" are also on the tip of her tongue. But how should she choose at this delicate moment?

The question is all the more important because the fate of the relationship stands in the balance. Each term of self-revelation has different implications for the future. To admit "attraction" is somewhat reserved; it suggests distance and judgments to be made. To say "stimulated" implies a more cerebral future. The terms "fascinated" and "intrigued" are comparatively dynamic, but still not very sensual. In contrast, to say she is "in love" could suggest that she is slightly irrational or out of control. It is also an expression of emotional dependency; to add "passionately so" might drive the man away. Perhaps he only wanted a good time. The terms "soul" and "lust" could carry the relationship in still different directions. Her expressions of self cannot be separated from their social consequences.

In English, we have a sizable vocabulary of emotional expression; but what if various terms were abandoned? What if "in love" were unavailable? If one hopes to move toward a deep and committed relationship, the expression "in love" is very useful. It paints a picture of a significant future, and invites the other to take part. To say that one is "attracted" or "stimulated" or "feeling turned on" simply does not accomplish the same end. In effect, "in love" can achieve a form of relationship not easily available to its competitors. Similarly, the alternative expressions can achieve other ends—such as maintaining distance, or restricting the relationship to the physical level—that "in love" cannot. To abandon any of these terms means to lose latitude of action in social life.

By the same token, if we expand the vocabulary of self-expression, new options for relationships become possible. For example, there is currently no emotional term available in English sufficient for establishing a relationship of periodic passion. If a couple wishes to see each other now and then, but they desire for these occasions to be "deeply moving," they have no easy options for self-expression. The terms "attraction," "stimulation," and the like do not describe a deeply moving interchange. And to say that one is "in love" does not permit periodic absences to pass with indifference. As the vocabulary of self-expression is expanded, so is the potential repertoire of relationships.

The Cambridge philosopher Ludwig Wittgenstein once wrote that "the limits of language . . . mean the limits of my world."[2] This insight carries special validity for the language of the self. The terms available for making our personalities intelligible—terms of emotion, motivation, thought, values, opinions, and the like—place important constraints over our forms of action. A romantic relationship is only one of an enormous array of instances in which our vocabulary of self insinuates itself into social life. Consider our courts of law. If we did not believe that people possessed "intentions," most of our legal procedures would make little sense. We determine guilt or innocence largely in terms of intent. If you aim at a bear while hunting, and accidentally fell a colleague instead, you will probably feel contrite for the rest of your life, but may face no greater punishment. You didn't "intend" to slay your friend. But if you aim at the colleague and "intentionally" shoot him, you may spend a lifetime in prison. If we were to abandon the concept of intention—arguing, for example, that all our actions are driven by forces beyond our control— we would render the difference in aims irrelevant.

Consider also the domain of education, and the difficulties that would face teachers if they could not speak of students' "intelligence," "interests," "span of attention," or "motivation." Such characterizations of persons are the means by which students are singled out for special attention—both positive and punitive. They form the vocabulary by which students are warned and praised, and indeed, they are crucial to our educational policies. If we did not believe selves to be constituted by such processes as "reason," "attention," and the like, our educational system might collapse for lack of rationale. Systems of democratic governance similarly depend on commitments of the citizens to certain definitions of the self. It makes sense for individuals to vote only if they are presumed to have "powers of independent judgment," "political opinions," and "desires for social good." Without certain shared definitions of human selves, the institutions of justice, education, and democracy could scarcely be sustained.[3]

The language of the individual self is also woven into virtually all our daily relationships. In speaking of our children we rely on notions such as "feelings," "temperament," "needs," and "wants." In marriage most participants define themselves as having "commitments," "love," "romance," and "trust." In our friendships we make frequent and important use of such terms as "liking" and "respect." Business relations are suffused with words such as "motivation," "incentive," "rational," and "responsibility." The clergy would have a difficult time dealing with their parishioners if they could not speak in terms of "faith," "hope," and "conscience." To put the case more squarely, without the language of the self—of our internal states, processes, and characteristics—social life would be virtually unrecognizable.

THE SELF: FROM THE ROMANTIC TO THE POSTMODERN

The thesis of this book is that the process of social saturation is producing a profound change in our ways of understanding the self. Cultural life in the twentieth century has been dominated by two major vocabularies of the self. Largely from the nineteenth century, we have inherited a *romanticist* view of the self, one that attributes to each person characteristics of personal depth: passion, soul, creativity, and moral fiber. This vocabulary is essential to the formation of deeply committed relations, dedicated friendships, and life purposes. But since the rise of the *modernist* worldview beginning in the early twentieth century, the romantic vocabulary has been threatened. For modernists the chief characteristics of the self reside not in the domain of depth, but rather in our ability to reason— in our beliefs, opinions, and conscious intentions. In the modernist idiom, normal persons are predictable, honest, and sincere. Modernists believe in educational systems, a stable family life, moral training, and rational choice of marriage partners.

Yet, as I shall argue, both the romantic and the modern beliefs about the self are falling into disuse, and the social arrangements that they support are eroding. This is largely a result of the forces of social saturation. Emerging technologies saturate us with the voices of humankind— both harmonious and alien. As we absorb their varied rhymes and reasons, they become part of us and we of them. Social saturation furnishes us with a multiplicity of incoherent and unrelated languages of the self. For everything we "know to be true" about ourselves, other voices within respond with doubt and even derision. This fragmentation of self-conceptions corresponds to a multiplicity of incoherent and disconnected relationships. These relationships pull us in myriad directions, inviting us to play such a variety of roles that the very concept of an "authentic self" with knowable characteristics recedes from view. The fully saturated self becomes no self at all.

To contrast with the modern and romantic approaches to the self, I shall equate the saturating of self with the condition of *postmodernism*. As we enter the postmodern era, all previous beliefs about the self are placed in jeopardy, and with them the patterns of action they sustain. Postmodernism does not bring with it a new vocabulary for understanding ourselves, new traits or characteristics to be discovered or explored. Its impact is more apocalyptic than that: the very concept of personal essences is thrown into doubt. Selves as possessors of real and identifiable characteristics—such as rationality, emotion, inspiration, and will—are dismantled.

As I shall propose, this eroding of the identifiable self is both supported by and manifest in a wide range of beliefs and practices. The postmodern condition more generally is marked by a plurality of voices vying for the right to reality—to be accepted as legitimate expressions of the true and the good. As the voices expand in power and presence, all that seemed proper, right-minded, and well understood is subverted. In the postmodern world we become increasingly aware that the objects about which we speak are not so much "in the world" as they are products of perspective. Thus, processes such as emotion and reason cease to be real and significant essences of persons; rather, in the light of pluralism we perceive them to be imposters, the outcome of our ways of conceptualizing them. Under postmodern conditions, persons exist in a state of continuous construction and reconstruction; it is a world where anything goes that can be negotiated. Each reality of self gives way to reflexive questioning, irony, and ultimately the playful probing of yet another reality. The center fails to hold.

Is such talk of "dramatic change" and "disappearance" to be taken seriously? After all, we speak about ourselves today pretty much the same way we did last year, or even twenty years ago. And we can still read Dickens, Shakespeare, and Euripides with a sense that we understand the characters and their actions. Why should we anticipate important changes now, even if we are increasingly saturated by our social surroundings? This question is an important one, and an answer is a necessary prelude to all that follows.

Studies of the concept of self in other cultures and periods can begin to show us just how fragile and historically pliable our current beliefs and practices may be. We find that there is enormous variety in what people accept as "obviously true" about themselves, and many of our current truisms are surprisingly new. Let's consider some examples of this variety and change.

THE CULTURAL LOCATION OF SELF

Emotional meaning is a social and cultural achievement.
—Catherine Lutz, *Unnatural Emotions*

If there is one message writ large within the annals of anthropology, it is to beware the solid truths of one's own culture. If we contrast our views with those of others, we find that what we take to be "reliable knowledge" is more properly considered a form of folklore. Consider the very definition we hold of a single, autonomous individual. We more or less take it for granted that each of us is a separate individual possessing the capacity for self-direction and responsibility. We grant inalienable rights to individuals—not to families, social classes, or organizations. Our moral system holds single individuals responsible for their actions, and not their friends, families, or professional associates. In our traditional concept of romantic love, the appropriate target is the single individual; to be romantically engaged with several persons simultaneously is thought to be either inconceivable or immoral.

Our view of the individual would be extraordinary in many cultures of the world, however. Consider the Balinese. As the Princeton anthropologist Clifford Geertz describes Balinese culture, the concept of the unique or individual self plays but a minimal role in everyday life.[4] Rather, individuals are considered representatives of more general social categories. It is the social category that is of critical significance in cultural life. In Geertz's terms, "It is not . . . their existence as persons—their immediacy and individuality, or their special, never-to-be-repeated impact upon the stream of historical events—which [is] played up, symbolically emphasized: it is their social placement, their particular location within a persisting, indeed an eternal, metaphysical order."[5] In effect, to love or despise, honor or humiliate, someone because of the state of his or her individual mind (feelings, intentions, rationality, etc.) would border on the nonsensical. It is not the personalized individual to whom one relates, but what we in Western culture would view as the depersonalized being.

As pointed out earlier, ways of talk are embedded within forms of cultural life. Consider, for example, Balinese patterns of naming. In the West, each individual receives at least one name that will identify him or her for a lifetime. But for the Balinese, names are primarily used to designate the kinds of groups to which the individual belongs. Infants do not receive a personal name until 105 days after birth. Such names are used only sporadically to refer to the child, and once the child has reached adolescence these names virtually disappear from use. Other names dominate, which primarily designate social status. For example, there are names to designate the individual's placement in the birth order—Wayan for the firstborn, Nioman for the second, and so on. There are also kinship names that define the generational group to which one belongs. In this system one receives the same name as all one's siblings and cousins within a given generation.

One of the most prominent designations is the "tekonym," a name that may change several times during one's life. An adult who becomes a parent is called "Father of . . ." or "Mother of . . ." (followed by the child's name). Later, when a grandchild is born, the person's name changes again, to "Grandfather of . . ." or "Grandmother of . . .", and once again if a great-grandchild is born. Meanwhile, status titles indicate one's social standing, and public titles indicate one's function or service in the community (e.g., postman, teamster, politician).

This socially embedded view of the self is also revealed in relationship patterns. Because the social group is central, relationships tend to be general and formal rather than specific and personal. We in Western culture, concerned with the unique character of individuals, typically pay more attention to the momentary character of our friends. We are continuously concerned with how they are "feeling," what they are "thinking," and so on. For us friendships often seem open-ended and suffused with potential; we cannot always predict where a friendship will lead. In contrast, among the Balinese, relationships are viewed as links between representatives of different groups or classes. As a result the relationships tend to be ritualized. Particular patterns of action may be repeated again and again, with only the cast of characters changing. Unpredictable outcomes are unlikely. Westerners carry out similar rituals with people in professional roles—doctor, garage mechanic, or waiter. (Yet even these ritualized relationships cannot always withstand the intense pressures toward personalization, as when a waiter introduces himself by first name to a table.) In Bali, according to Geertz, even the closest friendships may be conducted like well-mannered ceremonies.

Not only the emphasis on individuality varies from one culture to another.[6] So do assumptions about the makeup of a person. Consider the emotions, for example. In Western culture our emotional expressions can usually be sorted into less than a dozen broad categories. We can legitimately say, for example, that we feel anger, disgust, fear, joy, love, sadness, shame, or surprise (or we can use various alternative terms, such as saying "depressed" instead of "sad").[7] Further, we treat these emotional terms as representing biological givens. Thus we say that people inherit the capacities for these emotional feelings, and that we can literally "see" the expressions of these emotions in people's faces. Any adult who did not have the capacity to feel sadness, fear, or love, for example, would be considered psychopathic or autistic.

Yet when we look at other cultures, we become painfully aware of just how parochial these "biological givens" are. In some cultures, investigators find it difficult to locate any terms referring to "inner states." In others, the vocabulary is very limited, including only one or two terms that Westerners would identify as emotions. In still other cultures, many *more* terms are used to depict emotions than are found in the West. And often when another culture does have terms that seem to correspond to our own, their meanings turn out to be quite different.[8]

Consider the Ilongot people of the northern Philippines, for whom one of the most basic ingredients of the mature male psyche is a state called *liget*. As the anthropologist Michelle Rosaldo describes liget, it is roughly akin to the English terms "energy," "anger," and "passion."[9] However, the state is not identical to any of these, nor to any combination thereof. Liget is a distinct possession of the male, and we in Western culture could scarcely imagine its expression among us. A young Ilongot possessed by liget might weep or sing or sulk. He might stop eating certain foods, slash baskets, yell, spill water, or demonstrate irritation or distraction. And, when liget has reached its peak, he will be moved to slice the head from a neighboring tribesman. Having taken a head, he feels his liget transformed and transforming. His resources of energy are increased, he feels passion for the opposite sex, and he acquires a deepened sense of knowledge. Surely it is difficult for us to imagine that liget is basic to the biological constitution—that it somehow lurks within us, seeking expression, inhibited only by artificial layers of civilization. Liget appears to be a construction of the particular Ilongot culture, just as feelings of romantic love, anxiety, and envy are constructions of our own.

THE SELF THROUGH HISTORY

Like anthropologists, historians take a keen interest in people's conceptions of the self. For many historians, such explorations have an emancipatory aim. If we can comprehend the origins and changes in our

Western beliefs about the person, they reason, we can soften the grip of what is currently taken for granted. If what we take to be solid facts about human beings turn out to be by-products of a particular social condition, then such "facts" are more appropriately considered opinions or myths. Thus, they hope, historical awareness might release us from the prisons of our current conventions of understanding.[10]

Many historians find the Western preoccupation with the unique individual both extreme and restricting. How did our culture come to place such importance on individual selves? In one fascinating account of this development, John Lyons proposes that the centrality of the self was largely a product of late-eighteenth-century thought.[11] Before then, people tended to view themselves as exemplars of more general categories—members of a religion, class, profession, or the like. Even the soul, argues Lyons, was not quite an individual's possession. It was fabricated by God and placed in mortal flesh for a transient period. In the late eighteenth century, however, common sensibilities began to change. The evidence can be found in such diverse sources as philosophical treatises, biographies, confessional records, and tales of rogues and adventurers.

Consider the reports made of travels to exotic climes. For centuries, argues Lyons, a traveler reported what anyone would be expected to report, speaking as a representative of everyone. But in the late eighteenth century, the manner of reporting starts to change. When Boswell describes his visit to the Hebrides, for example, he is attracted to the special details that move him personally. He writes at length of his individual feelings and of why he is moved. It was during this period that people began to "take a walk to take a walk—not especially to get somewhere. . . . Seeing became a confirmation of the self rather than a process by which the outer world of nature was understood."[12] This is the conception of the individual self that has by now seeped into virtually every corner of Western cultural life.

At the same time, the set of characteristics attributed to individual selves has also changed dramatically over the centuries. Once-cherished characteristics have vanished, and new ones have come to take their place. Consider the child, for example. Today we believe that babies are born with the ability to feel many emotions, but their capacities for rational thought are not yet developed. Western parents tend to believe that their children don't demonstrate the capacity for abstract thought until they are over three years old. In effect, we believe that the child's mind must "mature."[13] Yet as the historian Philippe Aries demonstrates, for much of Western history—roughly until the seventeenth century—childhood was not considered to be a state of mental immaturity, a state somehow different or separated from that of the adult.[14] Instead, the Dutch psychologist J. H. van den Berg proposes, the child was more typically viewed as an adult in miniature—fully in possession of adult faculties, but simply without the experience to make full use of them.[15] Thus Montaigne wrote in his essay on children's education that philosophical discourse should be introduced at a very early age—in fact, "from the moment it is weaned the child will, in any case, be able to understand philosophical discourses."[16] Later, John Locke stated that children desire "gentle persuasion in reasoning," for "they understand it as early as they do language; and if I misobserve not, they like to be treated as rational creatures."[17] These understandings of the child corresponded to patterns of conduct. Montaigne wrote of a friend's child who read Greek, Latin, and Hebrew when he was six years old, and translated Plato into French before he was eight. Goethe was able to write in German, French, Greek, and Latin before he was eight. In the upper classes, reading and writing were common by the age of four; children were able to read the Bible and discuss complex matters of moral principle before they were five. Looking through the lens of contemporary beliefs about the "maturing mind," such abilities border on the incomprehensible.

Other historical work has examined cultural beliefs about motherhood. In modern times we tend to view mothers' love for their children as a basic aspect of human nature, much like our belief in a genetic basis for emotion. When a mother fails to demonstrate love for her children—abandoning them or selling them, for example—she seems something less than human. (Interestingly, if a man abandons his wife and children we generally do not see it as "unnatural.") And yet, argues the French historian Elisabeth Badinter, it was not always so.[18] In France and England during the seventeenth and eighteenth centuries, the child lived a marginal existence. Writings of the time demonstrate a pervasive antipathy for the infant, who was born in sin, often a burdening nuisance, and at best a plaything or potential laborer. For the poor, with no significant means of birth control or abortion, abandoning a child was common practice. Clearly the concept of "maternal instinct" would have seemed alien.

Indeed, in many circles, even nursing was considered a waste of the mother's time. If a family was rich enough, the newborn child was often sent to the countryside for care by a wet nurse. Because of the poor care and the insufficiency of the wet nurse's milk, infant mortality was common. Such deaths were seen as routine, and the child replaceable at a later date; family journals show little more concern for a child's death than for the death of a neighbor or even for the family's financial dealings of the day. As Badinter quotes Montaigne: "I lost two or three children during their stay with the wet nurse—not without regret, mind you, but without great vexation."[19] The concept of the mother's instinctive love for the child, concludes Badinter, is a recent development in Western history.

LANGUAGE AND ENCUMBERING THE SELF

Today common sense tells us that people differ in their reasoning abilities, that emotions are powerful forces in people's lives, and that it is important to be aware of a person's true intentions. Such assumptions represent what we take to be true and universal about human selves. Yet, as both cultural and historical study indicates, all such assumptions about "what we are really like" are precariously placed—products of a certain culture at a certain point in its history. Can our present conventions hold up against the forces of twentieth-century technologies that are set against all "truths about the self"?

At this point the skeptic may still reply, "Yes, such variations in belief and practice may be found, but Western cultural history is long, and our traditions of speaking and acting are deeply entrenched. Major change is unlikely." A final illustration, however, should indicate the rapidity with which change can occur—even within the present century. Consider the following characterizations of the self:

Low self-esteem	Authoritarian
Externally controlled	Repressed
Depressed	Burned out
Stressed	Paranoid
Obsessive-compulsive	Bulimic
Sadomasochistic	Midlife crisis
Identity crisis	Anxious
Antisocial personality	Anorexic
Seasonal affective disorder	Kleptomaniac
Self-alienated	Psychopathic deviate
Post-traumatic stress disorder	Voyeuristic

These are all terms commonly used by the mental-health professions and a significant sector of the public in making sense of the self. Two features of the list are especially noteworthy. First, all these terms have come into common usage only within the present century (several only within the past decade). Second, they are all terms of mental deficit. They discredit the individual, drawing attention to problems, shortcomings, or incapacities. To put it more broadly, the vocabulary of human deficit has undergone enormous expansion within the present century. We have countless ways of locating faults within ourselves and others that were unavailable to even our great-grandfathers.

In many respects this spiraling of deficit terminology can be attributed to the "scientizing" of human behavior characteristic of the modern era. As psychiatrists and psychologists try to explain undesirable behavior, they generate a technical vocabulary of deficit. This language is slowly

Anatidaephobia: The fear that somewhere, somehow, a duck is watching you.

disseminated to the public at large, so that they too can become conscious of mental-health issues. As people acquire the vocabulary, they also come to see self and others in these terms. They judge themselves and others as superior or inferior, as worthy or not of admiration or commitment. (How much can you trust an *addictive personality*, how much devotion does a *manic-depressive* merit, should you hire a *bulimic*, can you cherish a *hysteric*?) Worse, as this shift in understanding occurs, a spiraling cycle of enfeeblement is set into motion. For as people come to view themselves in these ways, they also come to see the professional as essential for cure. And, as the profession is asked for answers to life problems, it is pressed into developing a still more differentiated and expanded vocabulary. The new vocabulary enters the culture, engendering still further perceptions of illness, and so on in a continuous spiral of infirmity.[20]

To be sure, mental-health professionals take on an enormous burden of human suffering. Few professions are so humanely oriented. Yet, given the spiraling cycle of deficit, we need to give serious attention to the means of containing the language. At present it is difficult to see the limits. Recently I received an invitation to mental-health workers for a California conference on addiction. "Addictive behavior is arguably the number one health and social problem facing our country today," the announcement read. "Some of the leading clinical researchers in the field will present the 'state of the art' in research, theory, and clinical inter-ventions across the addictions, [including]: exercise, religion, eating, work, [and] sex." A century ago people could engage in all these activities without questioning their mental and emotional stability. If immersions in exercise, religion, eating, work, and sex are questionable today, what will be left untouched tomorrow? The languages of the self are malleable indeed, and as they change so does social life.

COMING ATTRACTIONS

The stage is set. We play out our lives largely within the languages of romanticism and modernism. These modes of understanding ourselves and others are built into the fabric of our daily relationships; without them daily life would be unlivable. Yet we are now bombarded with ever-increasing intensity by the images and actions of others; our range of social participation is expanding exponentially. As we absorb the views, values, and visions of others, and live out the multiple plots in which we are enmeshed, we enter a postmodern consciousness. It is a world in which we no longer experience a secure sense of self, and in which doubt is increasingly placed on the very assumption of a bounded identity with palpable attributes. What are the consequences? How are we to respond to the coming conditions?

To explore these issues, my plan is first to take stock of our cultural inheritance. What are the languages of romanticism and modernism, and what aspects of our lives do they sustain? I wish to explore the romantic language of personal profundity and to assess the difference it makes in human affairs. I will then contrast this view of the self with the modernist conception of humans as machines, a view set against the romantic backdrop but promising an optimistic and unbounded future.

It is these beliefs about the self that I see as the major victims of social saturation, a process that I describe in chapter 3. This chapter contains no major surprises. Rather, my attempt is to survey broadly much that we know in piecemeal. I wish to draw together the many isolated moments of awareness into a single global picture of the technological change that increasingly insinuates itself into our understandings and relationships. I end this chapter with a discussion of the fragmenting and populating of self-experience, a condition I call "multiphrenia."

Critical to my argument is the proposal that social saturation brings with it a general loss in our assumption of true and knowable selves. As we absorb multiple voices, we find that each "truth" is relativized by our simultaneous consciousness of compelling alternatives. We come to be aware that each truth about ourselves is a construction of the moment, true only for a given time and within certain relationships. This argument is most fully clarified by profound changes now taking place within the academic sphere. Thus, in chapter 4, "Truth in Trouble," I outline the ways in which the emerging multiplicity in perspectives is undermining longstanding beliefs about truth and objectivity. Many now see science as a sea of social opinion, the tides of which are often governed by political and ideological forces. And as science becomes not a reflection of the world but a reflection of social process, attention is removed from the "world as it is" and centers instead on our representations of the world. Many now argue that these representations are not the product of individual minds, but largely of literary traditions. And if scientific truth is the product of literary artifice, so are truths about the self.

This bursting of postmodern consciousness into the academic sphere is paralleled by a rich set of trends emerging within the broader cultural realm. These trends—in art, architecture, music, film, literature, and television—are the central focus of chapter 5. Of particular interest is the loss of identifiable essences, the increasing sensitivity to the social construction of reality, the erosion of authority, the growing disregard for rational coherence, and the emergence of ironic self-reflection. Each of these trends, traceable to the saturation of society by multiple voices, both contributes to and is supported by the breakdown of the knowable self. For as the sense of self as a singular, knowable set of essences is questioned, so doubt is cast upon the existence of other bounded entities, along with those authorities and rationalities claiming to speak beyond the limits of their parochial existence. And even these doubts become the victim of still other voices within.

I extend these arguments in the next chapter, "From Self to Relationship." Here I treat in greater detail what may be viewed as stages in the transition from the traditional to the postmodern sense of self. As the traditional individual is thrust into an ever-widening array of relationships, he or she begins increasingly to sense the self as a strategic manipulator. Caught in often contradictory or incoherent activities, one grows anguished over the violation of one's sense of identity. As saturation continues, this initial stage is superseded by one in which one senses the raptures of multiplicitous being. In casting "the true" and "the identifiable" to the wind, one opens an enormous world of potential. As I propose, the final stage in this transition to the postmodern is reached when the self vanishes fully into a stage of relatedness. One ceases to believe in a self independent of the relations in which he or she is embedded. Although this is not yet a pervasive condition, I touch on several important indicators that it is imminent.

At this juncture I indulge in two related explorations. In chapter 7, "A Collage of Postmodern Life," I consider several repercussions of the postmodern transition for daily relationships. Problems in intimacy, commitment, and coherent family life are all treated, as well as the implications for social movements of various kinds. I also explore the possible gains for the culture derived from the postmodern emphasis on "serious games." In the next chapter I turn to the possibilities of self-renewal—that is, the prospects for the culture holding fast to its traditional views of self and forms of relatedness.

In the final chapter, I step out of the storytelling role to evaluate the postmodern shift in self and relationships. While the book suggests many negative outcomes, there are also important exceptions. In this final chapter I attempt to let postmodernism speak on its own behalf, as it were, and to demonstrate why a certain degree of optimism is merited. Here I concentrate on the devastation produced by the modernist belief in truth and progress, and the liberating effects of postmodern pluralism— both for the self and for world culture more generally. In the final analysis it is the technology of social saturation, and the shift toward postmodern existence, on which global well-being will depend.

TWO

From the Romantic to the Modern Vision of Self

Each cultural form, once it is created, is gnawed at varying rates by the forces of life. As soon as one is fully developed, the next begins to form; after a struggle, long or short, it will eventually succeed its predecessor.
—Georg Simmel, *The Conflict in Modern Culture*

A s language flows among us, so are life patterns fastened or freed:

JAMES: The bottom line is clear: we don't have any choice but to close down the plant.

FRED: I just don't feel we can do that; it's too heartless for all those workers and their families.

MARGE: Be realistic, Sam. If you don't take more care of the baby, my whole career is going to be ruined.

SAM: What kind of a mother are you, anyway? You don't show one ounce of dedication or compassion to your own child—much less to me.

SUSAN: You really are dumb if you buy that house, Carol. It's in such bad shape and you'll be in debt forever.

CAROL: But Susan, somehow that doesn't bother me. There's just something deep inside that comes alive whenever I think about living there.

In confronting problems of plant closure, marital relations, or buying a house, each of these individuals relies on powerful linguistic forms. If they are heard, by either themselves or others, the consequences will be far-reaching—for workers, children, and the participants themselves. Most important for our present concerns, these languages derive their power from shared conceptions of the self—who we are, how we are constituted, and how we should perform. These beliefs about human personality are mainstays of contemporary life; they are infused within all manner of relationships, propelling them this way and that. Without such beliefs, cultural life would lapse into nonsense. There would be no rationale for closing plants, working, caring for children, or buying houses.

More specifically, these dialogues reveal two contrasting conceptions of human personality—both of enormous consequence to daily life. On the one hand, James, Marge, and Susan all rely on common beliefs in people as rational agents who examine the facts and make decisions accordingly. James's stress on "the bottom line" presumes that mature people base their action on sound reasoning; similarly, Marge assumes they will consider the consequences of their actions; and Susan's argument is powerful because of her belief that normal persons are both logical and practical. But if one does not share these beliefs about human nature, their arguments are insignificant. For Fred, Sam, and Carol, the ideal human being is not a creature of practical reason, but one who is guided by something deeper—moral feelings, loyalties, nurturing instincts, or a sense of spontaneous joy. Fred places the workers' welfare above the bottom line; Sam feels that his wife is less than human in placing her career above her child; and Carol is willing to be guided by her inner resonance with the house rather than by its physical condition.

This chapter will explore these opposing conceptions of the person. I propose that the vocabulary of moral feeling, loyalty, and inner joy is largely derived from a *romanticist* conception of the self. Although it reached its zenith in the nineteenth century, this view remains very much alive in the present world. It is a perspective that lays central stress on unseen, even sacred forces that dwell deep within the person, forces that give life and relationships their significance. Yet this conception of the person has fallen into disrepair in the present century, largely replaced by a *modernist* view of personality, in which reason and observation are the central ingredients of human functioning. This latter view pervades the sciences, government, and business, and has made many inroads into the sphere of informal relations. Both the romanticist and modernist traditions deserve closest attention, for not only are they among the most important of our lived vocabularies, but they form an important backdrop against which postmodernism must be evaluated. For, as we shall see in later chapters, postmodernism tends to extinguish the validity of both the romantic and modern realities.

ROMANTICISM AND THE REALITY OF THE
DEEP INTERIOR

The mind has a thousand eyes,
And the heart but one;
Yet the light of a whole life dies,
When love is done.

—Francis William Bourdillon (1852–1921)

Reason and observation were admired long before the twentieth century; both had acquired lofty status during the seventeenth and eighteenth centuries. The honor attached to reason can be traced, for example, to the writings of Descartes, Spinoza, Hobbes, and Newton. Using such writings as a springboard, thinkers of the so-called Enlightenment in the eighteenth century—Locke, Hume, and Voltaire, among others—placed central emphasis on the individual's powers of observation. The joint emphasis on these personal powers had enormous social and political implications. Authority by "divine right" or "divine inspiration" could most effectively be challenged through reason and observation. These ingredients of human nature ennobled the individual, and gave him (and more questionably *her*) the capacity for discerning truth and choosing appropriate action. This view of the self inspired democratic institutions, a commitment to science, and the hope of broad education. Pejoratives such as "mindless," "feather-brained," "irrational," and "feeble-minded" continue to express Enlightenment values.

Against this backdrop, we can only marvel at the literary and artistic accomplishments of the romantic period. For during the late eighteenth and nineteenth centuries the supremacy of reason and observation was challenged, and a new world was created—the world of the *deep interior*, lying beneath the veneer of conscious reason.[1] Wordsworth called the deep interior "a presence that disturbs me"; for Shelley it was an "unseen power," and for Baudelaire a "luminous hollow." Drawing from early Christian imagery, many romantics considered the central inhabitant of the deep interior to be the soul. This view linked the individual both to God and to the natural world of God's design, making the individual both divine and natural in aspect. For romantics of a more secular stripe, the central ingredient of the deep interior was a passionate force, given by nature but dangerous in potential. And for still other artisans of the deep interior, the emotions and the soul were indistinguishable: passion was an expression of the soul, while the soul was suffused with emotional energy.

Consider love. The concept of love had long been part of the Western tradition. However, the particular meaning and significance of the term changed over the course of the centuries. Love during the Enlightenment was often a matter of gallantry and strategic conquest for the upper classes, while puritanism was making strong headway among the common folk.[2] From the Enlightenment perspective, strong emotions were dangerous, interfering as they did with a balanced life of sound appraisal. Thus, in the late 1600s, the famous courtesan Ninon de l'Enclose wrote to her young lover,

> Shall I tell you what makes love dangerous? It is the sublime idea we are apt to form of it. But to speak the exact truth, love, considered as a passion, is nothing but a blind instinct that one must know how to appreciate properly—as an appetite which directs us toward one object rather than another without our being able to account for our taste.[3]

Contrast this cool appraisal with Shelley's nineteenth-century sentiments:

> What is love? Ask him who lives, what is life. Ask him who adores, what is God. . . . [Love] is that powerful attraction towards all that we conceive, or fear, or hope beyond ourselves, when we find within our own thoughts the chasm of an insufficient void, and seek to awaken in all things that are, a community with what we experience within ourselves.[4]

Or, consider Schiller's lines dedicated to Laura:

> Who and what gave me the wish to woo thee
> Still, lip to lip, to cling for aye unto thee?
> Who made thy glances to my soul the link?
> Who bade me burn thy very breath to drink,
> My life in thine to sink?[5]

Not only do such lines define love as a powerful union of souls, but asking "Who?" suggests that the moving power is beyond conscious knowledge. That which truly moves us exists at a mysterious depth.

Friendship, like love, was a matter of spirit. To be a genuine friend meant to be connected at the profoundest depths. As Keats wrote to his friend Benjamin Bailey, "I think you are thoroughly acquainted with my innermost breast in that respect, or you could not have known me even thus long and still hold me worthy to be your dear friend."[6] And Schiller's poem "Friendship" contains the following lines:

> Did not [God's spirit] urge and guide
> Our hearts to meet in love's eternal bond

FROM ROMANTIC TO MODERN VISION

Linked to thine arm, Oh Raphael, by thy side . . . ?
Do I not find within thy radiant eyes
Fairer reflections of all joys most fair?
In thee I marvel at myself—the dyes
Of lovelier earth seem lovelier painted there
And in the bright looks of the friend is given
Heavenly mirror even of the heaven![7]

Because individuals were capable of profound love, the loss of a loved one could engender profound grief. A high value was placed on the expression of such grief, because such expression gave voice to one's very depths and was thus ennobling. Diaries of the period reveal strong tendencies to keep the image of the deceased present and pervasive, and to communicate with the dead through prayer and séance.[8] One might also look forward to one's own death, because the immortality of the soul meant a possible union with the beloved after death. As William Barnes wrote in moments of deep grief,

Few be my days of loneliness and pain
Until I meet in love with thee again.

Such possibilities were already prepared in Goethe's early romantic work of the 1770s, *The Sufferings of Young Werther*. Goethe tells the story of a young man who is hopelessly in love with a young woman properly married to an older man. "She is sacred to me," writes the hero, Werther. "All desire subsides in her presence. I never know what I feel when I am with her; it is as though my soul were whirling in every nerve."[9] Werther's love goes unrequited, and after months of agonizing over the conflict between passion and morality, Werther takes his own life. The death, however, is heroic rather than futile. As Werther writes, "my heart . . . is really my sole pride, and . . . alone is the source of everything, of all my strength, all my bliss, and all my misery."[10] Thus, to take one's life becomes an act of self-realization. Werther goes on to attack the smug, sensible rationalists: "Oh you sensible people!" he exclaims. "Passion! Drunkenness! Madness! You stand there so calm, so unsympathetic, you moral people. You condemn the drunkard, abhor the man bereft of his reason, pass by like the priest and thank God like the Pharisee that He did not make you as one of these."[11] So popular and compelling did Goethe's slim volume prove, it is said, that a wave of suicides followed its publication.

Other concepts also came to populate the deep interior. The *imagi-*

nation was considered a prize possession, as it enabled one to escape the mundane givens of daily life.[12] Early in the romantic period, William Blake raised serious questions about the significance of "mere experience." What was given to the senses was not important to one's life, Blake proposed, but what was imagined was. For Blake, "Nature is imagination. . . . To me this world is all one continued vision of fancy or imagination."[13] Nor was imagination simply a peripheral aspect of human reason, as Enlightenment thinkers might have argued. Rather, for Blake, imagination was nothing less than a "spiritual sensation." Keats extended much the same theme as he wrote,

I am certain of nothing but of the holiness of the heart's affections and the truth of imagination. What the imagination seizes as beauty must be truth—whether it existed before or not—for I have the same idea of all our passions as of love: they are all in their sublime, creative of essential beauty.[14]

Genius was another honored resident of the inner reaches. This was not the genius of the modern age, indicated merely by a point toward the end of an intelligence scale. Rather it was a capacity to "see to the heart" of things, to inspire voice, art, music, and the like through one's insights: to impassion others with a sense of the sublime. As Schiller wrote, "Why are taste and genius so seldom . . . united? Taste of strength is afraid—genius despises the rein."[15] And again, demonstrating his antipathy toward the cool logic of the Enlightenment thinkers: "Understanding, indeed, can repeat what already existed,—That which Nature has built, after her she, too, can build. Over Nature can reason build, but in vacancy. . . . [G]enius, alone, nature *in* nature canst form." A belief in forms of superior inner being was also inherent in Nietzsche's philosophic writing. Nietzsche praised a form of "monumental history" that would threaten the banal complacency of present generations with historical accounts of truly great figures.[16] He proposed as a model figure the *Übermensch,* the superman who can integrate the chaos of the passions and give them creative expressions in life works.

The diaries of the time also provide a sense of the seriousness given to matters of psychological depth. For example, Delacroix wrote in 1824, "An interesting discussion at Leblond's about geniuses and outstanding men. Dimier thinks that great passions are the source of all genius! I think that it is imagination alone, or, what amounts to the same thing, a delicacy of the senses that makes some men see where others are blind."[17] In the same diary entry he also dismisses reason, so blessed in the discourse of previous centuries: "no rules whatsoever for the greatest minds;

rules are only for people who merely have talent, which can be acquired. The proof is that genius cannot be transmitted."

The romantic view of self was hardly limited to words alone; it was also a call to action. On its basis commitments were made, lives changed, and deaths hastened. We have glimpsed the possibility of grief-stricken suicide—indeed so significant an element of romantic culture that one could speak of a *mal du siècle*, a sickness of the century, characterized by anguish at the current decline of affairs and a search for death.[18] But the romantic view of self could also lead to exaltation. Delacroix plunges into the "deep interior" for inspiration: "When we surrender ourselves entirely to the soul it unfolds itself completely to us, and it is then that this capricious spirit grants us the greatest happiness of all. . . . I mean the joy of expressing the soul in a hundred different ways, of revealing it to others, of learning to know ourselves, and of continually displaying it in our works."[19]

It was just such beliefs that contributed to a major revolution in the artistic forms of the time. The neoclassicist emphases on exacting order, painstaking detail, subdued coloration, and frozen forms were abandoned. The concept of art as depiction or illustration of real-world affairs gave way to a concept of art as an external expression of inner feelings. The canvases of Delacroix, Gericault, Millet, Courbet, and others were often bold and vigorous.[20] Lively color or strong somber hues predominated; attention to detail was replaced by an expression of emotional content. The subject matter was often heroic, sometimes based on the works of romantic poets, Dante, or Goethe. The mysterious, fantastic, and morbid became familiar themes; pathos and tragedy were often celebrated.

Of special interest in much romanticist art is the creation of what might be termed a *presence of the absent*. As we saw, the romantic discourse of self created a sense of reality beyond immediate, sensory awareness; the unseen, inner depths were most substantial. Convinced of the reality and significance of these unseen resources, the artist was faced with the problem of conveying them through a visual medium. How can one use purely sensory devices to portray the reality of something beyond the senses?

The solution took many different forms. In England, J. M. W. Turner's canvases placed the viewer in the midst of turbulent mists or vapors. What is empty space for most artists became palpable substance in Turner's hands. Further, one sensed that something lay beyond the vapors— perhaps the sun, or a fire, or mystical beings from other lands. "The beyond" was thus the central subject matter of the paintings, but precisely what lay beyond was difficult to articulate. Other painters used different means to create the presence of the absent. The Pre-Raphaelites and symbolists often painted realistic pictures of mythical characters, thus transforming myth into reality. The German painter Casper David Friedrich often included figures looking off into the distance, or painted landscapes in which the viewer's eyes were directed toward a distant point itself not visible. One sensed "the beyond" but could never grasp its essence. In Norway, Edvard Munch sustained the romantic tradition in his faces contorted by anxiety and anguish from an internal wellspring far removed.

Music paralleled the visual arts. In many respects the music of both the baroque and early classical periods complemented the Enlightenment emphasis on powers of reason. Much has been written about the rational heuristics underlying the scores of Bach and Mozart. With such composers as Beethoven and Schubert, however, the emphasis shifts toward the world of deep emotion. For Beethoven music was ideally an *Ausdruck der Empfindung*, or an expression of feeling. (The *Moonlight* Sonata was dedicated to his "immortal beloved.") This view of music as an external expression of inner profundity came to dominate the scores of Brahms, Schumann, Mendelssohn, Verdi, and Chopin. But romanticism reached its zenith in the works of Richard Wagner. Not only did feasts of emotion inspire his works (*Tristan und Isolde* was written in anguish over his unrequited love for the wife of a rich patron), but he conceived of musical passages as "careers of feeling." The mythical and mystical were then given dramatic visual form on the operatic stage.[21]

Morality, religion, and mysticism also took on new dimensions during the romantic period. Debates on the moral good had long been part of the Western tradition, in religious, governmental, and scholarly circles. Prior to the romantic period the debate was often cast in terms of rationality. That is, people were confident that the power of reason could furnish answers to moral questions. If people could be trained to "think for themselves," it was held, each individual could function as a responsible moral agent. As the deep interior of the self became a reality, however, the vocabulary of moral decision making began to change. "Moral feeling" or "moral sentiment" began to take the place of rationality. Moral action was not simply the result of learning to think properly. Rather, as Shelley put it, "the essence, the vitality of [moral] actions, derives its color from what is no way contributed to from any external source. . . . The benevolent propensities are . . . inherent in the human mind. We are impelled to seek the happiness of others."[22] These inner propensities were most frequently traced to the soul, at that time not considered to be a fictional aspect of self but a God-given fact of human

For many romanticists, the material world of the senses is far less significant than the immaterial and unseen. In Wilhelm Amberg's *Contemplation*, the major drama is not given in the painting itself but in its intimations of the interior.

nature. And not only did the soul furnish connection between the individual and God, but its immortal existence made fast the possibility of supernatural emanations. As de Guerin wrote, "The soul sees through dense darkness [and] understands certain mysteries. . . . It converses with ghosts."[23] Thus the séance, haunted houses, and spiritual mediums became common fixtures of the nineteenth century.[24]

No account of the romanticist vocabulary of the self would be complete without mentioning Sigmund Freud. Freud was a transitional figure between the romantic and modernist sensibilities, and his significance is largely due to his ability to unify the opposing discourses. The background for Freudian theory was prepared by more than a century of cultural life. Not only had the deep interior of the mind become a matter of fact, but thinkers such as Schopenhauer had proposed a nonrational, dynamic center of human existence ("the will"), and poets such as Poe and Baudelaire had contended with the possibility of deep, inner evil. In this context, Freud could reasonably propose that the major driving force behind human conduct was essentially beyond the reach of consciousness. Largely blocked from direct expression, it wended its tortuous path to the surface through dreams, works of art, and distorted reasoning or neurotic action. The inner resource was essentially the energy of desire, and more focally the desire for sexual expression. To be sure, the mysterious passions took on a modernist cast, now transformed into the quasibiological language of "libidinal impulses." And where romantics found the inner reaches potently self-evident, Freud was moved by modernist demands for objective evidence of the unconscious.[25] However, the romanticist drama of personal depth remained firm and the analysand of today continues to quest for a self of a century past.

To summarize, much of our contemporary vocabulary of the person, along with associated ways of life, finds its origins in the romantic period. It is a vocabulary of passion, purpose, depth, and personal significance: a vocabulary that generates awe of heroes, of genius, and of inspired work. It places love in the forefront of human endeavors, praising those who abandon the "useful" and the "functional" for the sake of others. It fosters a belief in deep dynamics of personality—marriage as a "communion of souls," family as bonded in love, and friendship as a lifetime commitment. Because of romanticism we can trust in moral values and an ultimate significance to the human venture. For many the loss of such a vocabulary would essentially be the collapse of anything meaningful in life. If love as intimate communion, intrinsic worth, creative inspiration, moral values, and passionate expression were all scratched from our vocabularies, life for many would be a pallid affair indeed. Yet, as we shall see, it is just this vocabulary that is threatened by the modernist view that follows.

THE RISE OF MODERNISM

The sciences, pursued without any restraint and in a spirit of the blindest laissez-faire, are shattering and dissolving all firmly held belief. . . . The world has never been more worldly, never poorer in love and goodness.
—Friedrich Nietzsche, *Untimely Meditations*

Somewhere toward the end of the nineteenth century, romanticist energies began to wane. It is difficult to determine precisely why. Certainly romanticist raptures were poor company for the expansionist markets of the Western world. The romantic view of the person was similarly displaced by burgeoning mass production, and may have seemed preciously effete in a world of *realpolitik* and impending war.

In any case, as Western culture moved into the twentieth century, there emerged a new form of consciousness most frequently termed modernist. Much has been said about twentieth-century modernism, its roots, complexities, and variations. Analysts are scarcely unanimous in their views, and there are different stories to be told about architecture, the visual arts, literature, and so on.[26] My purpose here is not to review these

IT WAS TOM'S FIRST BRUSH WITH MODERNISM

developments in detail, but to foreground several critical themes bearing the modernist conception of the person.

Return of the Enlightenment

> *Love is a universal migraine*
> *A bright stain on the vision*
> *Blotting out reason.*
> —Robert Graves, *Symptoms of Love*

Although romanticism furnished a rich resource for cultural life, little about its vision was practical or levelheaded. As we saw, the very ideas of objective evidence and rational utility went against the romanticist grain. At the same time, however, the sciences were bearing impressive fruits. Medicine and sanitation were improving life chances, better weapons invited new conquests, and innovations in technology—electric lamps, washing machines, sewing machines, motion pictures, radio, motor cars, and then airplanes—promised a utopia on earth. Science was antiromantic. It traced its lineage to the Enlightenment, to powers of reason and observation. In the same way that such powers had, it was said, lifted humankind above superstition and ignorance in the past, they were enabling scientists to do so in the present. The success of science rests, it was argued, upon the capacities of the scientist for systematic observation and rigorous reasoning. If these assumptions now seem mundanely commonsensical, this can be attributed to the power and pervasiveness of modernist thought.

Darwin's compelling thesis gave more support to the notion of seeking truth through reason and observation. For the most potent message of *The Origin of Species* concerned species survival. If weak species perish and the strong survive, what is the status of humankind? How is the human species to sustain itself in an uncertain and continuously threatening world? The most obvious answer to Darwin's challenging question was science, with its cornucopia of technological by-products. Thus, in the early 1900s, philosophers—drawing on positivist thought from Bacon to Comte and James Mill—began to set out the basic rules for the generation of objective knowledge. In particular, logical empiricist philosophers from Vienna to Cambridge proposed that successful science was based on rational forms of procedure. If the rules of procedure used in successful sciences such as chemistry and physics were applied more broadly, the world could be liberated from all that was mystical, erroneous, and tyrannical—not only in the physical sciences but in the world of human affairs as well. The development of a broad array of "social sciences" was thus invited—sciences that, as Bertrand Russell put it, would produce a "mathematics of human behavior as precise as the mathematics of machines."[27] Rules for evidence and logical thinking might be extended to the realm of everyday decision making as well. For would business, government, and military institutions not operate far more effectively if they could base decisions on sound, scientific thinking?[28]

So promising were the possibilities that by the middle of the twentieth century the philosophy of science (and its handmaiden, analytic philosophy) had eclipsed all other forms of philosophic inquiry. Such topics as ethics, theology, and metaphysics virtually disappeared from university curricula. Such subjects failed to treat "observables," and it was argued that any terms not tied to the observable world were empty speculations— like the medieval disputes about how many angels could dance on the head of a pin. The social sciences flourished in this century. Psychology furnishes a good illustration—a century ago there was virtually no such science. Systematic concern with the mind was limited largely to a small band of philosophers and theologians. However, when the "study of the mind" was redefined early in this century as "science," and its participants adopted the methods, metatheories, and manners of the natural sciences, the horizons broadened dramatically. By 1940 psychology was a major feature in most university curricula in the United States. By 1970 psychology was one of the most popular student majors in the country. As a friend remarked, "Given present rates of growth, by the next century we will all be either Chinese or psychologists."[29]

The Grand Narrative of Progress

Can we doubt that presently our race . . . will achieve unity and peace, that it will live, the children of our blood and lives will live, in a world made more splendid and lovely than any palace or garden that we know, going on from strength to strength in an ever-widening circle of adventure and achievement?

—H. G. Wells, *A Short History of the World*

The optimism fueled by the neo-Enlightenment voices contributed to what many view as the *grand narrative* of modernism. It is a story told by Western culture to itself about its journey through time, a story that makes this journey both intelligible and gratifying. The grand narrative is one of continuous upward movement—improvement, conquest, achievement—toward some goal. Science furnishes the guiding metaphor. Had science not demonstrated the capacity to defy gravity, extend the lifespan, harness nature's energies, and carry voice and image through the stratosphere? Because of the individual's capacities for reason and observation, as expressed in the scientific attitude, utopias were now within our grasp.[30] To be sure, the narrative was more pervasive in the United States than in Europe. A Panglossian myth falls more easily on the ears when world wars are fought and "won" on foreign soil than amid recurrent waves of destruction. Yet Europe was hardly immune to utopian possibilities. The modernist period was one in which it was possible to believe that because reason and observation can reign superior, a single form of government—democracy or fascism—or a single economic system—capitalism or communism—might finally solve the accumulating and intractable problems dogging the steps of the species as it lurched through history.

The modernist narrative of progress was not limited to the sciences. Echoing Darwin, the British architect W. R. Lethaby wrote in 1918 that "design is a matter of progressive experiment, the working out of a principle by means of adaptation, selection, variation."[31] The Bauhaus school of arts and crafts in the 1920s attempted to create an environment where workers in all the arts—architects, metalworkers, sculptors, painters, potters, weavers, and the like—could investigate the fundamentals of aesthetic design.[32] The anticipated result would be not the generation of differing styles, but a general solution—an International Style. This concern with systematic, empirical investigation was also manifested in literary theory. With the emergence of the New Criticism, Cleanth Brooks, John Crowe Ransom, and their colleagues abandoned traditional critical attempts to reveal the mind and heart of the author.[33] Rather, literary analysis was to be an empirical investigation, focusing on the internal structure of the work.

In the domain of dance, classical ballet was scorned for its decorative formalisms, and the interpretive dance of the romantics seemed self-indulgent. Dance turned "modern" when, in one critic's words, it aimed to "externalize personal, authentic experience." And in the world of music, composers such as Schönberg and Stravinsky pushed emotional expression aside to experiment with atonality and twelve-tone technique. The audience of romantic music listened for the messages of the deep interior, for insight into the self and the mysteries of the cosmos. In modern music one hears an experiment in surfaces; the patterns of sound form an invitation to celebration. Or in Schönberg's terms, music "should be a direct and straightforward presentation of ideas."[34] It was this same faith in reason to move society forward that lay behind Le Corbusier's volume *The City of Tomorrow*, in which he argued for the redesign of urban life around principles of geometry. Urban planning as both a discipline of study and a professional niche was born of this belief that reason, not politics (being antirational), should direct the course of urban change. Similarly, the profession of public administration emerged to champion the cause of reason over emotion, method over impulse, and science over art in matters of the public good.

At the same time, a commitment to the grand narrative of progress was accompanied by a suspicion, ranging from disregard to antagonism, of the past—its knowledge, music, architecture, art, government, and so on. As Paul de Man expresses it, "The full power of the idea of modernity" was embodied in the "desire to wipe out whatever came earlier."[35] With tradition thrown into question, the modernist was freed to build toward a deliberated future. Marshall Berman vividly portrays this elixir of a glorious future in his account of the public-works development in New York from the 1920s through the 1940s.[36] In the spirit of modernism, Robert Moses, parks commissioner of New York, envisioned and then built some of the most monumental alterations of public space—and resulting life patterns—in human history. These include the creation of Jones Beach from a swampy wasteland on the edge of Long Island, the Northern and Southern State Parkways through farmland to Jones Beach, the West Side Highway, much of Riverside Park on land largely created at the edge of Manhattan, Flushing Meadow Park in a marsh in Queens, and the Cross-Bronx Expressway. It is the latter that Berman most bitterly regrets, for it cut through traditional close-knit, self-sustaining neighborhoods, destroying them and creating an urban jungle. But such regrets are for the reminiscent, for this was the era of the 1939 New York World's Fair, dedicated to "Building the World of Tomorrow" through scientific technology.

The Quest for Essence

If we can discover some quality common and peculiar to all objects that provoke [the aesthetic emotion], we shall have solved what I take to be the central problem of aesthetics. We shall have discovered the essential quality in the work of art, the quality that distinguishes works of art from all other classes of objects.

—Clive Bell, *The Aesthetic Hypothesis*

If one aspires to truth, then there must be something for truth to be about: the very concept of truth demands an object. And if truth is reached through successive approximations, then the search for knowledge proceeds toward an essence—a fundamental *thing-in-itself*. The concept of an essential unit of matter out of which the universe and all its conditions are constructed has a long history. That twentieth-century physics should rediscover the idea of the atom, the irreducible particle, is hardly surprising. However, the promise that reasoned observation will lead to the truth is intoxicating. Any discipline laying claim to scientific methods could also claim to search for its essence: the essence of the political process, the economy, mental illness, social institutions, foreign cultures, education, communication, and so on.

The pursuit of the essential was everywhere. Following the vision of the Chicago architect Louis Sullivan, for designers of everything from skyscrapers to chairs or forks, the watchword was "Form follows function." The hallmark of the modernist movement in architecture was the abandonment of all forms of decorative styling—rococo sumptuousness, Victorian gingerbread, neoclassic imitation, the elaborate symbolism of art nouveau—and its replacement by pure form. As the Bauhaus architect Mies van der Rohe put it, "Less is more." For generations of modern architects the key to superior design was practical, real-world utility.

In Vincent Kling's Du Pont Science Building, at Swarthmore College, each unit houses a different department and passageways connect the branches of knowledge. With purity of line and no decorative interferences, form follows function.

Modern dance abandoned the limited and stylized vocabulary of ballet, and sought the essentials of movement. For the dancer-choreographer Martha Graham, the guiding principle of expression was to be found in the act of breathing; for her contemporary Doris Humphrey, it was the dynamic conflict between change and stability. For later choreographers, dance ceased to be an expression or reflection of any other reality (including inner impulse) but was beholden only to itself. As Merce Cunningham phrased it, dance movement "begins to assume its own proportions."

Under the influence of Stockhausen in the 1950s, music also ceased to "be about" the world or the composer—an expression, as Wagner would have put it, of unarticulated emotions. Musical notes were simply, as John Cage put it, "organizations of sound." One could produce them electronically and experiment with their properties much as one would chemical elements. Musical composition could be based on a systematic, technical foundation. Since Stockhausen, this dehumanization of music has been aided by the use of mathematics, computers, and the electronic synthesizer.

The visual arts similarly pared away the accumulated, formerly unquestioned forms of representation in search of the essentials. Consider the impressionist movement of the turn of the century. In their spirited disregard for realistic depiction and formal rules, Monet, Renoir, Cézanne, Manet, and their colleagues were much indebted to their romantic forebears. As the object of the painting ceased to control the techniques of depiction, however, artists were freed to experiment with the possibilities of pigment in itself. This concern for the capacities of pigment in itself was accentuated in the work of the pointillists, Seurat and Signac. However, what was then but a shift in sensitivities from "the object" to "the impression of the object" set the stage for a transformation of momentous proportion in twentieth-century art. For, as artists from the cubists to the present increasingly asserted, art need not be pictorial; it creates its own reality—in Kandinsky's terms, "pure painting" or "object free" art. This view liberated figures such as Mondrian, Klee, Albers, and Rothko to explore the properties of color in itself. For Dubuffet it meant experimenting with raw materials as substitutes for pigment; for Pollack, dripping paint on canvas; and for optical (op) artists, investigating an array of disorienting visual effects. For the modernists the work of art was an essence within itself.[37] Or, as critic Clement Greenberg put it, each art is to be "rendered 'pure,' and in its 'purity' find the guarantee of its standards of quality as well as its independence."[38]

And finally, modernist poetry and fiction were affected. Echoing the architectural "Less is more," a reverberating theme among poets was "no

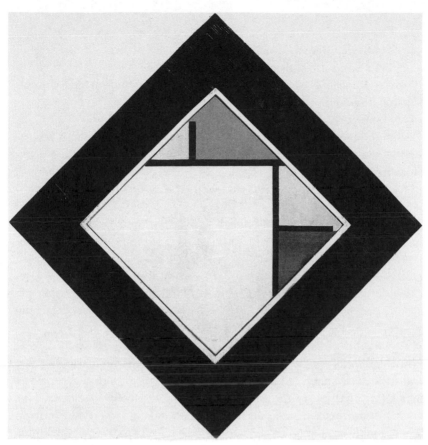

Theo van Doesburg's modernist *Composition* is not a representation of the world, but pure composition in itself.

unnecessary word." It is thus that modern poetry stands in stark contrast to the emotional outpourings of the romantics. Similarly, the modern novel often casts aside richly layered descriptions of characters and their settings, and brings into intense focus the obdurate "facts of the matter." For example, contrast the nineteenth-century adulation of the beloved quoted earlier with Ernest Hemingway's depiction of a lover's departure in *The Sun Also Rises*. Jake's lover, Brett, has just informed him that she is not going on with him but is remaining with the count (now off buying champagne). Brett says:

"Don't look like that, darling."
"How do you want me to look?"
"Oh, don't be a fool. I'm going away tomorrow."

FROM ROMANTIC TO MODERN VISION

"Tomorrow?"

"Yes. Didn't I say so? I am."

"Let's have a drink, then. The count will be back."

"Yes. He should be back. You know he's extraordinary about buying champagne. It means any amount to him."[39]

Within the modernist ethos it was appropriate that a newspaper reporter like Hemingway could turn novelist. Dialogue was essentially a dispassionate report of the "facts of the case." The possibility of "deeper significance," something beyond the given, was forced to the margins.[40]

The Metaphor of the Machine

Our civilization is taking on . . . the structure and properties of a machine. . . . This machine will not tolerate less than worldwide rule.
          —Paul Valéry, *The Outlook for Intelligence*

Rationality, observation, progress, and essentials—all of them modernist leitmotifs—were congenial companions to the increasingly potent and pervasive image of the machine. There were plenty of reasons to honor the machine in the modernist period. Not only could machines generate enormous incomes for their owners and operators, they provided jobs—a solid foundation for the national economy. They were also populist in their ends, able to work for the benefit of everyone. The large machines of industry could place telephones, radios, washing machines, electrical heaters, and the like into virtually everyone's hands. And each of those products was itself a machine, reducing labor and opening new and exciting opportunities.

In important respects the positivist conception of "truth through method" benefited from the metaphor of the machine. Guided by such a conception, fields of study could be viewed as "knowledge factories," generating objective truths like so many sausages. Scholars still apply such terms as "productive," "profitable," and "prosperous" to research programs. Machine imagery also rippled across the artistic scene. The Futurists, such as Marinetti and Malevich, saw in the machine the energy and strength sufficient for the construction of utopian societies. For cubist painters, human beings began to resemble complex mechanisms. Artists such as Léger, Feininger, Kandinsky, and Picasso began to fill the visual landscape with robotlike creatures. Similarly, when Schlemmer was asked to design costumes for a ballet, the outcome was a stage replete with automatons. In Paris the score of George Antheil's *Ballet Mécanique* was intended to be performed by a machine.[41]

The mechanical metaphor also left its mark on modern architecture. For late-nineteenth-century designers such as Ruskin and William Morris, great art was the product of high moral intention. Machines had no conscience, no soul; thus machine production was inherently inartistic.[42] However, partly because of the major demands placed on architects by both industry and science, and partly because machines themselves were producing a variety of new and substantial building materials (e.g., standardized metal and glass components), architectural thought became heavily mechanistic. By 1910 the design-oriented arts and crafts movement of Ruskin and Morris had been reconceptualized. It was now "a movement for the stamping out of [crafted designs] by sound production on the one hand and the inevitable regulation of machine production and cheap labour on the other."[43] For the Bauhaus group, familiarity with the machine was considered essential to all aesthetic study. As Le Corbusier summarized the case of architecture, "The house is a machine for living in."[44]

Fernand Léger's modernist-mechanist view of *Three Women.*

FROM ROMANTIC TO MODERN VISION

THE PRODUCTION OF MODERN MAN (*Sic*)*

In 1907 Dr. Duncan McDougall conducted an experiment to establish the objective existence of the human soul and to gauge its physical properties. His procedure was simple. He obtained the weight of human bodies immediately before death, and just after. He found that during the process of dying, bodily weight was systematically reduced (by approximately one ounce). What other conclusion was possible than the departure of a soul with a specifiable weight?

Such a conclusion seems quaint to the contemporary sensibility; McDougall's experiment was but an instance in the cultural transition from romanticism to modernism. Today we are little moved by romanticist talk of souls, but the modernist concept of human experimentation lives on robustly. If the physical world was subject to rational and objective scrutiny, and if progress could be made toward revealing the essence of art, architecture, and music, then should it not be possible as well to discover the basic character of human nature?

The twentieth century, then, was finally to answer the ancient challenge of the Delphic oracle: Know thyself. This challenge has been the chief occupation of scientific psychology, and psychologists have contributed much to the modernist vocabulary of self. Modernist views of the person now insinuate themselves into all corners of cultural life. Much that we hold dear and significant about ourselves and our relationships owes its intelligibility to such endeavors. Let us consider, then, what the present century has done both to obliterate the romantic preoccupation with the deep interior and to replace it with the rational, well-ordered, and accessible self.

The True and Accessible Self

In the social jungle of human existence there is no feeling of being alive without a sense of identity.
> —Erik H. Erikson, *Identity, Youth, and Crisis*

Science teaches that the world is composed of fixed and knowable entities. The same should be no less true of persons. For the romanticist the truly important features of the person lie beyond the bounds of observation and cannot be ensnared by simple practices of reason. For the

*N.B.: In this section I intentionally use sexist language, because as feminist scholars rightly observe, accounts of "human nature" in the present century have largely been accounts of male nature.

modernist, however, "murky interiors" no longer compel. The person is there, open to observation—"What you see is what you get"—and if you apply systematic powers of reason and observation you can know what sort of character you are dealing with. In the case of political figures— the Roosevelts, Churchill, de Gaulle, Dewey, and the like—one had a "sense of the man." Each possessed a firm and recognizable character. Even such popular entertainers as Jack Benny, Bob Hope, and Bing Crosby seemed to be "known." One expected that Jack Benny's life on the air did not differ distinctly from his life at home—surely Rochester and the violin were always there. By the same token, one could make relatively severe judgments about "goodness of character." There were the "honest" and the "dishonest," the "brave" and the "cowardly," the "moral" and the "wicked." There was no doubt that Will Rogers, Albert Einstein, Joe Louis, Doc Blanchard, Mahatma Gandhi, and Albert Schweitzer were "good guys." They were model human beings through and through. And they were to be contrasted with Dillinger and Capone, Laval and Mussolini, and of course the figure who "proved" the modernist thesis of basic character—Adolf Hitler.

In the literary realm, the sense of drama was often created by either the "growth" or the "revelation" of the protagonist's true nature. In Faulkner's *The Bear*, Salinger's *Catcher in the Rye*, and Hemingway's *Old Man and the Sea*, for example, the reader is caught up in the emergence of identity—the events leading to the crystallization of self. We learn how it is that persons come to be the individuals they truly are. In contrast, Miller's *Death of a Salesman*, O'Neill's *Long Day's Journey into Night*, and Williams's *Cat on a Hot Tin Roof* gain their dramatic impact by removing the trappings of a positive identity to reveal the true but discreditable character behind.[45] As the sociologist Kurt Back proposes, the "central attraction" of the mystery story in modern times is "the penetration of the unsuspected possibility of the other person."[46] The mystery relies on the reader's belief that there is "a truth about persons" and that it may be revealed by a thorough examination of the details of life.

It was psychologists who undertook the task of illuminating the nature of the basic self. The systematic application of reason and observation was to make "man's nature" known to "himself"—to generate fundamental knowledge of the knowledge-maker's foundations. Many attempted first to isolate and study basic "mechanisms" within "lower organisms," and then to move slowly to an understanding of human complexity. Thus, based on research with pigeons, rats, and primates, works began to appear with titles of staggering promise. B. F. Skinner's *The Behavior of Organisms*, Clark Hull's *Principles of Behavior*, and Edward Tolman's *Purposive Behavior in Animals and Men* were among the most influential.

In retrospect we find it disturbing that the scholarly world could believe the fundamentals of human nature could be laid bare by the antics of a small number of laboratory animals. Yet in the same way that experiments on souls were convincing to a romanticist mentality, so in the heyday of modernism the mind of man could be revealed by the behavior of the rat at a choice point.

Particularly for American psychologists, the image of the machine provided the dominant metaphor of the person. For if only the material world can be observed, then the knowledge of persons we seek must be the knowledge of material. And if machines are the most complex, powerful, and adaptive constructions of material known to man, then human beings must certainly be machinelike in their functioning. In this way it became comfortable to speak of "structures of thought," "perceptual mechanisms," "attitude structure," "association networks," the "stamping in" of habits, and so on. Each phrase connoted a being with a mechanical essence.[47] Much the same picture is repeated today in the cognitive sciences; the major change is in the form of machine. At present the mind is said to operate like a "dinky computer"—an effective and sophisticated "computational device," but no match for the fast machines. As the cognitive psychologist Ulrich Neisser points out, "The computer provided a much-needed reassurance that cognitive processes were real."[48] The computer metaphor is now placed into living practice in forms of cognitive therapy, "deprogramming" techniques, and "mind-building" computer toys for children.[49]

The immense attention devoted today to "cognitive processes" reveals a further dimension of the modernist view: man's essence is rational. Consider the fate of psychoanalysis in the present century. Freud's cauldron of seething and repressed motivational forces, so central to the romantic definition of the person, slowly dropped from view. In its place the ego, the beleaguered and obfuscated center of rationality for Freud, gained centrality. Among Freud's successors, Adler placed strong emphasis on conscious choice, Horney proposed that people can rationally conduct their own self-analysis, and Harry Stack Sullivan replaced psychosexual development with cognitive development as the central formative influence. With the advent of modernism, the torso was essentially severed at the waist, as "ego psychology," "object relations," and Kohut's "self-psychology" took over. Major problems were no longer buried so deeply within, but were typically attributed to the more accessible realm of thought. Perhaps the capstone theory of rationality was provided by the scholar and therapist George Kelly. For Kelly, emotional drives played no role whatsoever in human behavior. Rather, the ideal individual functioned exactly like a mature scientist, observing, categorizing, and testing hypotheses. "When we speak of man-the-scientist," wrote Kelly, "we are speaking of all mankind and not merely a particular class of men who have publicly attained the stature of 'scientists.'"[50] As a modernist, Kelly peered carefully into human nature, and lo—discovered a scientist.[51]

It is true that within therapeutic circles the machine metaphor was not widely prevalent. The assumption of basic essence was steadfast, however, and therapeutic theories and practice simultaneously revealed the positive value attached to this essence. Not simply did humans have an essence, but failing to possess one was tantamount to illness. Therapy functioned to build or restore essence. To illustrate, Erik Erikson proposed that the major achievement of normal development was a firm and fixed "sense of identity."[52] To cast about in a state of "identity diffusion" was to fail in the basic task of personality development. For Carl Rogers the quest for essence took the form of "becoming the self one fully is."[53] If others set conditions on their love, the victim begins to set conditions on the acceptance of self. The therapist's task is to restore a full sense of self-acceptance to the individual. Most existential therapists attempted to restore the individual's capacity for conscious choice—to establish the center of active being.[54]

Manufacturing the Individual

Human behavior is learned; precisely that behavior which is widely felt and characterizes man as a rational being, or as a member of a particular nation or social class, is learned rather than innate.
      —John Dollard and Neal E. Miller, *Personality and Psychotherapy*

If modern man possesses an essence, how are we to understand its origins? For the romanticist, such things as passion, genius, inspiration, and the like were largely inborn, inherent in the natural instincts of the individual. As romanticism waned, however, such explanations fell into disrepute. The modernist image of scientific progress offered an alternative solution: if knowledge of the world is built up through observation, as science makes apparent, then why isn't human behavior largely the result of external input? If we are rational creatures, we pay attention to the world and adjust our actions accordingly; thus, human actions must largely result from happenings in the surrounding world. In short, it is not by virtue of heredity that we are who we are, but by observation of the environment.

Freud may again be singled out for his significance in the transition from the romantic to the modern. The driving force behind all action, the energy of the id, was present at birth. However, this conception was coupled with a concern for the relationship of the child to his parents. The debilitating repression of the id was largely the result of prohibitions and restraints (e.g., castration threats) within the family. In effect, environmental forces bottled up the natural wellsprings of behavior; sickness was environmentally induced.

This same romanticist view of naturally good human beings corrupted by environmental conditions was carried on in the works of Erich Fromm, Karen Horney, and Carl Rogers. For each of them, social conditions were the causes of neurosis. This view lingers in more recent work on depression, in which depression is not seen as a natural or instinctive urge (as "melancholia" was for the romantics) but rather, as Seligman proposes in his popular volume *Learned Helplessness*, as the result of conditions in which one cannot exercise rational control over events.[55]

In the clinic, the environmentalist views led to techniques of "behavior modification." Problems such as phobias, homosexuality, depression, and the like were equivalent to malfunctions of machines. The therapist in this case operated much as a mechanic repairing a broken Maytag. For example, if the client wished to rid himself of his homosexual appetite, he might be seated at an apparatus delivering electric shocks when pictures of naked males appeared, but relief from shock when the female form was shown. Such primitive treatment was later replaced by techniques in which people learned to relax in situations previously found threatening (airplanes, elevators, tall buildings). For Freudian romantics, therapy required nothing less than total reconstruction of the psyche; ceasing to believe in "psychic depth," modernist therapists were free to tinker with the machinery at hand. Problems were to be confronted and solved, often with but a handful of treatment sessions.[56]

In the psychological laboratory, environmentalist leanings were even more pronounced. Research on learning played a pivotal role. Laboratory studies focused on a wide range of behavior—aggression, altruism, the understanding of self and others, memory, motivation, obedience, and the like—and in each case attempted to bring the behavior under experimental control. These behaviors were thought to be produced by environmental inputs; understanding the effects of various inputs in the laboratory would enable society to gain control over its destiny. These optimistic views also influenced advice given to the general public: In the case of child rearing, for example, parents were informed of the lifelong effects of their behavior on their children.

J. B. Watson, the "founder of behaviorism," proposed that it is through early learning experiences in the home that adult personality is formed. In a popular guide for parents, Watson wrote:

> It is especially easy to shape the emotional life at this early age. I might make this simple comparison: the fabricator of metal takes his heated mass, places it upon the anvil, and begins to shape it according to patterns of his own. Sometimes he uses a heavy hammer, sometimes a light one, sometimes he strikes the yielding mass a mighty blow, sometimes he gives it just a touch. So inevitably do we begin at birth to shape the emotional life of our children. The blacksmith has all the advantage. If his strokes have been heavy and awkward and he spoils his work, he can put the metal back on the fire and start the process over. There is no way of starting over again with a child. Every stroke, be it true or false, has its effect. The best we can do is to conceal, skillfully as we may, the defects of our shaping.[57]

Beliefs in the environmental production of personality were hardly limited to the learning laboratory. Industrial psychologists proposed improving worker output by altering environmental conditions. In this view, which Frederick Taylor called "scientific management," the worker is no less a machine than the machines with which he works.[58] And just as machines require inputs of electricity, oil, and gas to operate effectively, so workers require specifiable intensities of illumination, air temperatures, noise levels, rest pauses, and so on. Although the crude techniques of early scientific management have largely been abandoned, the modernist image of human organizations as machines continues to be reflected both in Simon and March's Nobel Prize–winning view of organizations as information-processing brains and in cybernetic theories of organizational life (complete with feedback mechanisms and automatonlike self-structuring).

Images of producing people also underlay many social practices of the times. Consider the behaviorist overtones of a popular child-rearing manual, Jacob Azerrad's *Anyone Can Have a Happy Child.*

> Children's behavior, good or bad, is directly related to the consequences of that behavior. . . . It doesn't matter to children whether they're being rewarded for behavior adults think is "bad" or "good." In either case, the rewarded behavior is likely to continue. It's up to the parents to be selective about the kind of behavior that receives attention.[59]

Youth training was also favored by the environmentalist view. Parental efforts to construct good character were to be supplemented by organizations such as the Boy Scouts, Girl Scouts, the YM and YWCA, the 4-H Club, Daughters of the American Revolution, Daughters of the Confederacy, Bible schools, and summer camps. Nothing less was at stake than the production of personality and thus society.

Personality and the Autonomous Individual

In healthy people [motivation] usually is autonomous of its origins. Its function is to animate and steer a life toward goals that are in keeping with present *structure,* present *aspirations, and* present *conditions.*
—Gordon W. Allport, *Personality and Social Encounter*

If machine imagery lies at the center of modernist conceptions of the person, then autonomous reliability should be the hallmark of the mature man. The well-designed machine resists deterioration and functions reliably; in the same way, if properly molded by family and society, the mature person will be "self-directing," "solid," "trustworthy," "consistent." To know him is to know what to expect of him. His words will be an authentic expression of what he truly is—now and in the future.[60] The modernist man is genuine rather than phony, principled rather than craven, and stable rather than wavering.

A focal text of the 1950s, David Riesman's *Lonely Crowd* both captured the modernist spirit and foresaw its demise. Riesman distinguished among several major character types, including the *inner-directed* and the *other-directed.* The former type was essentially an image of modernist man; his "source of direction . . . is 'inner' in the sense that it is implanted early in life by the elders and directed toward . . . inescapably destined goals."[61] The behavior of the inner-directed man was controlled by a "psychological gyroscope . . . set by parents and other authorities," which keeps him on course, "capable of maintaining a delicate balance between the demands upon him of his goal in life and the buffetings of his external environment."[62] However, it is the emergence of the other-directed man that most concerns Riesman, for he is without an internal guide; rather, his actions are forever guided by the immediate social surroundings. Riesman's antipathy for the other-directed individual is revealed in his choice of descriptions: "superficial," a "conformist" who "submits to the power of the group" and who possesses an "insatiable—need for approval."[63] This is a modernist evaluation of what we shall find to be the early emanations of the postmodern mentality.

Similar championing of the reliable, self-contained, machine-produced man permeates the psychological literature of the day. While purporting to be "value-free," scientific descriptions inevitably harbor and sustain the values of their proponents. Thus, it is no accident that during the hegemony of modernism, psychological research painted a consistently bleak picture of the individual without "the courage of his convictions," "strong moral fiber," "commitment," or "consistency." For example, in Solomon Asch's classic experiments on social conformity, research subjects were asked to judge the relative length of various lines.[64] Often the other participants in the study—all well rehearsed— agreed unanimously that what was obviously the shorter of two lines was the longer. When it was time for the real subjects to express their opinions, they frequently agreed to the unanimous but incorrect decisions of the group. This behavior was branded "conformity" by Asch and the profession more broadly, and equated with the sheeplike complicity of those failing to speak out against Nazism. The implicit value posture of such research is revealed when one considers other, equally appropriate descriptions— the subjects' actions could also be called "socially sensitive," "socially integrated," or "harmony-seeking." But in a period when "standing up for your own beliefs" was cherished, such descriptions were never seriously considered.

Researchers at Yale University similarly sought to find out why people are gullible to propaganda messages.[65] Why could they not think through the evidence on their own and stick to their convictions? (Note that if the messages provided "real information," gullibility would not be gullibility but "adaptive learning.") Extensive investigation revealed a major source of such degraded behavior: flawed personality. If people possessed basic self-confidence, researchers concluded, they might resist the silver-tongued devils of the world.[66] The attitude-change specialist William McGuire went on to formulate an "inoculation theory," the aim of which was to "inoculate" people against what must presumably have been seen as the "disease" of vulnerability to others' opinions.[67]

Perhaps the most powerful tribute to the rhetoric of autonomous and enduring dispositions was furnished by the personality- and mental-testing movements. If one could assume that persons possess machinelike essences, located not too far from the surface, then it should be possible to measure them. And if these essences can be measured, it should be possible to explain all manner of behavior and to predict the future of persons and societies. Just such presumptions inspired Theodor Adorno and his Berkeley colleagues to measure the *authoritarian personality*.[68] Using a pastiche of scales and correlations, they profiled an individual who was intellectually rigid, obedient to authority, and ethnocentric.

Precisely this type of personality, they reasoned, not only was responsible for Nazism in Germany but is racially prejudiced in the United States. In effect, evils in the world were traceable to evil essences.

By the same token, positive actions could be traced to stable dispositions. For example, the Harvard psychologist David McClelland proposed that a nation's economic prosperity is largely due to individual personality types characterized as high in *achievement motivation*.[69] Large-scale testing was used to fortify the speculation and to generate information about the kinds of child-rearing practices that fostered such stable tendencies. In addition, McClelland and his colleagues mounted programs to assist economically disadvantaged nations, such as India, in developing this economically essential personality trait. With the "right stuff," it was reasoned, the future of Indian well-being might be improved. One senses in this work the fascination of the grand narrative of progress.

This same belief laid the foundations for what later became the mental-testing industry. Based on the assumption that people are basically consistent or stable through time, that their essences will manifest themselves like a fingerprint or a birthmark, personality tests have flowered across the land. The Minnesota Multiphasic Personality Inventory (MMPI), the Strong Vocational Interest Test, the Stanford-Binet and Wechsler intelligence tests, and the Edwards Personality Preference Inventory (EPPI) are among the most widely used. There are also tests to measure leadership abilities, chronic depression, stress level, cognitive complexity, coping abilities, creativity, self-esteem, and a vast array of other "basic characteristics." By now most of the adult population in the United States has been subjected to mental tests, for they are viewed as more or less reliable gatekeepers or watchdogs for determining entry into or exclusion from school, jobs, military service, government service, and more. Even the Scholastic Aptitude Test (SAT)—so powerful as a national sorting device in the United States—benefits from the mystique that it measures a solid and enduring core. If it were not so—if such tests were perceived only to be indicators of transient moods, whims, or posturings—they would be of scant interest.

Yet the means by which such tests demonstrate the "internal traits" of the person is as interesting as it is misleading. At the onset, no one knows what causes people to place various markings in various patterns on paper. No one has observed "interior essences," and in terms of evidence one would be equally justified to announce that test scores were caused by "spontaneous creative urges," "a torrent of insights," or even "God's hand." Yet, consistent with the modernist ethos, the tests are said to measure mental dispositions. The measure is then used for predictive purposes—grades in college, occupational success, amenability to therapy, success in marriage, and the like. To be sure, such scores can be useful for predictive purposes. An individual with marked indicators of schizophrenia on various tests is not likely to make a good job candidate or marriage partner. Students in the lowest 20 percent on the SAT are not likely to graduate from Harvard.

Such predictive success sets the stage for a rhetorical sleight-of-hand so subtle that it remains undetected even by most investigators themselves. Successful predictions are called "evidence" that a test measures what it says it measures. "Something" caused the person to score as he did, and if the scores predict the future, then that "something" must be what the test-maker says it is. The logic is not unlike arguing that the internal voice of Satan causes people to have loose morals, and thereby concluding that a high correlation between a morality scale and, let us say, the frequency of extramarital intercourse is proof of the work of Satan in everyday life. In the modernist period, stable, machinelike essences replaced Satan as the fundamental source of human activity. But what essence, what "something," causes the test-taker to score as he does? We don't know; successful prediction in fact says nothing about the "underlying cause"—or indeed, whether behavior is even *caused* in the first place.

Many lament the loss of the romanticist languages of the person. However, it is also possible to appreciate the allure of the modernist replacement. In many ways modernism is both more optimistic and more democratic. The romantic individual was forever a mystery—the vital essence quixotic and out of reach. The modernist self, by contrast, is knowable, present in the here and now, just slightly below the surface of his actions. He is not likely to be transported by sudden inspiration, be smitten by some great passion, or give way to a rush of suicidal urges. Rather, he is reliable and trustworthy. His word today is good tomorrow and the next. The modernist self is not likely to have his reason clouded by intense emotional dramas; his reasons guide his actions and his voice is clear and honest. And we must not await the arrival of some naturally gifted, inspired, or insightful man to lead our nation or our institutions. Everyone is created equal, and it is up to us as parents and good citizens to mold the young. With proper molding, and the help of science, we create the future of our dreams. It is this modernist place in the sun that we shall find eclipsed by the rise of postmodernism.

THREE

Social Saturation and the Populated Self

Random moments from contemporary life:

- You find your mailbox stuffed with correspondence—advertisements for local events, catalogues from mail-order houses, political announcements, offers for special prizes, bills, and, just maybe, a letter.
- You return from a weekend away to find your answering machine overflowing with calls to be returned.
- You try to arrange a meeting with a business colleague in New York. She is attending a meeting in Caracas. When she returns next week you will be in Memphis. When all attempts to arrange a mutually convenient meeting place fail, you settle for a long-distance phone meeting in the evening.
- An old friend calls, passing through on business, and wants to meet for a drink or dinner.
- You think about planning a New Year's Eve party, but most of your good friends are away in Colorado, Mexico, or other vacation spots.
- You are away for the evening, but you program your VCR so that you won't miss a favorite program.
- You are in Montreal for a few days, and are surprised to meet a friend from back home in Atlanta.

Most of these events are commonplace in contemporary life, scarcely worth comment. Yet none of them were commonplace twenty years ago, and several have only entered our lives within the past five years. Such events are manifestations of a profound pattern of social change. The change is essentially one that immerses us ever more deeply in the social world, and exposes us more and more to the opinions, values, and life-styles of others.

It is my central thesis that this immersion is propelling us toward a new self-consciousness: the postmodern. The emerging commonplaces of communication—such as those just cited—are critical to understanding the passing of both the romantic and modern views of self. What I call the *technologies of social saturation* are central to the contemporary erasure of individual self. This chapter will explore the ways in which social saturation has come to dominate everyday life. However, we shall also see that as we become increasingly conjoined with our social surroundings, we come to reflect those surroundings. There is a *populating of the self*, reflecting the infusion of partial identities through social saturation. And there is the onset of a *multiphrenic* condition, in which one begins to experience the vertigo of unlimited multiplicity. Both the populating of the self and the multiphrenic condition are significant preludes to post-modern consciousness. To appreciate the magnitude of cultural change, and its probable intensification, attention must be directed to the emerging technologies.

THE TECHNOLOGIES OF SOCIAL SATURATION

Communication . . . defines social reality and thus influences the orga-nization of work, . . . the curriculum of the educational system, formal and informal relations, and the use of "free time"—actually the basic social arrangements of living.
  —Herbert I. Schiller, *Communication and Cultural Domination*

In the process of social saturation the numbers, varieties, and intensities of relationship increasingly crowd the days. A full appreciation of the magnitude of cultural change, and its probable intensification in future decades, requires that one focus first on the technological context. For in large measure, an array of technological innovations has led to an enormous proliferation of relationships. It is useful to survey two major phases in technological development, specifically what may be roughly called *low-tech* and *high-tech* phases. Preliminary advice to the reader is in order. Read the following section on technological change as rapidly as possible, for an experiential immersion in the enormity of the whole.

Life in Low Tech

Perhaps the most dramatic aspect of the low-tech phase is the simultaneity of its many developments. Here we are speaking of no less than seven sweeping and overlapping developments within the century, each of which casts us further into the social world. Consider their impact on social life:

1. *The railroad* was one of the first significant steps toward social saturation. The first surge in rail travel began in the mid-1800s. In 1869 it became possible for Americans to cross the continent by train.[1] Although rails are less used in the United States than other modes of transportation, most nations continue to improve their systems. Major new track lines are being laid in Russia and China. Fast rail systems have been installed in Japan, France, Italy, and Sweden, and an under-Channel system will soon link London and Paris. The number of rail passengers in Europe reached an all-time high in 1988, almost doubling the volume in 1970.[2] At the same time, urban mass transit—including elevated and underground rail—moves a steadily increasing volume of persons. Underground systems now operate in such diverse cities as Cairo, Prague, Minsk, and Beijing. More than sixty major cities around the world are now expanding their urban rail systems, and twenty-five new systems have opened in the last two years. With the recent development of the "maglev" (or "flying train"), capable of carrying 1,000 passengers at a speed of over 300 mph, rail transportation may be facing a renaissance.

2. Although *public postal services* were available in the eighteenth century, they did not truly begin to flourish until the advent of railroads in the nineteenth century and then airlines in the twentieth. In the early 1800s there were only about two thousand miles of postal routes in the United States[3]; by 1960 the figure had jumped to over two million miles. The volume of mail is also expanding rapidly; Americans receive almost three times more mail now than in 1945. At present the volume of mail is so great that the U.S. Postal Service is considered the largest single business in the world. In the early 1980s it employed over 700,000 workers, and it now moves over eighty billion items a year—nearly four hundred pieces of mail for every citizen of the nation.

3. At the beginning of this century *the automobile* was virtually unknown. Less than 100 cars had ever been produced in the entire world. Production increased only slowly until the assembly line was perfected in the 1920s. By 1930 world production of motor vehicles had reached the four-million mark, with more than three quarters of them produced in the United States. Fifty years later, in 1980, the annual production figure had jumped to almost 40 million—of which approximately a fifth

were made in the States.[4] Improvements in roads have also expanded the number of locations within reach. At the turn of the century there were only a hundred miles of hard-surface roads in the United States; by 1970 there were over two million miles of paved roads. Within recent decades the superhighways—more than 44,000 miles of them—have added new dimensions to long-distance travel.[5] Because of the expanding number of cars and people's increased dependency on them, traffic has become a major policy issue. Highway congestion is now so intense that the average speed on the Los Angeles freeways has dropped to 35 mph. In the next twenty years the volume of traffic is expected to rise by another 42 percent.[6]

4. *The telephone* made its entry into daily living at the turn of the century; within five decades there were some 90 million phones in the United States[7]; in the next decade, the number of phones almost doubled. There are now about 600 million telephones in the world (even though two thirds of the world's population still has no access to telephones). And the miles of telephone wire continue to expand (from 316 million miles of wire in 1960 to 1,290 million miles in 1984). The pattern of telephone relationships is also changing. Most dramatic is the shift in the function of the telephone from a community, to a national, to an international resource. The number of overseas calls from the United States in 1960 was approximately 3 million; by 1984 this figure had multiplied by almost 130 times, to almost 430 million calls.[8] And, within the 1980s, international telephone calls increased sixfold. As we shall see, high tech is in the process of sending this figure upward by untold magnitudes.

5. *Radio broadcasting* began in the United States and Great Britain in 1919. Since that time it has insinuated itself into virtually all aspects of social life. It has altered social patterns in living rooms, dining rooms, bedrooms, automobiles, beaches, workshops, waiting rooms, and city streets. In 1925 there were 600 stations in the world. This figure doubled in the next ten years, and by 1960 there were over 10,000 stations.[9] With miniaturization and mass production radios became increasingly affordable. By the mid-1980s there were some two billion radios in the world. In recent years "personal audio" has also become a major cultural phenomenon. There are now more than 12 million personal stereos moving about the globe, some to the very edges of civilization: An anthropologist visiting hill tribes along the Burmese border recently reported that the tribespeople offer to trade local handicrafts for personal stereos.

6. At the turn of the century *motion pictures* scarcely existed. The first moving pictures were shown in scattered music halls. With improvements in photography, projection, and sound recording, however, motion pic-

tures became increasingly popular. Even during the depression, box-office receipts remained relatively high. By the 1950s the weekly film audience in the United States alone reached 90 million.[10] Although film attendance at theaters has declined substantially as a result of television, both television and videocassettes continue to expose vast numbers of people to commercial films. (Over 60 percent of those American households with television also own a videocassette recorder.) In 1989 more new films were made in the United States than ever before—and even more were produced in India.

7. *Printed books* have been disseminating ideas, values, and modes of life for over 400 years. By the mid-1700s, for example, England produced some 90 titles a year; a century later, it produced 600.[11] With the development of the rotary printing press and factory production systems, commercial publishing has become a dominant force in the twentieth century. Particularly in the 1950s, with the emergence of paperback books, ownership of books became possible for vast segments of the population: by the 1960s English publishers printed over 20,000 titles a year, and by the 1980s, five nations (Canada, England, West Germany, the United States, and the USSR) were publishing between 50,000 and 80,000 titles a year.[12]

So we find seven technologies of social saturation—rail, post, auto-

Even in the smallest villages, one is seduced by values, attitudes, and aspirations from afar.

mobile, telephone, radio, motion pictures, and commercial publishing—all rapidly expanding within the twentieth century. Each brought people into increasingly close proximity, exposed them to an increasing range of others, and fostered a range of relationships that could never have occurred before.

High Life in High Tech

The seven low-tech alterations only began the saturation process. The past two decades have added untold potential for relatedness. We must briefly consider, then, the second, or high-tech, phase in the technology of social saturation, specifically developments in air transportation, television, and electronic communication.

Air Headings

Airport Gridlock Near, Aviation Experts Warn
—Headline, *New York Times*

The stories are told with increasing frequency: An executive flies from Washington, D.C., to Tokyo to represent his firm at a cocktail party; he returns the next day. Frankfurt couples fly to New York for the weekend to watch Boris Becker play in the U.S. Open. A New York executive flies to San Francisco to spend the day in consultation, and returns that night to Scarsdale on "the redeye." University officials wish to meet with candidates for an executive position; all are flown from locations across the continent for a single afternoon of meetings in an airport hotel. For a family reunion, eighteen people fly to St. Louis from five states across the nation.

For steadily increasing numbers air travel is becoming a casual matter. Businesses routinely think in terms of global expansion. Multinational corporations are so powerful that their budgets exceed that of many nations. Large cities are increasingly dependent on revenues from conference centers, international fairs, and tourism. For many academics, global conference-going is now a way of life. The reader of the Sunday *New York Times* in the 1930s would find no travel section. Today the section typically offers low-budget escapes to more than two hundred exotic locations. A high-school class reunion in North Carolina can pull graduates of over thirty years from as far away as Hawaii. Americans of Irish, Italian, German, and Scandinavian descent go to Europe in large numbers to locate relatives they have never met.

Such dramatic changes in social pattern have occurred only within the lifetime of most readers. Passenger travel by air was scarcely available before 1920. By the year 1940, however, there were approximately 3 million passengers in the United States.[13] Within ten years this figure jumped by six times. By 1970 the number of passengers reached almost 160 million. That figure again doubled in the next ten years. Almost eight of ten Americans have now flown. And, even though air traffic approaches gridlock, the FAA estimates 1990's total at 800 million passengers.[14] The number of passengers boarding planes in such cities as Dallas, Denver, Memphis, and Washington is expected to double by the year 2000. The Concorde now reaches speeds of Mach 2, transporting passengers from London to New York in less than four hours; a new generation of SSTs may bring Tokyo as close.[15]

Vistas of Video

A timid appearing junior college student meets a tall, blond, drug-using housepainter . . . and invites him to dinner. He gets amorous and rapes her in the bedroom of her apartment. She files charges but less than a month later she posts his bail and moves in with him and plans to be Mrs. Rapist. . . . When asked how she could marry [him] after what he did to her, she referred to a soap opera in which one character rapes another and later marries her. "It's like Luke and Laura on 'General Hospital,'" [she] said. . . . In keeping with the . . . TV flavor of the whole affair, [he] asked her to marry him while they were watching the Oprah Winfrey show, and they are considering an invitation to appear on the Phil Donahue show . . .

—*Philadelphia Daily News*

The year 1946 is a watershed, the first year of commercial television. In 1949 over a million television sets were sold in the United States. Two years later there were ten million; by 1959, fifty million.[16] By the early 1980s there were some 800 million television sets in use throughout the world. And they are watched. In the United States the average television set brings the outside world into the home for seven hours a day.

All that is well known. But two more subtle issues deserve attention, both significant to the understanding of social saturation.

First, it is important to consider a phenomenon with beginnings in the low-tech period of radio, film, and commercial publishing, but which becomes paramount in the high-tech era of television. This is the phenomenon of *self-multiplication*, or the capacity to be significantly present in more than one place at a time. In the face-to-face community one's capacities to carry on a relationship or to have social impact were restricted in space and time. Typically one's identity was manifest to those immediately before one's eyes, though books and newspapers made "multiples" of powerful individuals. With the development of radio and film, one's opinions, emotions, facial expressions, mannerisms, styles of relating, and the like were no longer confined to the immediate audience, but were multiplied manifold. Insights murmured into a microphone in Denver's Brown Palace Hotel could be heard by thousands in St. Louis, Minneapolis, and Grand Rapids. Manners of courting, arguing, deceiving, or playing the hero in a Hollywood studio were available for small-town millions across the country.

Television has generated an exponential increase in self-multiplication. This is true not only in terms of the increased size of television audiences and the number of hours to which they are exposed to social facsimiles, but in the extent to which self-multiplication transcends time—that is, in which one's identity is sustained in the culture's history. Because television channels are plentiful, popular shows are typically rebroadcast in succeeding years. The patient viewer can still resonate with Groucho Marx on *You Bet Your Life* or Jackie Gleason and Audrey Meadows on *The Honeymooners.*

Further, the VCR has made video-rental libraries possible—perhaps 500,000 throughout the country. Now people need not wait for a given film to be screened or televised; it lies waiting close by for the further duplication of its personages. People can choose the actors they wish to identify with or the stories that will bring fantasies to life. Increasingly this also means that in terms of producing a sense of social connection, any given actor may transcend his or her own death; viewers can continue their private relationships with Marilyn Monroe and James Dean long after the physical demise of the performers. With television, a personage may continue a robust life over eternity.

A second issue follows quickly from the first. I am proposing that the media—especially radio, television, and the movies—are vitally expanding the range and variety of relationships available to the population. Yet, the critic may reasonably respond, do such exposures count as *real* or important relationships? After all, there is no give-and-take, no reciprocal interchange. The answer to this challenge depends largely on what one counts as "real or important." Surely face-to-face encounter is not a requirement of what most people would consider "real and important" relationships. Some of the world's most intense affairs of the heart (Héloïse and Abelard, Elizabeth Barrett and Robert Browning) were carried on largely by written word. Nor does reciprocal interchange seem essential for significant bonding; consider people's relationships with religious figures such as Jesus, Buddha, and Mohammed. If palpable presence is not essential to such relationships, then one must be prepared for the possibility that media figures do enter significantly into people's personal lives.

There is good reason to believe so. Social researchers have long been concerned with the impact of televised violence on the attitudes and behavior of the young. Numerous instances of people acting out what they've seen on television have been documented, even when the models engage in theft, torture, and murder.[17] More directly, Richard Schickel's *Intimate Strangers* explores the manner in which the media generate an illusionary sense of intimacy with celebrity figures.[18] Not only are famous people available to us on television, in the movies, in autobiographies, and in celebrity magazines, but often these media furnish intimate details of their personal lives. We may know more about Merv, Oprah, Johnny, and Phil than we do our neighbors. At one point, according to a national survey, newsman Walter Cronkite was the "most trusted man in America." And, because such figures do become so well known, people absorb them into their cast of significant others—loving, sympathizing with, and loathing them. It is thus that David Letterman sought a court injunction against a woman who claimed to be his wife, John Lennon was killed by an unknown fan, President Reagan was shot by John Hinckley, and the television star Rebecca Schaeffer was killed by a fan who had written unanswered letters to her for two years. The columnist Cynthia Heimel argues that because celebrity figures are known by so many people, they serve as forms of social glue, allowing people from different points of society to converse with each other, to share feelings, and essentially to carry on informal relations. "Celebrities," she proposes, "are our common frames of reference, celebrity loathing and revilement crosses all cultural boundaries. Celebrities are not our community elders, they are our community."[19]

Also relevant are the immense amounts of time, money, and personal effort that go into maintaining media relationships. Millions are spent each year on magazines, books, posters, T-shirts, towels, and photographs bearing likenesses of the favored idol. When *Batman* opened, a crowd of 20,000 stood for hours to glimpse celebrities for a few seconds in person. How many of one's neighbors elicit such dedication? It may also be ventured that with the advances in film technology, the movies have become one of the most powerful rhetorical devices in the world. Unlike most of our acquaintances, films can catapult us rapidly and effectively into states of fear, anger, sadness, romance, lust, and aesthetic ecstasy—often within

the same two-hour period. It is undoubtedly true that for many people film relationships provide the most emotionally wrenching experiences of the average week. The ultimate question is not whether media relationships approximate the normal in their significance, but whether normal relationships can match the powers of artifice.

For many, the powers of artifice may indeed be in the superior position. So powerful are the media in their well-wrought portrayals that their realities become more compelling than those furnished by common experience. The vacation is not *real* until captured on film; marriages become events staged for camera and videotape; sports fans often prefer television because it is more fully lifelike than the eyeball view from the stands. It is to the media, and not to sense perception, that we increasingly turn for definitions of what is the case.

Electronic Innovation and the Proliferation of Relationships

Tomorrow's executives will have to feel as "at home" in Sapporo as Strasbourg as San Francisco . . . asserts Lester Thurow, Dean of MIT's Sloan School of Management. . . . "To be trained as an American manager is to be trained for a world that is no longer there."
                                                                    —*U.S. News and World Report*

Two of the greatest impediments to communicating, and thus relating, over long distances are slowness and expense. In the 1850s it was possible to convey a message across the American continent, but the speed of transmission was approximately ten miles an hour. The Pony Express required nine days to carry mail from Missouri to California, and the cost for half an ounce was $5.[20] The telegraph system later increased the speed of transmission by an enormous magnitude, but it was still expensive. In recent decades, electronic transmission has cut sharply into these two barriers, and current developments stagger the imagination.

In the late 1950s the development of the digital computer brought great advantages: it could store immense amounts of information in a relatively small space, and could process and transmit this information very quickly. The computer has now become a mainstay for most businesses of any magnitude. With the development of the microchip in the late 1970s, the efficiency of information storage, processing, and transmission increased by an additional magnitude. In the space required by a single handwritten letter, the equivalent of 500 books—two good-sized bookcases—can now be stored on a microchip.[21] With the perfection of laser processing, the microchip will be replaced by a process enabling a single disk on a home computer to store the entire works of Shakespeare several times over. In a single suitcase could be deposited the entire contents of the Library of Congress. Where days might be required to transmit the contents of a single book by telegraph or even phone, microprocessing enables such contents to be transmitted within a matter of seconds. Further, the microchip has meant that computers could be cheap enough for home use; the personal computer business is now a major growth industry in many countries. In 1981 there were slightly over 2 million personal computers in America.[22] By 1987 the figure jumped to almost 38 million, some 10 percent of which allows laptop work to continue in trains, planes, and hotel rooms. And sales continue to rise . . .

With low-cost electronic printing equipment (including home printers and copy machines), every computer owner is now a potential book publisher. Through desktop publishing, computer owners become direct agents of their own self-multiplication. Proponents of electronic communication had expected use of paper to dwindle in the 1990s, but largely because of desktop publishing, more paper is now used than ever before. With the development of the modem, any computer could be linked via existing phone cables to any other computer with a modem. This development, in turn, gave birth to electronic mail, computer teleconferences, and on-line databases (or information services).

Electronic mail first served mainly those within one city or organization. Most large cities offer bulletin-board services, which allow individuals to place an announcement of their interests on a file open to all users of the system. In this way computer conversations develop, and fanciful sub-cultures spring to life, sharing interests—at any time of day or night—in areas ranging from African art to aphrodisiacs, backgammon to banjos, philately to fellatio. There is almost always someone "out there" to talk to. Many local bulletin boards are also connected to national routing services that transmit messages overnight and free of charge from one board to another across the country. Many participants speak of the warm and accepting relations that develop within these contexts—much like a corner bar, where there are always old buddies and new friends. Estimates are that up to a billion messages a year are now being transmitted in the United States by electronic mail.[23]

Teleconference services enable groups of persons from across the country simultaneously to converse with one another. Over a half million Americans also make use of national, on-line information services or videotex—CompuServe, Dow Jones, or the Source—with databases that rapidly inform their users of airline schedules, movie reviews, world weather, the national news, and more. In France there are over 3,000 such home services available, including home banking, shopping, real-estate listings, and magazine contents.

In the 1960s rockets made it possible to place communication satellites into orbits that keep them in a fixed position relative to points on earth. While in orbit, they can bounce continuous electronic transmissions from one point on earth to another over almost one-third of the planet's surface At present these satellites transmit radio signals, telephone communication, digital data, and the like instantaneously to the far corners of the globe. Governments rely on such services to carry out their foreign policies, multinational corporations to conduct business, and individuals to sustain friendships. In poor rural areas in Mexico, satellite dishes allow Mexican families to receive as many as 130 TV channels from at least seven nations and in five languages. Satellite television reception is only in its infancy. In the mid-1980s it involved 130 satellites; twice as many are anticipated by the early 1990s.[24] To help business and government take advantage of the satellite capabilities, new companies are springing to life. These enterprises, some now boasting over 100,000 employees, install globe-spanning communications networks.

Worldwide electronic linkages, in combination with computer and telephone, have enabled the development of further social linkages via fax machines, which can convey printed matter rapidly and inexpensively throughout the world. A letter written by a political figure in Iran can, within seconds, be received in embassies around the globe. And with the aid of photocopy and mail, the same message can be in the hands of thousands the following day. Fax machines are rapidly gaining the capacity to transmit complex visual materials (such as maps and photographs), and the cost is dropping enough for fax services to be offered in hotels, in airports, and on trains. Low-cost, personal fax facilities are now advertised in flight magazines; the next step is clear.

These developments—computers, electronic mail, satellites, faxes—are only the beginning. Innovations now emerging will further accelerate the growth in social connectedness. At the outset is the digitization of all the major media—phonograph, photography, printing, telephone, radio, television. This means that the information conveyed by each source—pictures, music, voice—is becoming translatable to computer form. As a result, each medium becomes subject to the vast storage and rapid processing and transmission capabilities of the computer.[25] Each becomes subject to home production and worldwide dissemination. We now face an age in which pressing a button will enable us to transmit self-images—in full color and sound—around the globe.

Fiberoptic cables increase the amount of information that can be received a thousandfold. This opens the possibility for a virtual infinity of new television and radio bands. Further, fiberoptic cable will allow the transmission of a television picture of twice the fidelity of what is now available (approximating 35mm motion picture film). Digital phone services can be carried on the cable, not only reproducing the voice with fidelity, but also enabling subscribers to see the other person. So much information can be carried on the cable that all these various services could be taking place while subscribers were simultaneously having their utility meters read and their electronic mail collected. With a home fax receiver, one could also have an instant *Los Angeles Times* or *National Geographic* at one's fingertips.[26] Plans are now under way for people to designate the kinds of news they wish to see, and for computers to scan information services and compose individualized newspapers—to be printed on reusable paper.[27]

Over a hundred nations (including the USSR) are now involved in linking all the world's phone systems. Simultaneously, the development of the cellular phone is mobilizing possibilities for communication. With the development of point-to-point contact around the world, the 12 million cellular phones now in use will represent but a bare beginning. One could be anywhere—from a woodside walk in Maine to a hut in the Malaysian jungle—and speak with a loved one or colleague on the other side of the globe. Plans are now afoot for the world system to carry *all* electronic signals—including phone, television, recorded music, written text. This would enable a user to plug into the system anywhere from Alabama to Zaire and immediately transmit and receive manuscripts, sound recordings, or videotapes. The process of social saturation is far from complete.

THE PROCESS OF SOCIAL SATURATION

Monocultural communication is the simplest, most natural, and—in the contemporary world—most fragile form of communication. At its best, it is a rich, satisfying, and effortless way of communicating; at its worst, it can be narrow-minded and coercive.
        —W. Barnett Pearce, *Communication and the Human Condition*

A century ago, social relationships were largely confined to the distance of an easy walk. Most were conducted in person, within small communities: family, neighbors, townspeople. Yes, the horse and carriage made longer trips possible, but even a trip of thirty miles could take all day. The railroad could speed one away, but cost and availability limited such travel. If one moved from the community, relationships were likely to end. From birth to death one could depend on relatively even-textured social surroundings. Words, faces, gestures, and possibilities were relatively consistent, coherent, and slow to change.

For much of the world's population, especially the industrialized West, the small, face-to-face community is vanishing into the pages of history. We go to country inns for weekend outings, we decorate condominium interiors with clapboards and brass beds, and we dream of old age in a rural cottage. But as a result of the technological developments just described, contemporary life is a swirling sea of social relations. Words thunder in by radio, television, newspaper, mail, radio, telephone, fax, wire service, electronic mail, billboards, Federal Express, and more. Waves of new faces are everywhere—in town for a day, visiting for the weekend, at the Rotary lunch, at the church social—and incessantly and incandescently on television. Long weeks in a single community are unusual; a full day within a single neighborhood is becoming rare. We travel casually across town, into the countryside, to neighboring towns, cities, states; one might go thirty miles for coffee and conversation.

Through the technologies of the century, the number and variety of relationships in which we are engaged, potential frequency of contact, expressed intensity of relationship, and endurance through time all are steadily increasing. As this increase becomes extreme we reach a state of social saturation. Let us consider this state in greater detail.

Multiplying Relationships

In the face-to-face community the cast of others remained relatively stable.[28] There were changes by virtue of births and deaths, but moving from one town—much less state or country—to another was difficult. The number of relationships commonly maintained in today's world stands in stark contrast. Counting one's family, the morning television news, the car radio, colleagues on the train, and the local newspaper, the typical commuter may confront as many different persons (in terms of views or images) in the first two hours of a day as the community-based predecessor did in a month. The morning calls in a business office may connect one to a dozen different locales in a given city, often across the continent, and very possibly across national boundaries. A single hour of prime-time melodrama immerses one in the lives of a score of individuals. In an evening of television, hundreds of engaging faces insinuate themselves into our lives. It is not only the immediate community that occupies our thoughts and feelings, but a constantly changing cast of characters spread across the globe.

Two aspects of this expansion are particularly noteworthy. First there is what may be termed the *perseverance of the past*. Formerly, increases in time and distance between persons typically meant loss. When someone moved away, the relationship would languish. Long-distance visits were arduous, and the mails slow. Thus, as one grew older, many active participants would fade from one's life. Today, time and distance are no longer such serious threats to a relationship. One may sustain an intimacy over thousands of miles by frequent telephone raptures punctuated by occasional visits. One may similarly retain relationships with high-school chums, college roommates, old military cronies, or friends from a Caribbean vacation five years earlier. Birthday books have become a standard household item; one's memory is inadequate to record the festivities for which one is responsible. In effect, as we move through life, the cast of relevant characters is ever expanding. For some this means an ever-increasing sense of stress: "How can we make friends with them? We don't even have time for the friends we already have!" For others there is a sense of comfort, for the social caravan in which we travel through life remains always full.

Yet at the same time that the past is preserved, continuously poised to insert itself into the present, there is an *acceleration of the future*. The pace of relationships is hurried, and processes of unfolding that once required months or years may be accomplished in days or weeks. A century ago, for example, courtships were often carried out on foot or horseback, or through occasional letters. Hours of interchange might be punctuated by long periods of silence, making the path from acquaintanceship to intimacy lengthy. With today's technologies, however, it is possible for a couple to maintain almost continuous connection. Not only do transportation technologies chip away at the barrier of geographic distance, but through telephone (both stable and cordless), overnight mail, cassette recordings, home videos, photographs, and electronic mail, the other may be "present" at almost any moment. Courtships may thus move from excitement to exhaustion within a short time. The single person may experience not a handful of courtship relationships in a lifetime but dozens. In the same way, the process of friendship is often accelerated. Through the existing technologies, a sense of affinity may blossom into a lively sense of interdependence within a brief space of time. As the future opens, the number of friendships expands as never before.

Bending the Life-Forms

Our private sphere has ceased to be the stage where the drama of the subject at odds with his objects . . . is played out; we no longer exist as playwrights or actors, but as terminals of multiple networks.
       —Jean Baudrillard, *The Ecstasy of Communication*

New patterns of relationship also take shape. In the face-to-face community one participated in a limited set of relationships—with family, friends, storekeepers, clerics, and the like. Now the next telephone call can thrust us suddenly into a new relationship—with a Wall Street broker, a charity solicitor, an alumni campaigner from the old school, a childhood friend at a nearby convention, a relative from across the country, a child of a friend, or even a sex pervert. One may live in a suburb with well-clipped neighbors, but commute to a city for frequent confrontation with street people, scam merchants, panhandlers, prostitutes, and threatening bands of juveniles. One may reside in Houston, but establish bonds—through business or leisure travel—with a Norwegian banker, a wine merchant from the Rhine Pfalz, or an architect from Rome.

Of course, it is television that most dramatically increases the variety of relationships in which one participates—even if vicariously. One can identify with heroes from a thousand tales, carry on imaginary conversations with talk-show guests from all walks of life, or empathize with athletes from around the globe. One of the most interesting results of this electronic expansion of relationships occurs in the domain of parent-child relationships. As Joshua Meyrowitz proposes in *No Sense of Place*, children of the preceding century were largely insulated from information about the private lives of adults.[29] Parents, teachers, and police could shield children from their adult proceedings by simply conducting them in private places. Further, books dealing with the misgivings, failings, deceits, and conflicts of the adult world were generally unavailable to children. Children remained children. Television has changed all that. Programming systematically reveals the full panoply of "backstage" trials and tribulations to the child. As a result the child no longer interacts with one-dimensional, idealized adults, but with persons possessing complex private lives, doubt-filled and vulnerable. In turn, parents no longer confront the comfortably naive child of yesteryear, but one whose awe is diminished and whose insights may be acute.

The technology of the age both expands the variety of human relationships and modifies the form of older ones. When relationships move from the face-to-face to the electronic mode, they are often altered. Relationships that were confined to specific situations—to offices, living rooms, bedrooms—become "unglued." They are no longer geographically confined, but can take place anywhere. Unlike face-to-face relationships, electronic relationships also conceal visual information (eye movement, expressive movements of the mouth), so a telephone speaker cannot read the facial cues of the listener for signs of approval or disapproval. As a result, there is a greater tendency to create an imaginary other with whom to relate. One can fantasize that the other is feeling warm and enthusiastic or cold and angry, and act accordingly. An acquaintance told me that he believed his first marriage to be a product of the heavy phoning necessary for a long-distance courtship. By phone she seemed the most desirable woman in the world; it was only months after the wedding that he realized he had married a mirage.

Many organizations are now installing electronic-mail systems, which enable employees to carry out their business with each other by computer terminals rather than by traditional, face-to-face means. Researchers find that employee relations have subtly changed as a result. Status differences begin to crumble as lower-ranking employees feel freer to express their feelings and question their superiors electronically than in person. Harvard Business School's Shoshana Zuboff suggests that the introduction of "smart machines" into businesses is blurring the distinctions between managers and workers. Managers are no longer the "thinkers" while the workers are consigned to the "doing."[30] Rather, out of necessity the workers now become managers of information, and as a result, they considerably augment their power.

Relating in New Keys

Of the new forms of relationship that the saturation process has helped create, two are of special interest. First is the *friendly lover* relationship. For the essential romanticist, the object of love was all-consuming. He or she possessed value of such immense proportion that a lifetime of steadfast commitment could be viewed merely as preparation for an eternity of spiritual communion. The belief in marriage for "true love" is still pervasive, but as the social world is increasingly saturated, such relationships become unrealistic. Rather, men and women (especially professionals) are often in motion—traveling to business meetings, conferences, sales campaigns, consultations, vacations, and so on. Murmurings of "I can't live without you" lose their authenticity when one must add, "except until next Tuesday, and possibly again until the following Wednesday." And because many attractive members of the opposite sex are encountered along the way—providing professional benefits and companionship as well—a multiplicity of low-level, or "friendly," romances is invited. To illustrate, a single professional woman from Maryland disclosed that she was "seeing" a local lawyer (unhappily married) because it was fun and convenient. At the same time, he took a back seat when a favorite "old friend" in her profession came in from Oklahoma. However, especially during the summer, she was keen to spend her weekends with a Boston consultant (relevant to her line of work) whose boat was moored at Martha's Vineyard. Each of these individuals, in turn, had other friendly lovers.

A second interesting pattern, the *microwave relationship*, is found increasingly on the domestic front. The ideal family unit has traditionally included a close, interdependent "nucleus," composed of a father-provider, a caretaking mother, and children whose lives are centered in the home until early adulthood. Social saturation has cut deeply into this traditional view. Husband and wife are now both likely to have work and recreational relations outside the family; day-care and babysitting facilities are increasingly required; children's social activities may be scattered across city and countryside; evening obligations or indulgences are frequent both for parents and for children over the age of six; and family members are typically drawn into outside activities—sports, religious, community, hobbies, visits—on the weekends. Differing television needs often thrust various family members into different trajectories even when they are at home together. In many families the crucial ritual of interdependence—dinner together—has become a special event. (In some households the dining-room table, once a family center, is strewn with books, papers, letters, and other objects dropped there by family members "passing through.") The home is less a nesting place than a pit stop.

At the same time, however, many parents are loath to give up the traditional image of the close-knit family. As a result, a new form of relationship emerges in which family members attempt to compensate for the vast expanses of nonrelatedness with intense expressions of bondedness. As many understand it, quantity is replaced by quality. The microwave oven is more than a technological support for those living a socially saturated life. It is also a good symbol of the newly emerging form of relationship: in both cases the users command intense heat for the immediate provision of nourishment. The adequacy of the result is subject to debate in both cases.

Intensifying Interchange

Modern society is to be distinguished from older social formations by the fact that it affords more opportunities both for impersonal and for more intensive personal relationships.

—Niklas Luhmann, *Love as Passion*

Interestingly, technology also intensifies the emotional level of many relationships. People come to feel more deeply and express themselves more fully in an increasing number of relationships. This proposal may seem suspect. If persons pass through our lives in increasing numbers and speeds, wouldn't the outcome be a sense of superficiality and a disinclination to get involved? The attractive stranger you meet in Seattle is regrettably from Omaha; the fascinating new neighbors are returning in the spring to London; the absorbing seatmate on the plane is flying on to Bombay. What is there to do but keep it light and cool? To be sure, the vast share of the passing parade remains simply that. However, consider two aspects of the traditional, face-to-face community.

First, as relationships continue over a period of years they tend toward normalization. People choose to do things that reliably give them satisfaction. Changes in pattern mean risking these satisfactions. Thus, relationships over time tend toward a leveling of emotional intensity. As many married couples put it, "Exciting romance is replaced by a comfortable depth."

Second, the face-to-face community lends itself to a high degree of informal surveillance. People tend to know what the others are doing most of the time. They see each other across a room, through their windows, passing in the street, and so on. And where the social world remains stable, and new information is scant, the smallest details of one's life become everyone's topics of conversation. Petty gossip and strong community norms walk hand in hand. The intensity generated by the new, the novel, and the deviant is in scarce supply.

In the present context of saturation, neither of these conditions prevails. Because all relationships are constantly being disrupted, it is more difficult for any given relationship to normalize. The evening at home, once quiet, relaxed, and settling, is now—by dint of telephone, automobile, television, and the like—a parade of faces, information, and intrusions. One can scarcely settle into a calming rut, because who one is and the cast of "significant others" are in continuous motion. Further, because relationships range far and wide, largely through various electronic means, they cannot easily be supervised by others who care. One can find the intimacy of "telling all" to a close friend in Chicago, because those who would be horrified in Dallas or Topeka will never know. One can let the internal fires rage in Paris, because the folk in Peoria will never see the glow. One academic colleague spoke of his conversation with a woman while waiting in a check-in line for a return journey to the United States. The plane was to stop over in Iceland, and passengers had the choice of continuing the journey directly or remaining in Iceland and catching the next plane two days later. The professor found himself attracted to the lady and emboldened by the anonymity of the situation. Suddenly he found himself stammering a proposal to the woman to remain with him in Iceland for two days. Her complex smile gave him no answer. They silently approached the baggage carts on which travelers had to place their bags for either the direct flight or the layover. To his speechless amazement, she maneuvered her bag into the latter cart. After two days of bliss they parted company, never to communicate with each other again.

The press toward intensity is not limited to normalization and the breakdown of surveillance. There are also factors of fantasy and fleetingness at play. As the romanticists were well aware, little inspired the pen so much as the absence of the adored one. In the other's absence, one's fantasies were free to roam; one could project onto the favored person all virtues and desires. In this respect, nineteenth-century romanticism can be partially attributed to the combination of a cultural morality that discouraged a free play of relationships and the number of individuals educated in writing. Although standards of morality have liberalized since then, the increased possibility for relationships at a distance has had much the same effect as it did on the romantics. Relations at a distance can thus glow more brightly, and interchanges remain more highly charged.

The occasional meeting is intensified, finally, by its shortness. If it is agreed that the other is a "good friend," "very close," or a "special person," then the short periods of meeting must be similarly expressive. One must somehow demonstrate the significance of one's feelings and the high esteem in which the relationship is held. And, because there is little time, the demonstrations must be loud and clear. The result may be an elegantly prepared dinner, reservations at an unusual restaurant, entertainments or excursions planned, selected guests invited for sharing, and the like. Friends living in a central European city recently complained of what amounted to a delirium ad exhaustion. So frequently did visiting friends require a "display of significance" that both spirits and pocketbooks were depleted. Couples in frequently visited cities such as New York and Paris speak of the measures they take to ensure they have no spare bedrooms. With frequent visitors, no time remains for their nurturing capacities; spare rooms risk the evisceration of their private relationship.

POPULATING THE SELF

The very din of imaginal voices in adulthood—as they sound in thought and memory, in poetry, drama, novels, and movies, in speech, dreams, fantasy, and prayer . . . can be valued not just as subordinate to social reality, but as a reality as intrinsic to human existence as the literally social.

—Mary Watkins, *Invisible Guests*

Consider the moments:

- Over lunch with friends you discuss Northern Ireland. Although you have never spoken a word on the subject, you find yourself heatedly defending British policies.
- You work as an executive in the investments department of a bank. In the evenings you smoke marijuana and listen to the Grateful Dead.
- You sit in a café and wonder what it would be like to have an intimate relationship with various strangers walking past.
- You are a lawyer in a prestigious midtown firm. On the weekends you work on a novel about romance with a terrorist.
- You go to a Moroccan restaurant and afterward take in the latest show at a country-and-western bar.

In each case individuals harbor a sense of coherent identity or self-sameness, only to find themselves suddenly propelled by alternative impulses. They seem securely to be one sort of person, but yet another comes bursting to the surface—in a suddenly voiced opinion, a fantasy, a turn of interests, or a private activity. Such experiences with variation and self-contradiction may be viewed as preliminary effects of social saturation. They may signal a *populating of the self*, the acquisition of multiple and disparate potentials for being. It is this process of self-population that begins to undermine the traditional commitments to both romanticist and modernist forms of being. It is of pivotal importance in setting the stage for the postmodern turn. Let us explore.

The technologies of social saturation expose us to an enormous range of persons, new forms of relationship, unique circumstances and opportunities, and special intensities of feeling. One can scarcely remain unaffected by such exposure. As child-development specialists now agree, the process of socialization is lifelong. We continue to incorporate information from the environment throughout our lives. When exposed to other persons, we change in two major ways. We increase our capacities for *knowing that* and for *knowing how*. In the first case, through exposure to others we learn myriad details about their words, actions, dress, mannerisms, and so on. We ingest enormous amounts of information about patterns of interchange. Thus, for example, from an hour on a city street, we are informed of the clothing styles of blacks, whites, upper class, lower

Invited from wide-ranging locales, each representing a different profession, speakers meet for a single evening at Swarthmore College to address a large audience on current conflicts in education. Sara Lawrence Lightfoot speaks.

class, and more. We may learn the ways of Japanese businessmen, bag ladies, Sikhs, Hare Krishnas, or flute players from Chile. We see how relationships are carried out between mothers and daughters, business executives, teenage friends, and construction workers. An hour in a business office may expose us to the political views of a Texas oilman, a Chicago lawyer, and a gay activist from San Francisco. Radio commentators espouse views on boxing, pollution, and child abuse; pop music may advocate machoism, racial bigotry, and suicide. Paperback books cause hearts to race over the unjustly treated, those who strive against impossible odds, those who are brave or brilliant. And this is to say nothing of television input. Via television, myriad figures are allowed into the home who would never otherwise trespass. Millions watch as talk-show guests—murderers, rapists, women prisoners, child abusers, members of the KKK, mental patients, and others often discredited—attempt to make their lives intelligible. There are few six-year-olds who cannot furnish at least a rudimentary account of life in an African village, the concerns of divorcing parents, or drug-pushing in the ghetto. Hourly our storehouse of social knowledge expands in range and sophistication.

This massive increase in knowledge of the social world lays the groundwork for a second kind of learning, a *knowing how*. We learn how to place such knowledge into action, to shape it for social consumption, to act so

that social life can proceed effectively. And the possibilities for placing this supply of information into effective action are constantly expanding. The Japanese businessman glimpsed on the street today, and on the television tomorrow, may be well confronted in one's office the following week. On these occasions the rudiments of appropriate behavior are already in place. If a mate announces that he or she is thinking about divorce, the other's reaction is not likely to be dumb dismay. The drama has so often been played out on television and movie screens that one is already prepared with multiple options. If one wins a wonderful prize, suffers a humiliating loss, faces temptation to cheat, or learns of a sudden death in the family, the reactions are hardly random. One more or less knows how it goes, is more or less ready for action. Having seen it all before, one approaches a state of ennui.

In an important sense, as social saturation proceeds we become pastiches, imitative assemblages of each other. In memory we carry others' patterns of being with us. If the conditions are favorable, we can place these patterns into action. Each of us becomes the other, a representative, or a replacement. To put it more broadly, as the century has progressed selves have become increasingly populated with the character of others.[31] We are not one, or a few, but like Walt Whitman, we "contain multitudes." We appear to each other as single identities, unified, of whole cloth. However, with social saturation, each of us comes to harbor a vast population of hidden potentials—to be a blues singer, a gypsy, an aristocrat, a criminal. All the selves lie latent, and under the right conditions may spring to life.

The populating of the self not only opens relationships to new ranges of possibility, but one's subjective life also becomes more fully laminated. Each of the selves we acquire from others can contribute to inner dialogues, private discussions we have with ourselves about all manner of persons, events, and issues. These internal voices, these vestiges of relationships both real and imagined, have been given different names: *invisible guests* by Mary Watkins, *social imagery* by Eric Klinger, and *social ghosts* by Mary Gergen, who found in her research that virtually all the young people she sampled could discuss many such experiences with ease.[32] Most of these ghosts were close friends, often from earlier periods of their lives. Family members were also frequent, with the father's voice predominating, but grandparents, uncles, aunts, and other relatives figured prominently. Relevant to the earlier discussion of relations with media figures, almost a quarter of the ghosts mentioned were individuals with whom the young people had never had any direct interchange. Most were entertainers: rock stars, actors and actresses, singers, and the like. Others were religious figures such as Jesus and Mary, fictitious characters such as James Bond and Sherlock Holmes, and celebrities such as Chris Evert, Joe Montana, Barbara Walters, and the president.

The respondents also spoke of the many ways the social ghosts functioned in their lives. It was not simply that they were there for conversation or contemplation; they also served as models for action. They set standards for behavior; they were admired and were emulated. As one wrote, "Connie Chung was constantly being used as a role model for me and I found myself responding to a question about what I planned to do after graduation by saying that I wanted to go into journalism just because I had been thinking of her." Or, as another wrote of her grandmother, "She showed me how to be tolerant of all people and to show respect to everyone regardless of their state in life." Ghosts also voiced opinions on various matters. Most frequently they were used to bolster one's beliefs. At times such opinions were extremely important. As one wrote of the memory of an early friend, "She is the last link I have to Christianity at this point in my life when I am trying to determine my religious inclinations." Still other respondents spoke of the way their ghosts supported their self-esteem: "I think my father and I know that he would be proud of what I have accomplished." Many mentioned the sense of emotional support furnished by their ghosts: "My grandmother seems to be watching me and showing that she loves me even if I am not doing so well."

In closely related work, the psychologists Hazel Markus and Paula Nurius speak of *possible selves*, the multiple conceptions people harbor of what they might become, would like to become, or are afraid to become.[33] In each case, these possible selves function as private surrogates for others to whom one has been exposed—either directly or via the media. The family relations specialists Paul Rosenblatt and Sara Wright speak similarly of the *shadow realities* that exist in close relationships.[34] In addition to the reality that a couple shares together, each will harbor alternative interpretations of their lives together—interpretations that might appear unacceptable and threatening if revealed to the partner. These shadow realities are typically generated and supported by persons outside the relationship—possibly members of the extended family, but also figures from the media. Finally, the British psychologist Michael Billig and his colleagues have studied the values, goals, and ideals to which people are committed in their everyday lives.[35] They found the typical condition of the individual to be internal conflict: for each belief there exists a strong countertendency. People feel their prejudices are justified, yet it is wrong to be intolerant; that there should be equality but hierarchies are also good; and that we are all basically the same, but we must hold on to our individuality. For every value, goal, or ideal, one holds to the converse as well. Billig proposes that the capacity for contradiction is essential to the practical demands of life in contemporary society.

This virtual cacophony of potentials is of no small consequence for either romanticist or modernist visions of the self. For as new and disparate voices are added to one's being, committed identity becomes an increasingly arduous achievement. How difficult for the romantic to keep firm grasp on the helm of an idealistic undertaking when a chorus of internal voices sing the praises of realism, skepticism, hedonism, and nihilism. And can the committed realist, who believes in the powers of rationality and observation, remain arrogant in the face of inner urges toward emotional indulgence, moral sentiment, spiritual sensitivity, or aesthetic fulfillment? Thus, as social saturation adds incrementally to the population of self, each impulse toward well-formed identity is cast into increasing doubt; each is found absurd, shallow, limited, or flawed by the onlooking audience of the interior.

MULTIPHRENIA

Modern man is afflicted with a permanent identity crisis, a condition conducive to considerable nervousness.
—Peter Berger, Brigitte Berger, and Hansfried Kellner, *The Homeless Mind*

It is sunny Saturday morning and he finishes breakfast in high spirits. It is a rare day in which he is free to do as he pleases. With relish he contemplates his options. The back door needs fixing, which calls for a trip to the hardware store. This would allow a much-needed haircut; and while in town he could get a birthday card for his brother, leave off his shoes for repair, and pick up shirts at the cleaners. But, he ponders, he really should get some exercise; is there time for jogging in the afternoon? That reminds him of a championship game he wanted to see at the same time. To be taken more seriously was his ex-wife's repeated request for a luncheon talk. And shouldn't he also settle his vacation plans before all the best locations are taken? Slowly his optimism gives way to a sense of defeat. The free day has become a chaos of competing opportunities and necessities.

If such a scene is vaguely familiar, it attests only further to the pervasive effects of social saturation and the populating of the self. More important, one detects amid the hurly-burly of contemporary life a new constellation of feelings or sensibilities, a new pattern of self-consciousness. This syndrome may be termed *multiphrenia*, generally referring to the splitting of the individual into a multiplicity of self-investments. This condition is partly an outcome of self-population, but partly a result of the populated self's efforts to exploit the potentials of the technologies of relationship. In this sense, there is a cyclical spiraling toward a state of multiphrenia. As one's potentials are expanded by the technologies, so one increasingly employs the technologies for self-expression; yet, as the technologies are further utilized, so do they add to the repertoire of potentials. It would be a mistake to view this multiphrenic condition as a form of illness, for it is often suffused with a sense of expansiveness and adventure. Someday there may indeed be nothing to distinguish multiphrenia from simply "normal living."

However, before we pass into this oceanic state, let us pause to consider some prominent features of the condition.[36] Three of these are especially noteworthy.

Vertigo of the Valued

Because of the constant change and feeling "off balance," it is essential for men and women to develop . . . coping skills. First, understand that you will never "catch up" and be on top of things and accept this as all right. . . . Put a high priority on spending time relaxing and enjoying life, in spite of all that needs to be done.
—Bruce A. Baldwin, *Stress and Technology*

With the technology of social saturation, two of the major factors traditionally impeding relationships—namely time and space—are both removed. The past can be continuously renewed—via voice, video, and visits, for example—and distance poses no substantial barriers to ongoing interchange. Yet this same freedom ironically leads to a form of enslavement. For each person, passion, or potential incorporated into oneself exacts a penalty—a penalty both of *being* and of *being with*. In the former case, as others are incorporated into the self, their tastes, goals, and values also insinuate themselves into one's being. Through continued interchange, one acquires, for example, a yen for Thai cooking, the desire for retirement security, or an investment in wildlife preservation. Through others one comes to value whole-grain breads, novels from Chile, or community politics. Yet as Buddhists have long been aware, to desire is simultaneously to become a slave of the desirable. To "want" reduces one's choice to "want not." Thus, as others are incorporated into the self, and their desires become one's own, there is an expansion of goals—of "musts," wants, and needs. Attention is necessitated, effort is exerted, frustrations are encountered. Each new desire places its demands and reduces one's liberties.

There is also the penalty of being with. As relationships develop, their participants acquire local definitions—friend, lover, teacher, supporter, and so on. To sustain the relationship requires an honoring of the definitions—both of self and other. If two persons become close friends, for example, each acquires certain rights, duties, and privileges. Most relationships of any significance carry with them a range of obligations— for communication, joint activities, preparing for the other's pleasure, rendering appropriate congratulations, and so on. Thus, as relations accumulate and expand over time, there is a steadily increasing range of phone calls to make and answer, greeting cards to address, visits or activities to arrange, meals to prepare, preparations to be made, clothes to buy, makeup to apply . . . And with each new opportunity—for skiing together in the Alps, touring Australia, camping in the Adirondacks, or snorkling in the Bahamas—there are "opportunity costs." One must unearth information, buy equipment, reserve hotels, arrange travel, work long hours to clear one's desk, locate babysitters, dogsitters, homesitters . . . Liberation becomes a swirling vertigo of demands.

In the professional world this expansion of "musts" is strikingly evident. In the university of the 1950s, for example, one's departmental colleagues were often vital to one's work. One could walk but a short distance for advice, information, support, and so on. Departments were often close-knit and highly interdependent; travels to other departments or professional meetings were notable events. Today, however, the energetic academic will be linked by post, long-distance phone, fax, and electronic mail to like-minded scholars around the globe. The number of interactions possible in a day is limited only by the constraints of time. The technologies have also stimulated the development of hundreds of new organizations, international conferences, and professional meetings. A colleague recently informed me that if funds were available he could spend his entire sabbatical traveling from one professional gathering to another. A similar condition pervades the business world. One's scope of business opportunities is no longer so limited by geography; the technologies of the age enable projects to be pursued around the world. (Colgate Tartar Control toothpaste is now sold in over forty countries.) In effect, the potential for new connection and new opportunities is practically unlimited. Daily life has become a sea of drowning demands, and there is no shore in sight.

The Expansion of Inadequacy

Now You Can Read the Best Business Books of 1989 in Just 15 Minutes Each!
—Advertisement, *US Air Magazine*

Information anxiety is produced by the ever-widening gap between what we understand and what we think we should understand.
—Richard Saul Wurman, *Information Anxiety*

It is not simply the expansion of self through relationships that hounds one with the continued sense of "ought." There is also the seeping of self-doubt into everyday consciousness, a subtle feeling of inadequacy that smothers one's activities with an uneasy sense of impending emptiness. In important respects this sense of inadequacy is a by-product of the populating of self and the presence of social ghosts. For as we incorporate others into ourselves, so does the range of proprieties expand— that is, the range of what we feel a "good," "proper," or "exemplary" person should be. Many of us carry with us the "ghost of a father," reminding us of the values of honesty and hard work, or a mother challenging us to be nurturing and understanding. We may also absorb from a friend the values of maintaining a healthy body, from a lover the goal of self-sacrifice, from a teacher the ideal of worldly knowledge, and so on. Normal development leaves most people with a rich range of "goals for a good life," and with sufficient resources to achieve a sense of personal well-being by fulfilling these goals.

But now consider the effects of social saturation. The range of one's friends and associates expands exponentially; one's past life continues to be vivid; and the mass media expose one to an enormous array of new criteria for self-evaluation. A friend from California reminds one to relax and enjoy life; in Ohio an associate is getting ahead by working eleven hours a day. A relative from Boston stresses the importance of cultural sophistication, while a Washington colleague belittles one's lack of political savvy. A relative's return from Paris reminds one to pay more attention to personal appearance, while a ruddy companion from Colorado suggests that one grows soft.

Meanwhile newspapers, magazines, and television provide a barrage of new criteria of self-evaluation. Is one sufficiently adventurous, clean, well traveled, well read, low in cholesterol, slim, skilled in cooking, friendly, odor-free, coiffed, frugal, burglarproof, family-oriented? The list is unending. More than once I have heard the lament of a subscriber to the Sunday *New York Times*. Each page of this weighty tome will be read by millions. Thus each page remaining undevoured by day's end will leave one precariously disadvantaged—a potential idiot in a thousand unpredictable circumstances.

Yet the threat of inadequacy is hardly limited to the immediate confrontation with mates and media. Because many of these criteria for self-evaluation are incorporated into the self—existing within the cadre of social ghosts—they are free to speak at any moment. The problem with values is that they are sufficient unto themselves. To value justice, for example, is to say nothing of the value of love; investing in duty will blind one to the value of spontaneity. No one value in itself recognizes the importance of any alternative value. And so it is with the chorus of social ghosts. Each voice of value stands to discredit all that does not meet its standard. All the voices at odds with one's current conduct thus stand as internal critics, scolding, ridiculing, and robbing action of its potential for fulfillment. One settles in front of the television for enjoyment, and the chorus begins: "twelve-year-old," "couch potato," "lazy," "irresponsible" . . . One sits down with a good book, and again, "sedentary," "antisocial," "inefficient," "fantasist" . . . Join friends for a game of tennis and "skin cancer," "shirker of household duties," "underexercised," "overly competitive" come up. Work late and it is "workaholic," "heart attack–prone," "overly ambitious," "irresponsible family member." Each moment is enveloped in the guilt born of all that was possible but now foreclosed.

Rationality in Recession

A group of agents acting rationally in the light of their expectations could arrive at so many outcomes that none has adequate reasons for action.
—Martin Hollis, *The Cunning of Reason*

LATIN DEBTS: LACK OF CONSENSUS
Washington Awash in Arguments,
Dry on Agreements
—Headlines, *International Herald Tribune*

A third dimension of multiphrenia is closely related to the others. The focus here is on the rationality of everyday decision making—instances in which one tries to be a "reasonable person." Why, one asks, is it important for one's children to attend college? The rational reply is that a college education increases one's job opportunities, earnings, and likely sense of personal fulfillment. Why should I stop smoking? one asks, and the answer is clear that smoking causes cancer, so to smoke is simply to invite a short life. Yet these "obvious" lines of reasoning are obvious only so long as one's identity remains fixed within a particular group.

The rationality of these replies depends altogether on the sharing of opinions—of each incorporating the views of others. To achieve identity in other cultural enclaves turns these "good reasons" into "rationalizations," "false consciousness," or "ignorance." Within some subcultures a college education is a one-way ticket to bourgeois conventionality—a white-collar job, picket fence in the suburbs, and chronic boredom. For many, smoking is an integral part of a risky life-style; it furnishes a sense of intensity, offbeatness, rugged individualism. In the same way, saving money for old age is "sensible" in one family, and "oblivious to the erosions of inflation" in another. For most Westerners, marrying for love is the only reasonable (if not conceivable) thing to do. But many Japanese will point to statistics demonstrating greater longevity and happiness in arranged marriages. Rationality is a vital by-product of social participation.

Yet as the range of our relationships is expanded, the validity of each localized rationality is threatened. What is rational in one relationship is questionable or absurd from the standpoint of another. The "obvious choice" while talking with a colleague lapses into absurdity when speaking with a spouse, and into irrelevance when an old friend calls that evening. Further, because each relationship increases one's capacities for discernment, one carries with oneself a multiplicity of competing expectations, values, and beliefs about "the obvious solution." Thus, if the options are carefully evaluated, every decision becomes a leap into gray vapors. Hamlet's bifurcated decision becomes all too simple, for it is no longer being or nonbeing that is in question, but to which of multifarious beings one can be committed. T. S. Eliot began to sense the problem when Prufrock found "time yet for a hundred indecisions/And for a hundred visions and revisions,/Before taking of a toast and tea."[37]

The otherwise simple task of casting a presidential vote provides a useful illustration. As one relates (either directly or vicariously) to various men and women, in various walks of life, and various sectors of the nation or abroad, one's capacities for discernment are multiplied. Where one might have once employed a handful of rational standards, or seen the issues in only limited ways, one can now employ a variety of criteria and see many sides of many issues. One may thus favor candidate A because he strives for cuts in the defense budget, but also worry about the loss of military capability in an unsteady world climate. Candidate B's plans for stimulating the growth of private enterprise may be rational from one standpoint, but the resulting tax changes seem unduly to penalize the middle-class family. At the same time, there is good reason to believe

that *A*'s cuts in defense spending will favor *B*'s aims for a stimulated economy, and that *B*'s shifts in the tax structure will make *A*'s reductions in the military budget unnecessary. To use one criterion, candidate *A* is desirable because of his seeming intelligence, but from another, his complex ideas seem both cumbersome and remote from reality. Candidate *B* has a pleasing personality, useful for him to garner popular support for his programs, but in another sense his pleasant ways suggest he cannot take a firm stand. And so on.

Increasing the criteria of rationality does not, then, move one to a clear and univocal judgment of the candidates. Rather, the degree of complexity is increased until a rationally coherent stand is impossible. In effect, as social saturation steadily expands the population of the self, a choice of candidates approaches the arbitrary. A toss of a coin becomes equivalent to the diligently sought solution. We approach a condition in which the very idea of "rational choice" becomes meaningless.

So we find a profound sea change taking place in the character of social life during the twentieth century. Through an array of newly emerging technologies the world of relationships becomes increasingly saturated. We engage in greater numbers of relationships, in a greater variety of forms, and with greater intensities than ever before. With the multiplication of relationships also comes a transformation in the social capacities of the individual—both in knowing how and knowing that. The relatively coherent and unified sense of self inherent in a traditional culture gives way to manifold and competing potentials. A multiphrenic condition emerges in which one swims in ever-shifting, concatenating, and contentious currents of being. One bears the burden of an increasing array of oughts, of self-doubts and irrationalities. The possibility for committed romanticism or strong and single-minded modernism recedes, and the way is opened for the postmodern being.

FOUR

Truth in Trouble

We burn with desire to find solid ground and an ultimate sure foundation whereon to build a tower reaching to the infinite. But our groundwork cracks, and the earth opens to abysses.

—Blaise Pascal, *The Two Infinities*

A cademic life at this small American college was normally gentle and unperturbed. But several years ago came a startling event. It began simply enough: two scholars were invited to speak on the problem of understanding language, one a German sociologist and the other a French literary analyst. Such a topic hardly seems explosive, the talks were not widely publicized, and given the foreign origins of the speakers one might even worry about pulling a decent audience. Yet, as the date grew closer, news of the talks seemed to be spreading broadly. Queries by phone and letter, from scholars and students alike, steadily mounted. Excited discussion ensued from all corners of academia—philosophy, psychology, sociology, anthropology, literary studies, women's studies, religion, and communications among them—and resonated for hundreds of miles. The talks were finally scheduled in the largest auditorium in the vicinity. And when the event took place, even this location proved inadequate for the throngs—standing, sitting, crouching wherever space permitted.

Why should such a debate create this kind of excitement? The major reason is an emerging crisis in the common conception of human understanding. The problem of how people understand each other and the world about them once seemed relatively clear. Language expresses ideas and sentiments, it was held; to understand language is to understand the mind of the speaker. And a speaker's language is capable of carrying objective truth. Yet, because of various turns in intellectual life, it is now difficult to see how these assumptions can be sustained. It is unclear how people gain knowledge of each other's minds and how they can objectively describe the world outside themselves. All that seemed clear a decade earlier is now murky . . . Perhaps these foreign scholars might have insights not fully understood on this side of the Atlantic.

In this chapter I propose to explore this emerging crisis in academia. These are some of the most significant debates to occur in intellectual life within the past century. Most of the cherished beliefs that undergird the traditional goals of research and teaching are in eclipse. Some consider the demise of the traditional assumptions to be an event little short of catastrophe; to part with the longstanding ideals of truth and understanding is to invite chaos, first in the academic world and then in society more generally. Others feel an innervating sense that history is at a turning point, that a new and exciting era is in the making.

I focus on these developments at this juncture because the crisis in the academy about beliefs in objective knowledge has profound implications for beliefs about the self. Most of us cling to the romantic view that persons possess a depth of passion, moral beliefs, and creative inspiration. To the modernist it seems utterly obvious that rationality guides most human action. In large measure these beliefs derive their credibility from the assumption that they are objectively true (or, in principle, can be proven so). But as I argued in chapter 1, there is ample reason to doubt such claims in the case of human personality. The present crisis in the academy presses the argument to its radical extreme. We are not dealing here with doubts regarding claims about the truth of human character, but with the full-scale abandonment of the concept of objective truth. The argument is not that our descriptions of the self are objectively shaky, but that the very attempt to render accurate understanding is itself bankrupt. And if objective accounts of human personality are beyond possibility, then why continue the search for human essence? Whatever we are is beyond telling.

I shall further propose that the crisis in the academy is in large part a result of social saturation. The technologies that play an ever-increasing role in cultural affairs also have a major impact on discussions in the academic world. Thus, to understand the academic revolution currently taking place is an important preliminary to understanding what is occurring in the culture more generally. The demise of the true and knowable self in academia is the first and most articulate signal of changes of broad consequence. To explore these issues, we must first trace the link between the populating of the self and the demise of objectivity. How is it that the social saturation of our personal existence leads to a breakdown in our sense of objective reality? We can then explore the ramifications of this condition within the academic setting.

MODERNISM AND THE COMING OF MULTIPLICITY

Economics has . . . become so broad and so complicated that, within the fields, one group of specialists barely speaks the same language as the Ph.D.s across the hall. And so much of what is published seems more to proselytize for an ideology than to make sense of the chaotic world. . . . It's no wonder that a single economic development can be interpreted as a godsend or a disaster, depending on the interpreter's frame of reference.

—Peter Passell, *Economics: Reading Your Way Out of Chaos*

Increasingly we emerge as the possessors of many voices. Each self contains a multiplicity of others, singing different melodies, different verses, and with different rhythms. Nor do these many voices necessarily harmonize. At times they join together, at times they fail to listen one to another, and at times they create a jarring discord. But what are the consequences of the multiply populated self? Central to the modernist view was a robust commitment to an objective and knowable world, and to the promise of truth about this world. Natural scientists were to furnish objective knowledge of physical matter, economists were to discover basic laws for the world of money, and the other disciplines—psychology, economics, sociology, anthropology, history, and so on—were likewise assigned domains about which truthful and honest reflections were anticipated. In the realm of daily life one also believed in knowable selves. Individuals possessed a basic personality or character, and in most normal relationships this essential self was made known. One who fails to be himself or herself is a superficial sham, possibly neurotic (trying desperately to be somebody else), or downright dishonest.

But consider how objective truth is established in each of these domains. Let us begin with a simple case, that of Robert, a twelve-year-old shoplifter. Robert is caught in the act of stealing, and when his parents search his room they find evidence of earlier crimes. Their distress is intensified when they talk with their son and he seems to have no remorse. Robert's only concern seems to be the price he must pay for his crimes. The parents conclude that their son is lacking in moral character. They discuss the problem with their minister, several close friends, and a school counselor. All corroborate their views. It is clear that Robert lacks moral perspective, and steps must be taken toward improvement. For this small community, Robert's lack of moral character is an objective fact.

Now contrast this tidy scenario with a second: confronted with the same problem, the parents receive the following assessments:

MINISTER: Robert is basically a very good boy. However, you, his parents, have been so caught up in your own projects that he has been severely neglected. He is feeling unloved and resentful. His shoplifting is his way of showing it.

FRIEND 1: The two of you haven't been getting on very well for two years now. Robert was always a good kid, but now he senses this terrible tension in the house. This is his way of asking for help.

FRIEND 2: All of Robert's friends seem to have most of the things they want—good clothes, playthings, opportunities for fun. Robert suffers by comparison. This is his way of trying to get what he needs to be OK in the eyes of his friends.

SCHOOL COUNSELOR: Twelve is a difficult age for all kids. It's normal for kids this age to search around to find out who they are, what their environment is like. They test themselves and each other. Not to worry. It's a passing phase.

What are Robert's parents then to conclude? Is it an *objective truth* that Robert is morally deficient? As opinions become more varied, it becomes increasingly difficult to determine precisely what is true. As the social world loses its homogeneity, the "objective fact" that Robert is lacking in moral perspective slowly gives way to "mere opinion."

More generally, it may be said that the sense of objectivity is a social achievement. That is, to count something as factual or true demands that others also reach the same conclusion. You may proclaim that you see a full moon. It is an obvious fact. However, if no one else agrees with you, chances are you will reconsider. Are your eyes functioning properly? Did you mistake a streetlight for the moon? Did your imagination trick you? At this point, what seemed an ordinary statement of fact might become grounds for seeking professional help. Scientific objectivity is based on the same presumption of univocal assent. A single scientist may proclaim a discovery, but before this discovery is allowed to count as *fact*, numerous other scientists will examine the evidence, repeat the research, or otherwise attempt to "see for themselves." Objectivity, then, is achieved through a coalition of subjectivities.

In this light, let us consider the process of social saturation described in the preceding chapter. The expansion of telephonics, air travel, television, radio, computer networks, fax systems, and the like are dramatically increasing our exposure to others, and we absorb opinions, beliefs, attitudes, and values from all points of the globe. It is precisely this exposure that undermines commitments to objectivity. For as the range and variability of reactions to any condition are increased, so does "the truth of the matter" become increasingly cloudy. What is the truth about our economic condition, when a stockbroker friend says the market is going into serious decline, a television analyst predicts a bull market, and foreign investors view the situation as stable? What can truly be said about the "loss of the ozone layer" when scientists from differing fields disagree on the evidence, representatives from differing nations disagree on the outcome, and opinions continuously change with time?

Yet the erosion of objectivity goes deeper than the level of public debate. Social saturation does more than bring us face to face with disagreements about the nature of things. As we begin to incorporate the dispositions of the varied others to whom we are exposed, we become capable of taking their positions, adopting their attitudes, talking their language, playing their roles. In effect, one's self becomes populated with others. The result is a steadily accumulating sense of doubt in the objectivity of any position one holds. For as opinions are expressed, one becomes aware of the alternative voices lurking under the eaves of consciousness, like Herman Hesse's subterranean Steppenwolf, howling its mocking disapproval. In the face of continuous point and counterpoint— both in the public and private spheres—one slowly approaches the awareness that perhaps the monument to objectivity is hollow.

CRISIS IN THE ACADEMY

The signals emerge with increasing frequency:

- The *New York Times* reports on the "critique of the canon" in literary studies. Faculty and students alike reject the view that there are "truly great works of English literature," that these works teach values that transcend time, and that all educated students in the United States should be exposed to these works.
- Allan Bloom's *Closing of the American Mind,* an excoriating attack on the deterioration of higher education, becomes a best-seller.
- Women's-studies programs mushroom across the country, as women reject the traditional courses of study as dominated with masculine biases.
- New curricula in cultural studies emerge with increasing frequency,

dedicated to questioning the fundamental assumptions and institutions of Western culture.
• The Ford Foundation sponsors a major symposium at the City University of New York on the disappearance of authority in the university.

These events are manifestations of the increasingly pervasive doubt in the modernist views of objective truth, rational foundations of knowledge, and the grand narrative of progress. In major respects this erosion in confidence may be traced to the steadily increasing awareness of other voices, other perspectives, other points of view.

The technology of social saturation is centrally implicated in this erosion in two ways. The first is the expansion of viable viewpoints within fields of study. A century ago most scholars confined their activities to their local communities and a handful of correspondents. As travel grew easier, learned societies proliferated. As long as membership in them was circumscribed, the kind of agreement necessary to achieve a sense of objectivity was relatively easy to achieve. However, with air travel, mass publication of journals, international conferences, low-priced long-distance phones, and electronic mail, communal insularity became increasingly difficult to maintain. All that was "avowed fact" in one locale became food for criticism and replacement in another. It became no more a question of "the facts," but "whose facts?" Broad opposition breeds doubt.

The technologies of social saturation have also enabled a range of new voices to be heard, voices daring to question the old and institutionalized truths. Minorities across the nation could begin to organize, develop a sense of group consciousness, articulate values and goals, publicize injustices, seek legal help, and change laws. They were joined by a rapidly expanding influx into the universities of non-Western students and faculty. Undergraduates were increasingly exposed to the views of Asians, Indians, Arabs, and so on. In traditional communities, relatively closed to outside communication, oppressed and alien minorities simply remained so. However, when such minorities employ the technologies to unite with similar groups across the land, and to publicize their condition to the public at large, the fulcrum for social change shifts. Within the university setting, concerted efforts have been made to increase the presence of blacks, Hispanics, women, Native Americans, Asian-Americans, and others on both the faculty and student levels. New programs of study have developed—women's studies, black studies, cultural studies, and the like—each seeking to define itself, the world, and a coherent system of values. With each new community, the established truths—with their longstanding sense of objectivity—are thrown into suspicion.

Yet we must also take account of the structure of knowledge within the modernist ethos. For the modernist orientation itself has done much to generate this competition among competing truths. From the modernist perspective, the world is made up of various "natural kinds," each deserving its own form of study. There is the world of physical objects, for example, which demands physics and chemistry as basic disciplines. Living beings require different disciplines—for example, biology and sociology. And if each kind of thing requires a particular form of study, there was a ready-made rationale for an enormous array of self-sustaining subdisciplines. Thus some psychologists worked in the area of learning, others in perception, motivation, child development, and so on. (The American Psychological Association now lists thirty-four separate specialties.) Much the same pattern is duplicated in other disciplines. Between 1978 and 1988 over 29,000 new scientific journals were launched, almost quadrupling the previous number.[1] An enormous assortment of subdisciplines each claims truth.[2]

If each discipline were to remain content with its small slice of reality, one's trust in truth claims might be undaunted. As disciplinary viewpoints become accepted realities, however, those who share them become suspicious of the alternatives. If one believes that the world is purely material, then any discipline claiming to study "the mind," "metaphysics," or "spirituality" is suspect: such disciplines cannot be studying anything that exists. On the other hand, if one believes that there is no other world outside conscious experience, then "material" as a thing in itself becomes suspect. What we take to be material must be a construct of our individual experience. As disciplinary vocabularies strengthened, they began to threaten adjoining disciplines through annexation. Thus, chemistry could annex sections of biology, biology could claim sectors of psychology, psychology attempted to reduce sociology to its terms, sociology claimed expertise in linguistics, linguists claimed that their work could replace sections of philosophy, and so on.

Modernism, then, served as an incubator for the multiplication of competing perspectives.[3] And as perspectives became self-convincing, expansionary, hierarchical, and predatory, who was to declare the "really real"? Who could be trusted to rule among the antagonistic voices, and in whose terms was such a ruling to be justified? Or, as Jean-François Lyotard summarizes the problem of scientific legitimacy,

"How do you prove the proof?" or, more generally, "Who decides the conditions of truth?" It is recognized that the conditions of truth, in other words, the rules of the game of science, are immanent in that game, that they can only be established within the bounds of a debate that is already scientific

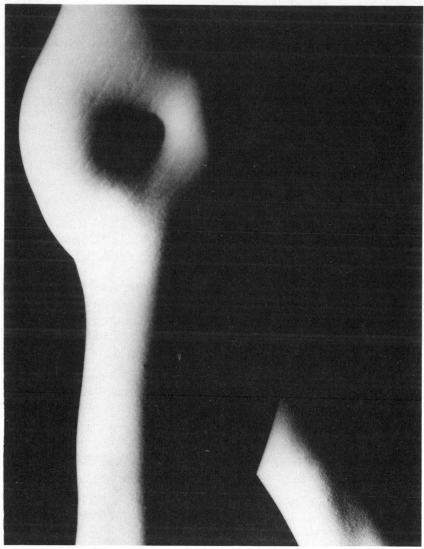

If each discipline claims a different truth about the human body, then what is truly true? Here Tom Sherman transforms the human body into patterns of light and shade. Even photographic images create the world they depict.

in nature, and that there is no other proof that the rules are good than the consensus extended to them by the experts.[4]

The groundwork was thus laid for challenging the very form of modernist intelligibility that had generated the chaos of competing voices. The very assumption that there are natural kinds, each of which demands a particular form of study, and the truth of which will ultimately be laid bare, was rendered vulnerable. The remainder of this chapter will explore three major academic challenges to the modernist presumption of objective knowledge. As we shall find, each simultaneously threatens traditional beliefs in basic, true, or knowable selves.

FROM FACTS TO PERSPECTIVES

The "data" [given] of research are not so much given as taken *out of a constantly elusive matrix of happenings. We should speak of* capta *rather than data.*

—R. D. Laing, *The Politics of Experience*

One of the major aspirations of modernist philosophers of science was to furnish rational foundations for knowledge. Rules of scientific conduct were developed so that all the disciplines might proceed more efficiently to build objectively grounded knowledge of their subject matter. This assumed first that there were basic subject matters to be known about, and second that it was the task of scholars to produce accurate accounts of these domains. Thus, such topics as "the solar system," "the biological system," "economic behavior," and the like are "out there," existing independently of the scholar. And proper research should bend itself toward true portrayals of what is there.[5]

The first important hint of trouble with the modernist view of objective truth actually occurred during the modernist period itself. It had long been assumed that objects in the world are defined largely by points in time and space. If something does not occupy space and occur within time, it is indeed difficult to call it "something" at all. Yet, as the physicist Werner Heisenberg convincingly demonstrated in the mid-1920s, it is theoretically impossible to determine the position and velocity of the basic units of matter. We do so in practice, proposed Heisenberg, only because we limit most of our interests to cases so crude (those seen with the naked eye) that we do not detect the impossibility. However, when one moves to the level of subatomic physics, the impossibility of locating the positions of atomic particles becomes clear. The very attempt to measure the position and velocity of a particle will knock the particle about in unpredictable ways. In effect, there is no basic unit of matter to be observed independent of those who make the observation. Subject and object are inextricably linked.

Although the broad commitment to objectivity made it necessary to disregard the unsettling implications of Heisenberg's demonstrations, concern with the observer's perspective continued to mount. And so it should, given a century in which technology ensured a steadily increasing exposure to a multiplicity of other perspectives. By the time of the 1962 publication of Thomas Kuhn's *The Structure of Scientific Revolutions*, there was wide receptivity to a critique that was to revolutionize the conception of knowledge itself.[6] Recall the modernist myth of progress: Science is preeminently rational. As the scientist tests theories against reality, those that fail to be verified are abandoned. Those that stand up to scientific test are retained. Thus, science moves inexorably in a self-correcting, progressive direction. Any scientist or citizen who employs the scientific method will inevitably move toward increased knowledge and an enhanced capacity for adaptation.

Kuhn's reply to the modernist conception of progressive knowledge was to use the conception in order to abuse it. What do we find, he asked, if we examine historical incidents or periods credited with major breakthroughs in science? If we take a hard look at these cases, do we find that scientific progress was achieved according to modernist conceptions? Can shifts in scientific perspective properly be traced to the rational procedures touted by the modernists? In effect, if we "observe the historical facts" (a modernist assumption), can we improve on the modernist concept of accumulating knowledge?

Kuhn concluded that what we view as great scientific advances cannot be credited to a modernist account of rational procedure. Rather, mainstream scientists of a given age are committed to a particular perspective of the world (along with associated practices)—a *paradigm*, in Kuhn's terms. At the same time, anomalous findings are generated by scientists outside this paradigm. These findings neither verify nor falsify the existing paradigm; they are simply irrelevant to it. At some point, when enough findings accumulate, the marginal group of scientists will develop an alternative way of thinking about the world, one in which their findings make sense. The new theory cannot be compared with the old in terms of its empirical truth; it is simply a different way of viewing the world, wedded to a different realm of facts. As Kuhn concludes, "we may . . . have to relinquish the notion . . . that changes of paradigm carry scientists and those who learn from them closer and closer to the truth."[7]

The shift from the Ptolemaic to the Copernican theory of the cosmos is a good case in point. Galileo is typically credited with carrying out the experiments essential to proving that the sun rather than the earth lies at the center of our solar system. Yet, argues Paul Feyerabend in his caustic volume *Against Method*,[8] if one scans the actual data available to Galileo and his critics, there is no way to credit him with empirically disproving that the sun revolves around the earth. Galileo's attackers had much evidence on their side. (Do we not "see" the sun "rise" and "set"?) Also, the means by which Galileo demonstrated the "truth" of his conclusions was novel. The force of his arguments depended largely on information collected through the telescope. On what grounds are such data to be trusted? Are there not myriad interpretations to be made of telescopic data? (Consider the unquestioning trust we now place in biology teachers who tell us that the mysterious and confusing blurs we see through a laboratory microscope are *actually* amoebas.) So Galileo had to make numerous unsupported assumptions about what kind of information the telescope provided him. Or more broadly, one had to be committed to numerous unwarranted assumptions in order for telescopic data to "count" for or against Galileo's position. "Good evidence" thus depends on the paradigm in which one is immersed.

Support for Kuhn's position was widespread. One of these arguments cut directly into the jugular of modernism. Modernism was deeply committed to the view that the facts of the world are essentially *there* for study. They exist independently of us as observers, and if we are rational we will come to know the facts as they are. Yet, as Kuhn suggested, what counts as a fact depends on one's perspective. This emphasis on perspective is sharpened in Norbert Hanson's *Patterns of Discovery*.[9] Hanson proposes that we come to each situation with practiced ways of perceiving, so that in the very act of perception we produce "the events" of consciousness. To illustrate, consider the accompanying figure. How is it to be identified? If one were an avid ornithologist, one might well see a bird with its beak open, ready for a tasty worm. A zoologist, however, might

identify it as a rudimentary sketch of an antelope. The figure is the same in both cases, but depending on the conceptual interests and knowledge of the observer, it can be identified in wholly different ways. As Hanson proposes, in the case of science, "The infant and the layman can see: they are not blind. But they cannot see what the physicist sees; they are blind to what he sees. . . . Seeing is a theory-laden undertaking. Observation of X is shaped by prior knowledge of X."[10]

If what we take to be objective knowledge is a result of perspectives rather than brute "facts in themselves," how is it that certain views come to be accepted as "knowledge" and others are cast aside as "erroneous" or "misleading"? It is this concern that has occupied a virtual army of historians and sociologists of knowledge since the publication of Kuhn's volume. They see no genuinely rational way to decide whether one theoretical perspective is more accurate than another. Therefore, these decisions may be properly traced to various social processes. Scientists exist in communities, and what is taken for "the truth" in these communities depends primarily on social factors such as power, social negotiation, and prestige.

Groundbreaking work by the UCLA sociologist Harold Garfinkel focused on *ethnomethodology*, that is, the conversational conventions used by people in everyday life to determine what counts as "the factual world."[11] Consider, for example, the case of suicide. We take it for granted that there are various sorts of death, including death by natural causes, murder, and suicide. There are statistical compendiums that chart suicide rates in various countries; insurance companies are keen to determine into which category a death is properly placed; and it is of enormous significance to us if we are told that a friend has committed suicide. But how do we determine when a suicide occurs? Corpses carry no labels telling us how they came into this state. To make such determinations, argued Garfinkel and his colleagues, we must fall back on conversational conventions about such issues. Often such conversations are built around the concept of "intention." Did the individual *intend* to take his life or not? Yet it is very difficult to know about people's intentions. How are people to determine, for certain, what intentions underlie their behavior? And how, in the light of cultures in which the concept of intention is not found, can we be so certain that people even have intentions? An individual may write a note in which he says he intends to take his life, but on what grounds should we trust this as an accurate report on his mental condition? Perhaps he doesn't understand his situation and was being driven by forces beyond his control. And what about deaths that we call "natural"? If our only desire in life were for longevity, chances are we would not eat many of the foods we do, breathe the air in our city streets, or lead such stressful lives. Since we do, and indeed we die before our time, shouldn't our deaths be considered forms of suicide? What then counts as evidence for suicide? It depends on the social group in which such decisions are made. Suicides are not "facts in the world," but the products of group perspective.

This line of thinking has since been extended by a large number of scholars into the realm of natural science—the privileged reserve of objective truth. To illustrate but one of these investigations, the sociologists Bruno Latour and Stephen Woolgar entered the Salk Institute for Biological Studies to observe scientists at work.[12] Exactly how did the scientists determine what counted as truth, opinion, or falsity in their work? They spent months watching the communications between the scientists at the laboratory, not only the formal meetings but the informal interchanges that took place while the scientists scanned data or chatted about findings. Latour and Woolgar conclude that what counts as objective truth is not the result of rationally subjecting hypotheses to empirical test, but emerges from a network of social agreements. Examples from this and related research:

- A senior investigator insists that her assistants use theory X rather than theory Y to interpret their findings.
- An investigator cites others' findings as support for his work, even when such findings were based on other research methods or different samples.
- Investigators demonstrate the weaknesses in theory and method of all those who oppose their position, but do not admit their own shortcomings
- Investigators cite favorably those who were likely to review their work for publication, hoping to increase the chances that their own work will be published—that is, viewed as "accepted truth."
- One theory is preferred by a scientific team over competing possibilities because granting agencies have a preference for this theory. To carry out research under this theoretical banner is to improve the likelihood of receiving future funds, and thus of maintaining a central position in the field.

Thus, they conclude, it is not the "real world" that determines scientific description and explanation, but rather social processes within science and society.[13] It is largely this line of thinking that has reduced the once-flourishing field of the philosophy of science—which was to furnish foundational rules of scientific procedure—to a beleaguered discipline on the defense. It is not that the social theorists discount what are taken to be the advances of the natural sciences; one can scarcely argue that words like "moon landing" and "polio vaccine" don't stand for something, and that whatever that something is was not present in previous history (as we understand that term). From the social perspective, however, the words used in conjunction with such "events" are not determined by the events in themselves, and thus many alternative accounts are possible. The success of a technology has nothing to do with the truth of the scientific accounts used on its behalf. A "successful vaccine" (using the common vernacular) does not make such terms as "virus" and "vaccine" objectively true; nor does "unsuccessful witchcraft" (by Western standards) render such terms as "magic power" and "devil possession" untrue. These two forms of language simply happen to be used by such groups while carrying on disparate activities—which various people call more or less "successful." Western biologists could replace their concepts with a shaman's in all their equations without affecting the outcomes of the science.

Thus we find steadily mounting suspicion of the objective truths of science, or of any other group that proclaims the truth of its language. To claim superiority of position on the basis of factual accuracy is specious, for accounts of "the way the world is" don't grow from nature but from the application of a socially shared perspective. What, then, is a "fact" on this account? As Mary Hawksworth puts it, "A fact is a theoretically constituted proposition, supported by theoretically mediated evidence and put forward as part of a theoretical formulation of reality. A fact is a contestable consequent of a theoretically constituted order of things."[14] In effect, once a theory is embraced by a group, it is used to interpret events in such a way that it *seems* factually true. What is "objectively" true depends, then, not on what is the case, but on the community in which one happens to participate. And in light of the increasing availability of "other voices," we find an increasing range of "other truths."[15]

What then is to be said of all that we take to be self-knowledge, of all the propositions, both scientific and quotidian, that define who and what we are? We speak of our feelings, carry out research on cognition, and attempt to cure depression. On what grounds do we proceed with these ventures? The preceding arguments suggest that none of our assumptions—either in science or daily life—is derived from "what is the case." The terms "emotion," "reason," "depression," and so on are not present in our vocabulary because they reflect the facts of emotion, reason, and depression in the world. Rather, such terms gain their meaning, their sense of reality, from the perspectives we bring to events in present-day society. A final line of unsettling questions now surfaces: How is it possible to describe the self outside a perspective—to locate a transcendent language of the self as it *truly* is? And if we cannot do so, why do we presume a real, objectively knowable self at all? Such a presumption becomes a gratuitous addition to the use of the language.

THE KNOWER AS DEMAGOGUE

[That] which categorizes the individual . . . attaches him to [an] identity, imposes a law of truth on him which he must recognize and which others have to recognize in him . . . is a form of power which makes individuals subjects.

—Michel Foucault, *The Subject and Power*

These initial lines of argument are buttressed by yet another form of inquiry, one of more immediate concern to society. The issue in this case is the relationship between claims to truth and the distribution of power in society. Those groups to whom knowledge is attributed are generally granted the privilege of making decisions. We want knowledgeable people, rather than the ignorant and uninformed, to decide on matters of importance. Thus the power of decision making is often granted to scientists, experienced politicians, learned judges, medical doctors, and so on. Their words reflect the realities of accumulated experience. And because our educational curricula are largely controlled by "those who know," the educational system operates to sustain the existing structure of power. Students learn "the right facts" according to those who control the system, and these realities, in turn, sustain their positions of power. In this sense the educational system serves the interests of the existing power elite.

To the extent that cultures are homogeneous in their values and definitions of reality, this condition remains unproblematic. However, as increasing numbers of people gain voice, claims to knowledge and the right to power become points of contention. For example, if Darwinian theory is not objectively true, but merely a perspective shared by biologists, then by what right are creationist views dropped from school curricula in favor of evolutionary theory? Does such a decision not strengthen the power of the scientific establishment in dictating national policy, and weaken the voice of religion? If the cures produced by the medical profession are only "cures" from a given perspective, then why should insurance benefits be granted for medical treatment but not for various forms of psychotherapy? Does this decision not strengthen the medical (or biological) conception of human behavior and dismiss the ordinary person's experiences and feelings as unimportant? And if the literary works selected by a department of English as superior and essential are only a reflection of the department's white and economically privileged perspective, then why should such reading lists be accepted by blacks, Chicanos, or Asian-American students? Are their traditions not obliterated by such decisions?

More generally, then, if our discourses are not derived from the facts, but once embraced they create what we take to be the factual world, then a more critical look at these discourses is in order. Because these discourses support and sustain various structures of power and privilege, certain people are marginalized and oppressed by them. Such concerns have generated an enormous body of scholarship aimed at uncovering the political, ideological, or ethical biases underlying the authority responsible for knowledge otherwise taken for granted. The critical literature seeks to demystify the voice of authority, and to increase the range of voices in the sanctuaries of power.

Voices of demystification are now everywhere. Perhaps the strongest are those of feminist critics. Many feminist scholars argue that the traditional voices of authority have been almost altogether male. Science, government, religion, business, law, the military, medicine, the family— all the institutions are patriarchal, and thus the "truth" of male voices alone directs cultural life. If the male perspective has dominated—erroneously, in the name of truth or wisdom—this voice must be challenged. For, they argue, that voice has primarily served the desires of men to the detriment of women's interests.[16]

To illustrate these concerns, it is especially useful to consider formulations in the natural sciences, again because such sciences are considered exempt from value bias. Emily Martin's analysis of the ways in which biological science characterizes the woman's body is especially enlightening.[17] Martin's particular concern is in the way biological texts, in both the classroom and laboratory, represent or describe the female body. She concludes from her extensive analysis of such accounts that the woman's body is largely viewed as a "factory" whose primary purpose is to reproduce the species. It follows that the processes of menstruation and menopause are characterized as wasteful if not dysfunctional, for they are periods of "nonproduction." Note the negative terms in which the typical biology text describes menstruation (italics mine): "the fall in blood progesterone and estrogen *deprives* the highly developed endometrial lining of its hormonal support"; "*constriction*" of blood vessels leads to a "*diminished* supply of oxygen and nutrients"; and when "*disintegration* starts, the entire lining begins to *slough*, and the menstrual flow begins." "The *loss* of hormonal stimulation causes *decrosis*" (death of tissue). Another text says that menstruation is like "the uterus crying for lack of a baby."[18]

Martin makes two essential points. First, these scientific descriptions are anything but neutral. In subtle ways they inform the reader that menstruation and menopause are forms of breakdown or failure. These pejorative implications have broad social consequences. For the woman, to accept such accounts is to alienate herself from her body. Such descriptions furnish grounds for judging herself negatively—both on a monthly basis during most of her adult years and then permanently after the years of fertility have passed. Second, these characterizations could be otherwise. Such negative bias is not required by "the way things are" but results from an unthinking exercise of the masculine metaphor of the woman as a reproduction factory.

To secure the latter case, Martin points out that there are other bodily processes—some even exclusive to men—that could be described in the same manner but are not. The lining of the stomach is shed and replaced regularly, and seminal fluid picks up cells that have been shed as it flows through the male ducts. However, biological texts characterize the change in the stomach walls as a "renewal" and make no mention of males "losing" or "wasting" in describing ejaculation. In effect, there are many ways of describing the same set of processes, and the prevailing choice made by biological science is ideologically loaded—to the detriment of women.

A second illustration is useful, as it amplifies the concerns of anthropologists and historians with Western individualism (see chapter 1). Most authoritative accounts of "the way things are" contain hidden values, the critics surmise, and one of the most problematic of these is the value placed on individualism. Western culture has long placed a strong value on the individual's self-determination (usually limited to the male). It is the good person, it is said, who makes his own decisions, resists group pressure, and "does it his way." It is the spirit of individualism to which the culture pays tribute for economic prosperity, military victories, and a strong democracy. Yet, the critics point out, this same cultural value has many shortcomings. In particular, it invites people to think of themselves as fundamentally isolated, alone to ponder and create their own fate. Because cooperating with others means "sacrificing one's own desire" to the will of others, individualism also discourages cooperation and the development of community. A me-first attitude is also invited, because if we are all isolated individuals then self-gain is to be preferred to the gain of others. Indeed, propose the critics, if individualism remains the dominant value, the future well-being of the planet is jeopardized. We now possess the means for annihilating all human life, and values that stress independence, self-determination, and self-gain militate against cooperation for the good of all. They foster a context for destructive conflict.

With such views in mind, critics have examined various bodies of accepted knowledge for their implicit or unspoken celebration of individualism. In one of the strongest of these critiques, Edward Sampson has taken as his target the field of psychology.[19] To appreciate the force of Sampson's argument, consider the following commonly held propositions about human functioning:

- Each person possesses a set of basic personality traits that largely determine his or her actions in various situations.
- People's attitudes and values typically determine their choices.
- The mature person bases his or her ethical decisions on deep-seated moral principles.
- The well-adjusted person possesses a sense of self-worth on which he or she can rely in times of stress.

Such statements are virtual truisms in modern culture; in one form or another few would question them. Yet, Sampson reasons, each of these taken-for-granted principles lends support to the ideology of individualism. Each proposes that people possess inner tendencies—personality traits, attitudes and values, moral principles, sense of self-worth—and that these inner tendencies determine their behavior. In effect, each of these statements paints a picture of the ideal human as one who is self-directing and self-reliant. The statements seem innocent enough, but they contain subtle and unwitting biases. There is no way that such propositions could be derived from people's observed actions—the movements of their limbs, torso, mouth, and so on. Rather, these propositions are derived from forms of discourse used by large segments of the culture to support their institutions. They are favored ways of talking and writing. When scientists enter their laboratories to determine "the nature of man," they import this form of discourse and use it to interpret their findings. The result is that the scientists add sanctity to an ideology of potentially harmful consequence to the future.

THE DISAPPEARANCE OF THE KNOWER

What, therefore, is truth? A mobile army of metaphors, metonymies, anthropomorphisms; . . . which after long use seem firm, canonical, and obligatory to a people: truths are illusions of which one has forgotten that they are illusions.
—Friedrich Nietzsche, *On Truth and Falsity in Their Extramoral Sense*

In the face of the preceding arguments, assumptions of real selves begin to pale. If the properties of personality are by-products, not of persons themselves, but of our "ways of talk," then what is gained by presuming a real self, beyond the possibility of accurate description? And if each mode of discourse favors certain groups to the detriment of others, doesn't the presumption of real and actual selves render society more rigid, and oppression more compelling? These doubts are only a beginning. In still other quarters of academia, the powder has been readied for a full-scale demolition of the self. This line of reasoning is changing the entire landscape of literary study, and is held directly responsible for the "postmodern" turn in academic life. Many complex considerations are at stake, but as in previous cases, subtlety will be sacrificed for clarity.

At least since classical Greece, human beings in the West have credited themselves with internal or psychological processes of thought (or more formally, *cognition*). Over the centuries there have been many attempts to imbue thought processes with wondrous attributes or capacities. For Descartes and other rationalist philosophers, individual thought was the sole basis for indubitability, providing the guarantee of personal being—"I think, therefore I am." For many Enlightenment thinkers it was the power of individual reasoning, located within all normal beings, that granted them the right to challenge authority. And for modernists of the twentieth century, it is through powers of reason that one establishes knowledge. As individuals sift the evidence, propose hypotheses and antitheses, and evaluate the outcomes of their deductions, they build repositories of knowledge within. And, it is said, such repositories enable individuals to cut a successful path through the complexities of the world, and grant the human species an advantage in the competition for survival. It is this conception of the individual thinker, the center of knowledge and decision making, that is now in jeopardy.

To appreciate the force and implications of the arguments, it is useful to differentiate three separate but interlocking assumptions within the traditional belief system. As illustrated in the figure on p. 100 (Phase 1), we first presume a distinction between a real or objective world and a world within the mind, between the objective and the subjective. Thus, traditionally, the world exists as it is ("nature in itself"), and if a person is to survive, it is his or her task to perceive or apprehend the world as it is. It is also believed that when we speak or write, our words are external expressions of our inner thoughts—of what we believe or know to be the case (Phase 2). As we say, "He speaks his mind," "She told me what she thought," or "His lecture will be a good expression of his ideas." Finally, we presume that our expressions of thought—namely, our words—can furnish suitable guides or pictures of the world as it is (Phase 3). Thus, if we perceive the world correctly, and express our knowledge in plain language, others will gain in knowledge.

These assumptions are hardly academic in their implications. They provide the basis for the widespread faith in the ability of scientists to furnish objective knowledge of the world, and for holding scientific knowledge to be more trustworthy (based on real-world observation) than the opinions of poets, politicians, or spiritualists. They furnish the chief rationale for having schools and building the curriculum around the printed and spoken word. They underlie our conceptions of democratic process, in which each individual is credited with the ability to "think for himself." And on the more personal level, they shape the contours of intimacy. To "truly know" someone generally means that our private world of thoughts and feelings resonates with and is understood by the other, and vice versa—mind to mind, heart to heart.

But this traditional view of the individual knower no longer seems viable. Each of the necessary assumptions has been criticized, and criticisms in one domain have implications in the next. If it proves difficult, for example, to make sense of the distinction between external and internal levels of reality, then by implication doubt is also cast on the

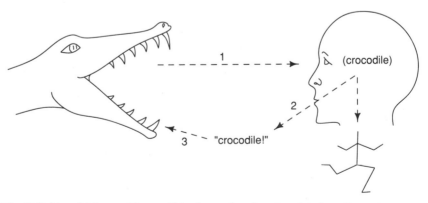

The Enlightened Man: 1. The world is observed and contemplated. 2. Concepts are expressed through words and actions. 3. Words carry a picture of the world to others.

assumption that knowledge of the external world is a possession of individual minds, and that words serve as external expressions of the inner world. Let us explore the emerging critiques of the individual as agent of knowledge.

Separating the Knower from the Known

These two terms, "sense-data" and "material things," live by taking in each other's washing—what is spurious is not one term of the pair, but the antithesis itself.

—J. L. Austin, *Sense and Sensibilia*

There is scarcely a reader who doubts that when he or she is asleep the world goes on as it is. The world is there, independent of us; we are but its spectators during our conscious hours. Yet in spite of the obvious fact that we are transient agents of experience in a world that will continue beyond our demise, can such a belief be justified? The distinction between the *real* world and the *perceived* world seems altogether self-evident, but is it? If all experience were removed from existence, would anything be left over to be called *real* "clouds" or "steeples"? If we removed from existence all that we call real-world, would anything remain that we call "seeing," "hearing," or "smelling"? To remove the entirety of one domain is to remove the whole of the other. Why then do we treat this unity as two realms of existence rather than one? And, as philosophers have long questioned, if each of us lives in our private experience, then on what grounds do we conclude that there is anything outside of experience? If all that we can know is in our experience, then we can know nothing beyond it—which would exclude the possibility of knowledge of an external, or nonexperiential, world.

We find, then, that philosophers have never been able to justify the distinction between the real world and the experienced world, nor the existence of a real world independent of experience. Most scholars cease to worry about such intractable problems. As is often proposed, the distinction between world and mind seems intuitively correct, and it seems to make sense of much that we know. By abandoning the problem of justifying this conclusion, a range of possibly more fruitful questions can be asked. Specifically, if we presume a dualism—a knower and a known—how can we explain how the real world comes to be represented in the mind of the knower; how can we determine when and where "misperception" occurs; and how do mental representations of the world influence the individual's actions? Such "problems of knowledge" have long occupied philosophers, and in this century psychologists have joined them, seeking experimental solutions to such questions as why people see constancy in a world of continuous change, what cues we use to estimate depth, and how we account for perceptual illusions. Curiously, despite the enormous effort expended on the problem, there are still no widely accepted solutions.[20] The riddle of how we correctly perceive or know what is the case persists.

Thus the ground is ready for a more skeptical question: Is the problem itself ill posed? Why do we presume a real world on the one hand and an experienced world on the other? Are those intractable problems not created by the form of the question itself? Such a possibility began to crystallize in Wittgenstein's later work.[21] As Wittgenstein proposed, our words are not pictures of what is the case. Words are not maps of reality. Rather, words gain their meaning though their use in social interchange, within the "language games" of the culture. We don't use words like *perception, thought,* and *memory* because they accurately map a world we call mental. Rather, such terms gain their meaning from the way they are used in social life. To say "John, you forgot my birthday" is not a report on the state of John's mental world; the words function as a chastisement for his errant behavior in a given relationship. From this standpoint it is no longer necessary to ask how it is that an individual "perceives" or "remembers," for example, because such terms do not stand for (or map) existing mental processes. *Perceive* and *remember* are words that derive their meaning from the language games of the culture. "Try not to think of understanding as a 'mental process' at all," says Wittgenstein. "For *that* is the expression which confuses you. But ask yourself: in what sort of case, in what kind of circumstances, do we say, 'Now I know how to go on.' "[22]

Interest in this possibility has grown and prospered since Wittgenstein wrote. Richard Rorty's more recent *Philosophy and the Mirror of Nature* brings the argument to its logical conclusion. He proposes that the view of the mind as an internal mirror of external reality is a metaphor elaborated largely by philosophers of the seventeenth century, designed at the time to defend the purpose of philosophical inquiry against the successful sciences of the day. It is only when one takes the metaphor as literal that the problem of knowledge is created. Rorty writes,

> to think of knowledge which presents a "problem," and about which we ought to have a "theory," is a product of viewing knowledge as an assemblage of representations—a view of knowledge which . . . was a product of the seventeenth century. The moral to be drawn is that if this way of thinking of knowledge is optional, then so is [the problem of knowledge].[23]

And so also is the concept of the individual self. For if it makes no sense to ask, as a matter of serious concern, how the *objective* world makes its imprint on the *subjective* world, how the individual mind comprehends external reality, why continue to grant honorific status to the distinction between subject and object at all? Why must we take seriously the presumption that there are individual minds about which we must gain knowledge? And what, after all, should we mean by knowledge in such a case? To eradicate the distinction between world and mind, object and subject, is to remove both from the field of existing essences. "World" and "mind" became entries in the discursive practices of the culture.

Fathoming Other Minds

Some revolutions occur quietly: no manifestoes, no marching and singing, no tumult in the streets; simply a shift in perspective, a new way of seeing what had always been there. [We] have been witnessing just such a change in the field of literary theory and criticism. The words reader and audience, once relegated to the status of the unproblematic and obvious, have acceded to a starring role.

—Susan Suleiman, *The Reader in the Text*

Given these critiques, we can no longer sustain the presumption that individual minds operate as mirrors of external reality. Why then must we presume that there is an internal world of the self—private and isolated—that thinks, knows, and expresses itself in words? Yet the assumption that people express their minds through words is a mainstay of Western cultural life. To understand another's words, we hold, is to have access to his or her mind or consciousness. When we interpret another's words correctly, we are grasping his or her "intention" or "meaning." A proper account of Shakespeare's *Othello*, then, should help us see what Shakespeare was "trying to say," what he "meant" by the play. A student's essay on Eliot's "The Waste Land" should strive to reveal Eliot's "intentions," what he was "trying to express" in the various symbols in the poem.

This assumption not only figures prominently in the Western educational tradition. It also forms the basis for legal decisions that depend on interpreting earlier judicial rulings. When the U.S. Supreme Court interprets the Constitution in a given case, it claims knowledge of the founding fathers' "intentions." Similarly, when the pope gives an interpretation of an earlier writ or biblical passage, he claims knowledge of the writer's "inspiration" or "meaning." And when a newswriter, historian, or political scientist furnishes an analysis of a given speech, the claim is that the speaker's "meaning" or "motives" will be revealed.

The problems with these assumptions begin with a consideration of the audience—the reader or listener. To make sense of another's words or actions, the audience must proceed from some perspective. Others' words do not come with labels indicating how they must be interpreted, and such interpretation must thus be based on a set of assumptions, or a perspective—concerning, for example, what people "have on their minds," how they are motivated, and so on. The German theorist Hans-Georg Gadamer proposes that people approach a text (or any other verbal expression) with a *forestructure* of understandings that form the basis for interpretation.[24] However, this forestructure is open to change through time. The *horizon of understanding*, as he puts it, is continuously changing over the course of history, favoring interpretations in one period that would seem woolly-minded or absurd in another. From our contemporary vantage point, a person's spoken opinions can be read as evidence of his unconscious desires; two centuries ago such an understanding would have been practically impossible. This is not to say that our ability to understand has improved with time, only that our horizon of understanding has changed. And it is for this reason, many maintain, that we can never know if we "understand" the great texts of the past—the Bible, Shakespeare, the Constitution. We can only understand such texts in terms of our present conventions of interpretation, and there is no means of assessing the similarity between them and those of the past—each attempt to interpret the conventions of the past would itself proceed on the basis of our contemporary conventions.[25]

Matters of *correct* interpretation are even more complicated. The literary theorist Stanley Fish notes that we now have many frameworks of interpretation to choose from.[26] Each derives its sense of validity from a particular *community of interpretation*—a group of individuals who by virtue of persuasion and consent come to share certain assumptions about the proper reading of a text. In effect, every reader approaches a book with certain styles of interpretation intact, styles that reflect the communities of which he or she is a part. The way the book is interpreted must inevitably depend on these styles.

Consider, for example, the line "Her boss approached her with steady gaze and ready smile." How is the reader to interpret the line? What is the author's intent? For a teenage subcommunity obsessed with romance, the "steady gaze" and "ready smile" are the obvious signals of a budding love affair, so clearly the author intends to write about love. In contrast, a business executive might assume the author was describing a popular managerial style. If the reader were a feminist, however, the "steady gaze" and "ready smile" might reveal the nuances of sexual harassment. And for a Marxist, the author might be describing the seductive exploitation of the working class. In effect, each reader incorporates the author into his or her own perspective. Or in the succinct terms of the literary analyst Morris Zapp, "Every decoding is another encoding."[27]

This argument is not a happy one for most teachers of literature, for it means that all readings of a text or poem—including those of neophyte students—are equally valid as insights into "true" meaning. We still have many conventions by which to speak of the superiority of one interpretation over another (aesthetic appeal, inclusiveness, subtlety, originality, value basis), but the traditional standard of accuracy no longer applies. This emphasis on communities of interpretation also poses difficulties in the judicial sphere. When the Supreme Court issues an interpretation of the Constitution, in what sense do the justices reflect the "true intent" of the founding fathers? Are they not simply reading their own values into the Constitution? How could they do otherwise?[28] (For those dismayed at the shifting opinion of the Court on such matters as abortion and civil liberties, these suspicions have now become realities.)

The implications of these lines of reasoning are of signal consequence to the traditional view of the self. For if words are interpreted according to community-based understandings, then of what value is the concept of the author's intention, meaning, or subjectivity? Our interpretations of another's words or actions cannot be judged in terms of their correspondence with the inner processes of the other and social life continues nevertheless. So why presume that there *are* psychological processes (intentions, desires) to which interpretations should be true? One may reply in protest, "But I do understand my intentions, what I mean when I speak; and if you are to interpret me correctly you must know my intentions." But what is it to "look inward" and to identify what one "really means"? Can one identify an "inner state" not already prefigured in the public language? Can an American look inward and identify an emotion for which there is no English word? To express what one believes one intends, it is necessary to use the public language. And when this language is communicated to others, they have little choice but to interpret it in terms of their local or commonsense conventions.

As scholars now ask, why do we privilege "the mind" behind the text as being its point of origin, its rational or creative source? If understanding a text is a matter of participating in ongoing conventions of culture, then why is writing (or speaking) not a similar process—a matter of joining in the language games? To write or speak is not, then, to express an interior world, but to borrow from the available things people write and say and to reproduce them for yet another audience. As the French theorist

Roland Barthes has put it, "a text is not a line of words releasing a single 'theological' meaning (the 'messages' of the author-God) but a multi-dimensional space in which a variety of writings, none of them original, blend and clash."[29] But if the idea of a creative mind behind the text is unworkable, where in Western history did we come to believe in the idea? The idea of single minds behind words is a cornerstone of Western individualism, and thus may date back to the seventeenth and eighteenth centuries. Before this time, many writings did not have single individuals who claimed sole authorship. Michel Foucault suggests that the desire to identify an author resulted in part from authorities' attempts to hold persons responsible for undesirable political writings. In any case, Foucault concludes, "The coming into being of the notion of 'author' constitutes the privileged moment of individualization in the history of ideas, knowledge, literature, philosophy, and the sciences."[30] And if the texts of the culture are without authors, so actions are without underlying agents.

The Deconstruction of Mind and Object

Language is not an instrument or tool in man's hands, a submissive means of thinking. Language rather thinks man and his "world."
— J. Hillis Miller, *The Critic as Host*

If it is difficult to justify the view that people have individual minds that reflect reality, and that their internal reflections are communicated via their words, what are we then to make of a third and related presumption: that individuals use their words to share their knowledge with others, to represent to others the world as it is? Can words accurately capture the world as it is, thus conveying to others what is the case? Does the very concept of truth-telling not depend on such a possibility? Yet, earlier in this chapter, we encountered suspicion of such a view—if one's choice of language is not determined by the contours of "the world as it is," then language can scarcely "mirror" or "map" what is the case. Recent literary theory raises the suspicion to the boiling point, and the results now spew from the literary realm across the sciences and humanities.

To appreciate the argument in this case, let us return for a moment to the fate of literature in the modernist period. As you will recall, the major attempt in the arts and sciences was to locate a fundamental essence, knowledge of "things in themselves." Knowledge of these essences was to be communicated through language, and thus books on physics should inform us of the nature of the physical world, lectures on economics of the economic world, and so on. This same search for essences was also taking place in the literary domain. The attempt in this case was to disclose the essential character of language—the chief vehicle used by all the other disciplines to "reflect," "record," or "communicate" the truth. The stage was thus set for the modernist quest for essences to cave in upon itself. For as literary theory developed along modernist lines, the conclusion was inevitably reached that language, too, was essentially a "thing in itself." That is, language is not "about the world"; it is not a simulacrum of reality, a mirror or a map. It operates according to an inner logic of its own, according to its own conventions. If this is so, then it is specious for all the other disciplines to claim that their languages carry truth. Languages principally carry themselves.

Perhaps the most powerful movement in this case, gaining initial momentum in France but rapidly attracting international attention, has been *deconstructionism*. Although it is impossible to do justice to the full line of deconstructionist writings (a task indeed prohibited by the deconstructionist writings themselves), the movement has influenced many scholars to conclusions of substantial consequence. The critical source has been the work of the French theorist Jacques Derrida.[31] One of Derrida's chief concerns is with what he terms the *logocentric* bias underlying the Western intellectual tradition—in our terms, the presumption that words reflect the workings of the mind as it converts the surrounding chaos into logical order. This traditional view demands reverence for the knower's words, for if such words are based on sound reason and observation, they can elucidate the essence of what is the case. It is largely by this rationale that students are assigned books and given lectures; these are the vehicles for communicating the accumulated knowledge of the culture. Derrida opposes the view of words as the individual's reflection of essences. Instead, he proposes, language is a system unto itself. Words derive their capacity to create a seeming world of essences from the properties of the system. This system of language (or of sense-making) preexists the individual; it is "always already" there, available for social usage. Thus, anything said about the world or the self should, in principle, be placed in quotations. If it is sensible, it has already been said. The most one can do is to rearrange the sayables.

Consider, for example, a term such as *democracy*. We speak about democracy as an existing essence—a form of government to be studied by scholars, appreciated by citizens, and maintained by force if necessary. Yet the meaning of the term is not derived from observing persons moving about in time and space. Rather, to use the term meaningfully depends on a literary distinction between democracy and, for example, contrasting terms such as *totalitarianism* and *monarchy*. Further, its meaning derives from other terms with which it is said to bear similarity, such as *equality* and *freedom*. And the meaning of democracy "at the present time" depends on its contrasts and similarities with other terms in the past. (*Democracy* in present-day America must be understood, for example, in terms of its contrast with what it meant when literacy tests were required for voting.) More succinctly, then, the meaning of a term depends first on a *difference* between this term and other terms in the system of language. At the same time, understanding a term requires a constant process of *deferring* to other terms within the system—to words such as totalitarianism, equality, and freedom. Yet what do these latter terms mean? To what essence do they refer? In order to clarify, we again resort to language, to a process of difference and deferral. "Equality" is the opposite of "inequality"; it is reflected in societies that are "fair" and "just." But what precisely is it to be "fair" or "just" . . . and the game of language continues. We never exit the texts of democracy to encounter "the real thing." In the end, for Derrida, "There is nothing outside text."

From this standpoint, words lose their capacity to describe things as they are, or to capture essences. For all the enormous scholarship on democracy, the constitutions guaranteeing it, and the rousing attempts to promote and defend it, there is no *it* about which such activities swirl. Democracy as an *in itself* lies empty; its life is confined to a history of textuality.

For many scholars this perspective invites forms of textual debunking, or deconstruction. Here one demonstrates how a broadly accepted thesis "about the nature of things" derives its meaning from subtle exercises in differing and deferring. In deconstructing a text, major propositions about the nature of things are often shown to depend on an implicit acceptance of the supplementary meaning that it denies. Thus, for example, deconstructing a thesis on the advantages of democracy over totalitarianism might involve showing how the thesis makes sense only if one accepts the hidden assumption that democracy itself is a totalitarian form. The argument for the superiority of one over the other then lapses into incoherence.

For many other scholars, deconstruction theory invites a revival of rhetorical study. If texts do not derive their persuasive power from "the way things are," but from textual maneuvers, then attention must be directed to the "world as represented." The rhetorical techniques of representation, of constructing the world, have a critical and often unwitting impact on social life. Our understandings become subject to the maneuverings of metaphor, narrative form, plain talk, irony, and the like. Consider the writing of history. We generally think of proper history as furnishing us with an accurate account of the past. It is through the teaching of history that we come to understand our heritage, our accomplishments and our failings, and enrich our wisdom for the future. Yet, proposes the historian Hayden White, if historians are to be intelligible they must inevitably rely on the existing conventions of writing within their culture.[32] These conventions are themselves subject to historical growth and decay, and our understandings of the past are thus rooted in the literary traditions of the day, particularly our traditions of storytelling, or narrative traditions.

When historians generate a picture of reality, they cannot possibly report every document, every movement of the body, every nuance of speech, and so on, that they believe to have existed. Rather, they select and interpret the evidence in a way that will fit the cultural demands for proper narratives. They can write without hesitation of the "rise and fall" of a civilization, and they can speak of the emergence of new social orders through revolution. Such accounts fit the presently acceptable forms of storytelling. On the other hand, our sense of a properly formed narrative does not permit a high degree of repetition. A historian could not write of a king who "looked skyward on April 14, 1672, again on April 15, again on April 16. . . ." Nor do we generally accept stories in which there is no *direction* or *point*. Historians cannot write of the past as a succession of "one damn thing after another"—the birth of a child, the braying of a donkey, the rolling tide, the family consuming the evening meal, the battle fought. This is not because repetition and pointlessness are not true of the world; they are simply inadequate techniques of storytelling. In White's terms, "historical narratives . . . are verbal fictions, the contents of which are as much 'invented' as 'found.'"[33]

(Reader beware, the same may be said of this book, and as well of the saying so . . .)

Yet embedded in the deconstructionist writings is a more subtle and far-reaching message concerning the durability of the self. Not only the object of a text is erased through such analyses, but the author as well. This is so in two respects. First, the process of deconstruction applies to all those terms that seem to describe the essence of mind: words such as "reason," "emotion," "attitudes," and "wants." To what do such terms refer? To understand their meaning we must again fall back on a process of differing and deferring, forever massaging and manipulating the language, but never locating the "real" thing. Why then do we presume that there is a real thing—an essence—to which the language of the individual mind is affixed? If there is nothing outside of text, this includes the minds of those who speak and write.

In addition, there is a second and more subtle way in which deconstructionist writings undermine the assumption of an essential self. From the traditional standpoint, the individual observes the world and transforms his or her thoughts into words that express these thoughts to others. For the deconstructionist, language is a system unto itself, a cultural form that owes its existence to a collectivity of participants. Its structure preexists any single individual, and if sense is to be made, the individual must essentially participate in the communal conventions. Thus, individuals are not the intentional agents of their own words, creatively and privately converting thoughts to sounds or inscriptions. Rather, they gain their status as selves by taking a position within a preexisting form of language. "I" am I only by virtue of adopting the traditional pronoun in a culturally shared linguistic system.[34] A language without the pronouns "I" and "you" might fail to recognize persons as having individual selves. If we could only speak as "we," there would be no "I" who was acting. Or, to put it in another way, people do not speak their experience; rather, without forms of speaking they could not claim to have an experience.

It is thus that the current turmoil in the academy prepares for the exit of the self. The rise of many voices creates a context in which claims to objective truth can no longer be warranted. Further, because claims to true and accurate description mystify the interests that they serve, the calm voice of objective assurance is all the more dangerous. Faith in objective knowledge about individual persons—about mind, emotion, intention, and the like—is thereby eroded. The image of the autonomous agent of knowledge, privately observing and sharing his or her thoughts with others, is also placed in jeopardy. Under current critical appraisal, the distinction between object and subject, mind and world, deteriorates; the assumption that words are external signs of internal meanings turns pale; the object of the individual's words is deconstructed; and the individual slowly disappears into the greater dance of communal life.

FIVE

The Emergence of Postmodern Culture

Modernism is dominant but dead.
—Jürgen Habermas, *Modernism: An Incomplete Project*

What is the relationship between the Greek columns sprouting from recent buildings and *Monty Python's Flying Circus*? What does new age music have to do with Milan Kundera's novels? And why does music television flourish at the same time as critical legal studies? These entries into cultural life seem disconnected, mere chance occurrences thrust upon us by historical circumstance. Yet in important ways they are of the same family. They are all outgrowths of what may be viewed as a postmodern consciousness. This consciousness now pervades the arts, sciences, leisure activities, news media, entertainment world, and political life, and its expansion seems as inevitable as the growing efficacy of communications technology. Most important, postmodernism undermines the modernist project and simultaneously subverts romantic visions of the self. Its implications for conceptions of human character are thus substantial, as threatening as they are intoxicating.

As we saw in the preceding chapter, modernist foundations of objective knowledge, so central to the institutions of science and education, are rapidly eroding. The increasing awareness of multiplicity in perspective undermines attempts to justify any transcendent criterion of the correct. Concepts of truth, honesty, and authenticity now turn strange. Not only do attempts at characterizing *the actual person*—the workings of the mind, the human spirit, or the biological individual—become suspect. The very concept of an internal core—an intentional, rational agent—

also begins to fray. This emergence of postmodern consciousness within the academic sphere is only a sign of social change of much greater proportion. The fallout from social saturation is everywhere in our culture, and the effects on cultural assumptions of self are broad.[1] This chapter will explore some of the major reverberations.

THE LOSS OF THE IDENTIFIABLE

Ms. Holcomb's music has roots in a great variety of styles. Many of the songs are couched in simple, folklike style. . . . From another end of the spectrum there are Gregorian-chant references. . . . And there are slightly off-color hymnlike sections. . . . Gospel music also finds its way into the work . . . but jazz and rock elements . . . are given fuller scope. . . . —Allan Kozinn, *The New Music Festival*

Central to the modernist view was the assumption of *things in themselves*. That is, the modernist believed that the world was made up of various essences or "natural kinds"—physical atoms, chemical elements, psychological states, social institutions. The various fields of endeavor—physics, chemistry, psychology, and the like—were each to inform the culture about the nature of a particular class of entities. Yet, as one becomes increasingly aware of multiplicity in perspective, things-in-themselves disappear from view. If "what there is" depends on the perspective one brings to the situation, if these perspectives are biased by values and ideology, constrained by literary conventions, and ambiguously related to a world outside themselves, then of what consequence is the assumption of a thing-in-itself? Proposals that the world is round, that infants experience emotions, or that people are motivated by economic incentives—all of which seem to say something about things in the world—appear on closer inspection to be language conventions favored by certain groups at certain times. Only social constraints make one way of talking seem superior to another. (If scientists agreed that the forces behind all material events were spiritual, and substituted spirit forces for such words as *gravity* and *ionization* in their account of events, scientific life could go on unimpeded, and students could intelligibly learn that "the world is governed by spiritual forces.")

Learning that there is no thing-in-itself to which our accounts of the world must be true can lead to an enormous sense of liberation. So long as there is at least someone or some group to say "That's interesting," "It seems possible," or "That sounds reasonable," one is free to construct, render, or depict the world as desired. For many academics, disciplinary constraints—the standard ways of "doing" anthropology, economics, psychology, and the like—lose their foundational justifications. The scholar is free to combine and synthesize in any way that communicates effectively. The Princeton anthropologist Clifford Geertz has called the newer forms of scholarship *blurred genres*.[2]

But can we in the culture as a whole detect the disappearance of things-in-themselves? Are cultural life-forms losing their identities, blending into ever-shifting and unnameable forms? One needn't look far to see positive indications. One of the most visible blurrings of traditional boundaries has taken place within the visual arts. Just as modernist literary theory led to deconstructionism, so modern art prepared the way for the postmodern. Many modern artists abandoned traditional pictorial modes to locate the "essence" beyond the vision of the eye; others eschewed the challenge of depiction altogether. Form and color themselves possessed essences to be explored; they should not be used in the service of portraying something else.

Partly because there were no binding agreements regarding what was "essential," and partly because acclaim was often accorded those whose pursuits of purity were most audacious, the definition of "art" soon began to melt. For conceptualists such as William Anastasi, mere layers of plaster and paint on an aging wall served as art; Joseph Beuys achieved fame through arrangements of metal scraps, used car batteries, and the like; other artists experimented with hanging large metal frames before landscapes, and defining as art all that the viewer scanned within the rectangle. And, of course, there was Andy Warhol's presentation of Campbell's Soup cans and Brillo boxes—icons of advertising or anti-art—as "fine art." A prominent graffito near the Pompidou Center captured the emerging conclusion: "Tout est art." Yet when all is art, the genre is dissipated.

Equally apparent to the eye is the blurring of traditional boundaries by architectural design. In the modernist period the major challenge was presented by fundamental forms. The decorative and the unessential were to be cut away to yield transcendent forms—the building-in-itself. Yet this "dream of pure form," as the Museum of Modern Art's Mark Wigley sees it, "has become a kind of nightmare."[3] The pure forms have become all too formalized and constraining—architecture for architects, deaf to the voices of those who must dwell within. Contrast the modernist quest for purity with the recent words of the popular Swiss architect Mario Botta: "The architect is no more than an interpreter of the time in which he or she lives. Architecture is a formal expression of history. It is a discipline that turns the spirit of the epoch into stone."[4] For Botta, as for many other postmodern architects, there is no essential or basic form to be revealed by one's designs. The architect is engaged in a cultural dia-

Although much postmodern architecture now tends toward the programmatic, architects such as Albuquerque's Bart Prince find the context an invitation to the imagination. Included here are shots of both the facade (left) and the interior stairs (right) of the Joe Price house in Corona del Mar, California.

logue in the here and now. Since many voices participate, a free play of architectural forms results. As the architect Philip Johnson puts it, "pluralism reigns, perhaps a soil in which poetic, original artists can develop."[5]

This emphasis on multiplicity of voice is captured for the postmodern architect by the concepts of *double* or *multiple coding.* In double coding, the design attempts at once to speak the language of professional archi-

tecture—an aesthetic language evolving over centuries of experience in design—and a second language, that of the people.[6] In effect, the postmodern building is designed to speak in multiple vernaculars. A postmodern structure may include classical columns and arches, dashes of bright color, ornamental ironwork, and friezes designed to speak in the common voices of the culture. The postmodern architect and theorist Robert Venturi finds Frank Lloyd Wright's modernist motto "Truth against the world" and Le Corbusier's search for the "great primary forms" arid in their implications. Rather, he says, "I like elements which are hybrid rather than 'pure,' compromising rather than 'clean,' distorted rather than 'straightforward,' ambiguous rather than 'articulated' . . . inconsistent and equivocal rather than direct and clear. I am for messy vitality over obvious unity."[7] To the dismay of many contemporaries, Venturi and his colleagues look at the sprawling chaos of Las Vegas boulevards and proclaim, "Main Street is almost all right."[8]

In writing, too, the borders blur. During the modernist period, one could make comfortable distinctions between *fiction* as opposed to *factual* or scientific writing. In the same way historical novels (mere entertainment) could be contrasted with serious historical reports, and literal or scientific writing was considered objective while metaphoric or "pretty" language was best reserved for the arts. With the breakdown of things-in-themselves, and the sensitivity to multiple realities, such borders begin to dissolve. Fiction, for example, begins to look like biography (Banville's *Keppler*), autobiography (Ondaatje's *Running in the Family*), and history (Rushdie's *Shame*).[9] Tama Janowitz's otherwise fanciful *A Cannibal in Manhattan* includes photographs ("real" pictures) of the protagonists attending a wedding party at Tavern on the Green. Historical writing, along with certain work in anthropology, sociology, and psychology, begins to resemble fiction. For example, the Princeton historian Natalie Zemon Davis teamed with French filmmakers to produce *The Return of Martin Guerre*, a story taken from the archives of sixteenth-century France. The result was an intriguing account of duplicity, replete with dramatic technique, and yet heralded by many historians as more fully expressive of the period than many scholarly treatises. Where in such an effort can one draw the line between artifice and objectivity?[10] Instead, a new genre emerges, neither fact nor fiction, but *faction*.[11]

To illustrate faction at work, consider the French author Georges Perec's *W: Or the Memory of Childhood*.[12] At first the book seems to be autobiographical, with alternate chapters giving apparently straightforward reports of Perec's childhood in Nazi Germany. However, at times Perec admits that he isn't able to discern when he is telling the truth and when he is giving the reader imaginative re-creations of what really happened. Is the reader to trust, then, that what he is writing is "truly" autobiographical? At the same time, these seemingly autobiographical accounts are interwoven with what are surely allegorical chapters. These alternating chapters tell a story of an island society where sport is king: athletic competition is the primary way of life. Winners are given enormous privileges and losers are mocked, starved, and even killed. As the barbarity of this society is revealed, the reader comes to feel that it represents emotional life under the Nazi regime, in a way that factual reporting cannot. However, if this is its intent (which Perec himself never admits), then the fictional account must be accepted as "truth-telling" while the "truthful account" is buried in the dust of doubt.

(And what is to be said of this book you are reading now? Is it a factual report, a fictional fantasy, scholarship, journalism, prose, poetry, history, psychology, sociology, anthropology, ideology . . . or is it all of the above? On what grounds can they be separated?)

Within modern music we again find the emergence of blurring genres. The modernist concern for "pure music," music-in-itself, set the stage for the postmodern disappearance of musical genres. For if music is only bits of sound, then traditional genres of music are no more than convention-alized arrangements of sound. To claim that certain music is "sacred," "transcendental," or "profound" is simply an exercise in rhetoric. In John Cage's words, "The lines between what is music and what is not are drawn by each individual, and they change according to the individual."[13] The works of Philip Glass and Terry Riley nicely illustrate the eroding dis-tinction between classical (or serious) music and popular fare. Glass's work with Robert Wilson, *Einstein on the Beach*, defies categorization. Not only is the music a polyglot of classical, popular, and modern idioms, but the performance also includes infusions from opera, ballet, poetry, the mass media, and rock-concert staging effects.[14] Echoing the theme of multiple perspectives, composers have developed the concept of *musical layering*. Most traditional compositions feature a single melodic line or hummable melody; musical layering places one idiom upon the other, just as several voices might sing together, each a different song. When one melody, tempo, or tonal range is superimposed upon the other, the resulting listening experience borders, for some, on cacophony. At the same time, such blurring is designed to expand the listener's listening capacity by maximizing the unexpected, or combining the uncombined.

At the level of popular music, the Beatles were perhaps the first im-portant indicator of modernism's demise. Rather than embracing a sin-gular musical tradition, or a circumscribed range of instruments, the Beatles moved at will across the musical spectrum. Interlaced within their rock-and-roll standards were doses of Indian sitar music ("Norwegian Wood"), the symphonic ("Eleanor Rigby"), the dancehall ("When I'm 64"), Elvis Presley ("Oh! Darling"), reggae ("Ob-La-Di, Ob-La-Da"), folk music ("Rocky Raccoon"), children's songs ("Yellow Submarine"), and psychedelia ("Lucy in the Sky with Diamonds").[15] This blending and blurring continues to pervade the world of pop music. Consider:

• The increasing tendency of musical groups to "sample" the work of other artists—that is, to insert snippets of previously recorded material into their own recordings. Thus a single album by the rap group De

La Soul samples, among many others, the country singer Johnny Cash, a French language lesson, Liberace live in concert, and the '60s soul star Otis Redding whistling.

• Torch songs for Jesus, a genre in which romantic musical idioms encourage religious devotion. One cannot be certain whether the object of such songs is Jesus or a lover.

• Jazz festivals featuring Latin American salsa, electrified gypsy violins, African drum groups, and Caribbean reggae.

• New age music, often blending classical, jazz, and romantic idioms with Asian, disco, and jungle sounds. In the case of groups like Shadowfax, the music is played on a range of electronic instruments that themselves are hybrid in form, and their sounds are combined, re-formed, and replayed through a synthesizer.

Even the traditional categories of cuisine are slowly eroding. In the place of such well-defined genres as French, Italian, and Chinese cooking, one increasingly finds the borders blurred: Ingredients from one genre are combined with those from disparate traditions in new and often interesting ways. Chefs no longer so much "master a tradition" as learn to have a voice of their own. The international columnist Patricia Wells calls it "comma cuisine," pointing to the commas distinguishing the miscellaneous ingredients found on many restaurant menus. For example, Michael's in Santa Monica offers "East Coast sea scallops, Maui onion confit, haricots verts, vine-ripened tomato, baby greens with balsamic vinegar, and del Gardo extra-virgin olive oil"—a single dish combining flavors from four different traditions.

Increasingly, then, the traditional categories of cultural life become blurred, the edges indistinct. No longer can we be sanguine in identifying what is art, characterizing good architectural design, distinguishing between fact and fiction, or recognizing separate musical genres. In this cultural climate, the concept of the individual person begins to lose its integrity. Romanticists and modernists could never agree on whether the essential self was spirit or material. But competing voices now propose that selves belong to the domains of the aesthetic, rhythmic, robotic, symbolic, economic, literary, and more. When the distinction between subject and object ceases to compel, and category boundaries lose their edges, we become less and less able to distinguish *me* and *mine* from *you* and *yours*.

We seem to be machinelike, but with a spiritual side; biologically determined, but in possession of conscious control; fundamentally motivated toward self-gain, but even more fundamentally motivated by high ideals; sheeplike creatures who are slavishly dependent on the mass media, but drawn deeply toward goals of uniqueness and independence. Where are we to draw the lines that define the human self? Portrayals of the self multiply, the lines grow increasingly complex, and with this mounting complexity the boundaries grow fuzzy.

THE SOCIAL CONSTRUCTION OF REALITY

Language allows me to objectify a great variety of experiences coming my way in the course of life.
—Peter L. Berger and Thomas Luckmann, *The Social Construction of Reality*

If the traditional categories are collapsing, and genres continuously blurring, blending, and re-forming, what are we to make of common claims to knowledge? Everyone, from family members to physicians and government leaders, confidently informs us of "what is the case." When the "objects of knowledge" acquire a puttylike character, how are such "reports," "factual descriptions," or "insights" to be regarded? At least one major answer drawn from the arguments set out in the previous chapter is that such claims are social constructions. That is, words are not mirrorlike reflections of reality, but expressions of group convention. Various social groups possess preferred vocabularies, or ways of putting things, and these vocabularies reflect or defend their values, politics, and ways of life. For participants in such groups, these forms of talking (or writing) take on a local reality. They seem totally convincing. Yet their very "reality" is their danger, for each renders the believer heroic and the nonbeliever a fool. This is not to say that modern medicine is no better than witchcraft; by contemporary Western conventions it surely is. However, the words employed by physicians are not thereby rendered *truer* (in the sense of more accurate depictions) than their exotic counterparts. To possess an effective procedure, according to certain definitions, does not render "true" or "objective" the words employed in carrying out the procedure.

This consciousness of construction is hardly limited to the academic sphere; it is increasingly pervading society. Daniel Boorstin's volume *The Image: A Guide to Pseudo-Events in America* offered an early contribution to this consciousness.[16] Boorstin laments that our confrontation with objective reality is gradually being replaced by a pseudo- or staged reality. For example, political events are staged for public consumption;

events are created to give the appearance that important things are happening; information is "leaked" to the press by political officials for purposes of strategic advantage. Nothing is actually happening, argues Boorstin; all is done for purposes of manipulating images. The importance of persons is clouded over by the race to *appear* important, to gain celebrity status by manipulating information. And those who travel to distant lands no longer encounter the real surroundings, but experiences specially prepared for the tourist. Susan Sontag's more recent writings on metaphors of illness sound a similar refrain.[17] As she deftly shows, in the last century tuberculosis was romanticized (with the cough and deteriorating body signals of a finer and more deeply tuned sensitivity); in the present century cancer and AIDS are construed as harrowing and uncontrollable predators, tainting their "victims" in repulsive hues. In effect, we live in a metaphoric world of illness and fail to engage the illness in itself.

In their laments both Boorstin and Sontag speak as modernists peering into the emerging miasma of the postmodern. Our plight, says Boorstin, is that "we have used our wealth, our literacy, our technology, and our progress, to create the thicket of unreality which stands between us and the facts of life." Similarly, Sontag wishes us to move past the metaphor to confront the disease as it is. For the postmodern, however, the very "facts of life" themselves are thrown into question; concepts of "unreality" and "metaphor-free experience" are both rendered suspicious. One cannot escape perspective.

In this light, consider the social construction of the news. High standards have traditionally been placed on accuracy in reporting. We distinguish between objective reporting and "yellow journalism," between unbiased reporting (expected from the *New York Times* or the *London Times*) and mere propaganda (served up, we believe, by the *National Enquirer*). As postmodern consciousness slowly pervades the culture, this view of the news begins to erode. Echoing the traditional beliefs in objectivity, the president of CBS News, Walter Salant, announced, "Our reporters do not cover stories from their point of view. They are presenting them from nobody's point of view."[18] Increasingly, however, we become aware of the social processes that bring about what we had previously taken to be accepted fact. This enhanced consciousness is dramatized in such films as *Network, Broadcast News, All the President's Men*, and *Good Morning Vietnam*. In each case the audience witnesses the various social, ethical, and political pressures that go into fashioning "the factual world." Similarly, in the book *Prime Times and Bad Times*, Ed Joyce, former president of CBS News, explores how the demand for higher ratings and the prima-donna personalities of anchormen shape what the viewer receives as news.[19] There are pressures to dramatize the news, to make it upbeat and entertaining, for if properly enthralling stories are not presented, ratings fall, sponsors are lost, and revenues slump. The "factual world" is thus replaced by a world constructed for entertainment and profit.[20]

As the political scientist Murray Edelman puts the case, "Those involved in making, reporting, and editing news . . . have an incentive to shape it so as to attract audiences, and sometimes to encourage particular interpretations through its content and form. Interest groups, public officials, and editorial staffs share an interest in making news dramatic; economic, psychological, and ideological concerns reinforce each other in this respect."[21] He goes on to propose that the entire picture of the political sphere—"crises" and "resolutions," "political problems" and "policies," "oppositions" and "coalitions," "successes" and "failures"—are *all* constructions rather than realities. They form the great "political spectacle" within which we live our lives. What we find, then, is that the entire sense of what may be termed the *national reality* is not a picture of "what is the case," but a massive linguistic production. There is no "East-West détente," no "election race," no "war on drugs," and so on; these are only words favored by particular groups for particular purposes. To be sure, the words may stand as signs for something. Events do occur, after all. But there is no description or label that is uniquely pictorial, that mirrors the world as it really is, no perspective-free position, no final voice that speaks beyond the interests of some community.[22]

For the French theorist Jean Baudrillard, this consciousness of construction finds its most powerful expression in the concept of *hyperreality*.[23] To appreciate Baudrillard's view, recall the treatment of literary deconstruction in the previous chapter. Deconstruction theorists propose that words gain their meaning through their reference to other words; literary works gain their significance by the way they are related to other writings. Thus language does not derive its character from reality, but from other language. Now consider the media—newspapers, television, the movies, radio. For Baudrillard, media portrayals of the world are driven not by the way the world "is," but by the steadily emerging histories of portrayal itself. As these histories unfold, each new lamination is influenced by the preceding, accounts are layered upon accounts, and reality is transformed into a hyperreality. For example, Baudrillard asks, what is the reality of "the Holocaust"? One cannot deny that certain events took place, but as time goes on these events become subject to myriad re-presentations. Diaries become subject to redefinition by television and movies; biographies influence the writing of historical novels; narrated history is transformed into plays, and each "telling" lays the experiential groundwork for subsequent retellings. Realities accumulate, accentuate, interpenetrate, and ultimately create the world of hyperreality—itself in continuous evolution into the future. We feel we possess an intimate acquaintance of the events in themselves; they are sharply etched in our consciousness. For Baudrillard, however, this consciousness moves increasingly toward hyperreality.[24]

And thus the culture opens to the possibility of selves as artifacts of hyperreality. As political events, health and illness, and world history slip from the realm of the concrete into the domain of representation, so a commitment to obdurate selves becomes increasingly difficult to maintain.[25] What, after all, is the reality of our motives, intentions, thoughts, attitudes, and the like? For example, we readily speak of love, dream of it, build lives around what we take love to be. But what is love, after all? We now have centuries of accumulated stories, accounts, illustrations, and poems, each feeding off what has preceded, each adding its own lamination of understanding. In the present century love provides the theme for hundreds of thousands of films, television dramas, and musical offerings, each of which adds, modifies, or complicates our understandings. Love, then, is a constituent of hyperreality. There are no means by which we can press past the enormous layers of sedimented understandings to confront the phenomenon face to face. There are no means by which "it" can be recognized except through the standards furnished by the domain of hyperreality. There are no means by which "it" could be characterized or expressed except in the terms offered by the present cultural constructs. A friend recently wrote enthusiastically of a party that was "like being in the movies." At one point in cultural history we asked whether movies furnished an adequate likeness of real life. The good movies were the more realistic. Now we ask of reality that it accommodate itself to film. The good person, like the good party, should be more "movieistic."

As we find, the current texts of the self are built upon those of preceding eras, and they in turn upon more distant forms of discourse. In the end we have no way of "getting down to the self as it is." And thus we edge toward the more unsettling question: On what grounds can we assume that beneath the layers of accumulated understandings there is, in fact, an obdurate "self" to be located? The *object* of understanding has been absorbed into the world of representations.

AUTHORITY CHALLENGED

It is reckless to believe that any given position is "most" sophisticated, particularly if the position in question is intuitively appealing to the person doing the judging. . . . The question of what is more or less sophisticated has got to be a matter . . . about which there can be several points of view, perhaps even points of view that differ—in what else?—levels of sophistication. —Robert Ryder, *The Realistic Therapist*

Reflections of current life:

- A White House assistant worries that the office of the president no longer carries the power of prestige it once had.
- Positions of university president become increasingly difficult to fill as the respect for the office diminishes.
- Jokes poking fun at lawyers become so popular that they are now published in book form.
- Churches in dozens of European cities raise funds by rentals to orchestras and theater groups, or are put up for sale.
- An East German minister laments, "We have no real leaders."
- New Jersey school principal Joe Clark is lionized for his tough treatment of students, as secondary schools lose their capacity to maintain order and drastic measures appear to be required.
- While the lower classes traditionally have aped the fashions of the wealthy and powerful, upper-class fashion images now draw frequently from the counterculture: the hip, black radicals, rock singers, motorcycle gangs, punkers, and clochards.

Such commonplace events suggest a generalized diminution in respect for traditional authority. To the extent that this is so, the roots can be traced first to the rise of modernism in the present century. In the romantic era one could readily believe that certain gifted individuals possessed "genius," "profound inspiration," and "moral insight." As "reason" and "objectivity" came into fashion, however, the denizens of the deep interior were increasingly discredited. Genius became the deviant end of an intelligence scale; inspiration and moral insight were viewed as mere emotional outpouring. Further, anyone claiming knowledge not based on the rigorous methods of science—including the clergy, government officials, judges—was also found wanting. Even within the sciences themselves, authority was suspect. All scientists were subject to the critical scrutiny of their peers, and scientific authorities were only as good as the latest facts. Finally, because modernism emphasized the machine production of individual qualities, authorities lost their claim to the romanticist attributes of intrinsic worth or capability. Authorities were not *by nature* wise, insightful, or virtuous, as the romanticists would have it; they were simply products of their educational and social backgrounds. For the modernist an authority is just a nobody turned somebody by virtue of training—but truly, beneath the veneer, a nobody after all.

Where modernism prepared the way for the suspicion of authority, a "legitimation crisis," in Jürgen Habermas's terms, postmodernism furnishes the coup de grâce. For if the subject of knowledge is deconstructed, and tellings cannot in principle be true or false, then all authoritative claims (and claims to authority) are placed in doubt. Scientists, elder statesmen, Supreme Court justices, ministers, rabbis, business leaders, medical doctors, psychiatrists, economists, professors . . . all those traditionally granted status as "knowing something" are brought into question. What are the grounds for the "tellings"? Are they not dishing out preferred perspectives, merely sugarcoated with claims to "truth," "experience," or "wisdom"? They are victims, like the rest of us, of communal tastes, values, and ideologies, all of which color the ways they understand the world. The range of voices commenting on the issues of the day should expand.[26]

A case in point is the recent emergence of what is termed the "critical legal studies movement." A vocal minority within law-school faculties, often joined by enthusiastic students, has come to challenge the very concept of justice as represented in the law and practiced in the courts. It is traditionally assumed that there are general legal principles, abstract bodies of reason that serve the ends of justice within the society. With due procedure, these legal principles will be manifested in judicial opinions—applied dispassionately, without political bias, and without personal prejudice. (The modernist cast of such assumptions is clearly evident.) Critical legal theorists, much to the consternation of their colleagues, counter that not one of these assumptions can be justified.[27] Worse, to make such assumptions blinds one to the ways in which existing legal codes are molded by political and personal interests. What pass for "correct" legal principles typically serve the class interests of the "haves," and the application of the laws is shot through with self-serving biases that oppress and disfigure significant sectors of the culture. In effect, they say, the justice system serves to protect certain classes and interest groups at the expense of others.

Similar disquiet can be discerned in the field of art history. As an increasingly vocal group of historians now claim, the writing of art history (and thus the way art is taught to the public and presented in museums) masks cultural biases under the guise of truth. Any American visiting art museums in Brussels, Berlin, or Oslo will rapidly discover that the "geniuses whose art transcends both time and culture" in the home country are replaced in foreign lands by a pantheon of local heroes—who, in turn, are scarcely noticed in neighboring nations. Further, the critics point out, standard art histories are typically blind to important aspects of the art they describe. As Henri Zerner at the Fogg Art Museum sees it, "Although established art history pretends to be objective, it is in fact allied to a conservative ideology and very involved with the art market."[28] This sensitivity to the social and political biases entering into the glorification (or condemnation) of art has begun to influence museum exhibition policies. Not only are many museums now opening their walls to the works of previously marginalized groups or individuals, but many exhibitions also include political or ethical commentary. For example, in a recent exhibition of the history of the nude in London's Victoria and Albert Museum, works by Botticelli, Ingres, and Degas were accompanied by sociopolitical critiques.[29] "The masters" were taken to task for portraying the female as a passive, helpless sex object, and close to nature; by contrast, the male nude is more often depicted in serious cultural pursuits (solving a problem, vanquishing a foe).

The same drama is now sweeping across American campuses. In most universities "core" courses aim to teach the masterworks of Western writing, works that bear the highest values and most discerning insights of the culture, essential landmarks in the civilizing process, works about which no educated person should be ignorant. Plato, St. Augustine, Dante, Milton, Shakespeare, Rousseau, Emerson, Melville, Eliot . . . the authors' names are all familiar. Although the existence of such a *canon* (with local variations in taste) has long been taken for granted, and its significance seldom doubted, its authority is now under attack by students and faculty alike. News headlines such as "The Battle of the Books" and "From Western Lit to Westerns as Lit" capture the flavor of the conflict. However, we can understand the problem in terms of the multiplication in voices. Consider again the specimen names in the above list: They are all male, white, and from Western civilization. As increasing numbers of females, nonwhites, and non-Western students and faculty gain voice, it is only natural for them to ask: "Where are our traditions; did they not contribute to the civilizing process?" More critically, the black scholar Henry Louis Gates, Jr., proposes that "the high canon of Western masterpieces represents . . . an order in which my people were subjugated, the voiceless, the invisible, the unrepresented and the unrepresentable."[30] Traditionalists such as Reagan's secretary of education, William J. Bennett, rise in defense of the canon: "The West . . . has set the moral, political, economic, and social standards for the rest of the world."[31] Yet in a world of pluralistic perspectives, by what criterion is such a defense to be mounted? Because traditional Western standards are in fact deplorable from certain vantage points and parochial from others, the canon continues to crumble, and curricula continue to add new, previously silenced voices.

Many believe that this movement in the universities means that the classics will be abandoned in favor of less challenging fare. Although it is true that many curricula now feature works of otherwise dubious nature (such as Zane Grey, romance novels, Marvel comics), it is important to note that these works, along with the classics, are being subjected to a different kind of reading than that which dominated the romanticist and modernist eras. In the postmodern context, the attempt is not so much to ascertain the underlying wisdom of the works (as in the romanticist case), or to locate their internal coherence (as favored by modernists), but to explore the works as expressions of ideology, culturally dominant values, and popular stereotypes. In this context there is little that renders the canon superior to the pop-culture products. Both are carriers of the myths and values of an era, and it is to these that the postmodern reader's attention is most fully drawn.

In this context of generalized deterioration of authority, no one is left to speak convincingly of the self. Even within the professions claiming specialized knowledge of individual minds, internecine struggle prevails. The clergy is distrusted by psychiatrists, and they by social workers and family therapists, who themselves are disparaged by clinical psychologists. And, of course, all these concur that experimental psychology is largely irrelevant to understanding the complexities of the individual. But with the advent of postmodern consciousness, the doubts creep more widely throughout the culture. Psychiatrists, for example, are criticized by former mental patients for their systematic misunderstanding; experimental psychologists are taken to task by animal-rights advocates; and welfare recipients speak out against the views of social workers. Even street people form advocacy groups and publish newspapers to protest against the lack of both professional and public understanding of their lives. As the articulation of understanding becomes increasingly democratized, no one remains to claim authority.

THE BREAKDOWN OF RATIONAL ORDER

Rationality is one tradition among many rather than a standard to which traditions must conform. —Paul Feyerabend, *Science in a Free Society*

The president of Swarthmore College, David Fraser (left), after handing out degrees to the senior class. Once a solemn ritual, this moment has become an opportunity for the seniors to decorate the president—the preceding year with condoms, and this year with building supplies.

Some recently found objects:

- Small shops selling unrelated items, such as photography books, karate outfits, and fans.
- Books with randomly distributed quotes or boxed materials—often tangential to the flow of argument.
- T-shirts displaying strings of nonsense phrases on front and back.
- The two- or three-sentence items that now constitute "the news" in *USA Today* and on many radio stations.
- Performances of the popular comedian Steven Wright, typically composed of a continuous stream of unrelated ideas. A sampler:

    "I was arrested today for scalping low numbers at the deli. I sold a number three for twenty-eight bucks."

    "I was once walking in the forest and a tree fell right in front of me and I didn't hear it."

    "I used to be a narrator for bad mimes."

Yet another victim of postmodern consciousness is the faculty of reason, a major player in the modernist vocabulary of the mind. Problems with the concept of reason began to appear in the discussion of multiphrenia in chapter 3. There we found that if one has multiple goals, and many ways to evalute them, the very concept of rational decision making is threatened. If everything is reasonable, then nothing is reasonable. In chapter 4, important questions were raised concerning the relationship of language to thought. The traditional assumption of language as an outer expression of an inward rationality was found wanting, and was replaced with a view of language as a possession of interpretive communities. Again, the concept of individual rationality is questioned. For if language is not an expression of reason, why do we believe that reason lies *there*, just below the surface of our actions, directing them in this way and that?

A third assault on rational process results from the arguments in this chapter. If any act, situation, or object is subject to multiple descriptions or perspectives, any given perspective can only be validated by reverting to still other perspectives. Not only does this undermine a rational foundation for any single position, but it suggests that the term *rationality* is a rhetorical device for the valorization of one's favored position. A statement or a behavior is "rational" if it is favored by "our kind." Such terms as *unreasonable* and *irrational* thus become means of social control and possible oppression. As Bruno Latour phrases it, "an irrational belief or irrational behavior is always the result of an *accusation*. Instead of rushing to find bizarre explanations for still more bizarre beliefs, we [should] simply ask who are the accusers, what are their proofs, who are their witnesses, how is the jury chosen [and] what sort of evidence is legitimate."[32] Rationality reduces to suspicious rhetoric.

In the academic world, the breakdown of rational standards has led to an anything-goes attitude. One of the most vocal advocates of this position, the Berkeley philosopher Paul Feyerabend, argues that if the sciences relied upon classic standards of rationality to carry out their work, little that we call progress would result.[33] The traditional demand that scientific thinking be "consistent with the state of existing knowledge" simply eulogizes the status quo, discouraging innovation. The view that scientific theories should be derived from observation also fails, because the way we understand our observations already presumes a range of theoretical commitments. Thus, to base theories on observation would simply be to favor our unspoken prejudices. By contrast, an anything-goes mentality—continuously challenging the rationally acceptable—favors flourishing sciences. For Feyerabend the implications of this view are hardly limited to the sciences. Because the dogma of science—favored by modernism—has become so powerful in society, all competing voices have been muted, causing society to become stagnant and stultifying.[34] Now, with reason in decline, an anything-goes mentality reverberates throughout the culture.

Take emerging trends in literature. In the literary realm, the novel has traditionally proceeded according to cultural roles of good storytelling—stories have recognizable plots, they proceed from a beginning to an end, there is typically a central protagonist, and the story has a point. Lacking these characteristics, the novel seems strangely if not frustratingly irrational. Yet it is precisely these features that are vanishing from the contemporary novel.

The demise of rational sense in the novel has important roots in modernism. If a literary work is a thing-in-itself, as modernist critics advocated, then a given work need only be true to itself. Works should be evaluated on the basis of their internal logic or rules. James Joyce's *Ulysses* served as perhaps the most dramatic invitation to experiment with traditional narrative logic. But Joyce broke the rules to express "a deeper meaning"—insights of profound implication. Postmodernism begins when "deep meaning" and "the author's intention" recede, and readers are invited to engage in the free play of the very forms that once held the sense of the real and the rational in place. The French author Alain Robbe-Grillet represents an important transition between the modern and postmodern. In his film *Last Year at Marienbad,* for example, there is virtually no plotline; events do not move through time in an orderly sequence. Rather, the viewer is presented with images of the preceding year, which might have been prior, but might also be visions of time future, or the present. One image is tumbled upon the other, and the viewer is lost in a vertigo of timelessness. For, as Robbe-Grillet writes, all we have is our consciousness of time present. Thus, our sense of past and future must necessarily be constructions of present consciousness.[35] Both are producible, controllable fictions of the moment—any moment. To believe that time proceeds in a smooth, linear sequence is to believe in a fictitious form, not in our actual experience.

Although Robbe-Grillet is not well known outside literary circles, the Czech author Milan Kundera's works have brought postmodern elements to a broad readership. In *The Unbearable Lightness of Being*, the narrator begins as if relating a story of his acquaintances; yet he knows things about the characters (the nuances of their private experiences) that are beyond the access of an outsider.[36] At times the story seems to be about Tomas, but at others the central character seems to be his girlfriend, Tereza; their stories are occasionally replaced by accounts of Franz, and then of his mistress Sabina. Few of these accounts proceed in linear time; rather, the clock is abandoned as childhood events are interspersed with adult actions and lives are lived after the reader learns of their termination. And from time to time, the writer inserts a bit of his own life and philosophy into the text. One moves through the novel as in a dream. The postmodern novel is "the art of shifting perspectives."[37]

A similar shift to incoherence can be located in the visual arts. Again, modernism prepared the way. As artists began to explore or proclaim a multitude of essences, standards of rational procedure began to evaporate. In the artist Suzi Gablik's words, "So many metamorphoses and revolutions of every kind, so many differing values presented simultaneously, have finally done away with the frame of things—destroyed the conviction that there are any limits to art at all. Having thus removed any standards against which we might any more measure ourselves, we no longer know what rules we might follow, much less why we might follow them."[38]

This modernist breakdown in rational coherence has opened the way to distinctly postmodern art. Two movements are particularly noteworthy. First is the advent of pastiche. Although the modernist quest for essence meant breaking the traditional rules about what constitutes a proper piece of art, most modernist works were coherent or singularly focused within themselves. In contrast, with postmodern pluralism, the emphasis shifts toward pastichelike multiplicity within a work. Rather than painting in an abstract, hard-edge, or expressionist mode, for example, postmodernism invites a stylistic free-for-all. The painter may include any or all modes. Robert Rauschenberg might include in a single work not only images from the old-master painters Velázquez and Rubens, but also a truck, a helicopter, a Coca-Cola bottle, or an eyeball. And many of these images are photographic reproductions: The Velázquez image is in fact Velázquez, photographed and partially reproduced as an original Rauschenberg. Here Rauschenberg, similar to literary theorists writing on "authorless texts" (chapter 4), poses a significant challenge to the traditional conception of authorship. Was Velázquez's work itself truly original? Yes, his hands held the brush, but the work is a product of a tradition with many participants. They, too, joined in the making of his work— just as Velázquez participates now in Rauschenberg's. Rauschenberg thus recedes from view as the individual "creator" of his work.[39]

The second shift toward incoherence can be viewed not in single works but in the field as a whole. When modernism invited a broad "madness" in the constitution of the art object, it was generally a chaos in search of the coherent. Each artist sought purity—either in representation or expression. In abandoning the modernist search for essences, postmodern artists are freed in a different way. Like postmodern architects, they are invited to draw from all traditions, to speak in any voice that appeals. As Charles Jencks sees it, this has inspired artists to return, for example, to

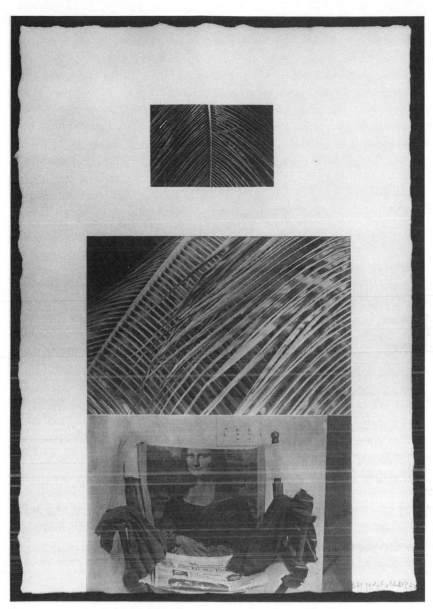

In Robert Rauschenberg's etching *The Razorback Bunch*, the *Mona Lisa* takes its place among the ordinary images of daily life, its reputed originality subverted by the process of infinite duplication and revision.

national or regional styles of painting, to recapitulate the mock-heroic style of the eighteenth-century allegory painting, and to experiment with photorealism.[40] Still others can more freely use the medium as an expressive device, giving voice, for example, to women's experience (as in Judy Chicago's *The Dinner Party*, a tribute to the great women of the world), ecological concerns (as in Jenny Holzer's neon advisories or Hundertwasser's designs for grass-roofed houses), or agonies over human brutality (as in Kiefer's visual critiques of German imperialism).

Finally, we must consider the infusion of the inchoate into popular culture. In particular, reconsider the logical story or narrative in the context of television. Early indications of the breakdown of linear plot were contained in the offbeat '60s drama *The Prisoner*, which for an avid cult audience engendered the same dreamlike state of compelling incoherence achieved by Kundera's novels. More significant because of their enormous appeal, however, are today's *multidramas*. Traditional television fare features a single storyline, often centering on a single hero or heroine and moving ineluctably toward a single, commodious ending. In contrast, the newly emerging multidrama launches an array of stories, partial stories, and tangential scenes, interspersed and interwoven, which simultaneously wend their way toward occasional conclusions. Perhaps the most tightly knit of the multidramas is *Hill Street Blues*. Within less than an hour, the viewer may be challenged with scenes from a half-dozen stories of crime, friendship, love, competition, and race relations. Although typically related by virtue of common protagonists, the scenes are heaped one upon another, and many of the stories are left uncompleted by traditional standards.[41]

The deterioration of the traditional narrative is carried a step further by the soap opera. In shows such as *Days of Our Lives*, *General Hospital*, and *Dallas* (a prime-time soap), stories of love, infidelity, murder, avarice, drug addiction, and the like are all interwoven, with characters often playing different parts (such as hero and villain) in different stories. The drama existing in any given scene often depends on the viewer's awareness of simultaneous stories in which the protagonists are enmeshed.[42] Although there is a sensed ending of what might be called "chapters," there is no grand narrative to be completed. Life simply goes on, with minor dramas sometimes postponed, sometimes abandoned, and new possibilities for "storiedness" emerging with each new scene.

While lacking the dramatic intensity of this compounding of plots, music television—MTV—has carried the postmodern breakdown of narrative rationality to its furthest extreme. MTV in the United States is a twenty-four-hour, nonstop cable-television channel that (aside from commercials) primarily features rock music videos. The channel was launched in 1981, and within three years it had acquired an audience of over 22 million viewers, largely between the ages of twelve and thirty-four. As E. Ann Kaplan proposes in her *Rocking Around the Clock*, music television is a quintessentially postmodern medium.[43] It relies heavily on the breakdown of objective reality: The shape or identity of an object or person may change several times within a given video clip, and what appears to be the reality of a photographed world may be revealed to be a drawing (an artistic reality), which then proves to be an artifact of a machine operation (computer graphics). Rock videos also revel in their challenge to authority—often celebrating life within youth culture or various minority or oppressed groups, attacking the economic class system, or revealing the foibles of parents and policymakers.[44] But most pertinently, rock videos represent a full breakdown in the sense of a rationally coherent world. Few of the videos offer a linear narrative; most will jolt the viewer with a rapid succession of images—often less than two seconds long— that have little obvious relation to each other. As Kaplan puts it, "MTV refuses any clear recognition of previously sacred aesthetic boundaries; images from German Expressionism, French Surrealism, and Dadaism . . . are mixed together with those pillaged from the noir, gangster, and horror films in such a way as to obliterate differences."[45] To enter the world of MTV is to abandon the concept of a coherent world.

With the demise of rational coherence, a longstanding demarcation of self-identity also recedes from view. For it is the sense of continuity— that I know I am I by virtue of my sense of continuous sameness—that for centuries has served as the chief criterion by which a self is to be identified. As David Hume, even in his skepticism, wrote, "Our notions of personal identity proceed entirely from the smooth and uninterrupted progress of the thought along a train of connected ideas." Thomas Reid saw the matter as virtually beyond the scope of philosophical analysis: "The conviction which every man has of his Identity, as far back as his memory reaches, needs no aid of philosophy to strengthen it; and no philosophy can weaken it, without first producing some degree of insanity." And so it is, even into the recent writings of Erik Erikson, for whom ego identity "connotes both a persistent sameness within oneself (selfsameness) and a persistent sharing of some kind of essential character with others." Yet, if coherence is simply "one kind of rationality" among many, and possibly oppressive in its social consequences, then from whence derives its honor? If linear sequence is the hobgoblin of the modernist mind, why should selfsameness be desired? For increasing numbers the attitude of anything-goes applies to the construction of selves. For the postmodern, life is rendered more fully expressive and enriched by suspending the demands for personal coherence, self-recognition, or determinant placement, and simply *being* within the on-going process of relating. We will return to these themes in later chapters.

SELF-REFLECTION AND THE INTRUSION OF IRONY

We must live an uneasy cerebral relation to the bric-a-brac of life—the
mundane forms and rituals whose function it is to make us feel at home,
to reassure us, to fill up the gap between desire and fulfillment.
 —Dick Hebdige, *Subculture: The Meaning of Style*

One final dimension of the cultural drift toward postmodernism demands attention, one that is critical to the waning of the self. As Hilary Lawson puts it, "The postmodern predicament is indeed one of crisis, a crisis of our truths, our values, our most cherished beliefs. A crisis that owes to reflexivity its origin, its necessity, and its force."[46] By reflexivity Lawson implies a sense of self-reflection or self-awareness. Why should self-reflection be thrust into such a central role in the postmodern era? At least one important answer follows directly from earlier proceedings. First we found the concept of objective truth to be wanting. How could one hold to a belief in a single, objective account, it was asked, in the face of a multiplicity of viewpoints? Claims to truth and right, it was later found, are more reasonably viewed as the constructions of communities with particular interests, values, and ways of life. As a result, the crucial questions shift from the world as it is to the world as represented. How do words and images gain their power to convince? Why are some ways of putting a case so much more compelling than others?

Indeed, with this shift from objects to objectifications, from reality to constructions of reality, we cross the threshold into a virtual vertigo of self-reflexive doubt. For the focus on how things get constructed is, after all, born of doubt—doubt of all authority and all claims to truth. Yet, once this doubt is unleashed, one confronts the awful irony that all one's doubts are also subject to doubt. After all, these doubts are themselves constructions of the world from a certain vantage point. All the attacks on modernist foundations, cunning and bold, sophisticated and searing, are constructed from language. Are not these offerings themselves born of particular interests and constrained by conventions of rhetoric? What saves them from their own criticism? And if this is so, these arguments can scarcely be true or accurate. Further, what of the doubt now voiced in these very self-reflexive criticisms—is this too not born of perspective, momentarily privileged, and subject in turn to deconstruction? Each new growth in doubt turns to bite its own tail.[47]

Postmodern reflexivity has been amply articulated within the intellectual world. Consider Roland Barthes's agony over his feelings of jealousy: "When jealous, I suffer four times over: because I'm jealous, because I reproach myself for being jealous, because I'm afraid my jealousy doesn't affect the person I'm jealous of, and because I'm being carried away by cliché."[48] Images of reflexivity echo across the cultural scape. Consider recent instances in theater. In the traditional play, the audience is invited into a single reality, and the success of the experience largely depends on the temporary suspension of disbelief. However, postmodern consciousness begins when the borders between the "dramatic" and "real" world grow thin, and the constructed character of both are revealed. Thus, for example, Alan Ayckborn's *The Norman Conquests* repeats the same time segment in three separate acts—with each act revealing events taking place offstage in the preceding acts. Each act thus demonstrates the limits of "suspended belief" in the reality of the preceding, and at the same time calls attention to the position of the writer in creating the realities. In Tom Stoppard's *The Real Thing*, the audience is drawn into the initial scene, where a wife's infidelity is slowly and painfully revealed, only to find in the second scene that the first was a scene from a play. This suggests that the second scene is the "really real"—while all the

while, of course, itself a scene from a play. Later in the play the actors of the first scene confront "real" infidelity in their lives, the contours of which make their way into yet another "staged" scene. At this point, however, the audience can scarcely be certain where the dividing line between stage and life is to be located, while simultaneously sensing Stoppard's hand in the laminating of realities.

Television has also become increasingly self-reflective over the decades. Consider an early Monty Python classic in which John Cleese and his companions find themselves lost in a jungle, without food and threatened by dangerous savages. At the height of desperation Cleese turns full face to the camera and announces to the viewers that this is, after all, a film story. And if it is, there must be a camera crew present that can show them the way to safety. The "local reality" of the film world is thus broken, and the camera crew appears on screen. Alas, the ensuing discussion reveals that they, too, are lost. And then, in a move of ultimate irony— crystallizing our utter incarceration in constructed worlds—the Python film crew concludes that they, too, are subjects in a film. There must be, then, a second film crew who is depicting their discussion. The second-order crew is then revealed, with the audience now standing at the edge of an infinite egress.

Self-reflection has since become commonplace. For example, in some interview shows (such as *David Letterman*) the cameras, crew, sets, and so on—all the devices used to create the reality of the event—are exposed to the audience. One sees both a "reality" and the devices of its creation. Single characters are also used to accomplish these ends. In the celebrated television series *Moonlighting*, which received sixteen Emmy nominations in one year, the male protagonist, played by Bruce Willis, periodically turns to the viewing audience and punctuates the unfolding story with winks or comments. The reality in which the audience has been immersed is thus deflated, while they are simultaneously invited into yet another—that of a private relationship with Bruce.

Perhaps the master of media self-reflexivity is Woody Allen. Such films as *Take the Money and Run*, *Manhattan*, and *Hannah and Her Sisters* are suffused by his often ironic and self-deflating reflections on himself. However, the art of reflexivity is extended to its extreme in *The Purple Rose of Cairo*. The film depicts a lonely female cinema viewer, played by Mia Farrow, who is shocked to find that her celluloid hero can actually step from the screen into the audience. Film reality and actuality blend. Her amorous relationship, filled with adventure, longing, and ultimate pathos, absorbs the audience for the remainder of the film. Yet the sensitive audience member is thereby thrust into the endless labyrinth of self-reflection. For, after all, isn't the viewer now in the same position as

Mia Farrow—living in one reality but deeply absorbed by "someone" from another reality? After the film, one almost expects to look back and find Mia Farrow among the viewers. And if so, would it *truly* be her? (And what would "truly" mean in this case?)

The reverberations hardly end here. A recent art exhibition in Berlin was devoted to the subject of making art exhibitions—a topic seeking its own origins, which then becomes a topic whose origins stand to be revealed. Escher graphics have returned to popularity, with their stairways into the beyond, violating the senses by returning to their origins. Even advertising has "gone reflexive." For example, a film advertisement shown before the main feature in an Australian movie house boasts the merits of a ski resort. Happy skiers, lessons, exciting runs, dining, and dancing are all featured. The final scene shows a group of chic young men and women gathered around an open fire, drinking, laughing, and smoking. The enthusiastic narrator presses on: "And what kind of cigarettes do they smoke?" His response suddenly thrusts the audience into self-consciousness of the "cardboard reality" of advertising, only to be beckoned on in spite of it: "I don't care what kind of cigarettes the wankers [often translated as 'masturbators'] smoke; just come and ski at the . . ."

Once we are aware of the ironies of self-reflection, how are we to regard them? What response can we make? Those working within the postmodern idiom have a common rejoinder—essentially an invitation to play. For once it is realized that all attempts to "tell the truth," to be wise, insightful, intelligent, or profound, are constructions of language—borrowed, ambiguous, and beaten about by ideological factions—then it becomes very difficult to make a deeply serious investment in such tellings. And when the critical analysis of such problems proves subject to the same shortcomings, even the colors of serious criticism grow pale. This is not to say that we can step outside language; to do so would be to step outside culture and thus ourselves. Instead, the favored option for many is to indulge in the communal constructions, but with humor, irony, and humility. We shall return to this option at the close of chapter 7.

Most important here, however, is the effect of reflexivity on the traditional commitment to individual selves. If one lives within the confines of a single reality—coherent through time and space—the objectivity of self seems unassailable. Yet when lived reality is continuously punctuated by consciousness of its limitations and artifice, commitment becomes arduous. When one's being as a professional, a spouse, or an American, for example, is constantly being doubted—its constructed and contingent character made evident through other standpoints—then daily existence as an objectively given self is threatened. It is difficult for most people to maintain a sense of sincerity when made conscious of others' doubts; the self-consciousness engendered by such doubts continuously intrudes and disrupts the sense of spontaneous or sincere being. With the proliferation of postmodern reflexivity, this undermining of being becomes a self-sustaining way of life. For the acutely sensitive, it is only a small jump to an awareness of the constructed contingency of the doubt, as it too is placed into yet another perspective. As one moves from one perspective to another, the objectivity of self recedes from view. And in the end one is left with perspectivity—itself a product not of the individual but of the surrounding communities in which one is embedded.

Thus we find that the postmodern turn within the academic sphere resonates throughout the culture. Belief in clear and separable things-in-themselves deteriorates across a broad spectrum. As the distinction between fact and fiction, culture and kitsch, a genre and its opposites disappears from art, architecture, and music, so do the boundaries of the self become blurred. If "what there is" depends on how it is conceptualized, then consciousness of construction is also sharpened. And as political events, news-reporting, and other realities are found increasingly to reflect the passions and prejudices of their makers, the replacement of real by constructed selves becomes increasingly plausible. If words cease to carry truth, then authorities also lose their command. All attempts to declare the nature of selves—their intentions, aspirations, and capabilities—become suspect. No transcendent voice remains to fix the reality of selves. As rational coherence is increasingly questioned, so does the traditional view of identity as fixed by cross-time continuity lose its appeal. When anything goes, so does personality as a discriminant category. In the end consciousness of construction turns reflexive. The very consciousness of self-construction must inevitably be viewed as a construction, and this sense as well . . . with no ultimate grounding in the one indivisible self.

SIX

From Self to Relationship

A report from a friend:

> On Saturday I went shopping with my teenage daughter. I needed a dress
> for a party the next week. I saw a very attractive dress, black, a daring cut,
> and with silver sequins. I was very excited until I tried it on. Dejectedly I
> had to tell my daughter that I just couldn't take it. It just wasn't me. My
> daughter responded with gentle mockery, "But Mom, that isn't the point.
> With that dress you would really *be* somebody."

A slight difference in opinion, yes, but a reflection of profoundly different
worlds. The mother is a modernist; the daughter is entering the world
of postmodernism. In the postmodern world there is no individual essence
to which one remains true or committed. One's identity is continuously
emergent, re-formed, and redirected as one moves through the sea of
ever-changing relationships. In the case of "Who am I?" it is a teeming
world of provisional possibilities.

In earlier chapters we explored the process of social saturation and the
emergence of postmodern consciousness in both intellectual life and the
cultural life more generally. Increasingly the individual has been deprived

of traditional markers of identity: rationality, intentionality, self-knowledge, and sustained coherence. Further, authority has increasingly been stripped from the voices traditionally informing the culture on matters of individual personality. Objectivity about such matters was replaced by a perspectivism; the concept of "individual persons" could not be a simple reflection of what there is, but a communal creation—derived from discourse, objectified within relationships, and serving to rationalize certain institutions while prohibiting others. Within this simmering stew, one begins to savor a newly emerging taste. As the ingredients coalesce, and the self vanishes with the rising vapors, one now detects a new reality— the reality of relationship. To appreciate the possibility, two preliminary steps are useful: first to bid final adieu to the concrete entity of self, and then to trace the reconstruction of self as relationship.

THE HUMAN BEING IN QUESTION

The indeterminateness of the individual self has been expanded to a world-wide condition.   —Kurt W. Back, *Thriller: The Self in Modern Society*

Under modernism, the individual seemed an isolated, machinelike entity—reliable, predictable, and authentic, propelled by a core mechanism embedded not too deeply within the interior. But today's increasing cacophony of competing voices creates a pervasive challenge to the assumption of "things (including people) in themselves." If each voice portrays the individual a little differently, then the very idea of an "isolated self," independent of the voices themselves, begins to teeter. Is the person "merely a biological creature," "a bundle of atoms," "an array of learned habits," "a computational automaton," "a pattern of personality traits," "a rational agent"? As the chorus of competitive voices builds, "the person" as a reality beyond voice is lost. There is no voice now trusted to rescue the "real person" from the sea of portrayals.

In the preceding chapter we found that the multiplication of perspectives led to a blurring of boundaries. If categories cease to be sacred, all that once seemed securely identifiable begins spilling across the borders, merging, melding, and mixing. The same may be said of our emerging conception of individual selves. Consider only a few threats to the integrity of persons from recent pages of cultural history:

• Widely popular among young television viewers, Max Headroom appears to be an electronically devised automaton. But his mechanical movements and glitch-filled voice are combined with an altogether human intelligence and personality.

- The box office hit *Who Framed Roger Rabbit?* found audiences readily accepting relationships of love and death between human beings and cartoon figures. A major challenge to the definition of "human being" was posed by the figure of Jessica Rabbit, a "toon" whose shapely figure and seductive manner generated far more sexual energy than did any of the "human" characters. The possibility that cartoon figures could replace the human as targets of desire hardly escaped the editors of *Playboy* magazine, who promptly featured Jessica as a cover girl— replacing her face with a human photograph.
- The replacement of human lovers with sexual facsimiles is now a major industry across Western culture. Men may acquire inflatable women dolls, plastic female faces with open lips, and Styrofoam vaginas complete with pubic hair.
- In the hands of the celebrated British artist Francis Bacon, figures appearing distinctly human are distorted or absorbed into the background. The human and the inhuman become one.
- Major cult figures among the youth include Tim Curry, star of *The Rocky Horror Picture Show*; Divine, a major protagonist of *Pink Flamingos* and *Hairspray*; and (for the very young) Michael Jackson. Handsome Curry wins major acclaim for his bisexual antics in drag. Film audiences are delighted to know that raucous and rotund Divine is— at least by conventional standards—a man. Through surgery, makeup, and other forms of artifice, Michael Jackson's appearance has increasingly approximated that of his sister.
- Female bodybuilders increasingly develop muscles that render them virtually indistinguishable from the traditional Charles Atlas model. At the same time, steroid use among male athletes now generates what amount to "superhuman" body forms.

These various occurrences all suggest a new cultural attitude toward the concept of the individual self. In each case the definitional boundaries are challenged—with curiosity, delight, and even zeal. Such cases are all drawn from the world of leisure. In other domains, however, the questions become more serious. Thousands of persons opt each year for artificial and biological *substitutions of self*. Replacements for limbs, noses, breasts, hair, teeth, and genitals may all be furnished to those with the need or desire. Chemical compounds may be substituted for hormones, and the heart may be sustained by machine. That which cannot be substituted by artifice can often be donated directly. Kidney and cornea transplants are common; heart transplants continue to improve, and the possibilities

What is it to be a human being? When one's erotic interests are aroused by the body of Toontown's Jessica Rabbit attached to the head of a *Playboy* model, are these interests still human?

seem unlimited. But as we witness the incremental potential for self-substitution, profound conceptual questions become salient. For example, does the permanently comatose patient whose life is maintained solely by machine retain his or her rights as a full person? What parts or how much of an individual's body can be replaced or remodeled before he or she ceases to be the same person?

The current debate over abortion may be viewed as an extension of the same issues of self-definition. Legally a fetus was not considered a viable "human being" until three months after conception. Technological developments make it possible to challenge this definition. Using *in utero* photography, ultrasound techniques, and electrical stimulation, pro-life groups attempt to demonstrate that the fetus both looks human and experiences pain far earlier. The individual *is* there after all, they reason, and abortion before the three-month period is thus tantamount to murder. But of course, whether the fetus "looks" and "feels" in the same way a *real* person does is not a matter of evidence but of definition.[1] The data in this case are merely rhetorical devices, and whether they are effective or not depends on the strength of the conventional definitions. With further bending, one may argue that indeed one becomes a person at the moment of conception. Or, because animals have "feelings," they too partake in humanness and thus deserve rights accordingly. These latter sentiments are hardly unfamiliar to the antivivisectionists and vegetarians of the culture.[a]

The erosion of self-definition is particularly vivid in the case of gender.

Gender Gerrymandering

One can never unveil the essence *of masculinity or femininity. Instead, all one exposes are . . . representations.*
— Linda Kauffman, *Discourses of Desire: Gender, Genre, and Epistolary Fictions*

A once obdurate and unquestionable fact of biological life—that there are two sexes, male and female—now moves slowly toward mythology. Thirty years ago the term "real man" was seldom heard. The reality was virtually unquestioned, and therefore undiscussed. For many, John Wayne, Gary Cooper, and Humphrey Bogart served as cultural exemplars. If modernism had masculine heroes of any kind, their portrayals were close to the mark: realistic, incorruptible, taciturn, yet capable of sentiment when the business at hand had been successfully completed. Such figures only infrequently roam the world of today's fantasy. Even John Wayne's performances took on the character of parody in his later years. The figure of Rock Hudson represented an early turning point. "Rock"—the name teemed with grit and power; and yet both personally and in performance one confronted a soft and gentle amiability. The male stars of the '60s, '70s, and '80s—Marlon Brando, Paul Newman, Robert Redford, Dustin Hoffman—could surely play the parts of "real men." However, because they played so many other parts—at times indeed effeminate—the audience was always aware of the unreality of the "real." With the appearance of such books as *Real Men Don't Eat Quiche*, one becomes cognizant of a passing image. Such sly warnings are only interesting when the species is endangered—when those who know they *should* be real men are in fact wearing aprons, sipping Perrier, and avoiding high-cholesterol foods.[3]

Early intimations of gender breakdown occurred when the Johns Hopkins psychobiologist John Money began publishing his work on transsexualism.[4] His studies, describing men who felt their bodies were not truly their own, that they had unfairly been given the wrong genital formations, informed the culture that biological features are questionable criteria for judging gender. As this minority voice reverberated through the mass media, one learned that a woman can be locked inside a man's body (or vice versa). The book should not be judged by the cover. Coupled with the growing consciousness of transsexualism has been an even more profound opening of the homosexual closet. Although the reasons are unclear, the increase in publicly declared homosexuality over the past twenty years has been a remarkable phenomenon. (How many residents of major cities do not suspect that, indeed, their city is "the gay capital"?) The homosexual challenges a second critical criterion for determining gender: sexual preference. Precisely who one is, the culture is informed, cannot be determined by the object of one's attraction.

But if biological differences and sexual preferences do not signify gender, how are we to distinguish? How can objective judgments be made in this matter? It was just such questions that inspired Suzanne Kessler and Wendy McKenna's volume *Gender*.[5] These investigators surveyed the criteria used in various cultural enclaves for making gender distinctions. They found that children do not use the same criteria as adults, transsexuals do not agree with heterosexuals, some cultures recognize more than two genders, and the Western medical profession uses criteria shared by virtually no one else—namely chromosomes. In the latter case, peculiar dislocations of conventional reality occur. For example, a Russian female athlete, actively heterosexual, is shocked to learn from medical officials at the Olympic trials that she cannot compete as a female. Medically, she is male.

At this point the postmodern plight begins in earnest. If there are multiple voices, each proclaiming a different reality, whose reality is to be privileged? On what grounds? And as one approaches the state of indeterminacy brought about by these plural realities, one confronts the possibility that the distinction is not essential at all. If the words *masculinity* and *femininity* do not mirror an "independent and palpable reality," the distinction is unnecessary. For many feminist thinkers such a conclusion is inviting. As they see it, gender differences are not inherent in nature. Gender is a category born of culture, and used for a wide variety of questionable purposes. In particular, there are political and ideological biases inherent in the current practices of gender assignment. Simple biological differences have come to signify a natural basis for an enormous range of behavioral and societal practices. Because persons with certain physical characteristics happen to occupy most positions of power in society, it is presumed that these traits and these positions should be related. Because those who bear children normally happen to raise them, it is presumed that child rearing is natural or instinctive for those who give birth. Such suppositions are analogous to proposing that persons with dark skins are biologically disposed to slum dwelling, or those with slanted eyes to running Chinese laundries. Many argue that, because the presumption of biologically based gender differences reinforces the existing structure of power, it is inimical to the interests of women and should be abandoned or reconstructed.

Gender is but one of the traditional categories of self-identification that now deteriorates. Categories of race, age, religion, and nationality are similarly suspect. As the boundaries of definition give way, so does the assumption of self-identity.

CONSTRUCTED SELVES

Anger is generated and reduced by how we interpret the world and the events that happen to us.
    —Carol Tavris, *Anger: The Misunderstood Emotion*

Although it grows increasingly difficult to be certain of who or what one is, social life proceeds. And in one's interactions one continues to identify oneself as this or that sort of person. One may identify oneself as American in one situation, Irish in another, and a mixture of nationalities in still others. One may be feminine for certain friends, masculine for others, and androgynous for still others. As these public characterizations of self are found effective in meeting the challenges of a complex social world, a new consciousness begins to develop. This is the consciousness of construction, which was so central to the discussion of the preceding chapters. For what is true of a culture's history (chapter 4) and of the national reality (chapter 5) is no less true of persons. That is, attempts to define or describe oneself inevitably proceed from a perspective, and different perspectives have different implications for how a person is treated. One may indeed feel that it is legitimate, from a certain perspective, to define oneself as American, Irish, or mixed in nationality—that from a certain vantage point one is masculine, feminine, or androgynous. Thus, interest in "true identities" and "actual characteristics" of persons can be replaced by concern with the perspectives in which they are constructed.

It is in this context that many scholars have become deeply interested in people's commonsense beliefs about themselves and others, and the impact of these beliefs on their actions. They ask, for example: How do people commonly conceptualize the nature of love, of intelligence, and of aging?[6] And how do these beliefs inform our patterns of romance, school testing programs, and the risks we are willing to take as we grow older? How do people conceptualize the nature of child development, the stability of personality, or the causes of homosexuality, and do these assumptions not influence the way we raise children, our attempts at self-change, and our relations with the "gay" and "straight" worlds? In all such cases the attention turns from the nature of *real* love, intelligence, aging, child development, and so on to how it is *constructed* or represented in the culture. For good or ill, it is the individual as socially constructed that finally informs people's patterns of action. And in the end, there is no means of moving past the constructions to locate the real.

As belief in essential selves erodes, awareness expands of the ways in which personal identity can be created and re-created in relationships. This consciousness of construction does not strike as a thunderbolt; rather, it eats slowly and irregularly away at the edge of consciousness. And as it increasingly colors our understanding of self and relationships, the character of this consciousness undergoes a qualitative change. In the pages that follow I wish to trace the character of this transformation, for in my view, there are subtle differences in the character of this consciousness as one moves from life in the modern to life in the postmodern world. It is especially important to follow this path, as one may discern in the trajectory a newly emerging sense of self. Where both the romantic and the modernist conceptions of identifiable selves begin to fray, the result may be something more than a void, an absence of self. Instead, if this tracing of the trajectory is plausible, we may be entering a new era of self-conception. In this era the self is redefined as no longer an essence in itself, but relational. In the postmodern world, selves may become the manifestations of relationship, thus placing relationships in the central position occupied by the individual self for the last several hundred years of Western history.

To be sure the changes I wish to discuss are unsystematic, occurring at irregular intervals and in different sectors of one's life. For analytical purposes, however, I shall separate the consciousness of self-construction into three major phases, each denoting a stage of development from the modern to the postmodern. One's commitment to the modernist self first weakens in a stage of *strategic manipulation.* The individual increasingly and distressingly finds himself or herself playing roles to achieve social gains. As modernist beliefs in the essential self are undermined through this process, a second stage of *pastiche personality* may be distinguished. Here the individual experiences a form of liberation from essence, and learns to derive joy from the many forms of self-expression now permitted. As the self as a serious reality is laid to rest and the self is constructed and reconstructed in multiple contexts, one enters finally the stage of the *relational self.* One's sense of individual autonomy gives way to a reality of immersed interdependence, in which it is relationship that constructs the self. Let us consider the three phases in more detail.

The Strategic Manipulator

Prepare a face to meet the faces that you meet
                —T. S. Eliot, *The Love Song of J. Alfred Prufrock*

Personality is an unbroken string of successful gestures.
                —F. Scott Fitzgerald, *The Great Gatsby*

In the traditional community, where relationships were reliable, continuous, and face-to-face, a firm sense of self was favored. One's sense of identity was broadly and continuously supported. Further, there was strong agreement on patterns of "right" and "wrong" behavior. One could simply and unself-consciously *be,* for there was little question of being otherwise. With social saturation, the traditional pattern is disrupted. One is increasingly thrust into new and different relationships—as the network of associates expands in the workplace, the neighborhood is suffused with new and different voices, one visits and receives visitors from abroad, organizations spread across geographical locales, and so on. The result is that one cannot depend on a solid confirmation of identity, nor on comfortable patterns of authentic action. One confronts scores of new and different demands. How is one to act polite, rational, firm, humorous, or affectionate, for example, with people from other countries, ethnic and age groups, economic backgrounds, religions, and so on? As one shuffles and searches for appropriate forms of action, identity is more likely to be questioned than confirmed. One confronts subtle hints of doubt: "Who are you? What do you hide? Give me proof." The result of this wrenching from the familiar is an enhanced sense of "playing a role," managing impressions, or acting a part to achieve goals.

Thus, as the modernist confronts the challenge of social saturation, he or she is continuously ripped from the security of an essential or unified self. As the sociologist Arlie Hochschild observes, "To manage private loves and hates is to participate in an intricate emotional system. When elements of that system are taken into the marketplace . . . they become stretched into standardized social forms. In these forms, a person's contribution of feelings . . . is seen as coming less *from* the self and less directed *to* the other. For this reason [one's feelings are] susceptible to estrangement."[7] In effect, as the modernist is pulled in myriad directions, one may feel a sickening sense that one's true emotions are being lost in the charade.

As explored in the earlier discussion of multiphrenia (chapter 3), social saturation also multiplies the standards available for self-comparison. As one interacts with persons from diverse backgrounds, and is exposed to various media representations of "good persons," the range of self-evaluative criteria expands manifold. It is not simply the local community that dictates the nature of the good, but virtually any visible community. In the traditional community a man might live in tranquility simply by being sincere, amiable, reliable, and reasonably effective at work—a "good guy," a mensch. In contrast, the middle-class male in a socially saturated context can scarcely claim self-respect unless he can demonstrate proficiency or participation in:

a profession	fitness training (jogging, tennis)
a love life	mechanics (car repair)
a circle of friendship	money management (investments)
being a good son	sports knowledge
being a responsible father	cultural events (art, music)
a personal hobby	food and wine sophistication
political savvy	outdoor cooking
functionless leisure (TV)	travel

With each expansion in the criteria of the good, the individual is again forced out of the comfortable patterns and univocal affirmation. Increasingly one senses the superficiality of one's actions, the strategic marketing of personality.

This sense of self as strategic manipulator has been articulated by numerous social sciences over the past decades. For many the works of the sociologist Erving Goffman most poignantly capture the nagging sense of guilt pervading the daily life of modernist beings struggling toward efficacy in a socially complex world. In such works as *The Presentation of Self in Everyday Life, Strategic Interaction,* and *Stigma,* Goffman placed in painful focus the minutiae of daily life—arriving at a neighbor's door, waiting on a table, holding hands, placing objects in a room—to demonstrate their darkly manipulative underpinnings.[8] No actions remain sincere, simple explosions of spontaneous impulse; all are instrumental. A quote Goffman cites from the delicately eviscerating work of William Sansom's *Contest of Ladies* bears retelling. The Englishman Preedy, vacationing in Spain, makes his first entrance on the beach of the summer hotel:

> But in any case he took care to avoid catching anyone's eye. First of all, he had to make it clear to those potential companions of his holiday that they were of no concern to him whatsoever. He stared through them, round them, over them—eyes lost in space. The beach might have been empty. If by chance a ball was thrown his way, he looked surprised; then let a smile of amusement lighten his face (Kindly Preedy), looked round dazed to see that there *were* people on the beach, tossed it back with a smile to himself and not a smile *at* the people, and then resumed carelessly his nonchalant survey of space.
>
> But it was time to institute a parade, the parade of the Ideal Preedy. By devious handling he gave any who wanted to look a chance to see the title of his book—a Spanish translation of Homer, classic thus, but not daring, cosmopolitan too—and then gathered together his beach-wrap and bag into a neat sand-resistant pile (Methodical and Sensible Preedy), rose slowly to stretch and ease his huge frame (Big-Cat Preedy), and tossed aside his sanduls (Carefree Preedy, after all).[9]

Each movement of the body, seemingly private and spontaneous, is orchestrated for social effect. In the modernist attempt at machinelike efficacy, claims to sincerity evaporate.

While they voice common experiences within the culture, such accounts of human action err in an important respect: they presume that experiences within a transient period of history are universal. They attempt to define the human being as a dramaturgic agent—one who by very nature is an actor upon life's stage. From the present standpoint, however, the sense of self as strategic manipulator is dependent on a specific cultural context. The sense of "playing a role" depends for its palpability on the contrasting sense of "a real self." If there is no consciousness of what it is to be "true to self," there is no meaning to "playing a role." The sense of self as strategic manipulator derives, then, from the modernist context, in which real, authentic selves existed—or should exist—and to act in any other way was a form of forgery or deceit. The sense of strategic manipulation also requires a range of invitations to act in other than the traditionally acceptable ways, invitations that are sufficiently enticing or commanding that one willingly though shamefully forsakes the path of authenticity. This invitation is furnished by the technology of social saturation.

The Pastiche Personality

We are eager to relinquish ourselves because it is a difficult and painful matter to become a self, and because we long for the rewards that our culture is only too ready to give us in exchange for that self.
—René J. Muller, *The Marginal Self*

The nausea of dissimulation is the burden of the modernist in an increasingly saturated society. As one casts out to sea in the contemporary world, modernist moorings are slowly left behind. It becomes increasingly difficult to recall precisely to what core essence one must remain true. The ideal of authenticity frays about the edges; the meaning of sincerity slowly lapses into indeterminacy. And with this sea change, the guilt of self-violation also recedes. As the guilt and sense of superficiality recede from view, one is simultaneously readied for the emergence of a pastiche personality. The pastiche personality is a social chameleon, constantly borrowing bits and pieces of identity from whatever sources are available and constructing them as useful or desirable in a given situation. If one's identity is properly managed, the rewards can be substantial—the devotion of one's intimates, happy children, professional success, the achievement of community goals, personal popularity, and so on. All are possible if one avoids looking back to locate a true and enduring self, and simply acts to full potential in the moment at hand. Simultaneously, the somber hues of multiphrenia—the sense of superficiality, the guilt at not measuring up to multiple criteria—give way to an optimistic sense of enormous possibility. The world of friendship and social efficacy is constantly expanding, and the geographical world is simultaneously contracting. Life becomes a candy store for one's developing appetites.

The invitations to open-ended and guilt-free construction of the self are many and varied in contemporary culture. Consider our changing attitudes toward the presidency. Voters in the modernist era hoped to select "a real man," a president who was realistic and rational, as powerful and reliable as a smoothly running turbo-jet. One's choice thus depended on a thorough assessment of "the real thing." Gradually, however, society became aware of strategic manipulation in the construction of the man. As Joe McGinniss's *The Selling of the President 1968* made clear, the days of "getting to know you" were rapidly vanishing.[10] Presidential candidates were "made" and "sold" like commercial goods; a contender's true character, ability, or political views were secondary to creating a winning image. From a modernist standpoint, such processes were detestable; presidential races were beginning to approximate a competition among unscrupulous advertisers. As we move into the postmodern era, however, interest in "true character" and disgust with "false advertising" diminish. The candidate's "true character" seems elusive, unknowable, even irrelevant. For success as a president can be a matter of style—saying the right thing with the right manners at the right time. If we learn that "seeming" rather than "being" enables one to attain the presidency, then marketing one's personality becomes the most reasonable orientation to daily life.

Research psychologists also lend a resonant voice to this image of the pastiche personality. Particularly interesting is the research of Mark Snyder and his colleagues at the University of Minnesota.[11] They compare the behavior and life-styles of persons termed high in *self-monitoring*— masters at self-presentation, sensitive to their public image and to situational cues of appropriateness, who are able to control or modify their appearance—with a contrasting group who are much less concerned or capable in these respects. The differences between the high and low self-monitoring individuals recall David Riesman's celebrated distinction between inner-directed (or self-determining) and other-directed (or socially malleable) personality types.[12] However, where Riesman took a modernist perspective—favoring the inner-directed over the other-directed—in Snyder's more contemporary account, the values are reversed. Thus, the research is used to demonstrate that those high in self-monitoring are— relative to those who are low—more positive in their attitudes toward others, less shy, less upset by inconsistencies, superior in remembering information about others, more emotionally expressive, and more influential. Snyder does not condemn self-monitoring strategy for its incoherence, superficiality, and deceit, but finds rather that it "gives the individual the flexibility to cope quickly and effectively with the shifting

Self-mutability gains expression in the works of Cindy Sherman. In this sample of "self-portraits," Sherman identifies herself not only as a photographer but also as the subjects of her photographs—in this case as both a bag lady and a housemaid.

situational demands of a diversity of social roles."[13] In the postmodern
world, research demonstrates merit in multiplicity.

The sociologist Louis Zurcher expresses much the same attitude toward multiplicity in his concept of the *mutable self*.[14] As he sees it, acceleration in the rate of cultural change demands a new orientation toward self, one that removes the traditional goal of "stability of self (self as object)" and replaces it with "change of self (self as process)." For Zurcher the mutable self possesses an "openness to the widest possible experience" and is characterized by tolerance, openness, and flexibility. Yet Zurcher falls short of full praise for the mutable self, for he and his colleagues find that this condition also gives rise to a form of narcissism.[15] Daily life becomes suffused with the search for self-gratification. Others merely become the implements by which these impulses are served.[16]

Nowhere is the sense of exhilaration and potential in multiplicity more evident, however, than in the world of fashion. During the modernist period concern for fashionable clothing was limited primarily to an affluent minority. Women might take an interest in the height of the hemline or the seams of their stockings, but economy, durability, and normalcy were the most important criteria for selecting clothing. Most shopping was done in department stores, which determined the minimal "fashion line" for large sectors of the culture, but supplied a large number of formless but popular housedresses. To be *styled* was for many to "look cheap" or to "put on airs." Men were even less style-conscious; sensitivity to style was tantamount to replacing the real self with an imposter. As a result, men had their wives shop for them, and they took great pride in making a suit last many seasons. Such attitudes toward clothing styles were compatible with the modernist conception of self as a fundamental, enduring entity. If the self is simply "there," known and trustworthy, then clothing is not considered a means of self-expression; it is merely practical.

As postmodern consciousness expands, these views of fashion recede. For the pastiche personality, there is no self outside of that which can be constructed within a social context. Clothing thus becomes a central means of creating the self. With proper clothing, one becomes the part. And if the clothing is orchestrated properly, it may also influence the very definition of the situation itself.[17] In this context, the replacement of department-store–reliable clothing by the remarkable array of apparel served up by "unique" boutiques becomes intelligible. Each international (meaning both exotic and universally acceptable) label promises a new and different statement of the self. And because making the same clothing statement season after season would be a mere repetition of the same old stories, the fashions must change. Many women rail against the prices paid for garments that must be abandoned scarcely before they deserve cleaning. Yet if women did not insist on new vocabularies of clothing—

in the same way they require fresh insights, new experiences, and informed opinions to properly construct themselves in ongoing relationships—Gucci, Pierre Cardin, Christian Dior, and the like would soon be facing lean years. It is not the world of fashion that drives the customer into a costly parade of continuous renewal, but the postmodern customer who seeks means of "being" in an ever-shifting multiplicity of social contexts.

Western culture has long tended to define the male as more unitary and solid in character than the female. Thus for the male the *fashioning up* of the culture is more radically dislocating. Men find the guaranteed-for-a-lifetime identity now challenged by Calvin Klein underwear, Gucci briefcases, Aegner belts, raincoats for spies, casual shoes for yachtsmen, bathrobes for playboys, and shirts for safaris. Aftershave lotion, a faintly scented skin medicinal in the modernist era, is now replaced by heavily scented men's cologne—with functions that are clearly interpersonal. (Elvis Presley *perfume* for men now presses the definition of *male* still further.) Even the domain of athletics, the last preserve of the "real man," is now invaded by designer warmup gear, shoes, sweatbands, and athletic supporters.

As social relationships become opportunities for enactment, the boundary between the real and the presented self—between substance and style—is erased. What seems to be true and substantial from one standpoint seems merely stylistic from another. The Russian premier's political statements seem true and authentic reflections of the man, but news commentators assure us that they are mere expediencies of the moment. One's tears seem to be authentic signals of deep grief until a sociologist demonstrates them to be constituents of a customary ritual, appropriate and desirable on certain occasions. One's anger seems real enough, until a mate points out that it is merely a routine means of getting one's way. When style and substance become matters of perspective, they cease to be actual ingredients of actions themselves. They are merely ways of looking at behavior. In the end, as the concept of the substantial self recedes, and increasing emphasis is placed on good form, there is no distinction to be made between the two. If all is style, the concept fails to signify difference; it is simply synonymous with what there is. At this point such terms as *style*, *superficiality*, and *self-presentation* may be abandoned, for they cease to be informative.[18]

The Arabian poet Sami Ma'ari nicely summarizes the spirit of the pastiche personality: "Identities are highly complex, tension filled, contradictory, and inconsistent entities. Only the one who claims to have a simple, definite, and clear-cut identity has an identity problem."[19]

The Emergence of the Relational Self

[We must] replace the starting-point in a supposed "thing" . . . located within individuals, with one located . . . within the general communicative commotion of everyday life.   —John Shotter, *Texts of Identity*

As the modernist is drawn into the socially saturated world, the dominant sense is that of being a strategic manipulator: committed to a sense of substantial self but continuously and distressingly drawn into contradiction. As the moorings of the substantial self are slowly left behind and one begins to experience the raptures of pastiche personality, the dominant indulgence becomes the persona—the image as presented. Yet as all becomes image, so by degrees does the distinction between the real and the simulated lose its force. At this point the concept of the true and independent self—whether constituted by a deep interior or a machine-like rationality—loses its descriptive and explanatory import.[20] One is thus prepared to enter a third and final stage, in which self is replaced by the reality of relatedness—or the transformation of "you" and "I" to "us."

To appreciate the force of this transformation, a certain recounting is useful. Both the romantic and modernist traditions place a central emphasis on the individual as autonomous agent. Individuals are the fundamental units of society; relationships are secondary or artificial, a by-product of interacting individuals. This sense of the self as autonomous individual is largely responsible for the severe stresses of multiphrenia. Traditionally, it is the "I" who must perform, who must present myself, who will achieve or fail, who will be enriched, who must be responsible, and who in every other way stands at the vortex of an enveloping sociality. Yet the postmodern turn—both within the academy and without—poses a profound challenge to the concept of the autonomous self. Concepts of the individual—as the center of knowledge ("one who knows"); as possessor of rationality; as author of his or her own words; as one who creates, decides, manipulates, or intends—are all placed in question.

At the same time, an alternative to this view emerges quietly at the edges of argumentation. As self-constructions cease to have an object (a real self) to which they refer, and one comes to see these constructions as means of getting on in the social world, one's hold on them is slowly relinquished. They slowly cease to be one's private possessions. The invitation for one construction as opposed to another is, after all, issued from the social surrounds; and the fate of this construction is also determined by other persons. One's own role thus becomes that of participant in a social process that eclipses one's personal being. One's potentials are only realized because there are others to support and sustain them; one has an identity only because it is permitted by the social rituals of which one is part; one is allowed to be a certain kind of person because this sort of person is essential to the broader games of society.

The case is clarified by focusing on the language of self-construction—the words and phrases one uses to characterize the self. As outlined in the preceding chapters, it is impossible to sustain the traditional view of language as an outer expression of an inner reality. If language truly served as the public expression of one's private world, there would be no means by which we could understand each other. Rather, language is inherently a form of relatedness. Sense is derived only from coordinated effort among persons. One's words remain nonsense (mere sounds or markings) until supplemented by another's assent (or appropriate action). And this assent, too, remains dumb until another (or others) lend it a sense of meaning. Any action, from the utterance of a single syllable to the movement of an index finger, becomes language when others grant it significance in a pattern of interchange; and even the most elegant prose can be reduced to nonsense if others do not grant it the right of meaning. In this way, meaning is born of interdependence. And because there is no self outside a system of meaning, it may be said that relations precede and are more fundamental than self. Without relationship there is no language with which to conceptualize the emotions, thoughts, or intentions of the self.

As the emphasis shifts from self to relationship, multiphrenia loses much of its lacerating potential. If it is not individual "I"s who create relationships, but relationships that create the sense of "I," then "I" cease to be the center of success or failure, the one who is evaluated well or poorly, and so on. Rather, "I" am just an I by virtue of playing a particular part in a relationship. Achievements and failures, expansions of potential, responsibilities, and so on are simply attributes assigned to any being who occupies a particular place in certain forms of relationship. If one does not participate fully and effectively, it makes little difference, since there is no fundamental "I" on whose character this reflects. And one's place in the games of life may always be filled by other players. Or, in Jean Baudrillard's terms, "Our private sphere has ceased to be a stage where the drama of the subject at odds with his objects and with his image is played out; we no longer exist as playwrights or actors but as terminals of multiple networks."[21]

It would be foolish to propose that a consciousness of relational selves is widely shared in Western culture. However, in many ways one senses its presence in everyday affairs. It is there in subtle ways—in the slight sense of dejection when one dresses for dinner out and finds the restaurant empty of imagined audience; the realization that an invitation to a party means that your active participation is required in order for there to be a party at all; the frustration at not being able to relate life's happenings because the lack of audience threatens erasure of the events themselves; or the sadness at another's death upon realizing that some part of the self has thereby passed away. It is also there in the realization that one cannot be "attractive" without others who are attracted, a "leader" without others willing to follow, or a "loving person" without others to affirm with appreciation.

This quiet consciousness is more fully accentuated on the public level. We find, for example:

- An emerging redefinition of the presidency—from the nation's "center of power" to the status of "figurehead." This shift is accompanied by an increasing focus on the presidential staff. In modernist times the White House staff were shadowy figures, scarcely known to the public. The president governed, and the staff simply played a supporting role. Increasingly, however, the presidential staff becomes a focus of media attention.
- In the business world the idea of "the self-made man," the firm and undaunted executive who valiantly forges ahead, is disappearing from the vocabulary. Rather, such terms as "organizational cultures" and "interpersonal systems" enter increasingly into the vernacular.[22] These coinages call attention to the web of interdependencies that make up an organization. Organizations exist as systems of meanings that establish what is real and good. Without negotiated agreements about the means and goals of organizational life, the system would lapse into dysfunction.
- Therapy for troubled persons has traditionally centered on the psyche of the single individual. However, increasing numbers of therapists, counselors, and social workers are abandoning the individual-centered approach. An individual's problems, it is proposed, are only the by-products of troubled relations with others—within the family, the workplace, the school. It is not the individuals who are "sick," but the social networks of which they are a part. Thus, rather than exploring the individual's unconscious (a holdover from the romantic period) or "modifying" his or her behavior (as in the modernist heyday), increasing numbers of therapists help individuals, families, and even communities to explore their forms of relationship and the effects of these relationships on the participants.[23]
- Popular dramas of both the romantic and modern periods centered on the individual—the hero, the leader, the lover, the tragic figure. Judging by common television fare, such dramas are being replaced by

themes of complementarity, cooperation, and collusion among persons. Prime-time television over the past few decades has featured a parade of collective dramas: *All in the Family, The Avengers, Dallas, Eight Is*

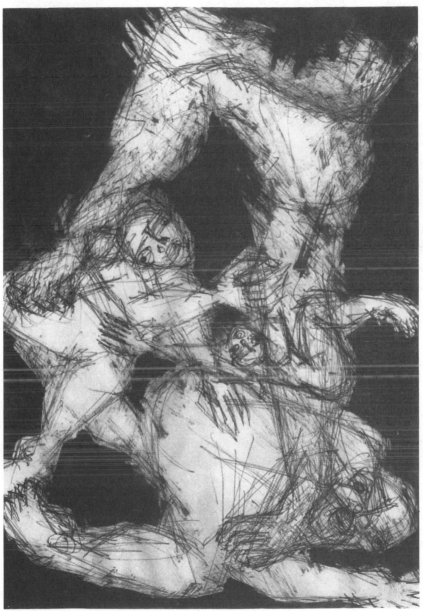

Eschewing the traditional focus on single, isolated individuals, the Zurich artist Regine Walter explores the possibilities of persons inseparable from relational forms.

FROM SELF TO RELATIONSHIP

Enough, Eastenders, Family Ties, Ponderosa, Precinct, Star Trek, Taxi,
and *The Waltons* are illustrative. We also find a substantial number of
films in which there is no single protagonist pursuing, risking, overcoming, and achieving. The emphasis turns to webs of interdependency,
whether in the so-called buddy films (*48 Hrs., Midnight Run*), female
equivalents (*Big Business, Beaches*), male teams (*Three Men and a Baby,
Seven Alone*), female enclaves (*Steel Magnolias, Crimes of the Heart*),
or complex relations within a group (*Hannah and Her Sisters, Sex, Lies,
and Videotape, Do the Right Thing*).

Still, the development of relatedness as a fundamental reality will proceed but slowly, for as we have seen, the Western vocabulary of understanding persons is robustly individualistic. The culture has long been
committed to the idea of the single, conscious self as the critical unit of
society. Descartes' dictum "I think, therefore I am" is emblematic. Decisions should issue from private thought, not authorities or other persons.
Private consciousness marks both the beginning and ending of our lives.
Thus we stand at the present historical juncture with a massive array of
terms to depict the individual. It is the individual who has hopes, fears,
wishes, thoughts, desires, inspirations, and the like. These are the terms
by which we understand daily life, and which are embedded within our
patterns of interchange. We ask about Bob's "feelings" toward Sarah, and
what Sarah "thinks" about Bob, and believe that a relationship is built
(or not) on these grounds. In contrast, we have an impoverished language
of relatedness. We cannot ask whether a *relationship* hopes, fears, or
wishes, nor can we understand how it is that a relationship could determine Bob's feelings and Sarah's thoughts rather than vice versa. It is as
if we have thousands of terms to describe the individual pieces in a game
of chess, and virtually none by which we can articulate the game itself.

LANGUAGES OF RELATIONSHIP

Relationships cannot become the reality by which life is lived until there
is a vocabulary through which they are realized. This vocabulary is slowly
beginning to emerge, and with it a sensibility that should render relationships as palpable and objective as the individual selves of previous
eras.[24] Because of the significance of this development to the future com-
plexion of social life, the remainder of this chapter is devoted to exploring
several domains in which the reality of the individual is giving way to
relational reality. Of focal interest are personal history, the emotions, and
morality.[25]

The Social Ownership of Personal History

We assume that life produces the autobiography as an act produces its consequences, but can we not suggest, with equal justice, that the auto-biography project may itself produce and determine life?
—Paul de Man, *Autobiography as Defacement*

Consider first your life story—the sort of account you might give if musing over how you got to be where you are, or if trying to make your past known to another. Traditionally we think of such a story as uniquely one's own, a private possession from which one draws sustenance and direction. In the romantic period persons often viewed their lives as driven by a mission, possibly directed by inner forces or personal muses deep within. One could speak unflinchingly of personal destiny. In the modern period, such discourse was replaced by a factorylike view of personal history. One had a production history that could be charted—as on a résumé—in terms of visible accomplishments (attained education, positions held, honors received, papers published). In both cases one could speak of possessing a life story, an accurate account of one's unique trajectory through life.

Yet such views of life history are ill suited to the postmodern temper. Recall Hayden White's critique of historical writing in chapter 4, in which he proposed that a culture develops modes of narration, and this array of rhetorical conventions largely determines how the past is understood. The past does not drive or determine the historical narrative; rather, the cultural practices of writing determine how we comprehend the past. This same line of thinking applies to autobiography.[26] Consider a five-year-old, asked by her parents about her day in kindergarten. She describes her pencil, then a friend's hair, then the school flag, and finally the clouds. Chances are this account would seem unsatisfactory to her parents. Why? Because the events are not related to each other; there is no direction or "point" to the account, no drama, no proper sense of beginning and ending. Yet none of these characteristics—relationship among events, direction, drama, and temporal containment—exist within the events of life. They are, rather, features of good stories in our culture, and without them one's tale is either boring or unintelligible. Chances are by the time she is six the child will have learned to describe her days *properly*, and by the time she is twenty-six, her sense of life history will acquire the same narrative character.

The genres of story offered by a culture at any given time are also likely to be limited. In Western culture most of our stories are built around events that go in either a positively or negatively valued direction.[27] In

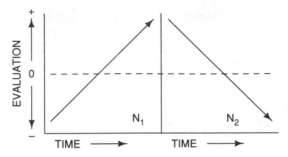

Fig. 1. Success and Failure Narratives.

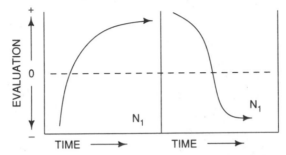

Fig. 2. Happily-Ever-After and Tragic Narratives.

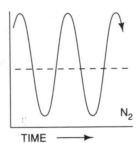

Fig. 3. Epic Hero Narrative.

the typical "success story," life events become continuously better, and in the "failure story," they go downhill (figure 1). Most other stories represent variations on these two rudimentary forms. In the "happily-ever-after" account, a success story (how I "won my man," "earned my rank," etc.) begins to level off; in a "tragedy," someone highly valued plummets very rapidly into failure (figure 2). Some individuals adopt the "epic hero" narrative, in which one strives toward success, only to be turned back, and then to battle again to the top, and so on in a series of heroic recoveries (figure 3). These are the common forms in which we see our lives. By contrast, you might tell someone that every third day of your life was hell, while the two intervening days were paradise, but no listener is likely to believe it. We are generally prepared to accept as "true" only those life stories that conform to existing conventions.

Yet one's personal history is not a cultural possession only in the sense of story forms. Indeed, the very content of such stories also depends on social relationships. Consider first the process of memory. As research on eyewitness testimony demonstrates, reports of the past are not like photographs, fixed and final. Rather, they are continuously in motion, altered with new information and experience.[28] When we make memories intelligible, either to ourselves or others, we must do so in the available language of the culture. This language essentially sets the limits over what we can legitimately count as a memory. In a given circumstance, we can say, "I remember seeing a man in a black coat," but not, "I remember black-gray-moving-large-to-small." This collage of words may actually express one's conjured image, but it does not count as a properly reported memory. What counts as an intelligible memory will depend on the culture in which the report is made. It is in this context that scholars have coined the term *communal memory* to refer to the process of social negotiation that occurs among persons in deciding "what happened."[29] Thus family members may discuss at length what counts as an accurate memory of family history; vacationing friends will energetically negotiate over the "right way" to report their adventures. Memory, then, becomes a social possession.

In his challenging volume, *Narrative Truth and Historical Truth*, Donald Spence has carried the implications of these arguments into the arena of psychiatric practice.[30] Spence was particularly curious about patients' attempts to explore their early life histories. In psychiatric circles, the key to successful treatment is thought to lie in the ability of the patient to recall early relationships with parents and siblings, and especially traumatic events long forgotten; such insights into childhood history presumably release the repressed forces causing our adult problems. Yet, asked Spence, how likely is the patient to locate historical truth—what really happened? Childhood events are murky, memories change as relationships with parents and siblings are altered over the lifespan, and what is "found" often depends on what one is seeking. Thus,

the analyst's construction of a childhood event can lead the patient to remember it differently, if he remembered it at all; and if he had no access to the event, to form a new memory for the first time. Within his private domain, the newly remembered event acts and feels like any other memory; thus it becomes true.

In effect, the patient develops with the psychiatrist a form of narrative or constructed truth as opposed to a historically accurate truth, and it is the narrative truth that largely determines the outcome of treatment. In the therapeutic setting and beyond, we find *auto*biography is anything but *auto*nomous; it is more properly *socio*biography.

The Emotions Among Us

The pursuit of love in the assumption that it is a pleasure that can be defined exclusively within ourselves is a major perversion of modern every-day activity. —Willart Gaylin, *Passionate Attachments*

Who can deny that our emotions are personal possessions, belonging to the private world of experience and not directly open to anyone? Surely the past centuries furnish ample support for such a belief. In the romantic period the emotions possessed an awesome quality. Their power could propel one toward a life commitment or to suicide. For the modernist, emotions were a nuisance—forces that interfered with reason and objectivity. They were not to be denied—built in, as they are, to the biological system—but the major hope was that scientific understanding would be able to properly channel or control them so that the society could march forward in an orderly manner. Thus, such well-known volumes as Lorenz's *On Aggression* and *Frustration and Aggression* by John Dollard and his Yale colleagues attempted to demonstrate scientifically how hostile passions could be systematically brought under social control.

With postmodernism one becomes suspicious of the view that emotions are essences of personal being, tucked within the biological system and awaiting explosive expression. Traditionally it is said that we experience our emotions—love, anger, fear, and so on. But what, after all, is the object of our experience, the "it" by which we are impressed? Is it our blood pressure, our heart rate, our flaming cheeks that we experience? If so, we are again placed in doubt, for scientists do not consider changes in blood pressure, pulse, and the like to be *the* emotions themselves. Rather, these are only signals or indicators of emotion. Where then is the "it" for which these are signals? Is the object of our experience, then, our behavior—our tears and slumped shoulders in the case of sadness, and our angry voice and clenched fist in the case of anger? This too seems doubtful, for these actions are not the "emotions in themselves," but mere expressions of the emotions. However, if we subtract all the indicators, expressions, and signals, what is left over to constitute the "real emotion"? Where is the "it" to be located?

The question aroused scientific interest in the early 1960s, with the publication of Stanley Schachter's research on emotional labeling.[31] After reviewing the full range of scientific studies on emotion, Schachter concluded that there was very little physiological difference among the emotions. There were not separate and distinct biological bases for love, fear, anger, and the like. Rather, the most that could be said was that a person in any state of high emotion demonstrates "generalized physiological arousal." People who are angry will experience the same increase in blood pressure, heart rate, and the like as those who are afraid or ecstatic. Thus, Schachter proposed that differences among the emotions stem from the labels we happen to assign to the state of arousal. If scolding an errant teenage son, a man might assign the culturally approved label of anger to his emotions; if running from a bear, the proper label for his emotion would be "fear." And, if he is locked in an intimate embrace, the very same physiological state would be experienced as "love."

While few scientists are content with Schachter's evidence for the theory, many have come to share his doubts that the emotions are simply "there in our nature," propelling us along willy-nilly. Some of the strongest evidence against emotions as natural essences of the individual has been furnished by anthropologists. Recall the various cases in chapter 1 in which the emotions experienced in one culture do not seem to be duplicated in others. Or consider the Ifaluk of Micronesia, a culture studied by the anthropologist Catherine Lutz.[32] For the Ifaluk, *fago* is a central emotion. It seems akin to love, as it is expressed toward those with whom one has close relationships. However, fago is not joyous and energizing; it carries a saddened hue, and indeed is often experienced when the other is absent or dead. Yet fago is not simply grief for a lost loved one, for it is also actively displayed in ongoing relations, particularly toward those who are weak. In this sense it seems more like compassion. In Western culture there is no precise equivalent for fago. Does this mean that our biology is differently structured? Not according to the University of Massachusetts psychologist James Averill. He concludes that what we call emotions are essentially *cultural performances*, learned and enacted on appropriate occasions.[33] We are not driven by forces bottled up within us; rather, we perform emotions much as we would act a part on stage. In "doing" an emotion we recruit biology in the same way an actor needs heightened blood pressure and pulse to enact properly the rage of King Lear. The biological system is required to carry out the emotion effectively, but the biology does not require the actions themselves.

Once ownership of the emotions is transferred from biology to culture, we are prepared to remove them from individual ownership as well. Consider again the emotional performance—doing anger, love, or sadness. The performance seems clearly enough an "in-itself," an expression of the autonomous being. But look again. One cannot simply perform an emotion in any circumstance. The pedestrian cannot simply stop in mid-stride to bellow "I am angry," nor can the dinner-party hostess suddenly writhe on the table in a state of passion. Emotional performances are limited to certain, socially sanctioned contexts. The pedestrian can (and is expected to) feel angry if a careless youth steps on his foot, but not on his shadow. The hostess may be moved to passion by a gallant staring steadfastly into her eyes, but would be scorned if she responded in the same way to his six-year-old son. Further, once the emotional performance has taken place, others are limited by cultural rules in the kinds of re-actions that are allowed. Thus, if a close friend says to you, "I am so depressed," you cannot respond (without endangering the friendship) with "Let me tell you about my great weekend" or "You deserve it." Western culture offers only a handful of sensible moves to be made under such circumstances, such as offering sympathy, suggesting solutions to the problem, or redefining the problem in a less serious way. Similarly, once performances of these kinds have been executed, the depressive is limited in the next action. If sympathy is offered to the depressive, he or she cannot speak of gardening or commence singing an anthem.

If we recognize that cultural rules govern when and where an emotional performance can occur, as well as others' reactions to these performances, the expresser's responses to these reactions, and so on, we can begin to see emotional performances as single movements within an elaborate dance or *emotional scenario*.[34] In the same way that Ivan Lendl's move-ments on the tennis court only make sense in terms of Boris Becker's actions on the opposite side of the net, so emotional performances gain their significance as components of ongoing relationships. To talk about "my depression," "John's anger," "Myra's joy," and the like is to misplace inside individual heads actions that form part of more extended scenarios. "My depression" is only mine in the sense that I am playing out this particular aspect of the emotional scenario in which we are both engaged. Without your complicity, often preceding, during, and following this performance, the act would be reduced to nonsense.

Morality Beyond the Individual

The self has to find its moral identity in and through its membership in communities such as those of the family, the neighborhood, the city, and the tribe. —Alasdair MacIntyre, *After Virtue*

Let us consider finally the case of morality—again a seemingly private and personal affair. The present century has inherited the Judeo-Christian view that morality is centered in the individual. More specifically, we commonly hold that an act derives its moral character from the intention of the actor. To harm another is not immoral if the harm is unintentional; to help another is not moral if accompanied by the intention to bring the other harm. We do not generally hold persons morally responsible for actions beyond their conscious control, either in daily life or in courts of law. Thus, morality is essentially a matter of one's intentions, and intentions exist somewhere in the individual's mind.

Neither romanticism nor modernism was particularly kind to this traditional conception of morality. For the romanticist, actions could be driven by powerful sources deep within the recesses of the mind, thrusting conscious intention aside. In this sense, Freudian theory is generally inimical to the traditional view of morality. Indeed, for Freud not only was religion a form of collective neurosis, but the superego (the seat of moral inclination) functioned primarily as an irrational defense against the unconscious and amoral forces of eros. Similarly, the concept of intention suffered with the modernist view of persons as machines. If one's actions are governed by causal inputs, as modernists held, then what part does voluntary intention play in a person's life? If acts of aggression and altruism, for example, are products of socialization and environmental stimulation, then there is no place for an "uncaused cause" like voluntary intention.

The deterioration of the intentions occurring in the romanticist and modernist periods is completed in the postmodern. Why, in the first instance, do we presume that because we use the word "intention," there is a state in people's minds to which it corresponds? As we found in chapter 1, such words as *intention* are not found in all cultures and in all historical periods. Nor can we look inward and identify through introspection when the state exists and when it doesn't. This view was reinforced in chapter 4, where we found that if intentions lay behind people's words, we could never grasp their meaning. To speak, then, was not to give an outward sign of an inward state, but to participate in a social relationship. Following the argument that language gets its meaning from the uses to which it is put within the relationships, one can conclude that the word is used in the practical activities of holding people responsible, seeking forgiveness, and so on.

If morality is removed from the heads of individuals, how can it be reconceptualized as a relational phenomenon? Consider a battle royal in recent psychology. One of the most innovative theories of moral behavior—bursting upon the field in the late 1960s—was that of Harvard's Lawrence Kohlberg. Kohlberg argued that there was a natural course of development in a person's capacities for moral decision making.[35] During the early years of life, before the child is capable of abstract reasoning, moral decisions are largely made on the basis of rewards and punishments meted out by parental authorities. As reasoning powers develop, the individual turns to social approval and rules of law as sources of moral decisions. The highest stage of moral development is achieved, proposed Kohlberg, when persons are able to develop their own universal philosophies of right and wrong. Kohlberg's theory views morality in its advanced form not only as an individual matter, but as a product of rational thought. In this sense the theory lends support to the traditional Western view of morality.

However, for Kohlberg's colleague Carol Gilligan, his theory also harbored another bias, an implicit sexism.[36] Not only did Kohlberg's studies generally fail to credit women with advanced, or principled, moral thinking, but they valorized the self-contained, autonomous individual—in effect, the typical masculine image of the hero. Thus Gilligan and her colleagues set out to explore the way in which women tend to solve moral dilemmas. How do they deal, for example, with the issue of abortion? Gilligan's team proposes that women typically reach solutions through relating to others—considering the feelings of their friends, families, and so on. Rather than searching for general moral principles, abstracted from daily relationships, they see themselves as existing in a web of relationships held together by bonds of caring. "In all of the women's descriptions," Gilligan concludes, "identity is combined in a context of relationship."[37]

There is a tendency among feminists to see this form of moral decision making as peculiarly feminine—an outgrowth of the way female, as opposed to male, children are traditionally raised in the family. For our purposes, however, the orientation of Gilligan and her colleagues can be extended to form the basis for a postmodern, relational view of morality, in which moral decisions are viewed not as products of individual minds, but the outcome of interchange among persons. This is obviously the case when moral decisions are reached through active dialogue and negotiation, but it is also true when moral decisions appear to emanate from a single person. An individual's "good moral reasons" necessarily derive from the culture's repository of sensible sayings. One would not normally say, for example, that theft is wrong because it pleases the devil—not because such reasoning is incorrect, but because it is not a sample of proper moral reasoning by contemporary Western standards. When individuals declare right and wrong in a given situation they are only acting as local representatives for larger relationships in which they are enmeshed. Their relationships speak through them.[38]

So far, a fully developed theory of relational morality has yet to appear.[39] The concept of lying might provide especially rich material for analysis. Lying is typically viewed as an individual decision; it is the individual who must examine his or her conscience, and who must be held responsible for prevarication. Can our present analysis be extended to remove the lie from its locus in the self, and replace it in relationships? The concept of the lie is intimately tied to a belief in truth. To lie is essentially to tell an untruth; and one who tells the truth cannot be lying. With postmodernism the distinction between truth and falsity lapses into indeterminacy. As we found in chapter 4, vast problems attend the view that words can accurately "picture" or "reflect" the world. What is the case ("the truth of the matter") primarily depends on what perspective you bring to bear. In daily life, for example, we call the rose before us "red." No one doubts this as an objective fact. Yet for psychophysiologists the rose is not red but "colorless." The experience of color, they argue, is the result of energy at specific wavelengths being reflected on the cornea. Is it a lie, then, to say the rose is not red? It depends on whether you are using the perspective shared by people in everyday life or participating in the culture of the laboratory. Neither perspective is true nor false except within a particular community of understanding.

In this context we are positioned to reconsider lying as a relational rather than an individual event.[40] Indeed, if all members of a culture were unanimous in their perspectives—or their understandings of the world—the problem of lying would never emerge. There would be no stealing in a culture where all agreed that "taking another's possessions" is "immoral" and thus taboo. When there is more than one perspective on the world, however, the stage is set for lying. What is called "stealing" and labeled as "immoral" by mainstream culture may be viewed as "just," "cool," "enterprising," "smart," or "life-sustaining" by other members of the same society, in which case a "thief" asked whether he "stole" confronts not a problem of individual conscience but of group allegiance. To answer from the perspective of mainstream culture—"Yes, I stole"—is to be forced into accepting a definition of the situation at variance with that of his subculture: friends at school, for example. It is to tell the truth in *their* system of understanding, but to deny the reality of his own. To say that he did *not* steal is a lie from the standpoint of mainstream culture, but within the shared understandings of his subculture is true. From their standpoint his actions were intelligent and perhaps heroic. The existence of lying in society is thus not an outcome of individual depravity, but of pluralistic social worlds.

With postmodern consciousness begins the erasure of the category of self. No longer can one securely determine what it is to be a specific kind of person—male or female—or even a person at all. As the category of the individual person fades from view, consciousness of construction becomes focal. We realize increasingly that who and what we are is not so much the result of our "personal essence" (real feelings, deep beliefs, and the like), but of how we are constructed in various social groups. The initial stages of this consciousness result in a sense of the self as a social con artist, manipulating images to achieve ends. As the category of "real self" continues to recede from view, however, one acquires a pastiche-like personality. Coherence and contradiction cease to matter as one takes pleasure in the expanded possibilities of being in a socially saturated world. Finally, as the distinction between the real and the contrived, style and substance, is eroded, the concept of the individual self ceases to be intelligible. At this point one is prepared for the new reality of relationship. Relationships make possible the concept of the self. Previous possessions of the individual self—autobiography, emotions, and morality—become possessions of relationships. We appear to stand alone, but we are manifestations of relatedness.

SEVEN

A Collage of Postmodern Life

Certainty is the exception in 20th century life, and adjusting to discontinuity is . . . the emerging problem of our era.
—Mary Catherine Bateson, *Composing a Life*

Encountered in recent months:

- A businessman on a plane from Detroit to New York tries to arrange a liaison with the woman in the next seat. In the airport he phones his wife in Florida. She is in shock because her sister in Des Moines has had an auto accident and may die. He is stunned as he passes through customs and immigration offices. On the overnight to London he seeks sympathy from a British dairyman in the next seat. His luncheon with colleagues the next day is mirthful and boisterous.
- Connie spent her childhood in New Jersey. After her parents were divorced, her mother moved with the children to San Diego. Connie's teen years were spent shuttling between father and mother on either coast. After she graduated from the University of Colorado, she moved to Alaska to work on a fishing boat, and then to Wyoming to become a ski instructor. Now Connie is working on a geological-survey vessel in the Antarctic, and is engaged to a man living in Portland, Oregon.
- Fred is a neurologist who spends many of his spare hours working to aid families from El Salvador. Although he is married to Tina, on Tuesday and Thursday nights he lives with an Asian friend with whom he has a child. On weekends he drives his BMW to Atlantic City for gambling.

- A philosophy professor from Ohio State spends his sabbatical in Norway. While skiing in Wengen, Switzerland, he shares a chairlift with a British contractor. The contractor's major firm is located in Miami, but their chief building sites are in Saudi Arabia. The seven minutes together are filled with lively camaraderie, and as they ski off with their companions they arrange to meet later for a drink.
- Louise is a lawyer from Boston. She has just married Tom, a Kansan, who now practices law in San Francisco. Tom's chief interest is in running a blues club with a black friend in Oakland. They invite to their wedding many of their former lovers—all of whom are women.

For those steeped in the romantic tradition, such scenes are disquieting. Where, the romanticist asks, are the profound passions that press the soul toward its singular and essential expressions? Where is the depth of character that demarcates the mature individual? Nor is the modernist comfortable with these conditions. Lost from view are the personality traits that endure across time and situation, the sense of personal stability and authenticity necessary for an effective and smoothly functioning life. In place of the enduring and identifiable self, we find fragmentation and incoherence, lives led without direction, movement from one locale and culture to another with little residual effect. Who are these individuals? How are they to be identified? It depends on where and when the assessment is made, for today is no necessary prelude to tomorrow, the present hour no companion to the next. As we move into the postmodern world, purpose is replaced with pastiche.

My aim in this chapter is to explore the relationship between the loss of self, as treated in the preceding chapters, and the emerging incoherence of cultural life. The erosion of the individual self and its gradual replacement with a relational consciousness imply far more than a shift in sensibility. The emerging consciousness of relational embeddedness creeps into our actions in numerous ways, informing us of the possible and the problematic. With shifts in our conceptions of who we are (and are not), certain patterns of cultural life lose their credibility and others gain admiration and adherence. To transform understandings of who we are is to alter the ways in which we live together. The emergent incoherence in life patterns thus clasps hands with the disappearance of the individual self.

Two major processes are at work in relating conceptions of the individual to ongoing patterns of conduct. In both cases this connection is fostered by the technologies of social saturation. The first has been described in preceding discussions: As we become ever more saturated with relationships, we become increasingly populated with *fragments of the other,* each of us harboring expanding congeries of potentials for relating and replacing the other. The cumulative result is that we are readied for participation in a world of incoherence, a world of anything-goes. We are prepared for variegated contexts and connections, and if they present themselves with the speed of flipping television channels, we may marvel at our adequacy of adaptation. Further, because each fragment we incorporate from others is also an acquisition of value (a small voice of "ought"), the "we" may indeed seek the inchoate; any stabilized pattern of being treads on the sensibilities of myriad ghosts within. Each cries out for an alternative, points to a missed potential, or mocks the chosen action for its triviality. Each mode of being thus becomes a small prison from which freedom of expression must be sought; yet each bursting of the bonds forms but one more containment. The postmodern being is a restless nomad.

Not only do the technologies of social saturation fashion "the individual without character," but at the same time, they furnish *invitations to incoherence.* In a humdrum moment, the Vancouver tax accountant can pick up the phone and rekindle a relationship in St. Louis; within less than an hour the restless engineer can drive to a singles bar thirty miles away; on a tedious Friday a New Jersey executive can decide to fly to Tortola for the weekend. Through these and other means, one confronts myriad avenues pointing the way out of the immediate context. Even if one fails to take these avenues, others may arrive on one's doorstep by these means. In the final analysis, we find technology and life-style operating in a state of symbiotic interdependence. The technology opens opportunities, and as these opportunities are realized, the person becomes increasingly dependent on the technology. The technologies engender a multiplicitous and polymorphic being who thrives on incoherence, and this being grows increasingly enraptured by the means by which this protean capacity is expressed. We enter the age of *techno-personal* systems.[1]

Any evaluation of the postmodern transformation from self to relatedness must necessarily take into account these alterations in social patterns. Of what variety and significance are they? Who is affected, and how much? I will not attempt to be inclusive, but rather will single out several regions of social life that seem both diagnostic of our present and portentous of our future. These snapshots will be as assorted as the conditions they are designed to express. At times the portrayals will move from gray to black—reflecting the antipathy for which my own roots in romantic and modernist culture prepare my sensibilities. I do not view these impoverished conditions as final so much as transitional, however, and thus alternative vistas will also be explored. As the chapter moves on, the ground will be prepared for a positive stance toward the emerging age, a stance that will be more fully explored in the final chapter of the volume.

BREAKING THE BINDS THAT TIE

Beverly's parents had stayed married like two dogs locked together in passion, except it wasn't passion. But she and Joe didn't have to do that. Times had changed. Joe could up and move to South Carolina. Beverly and Jolene could hop down to Memphis just for a fun weekend. Who knew what might happen or what anybody would decide to do on any weekend or at any stage of life? —Bobbie Ann Mason, *Love Life*

In traditional communities, with their relatively unchanging and interconnected cast of characters, coherence of personality was favored. Relationships tended to be reliable and repetitive, supporting consistency of action. In the romantic period, the belief in the deep interior contributed to the solidity of self and relationship. To believe in the communion of souls was to favor a lifetime of commitment. Modernist discourse on the self also supported a belief in identity and coherence. People were knowable, understandable, and predictable, and thus relationships among persons—in families, the workplace, friendships, and the like—were optimal when each participant functioned as a reliable cog in the machine. Stabilized identities contributed to a soundly structured society, and a structured society in turn supported a stabilized identity.

With the wheels of social saturation spinning at ever-increasing speeds, such patterns recede into history. Consider the attempt of a postmodern person to establish a relationship with others. At the outset, postmoderns are populated with a plethora of selves. In place of an enduring core of deep and indelible character, there is a chorus of invitations. Each invitation "to be" also casts doubt on the wisdom and authenticity of the others. Further, the postmodern person senses the constructed character of all attempts at being—on the part of both self and others. One may press toward the genuine and true; romanticism and modernism are hardly dead. But in the end, one realizes that the social images of self and other are portrayals without a portrayed, reflections without an object of reflection.

Even for those who are not fully populated or reflexively aware, the attempt at solidified relations or reliable rituals is beset with difficulty. One major problem is the insinuation of the technologies of saturation into the normal rituals of relationships. Consider deep friendship—the celebrated bond between two people, meant to endure through thick and thin. In the nineteenth century, devotion to a friend of the same sex might eclipse the bond of marriage. Although this intensity of friendship has waned in the present century, many strive to hold fast to the friendships of teen or college years. Many try to develop "best friends" within their communities, who can be fully trusted or relied upon in time of need. Yet it becomes difficult indeed to define a relationship as "closest" or "best" when for weeks, even months, the participants are both in motion. Both may long for lazy and undirected hours, when each nuance of experience is examined with careful attention, and chance comments open new vistas of fascination. But consider the difficulties of locating such hours, when you take your work home with you almost every night, you know you must have more exercise, you visit your parents on the weekend, a spouse and/or children are craving for more quality time, your wardrobe desperately needs to be brought up to date, your support group absorbs your Thursday evenings, and there are numerous books, games, concerts, and exhibits that are not to be missed. Under these conditions, meandering moments are seldom found, and because this is so, the very concept of "closest" or "best" friend undergoes a sea change. Rather than a communion of souls it becomes an occasional and compressed "catch-up." From a traditionalist viewpoint, we lose the capacity for "genuine friendship."

The Crisis in Intimacy and Commitment

Current runs through bodies
and then it doesn't.
On again.
Off again.
Always two things
switching.
One thing instantly replaces
another.

It (is) the language
of the Future.   —Laurie Anderson, *United States*

In the context of social saturation, one can see why both intimacy and commitment are slowly vanishing from relationships. This began when romanticist concepts of the person were eroded by modernism. In the romantic period one could build a life around "true love," or a "powerful passion." With the advent of modernism, however, expressions of mysterious depths began to appear dubious. The person as well-ordered machine harbored no secret sectors of the psyche where uncontrollable urges reigned. Nowadays, to tell a romantic partner, "It is for your soul I thirst," or "My passion is all-consuming," might send him or her into quick retreat. For the modernists, "love" became a measurable quantity. Rather than allowing it to remain deep, spontaneous, and mysterious, scientists redefined love variously as "a state of arousal labeled according to cultural rules," a form of "addiction," or a "culturally channeled sex drive."[2] Computer coupling services rapidly sprang up, offering to "assess your personality" and locate a scientifically appropriate love-mate. Love by thunderbolt was replaced by questionnaire compatibility.

And so it is that those seeking committed intimacy today enter such relationships with a vocabulary that is either suspicious (as in the case of romanticist discourse) or impoverished (in the case of modernist replacements). Committed intimacy of the for-better-or-for-worse-till-death-do-us-part variety has carried over from the romantic period, but if one has scant command of the expressions required for participation in such a relationship, and the terms that are available must be used with caution, the traditional pattern can scarcely be achieved. Rob the culture of its expression of personhood and its fabric of relationships begins to fray.[3]

Yet it is not simply that the old vocabulary of commitment has been eroded and discredited. Entering a relationship with a multiplicity of potentials, each a possible invalidation of the other, makes it enormously difficult to locate steady forms of relatedness. These difficulties are only intensified in the case of committed intimacy, for two important reasons. The first is related to the romanticist underpinnings of committed intimacy. From the romanticist perspective, people possess core identities locked away in the inner depths. Indeed, for the romanticist it is only when two people touch at this level that we speak of "deep relationships." True intimacy occurs when there is an "intertwining of souls," "a spiritual communion," or a mutual igniting of the passions. In the search for committed intimacy the postmodern individual confronts a startling and dismaying contrast between the search for an inner core of being and the scattered multiplicity of the populated self. Longing to locate the "inner depths" of the other, one finds only a shimmering array of evanescent surfaces. Where, in the shifting presentations of sensitivity and boldness, emotion and cool rationality, seriousness and frivolity, sophistication and cultivated mannerliness, impulsiveness and control, is one to locate a true and indelible spirit?

One becomes similarly suspicious of oneself. If one is in continuous motion, always shuffling the cards of identity, it seems doubtful that the other has really "found the core" of oneself. If one sees oneself as manipulative agent, or as simply expanding the richness of one's capacities, then one questions, "Can the other truly know me?" And if one plays but a limited set of cards—continuously attempting to create the image of a "true center," the inner voices stifled by the play soon begin to murmur their message of disingenuousness: "This is sham, a lure, mere bait for commitment."

A second barrier to committed intimacy stems from the central place of evaluative criteria in such relationships. If one is simply "playing around," it is not so important to make critical judgments of the other. So what if he or she is a little self-centered, crude, or overly ambitious? The relationship is only for fun, not for keeps. But when it is not "just for fun," when one thinks of long-term, in-depth commitment, then each of these shortcomings deserves attention. "How long can I live with these tendencies? Can I change those annoying habits? Won't I grow tired of this?" are all significant questions. One pays the price of self-population, for each new fragment of the self has the capacity to generate a self-debilitating array of judgmental criteria. With each attempt "to be," one finds another voice within that is scornful. This same multiplicity in evaluative criteria affects one's perception of others. "Can he or she resonate," one asks, "with my sensitivities . . . with my boldness . . . with my emotional capacities . . . with my calculating self . . . with my seriousness . . . with my frivolity . . ." and onward. Each aspect of self raises new hurdles of acceptability for the other. The likelihood of a fully successful leap, at least for anyone of human scale, is small. And the result is an inevitable leadenness of "just settling," compromising for the sake of a commitment in name alone.

Beset with doubts in self and other, one may find that attempts at commitment seem aggravating. In any commitment may lurk a multitude of small deaths. And it is at this point that the technologies of social saturation again begin to churn. In earlier times one's range of available mates was geographically circumscribed. Sociologists found a high probability that one would marry someone living nearby; "geographic propinquity" was the best predictor of marriage. Yet the technologies of social saturation dramatically alter the concept of "nearby." One's neighborhood spreads from uptown to downtown, from across town to the suburbs, from city to city, and at times across continents. Even with the smallest amount of mobility, one is forever on the verge of "new prospects." And each new face may underscore the inevitable shortcomings of one's current companion, haunting one with doubts and issuing subtle invitations to yet another Valhalla of committed intimacy.

Fractional Relationships: "Why Not Take One-Eighth of Me?"

Select single w/m, 38, 6′, 160 lbs, good-looking, hung, safe. Seek trim, fun-loving couple, 30–45, for hot times and friendship. Am warm, considerate, discreet. I travel all over the U.S. and Canada, and can also entertain in my N.Y. apt. —Personal, *Odyssey Magazine*

In the early 1970s Bernardo Bertolucci's *Last Tango in Paris* became one of the most widely discussed films of the decade. Its success resulted not only from Marlon Brando's consummate performance, and the torrid sexual interplay between the aging Brando and the younger Maria Schneider. The dramatic narrative was equally absorbing—a relationship between two total strangers, mismatched by virtually all traditional standards, intense beyond propriety, and yet wholly confined to their occasional meetings within the walls of a single apartment. The climax of the film occurred when the relationship broke the boundary of the plaster enclosure. With images of the tango hall still reverberating, Schneider repels Brando's amorous approach by shooting him to death. With the postmodern turn, the stuff of drama becomes the staff of life. Contained and partial relationships—vital within their circumscribed domains, and moribund beyond—became modal.

The postmodern sensibility questions the concept of a "true" or "basic" self, and the concomitant need for personal coherence or consistency. Why, the postmodern asks, must one be bound by any traditional marker of identity—profession, gender, ethnicity, nationality, and so on? Liberated from the traditional demands for coherence, the postmodern is undaunted by such charges as "spineless," "plastic," "wishy-washy," and the like. Indeed, to use any of these traditional epithets begins to smack of narrow parochialism.

Most important for the present analysis, the disappearance of "true self" encourages one to search for the kinds of persons or situations that will enable the various actors in one's ensemble to play their parts. One requires a supporting cast for the Hamlet, Hemingway, and Hank Williams within, or the emerging Juliet, Jackie O., or Jane Fonda. For the postmodern, social complicity and identity walk hand in hand; without others there is no self. In effect, with the disappearance of true self, the stage is set for the *fractional relationship*, a relationship built around a limited aspect of one's being.

The same technology that favors the populating of the self also facilitates the development of partial relationships. National magazines, television, mass mailings, and the like inform the individual about the telephone, postal, and electronic services whereby one may locate partners prepared to play their proper but partial roles. Auto, rail, and air services then bring the cast together for the play's limited engagement. Thousands converge on Marbella, Southern Pines, or Phoenix to meet their golf mates; on cruise ships to the Caribbean to find passing intimates; on the Club Meds of the world to revel with strangers; on Caracas, Paris, or Maui to meet at conferences with those sharing religious beliefs, political opinions, professional interests, or therapeutic techniques. People traverse long distances to explore their mutual investments in everything from antique autos to Zen meditation. (In one sublime moment I recently spied an announcement for meetings of the International Society for the Study of Human Ideas on Ultimate Reality and Meaning.)

Yet most of these encounters are held separate from the remainder of one's existence. Indeed, their attraction is often based on their very limitations. Such relationships don't require full expression of self; one is free to express a delimited aspect without responsibility to the remainder, to coherence or consistency. One needn't worry that "this is only a misleading token of who I am," for in the context only a partial, provisional self counts. One needn't be concerned that "it's only superficial," because in the circumstance the partial is profound. Under these circumstances, the prospects of an expanded relationship, long hours shared exploring life's facets, would likely send the participants into recoil. Thus one hears, "I love to play bridge with him, but otherwise he's a bore." "He's the greatest at parties, but he's totally incapable of serious conversation," or "We share our deepest feelings in these workshops, but I would hate to have him around for a weekend." When the relational show is over, it is time for all to exit.

The family as an institution perhaps suffers most from the fractionalism of relationships. By the late nineteenth century, the family as an enduring unit of significant interdependencies was already in disrepair. With the industrial revolution, and the concomitant departure of the father (along with adolescent sons) from the farm or cottage industry to a remote workplace, the family suffered a sea change. Modernism also inflicted its toll. From the modernist standpoint, the person requires careful molding, much like a machine product. While the family was to serve as the major vehicle for personality production, its capacities were limited; it was considered unsystematic and untrustworthy as a source of influence. The individual could be shaped for a far more productive life if specialized skills and dispositions could be instilled. Thus within the modernist era a multitude of shaping programs became popular—school athletic teams, Boy Scouts, the YWCA, the 4-H Club, teen cotillions, summer camps. In each case the young were removed from the family, and interdependency diminished. In addition, since personal problems were perceived

"*Just go home and change, Worthington, and spare me any more talk about postmodernism.*"

Drawing by C. Barsotti; © 1990 The New Yorker Magazine, Inc.

as "machine failures" requiring repair by a well-trained mechanic, psychiatrists, psychologists, school counselors, social workers, and other mental-health professionals became popular. As people began pouring their secret longings and deep anguish into the ears of professionals, it no longer seemed necessary (or even desirable) to do so at home. Personally significant relationships were (and continue to be) developed with the professional—usually far warmer and more tolerant than those with spouses or siblings. Often one's most intense feelings and exciting self-insights are "saved" for the therapeutic hour. The professional can maintain dozens of such relationships simultaneously; however, the client's family is deprived of its traditional function.

As the technology of saturation becomes more effective, the range of fractional relationships further dissipates family functions. Day care furnishes partial mothers, big brother programs furnish sibling companionship, latchkey mothers are available while parents work, party lines give teenagers hours of engaging talk with strangers, crisis centers provide round-the-clock assistance to those in personal turmoil, rape hotlines provide instant advice in times of need, reproduction hotlines give advice on birth control, televised advertisements help people to reach others around the clock for personal warmth, and national clubs furnish support to those troubled by alcoholism, drugs, runaway children, and alternative life-styles. There are support groups for adult children of alcoholics; for those abused as children; for those troubled by their gambling; for those smothered in debt; for those bothered by their eating habits; and for those who feel tormented by their sexuality. In each case virtual strangers provide a personal service, often an emotionally significant one, matched to a particular facet of one's being.[4] At the same time, dependency on family members diminishes—which is only appropriate, because they are seldom at home.

Most unsettling to many is the invasion of the fractional relationship into the arena of sexual intimacy. Again, traditionally the family was to serve as the major (if not exclusive) domain of sexual intimacy. Even the unmarried sought an exclusionary relationship in which one's partner fulfilled all needs and desires. Crooners sang of "getting to know you" and not "a side of you," "I love you truly" rather than "I love part of you with part of me," and "why not take all of me" and not "one-eighth of me." The postmodern turn considerably alters the landscape. There are swingers' clubs in most major American cities, allowing couples sexual intimacies with new partners as often as they please. For those unable to join a club, there are national newspapers, magazines, and hotlines in which couples list their geographic availability and range of exotic desires. For those not wishing to risk personal contact, videotapes may be swapped so that couples may watch each other in intimate pursuits. Phone services allow lengthy erotic conversations with either male or female partners; so specialized are such services that specific numbers may be called for slavery, masochism, bisexuality, transsexualism, and so on, and in tribute to the technology of saturation, the services can be billed by phone to the client's credit card. Again, all such relationships are limited in scope; they exist as an expression of one important aspect of self; and functions previously assigned to enduring and exclusive relationships are lost.

Many are dismayed by the current state of events. It is painful to find the old rituals of relationship—deep and enduring friendships, committed intimacy, and the nuclear family—coming apart by the "seems." Continuity is replaced by contingency, unity by fragmentation, and authenticity by artfulness. Yet there is no obvious means of return at hand. Our consciousness of loss does not mean that we can now decide to escape the technologies of "progress." Nor, among the young, who are less aware of "the good old days," would such a return be desirable. When one grows up postmodern, "Main Street is just about all right." So, even though the emerging array of fractional relationships hastens the destruction of the traditions, the contemporary functions of these relationships must not be forgotten. The traditions are undergoing decay in any case. And for most people, even fractional relationships are vastly better than no relationships at all.

Ersatz Being

We should help our students . . . (1) Learn how to develop intense and deep human relationships quickly—and learn how to "let go." . . . (2) Learn how to enter groups and leave them.
            Warren G. Bennis and Philip E. Slater, *The Temporary Society*

As we have seen, social saturation and self-population throw traditions into disarray; committed forms of relationship become antiquated, and a multiplicity of partial relationships is favored. Yet ironically, the post-modern turn also favors the maintenance of traditional forms. Extending the arguments of chapter 3, we find that the technology of saturation renders the traditions of relationship available to the culture as never before. Television, films, mass publications, and radio are among the chief sources of such exposure. On any given evening one may "drop into" a dozen or more forms of traditional relationship. Within a relatively short period, one may savor an old-fashioned courtship, a collapsing marriage, the romance of young persons from opposite sides of the track, family rivalry, father and son alliances, and so on. As a result, one becomes acutely aware of "how it all goes." Contemporary culture may be unique in the fact that the phrase "blah, blah, blah" serves as an informative description of a conversation.

Half a century ago a young woman might nurse a romantic novel during the week and escape into a filmed romance on the weekend. Many young men of the time remained ignorant of romantic forms of relationship until their twenties. In contrast, today's adolescent may view as many as thirty such relationships a week during the average television viewing hours alone. And this is to say nothing of the supermarket sale of romance novels, the millions who watch the daytime soaps, and the latest romance gossip in *People* magazine. So acute is the knowledge of such relational forms that within the briefest moments modern television dramas can successfully explicate the most complex relationships. The average scene in a show such as *Dallas*, replete with a multiplicity of interdependent plots, is approximately sixty seconds. So sophisticated is the audience at recognizing the various relational genres (romance, duplicity, family bonding), that scene recognition (understanding what must have preceded and what is likely to follow) is almost instantaneous. To spell it out would only be a bore. It is thus that all the moves in the varied rituals of romance are ready and available for postmodern adolescents.

It is this sophistication in forms of relatedness that sets the stage for *ersatz being,* that is, the capacity for entering immediately into identities or relationships of widely varying forms. In ersatz being, the traditional forms are sustained; in the postmodern world, however, such forms may be ripped out of customary contexts and played out wherever time and circumstance permit. Thus, old-fashioned romance is not lost as a cultural form; unlike the past, however, there are few dictates as to when and where it is appropriate. No longer is it a matter primarily for unmarried young adults. It may be played out with but minimal cues from the age of eight to eighty, and between persons of varying age and economic, ethnic, and marital status. And so it is that one can immediately step into a family and play the part of an older brother or sister, give sympathetic and knowing advice at a crisis center, become a surrogate mother, offer therapy in a support group, or moan erotically to paying customers at the other end of a phone. And we find increasingly such events as an article in a London art magazine on "how to be Andy Warhol" and an Elvis Presley impersonation convention in Roseworth, Idaho, drawing participants from Italy and Australia. We confront each other increasingly as an array of hair-trigger potentials.

Two playgrounds for ersatz being are worthy of special attention, the first on a personal level and the second on a societal one. In the former case, consider the traditional concept of "the career." For both romanticists and modernists the career was considered a unified or singular endeavor. That is, one's life could properly be built around a particular goal or endpoint. For the romanticist the endeavor was often fraught with mystery and laced with value. One might speak of "having a calling," of aspiring to greatness, having the courage to persevere, or being inspired. Under modernism such language was largely replaced by a more functional conception of career. Persons had particular functions to fulfill within the society, and educational institutions and families were to play the major role in shaping each person to specification. If doctors or teachers were needed, for example, institutions should be arranged to produce them. One could also speak of a career trajectory in which one showed steady progress toward some goal (usually economic). In both periods, however, to have a career was to have a singular and recognizable identity.[5]

With the emergence of ersatz being, both romantic and modernist conceptions of career begin to recede. If one carries a multiplicity of potentials (having seen on television everything from taxi-driving, trucking, and drug-dealing to ranching, brokering, and doctoring) then almost no profession seems alien, mystical, or closed. They are all open possibilities, at least in fantasy. Further, because no concept of fixed or deep identity anchors one's choice, there is no powerful necessity to select one form of pursuit over another. And if identities are essentially forms of social construction, then one can be anything at any time so long as the roles, costumes, and settings have been commodiously arranged. Thus, entertainers and astronauts can become politicians, athletes become movie stars, and scholars become entertainers with but a modicum of public suspicion of superficiality. The transitions are possible because such individuals were not, from the postmodern perspective, "basically" entertainers, athletes, or scholars at the outset.

In 1986 alone over 10 million Americans switched their occupations. One increasingly meets persons like Nancy, an acquaintance who married and had four children, then, as they grew up, returned to college and became a drama teacher. Within a few years Nancy gave up teaching to become a fundraiser for a university. At the same time she began taking courses in brokering, and later gave up fundraising to become a stockbroker. Several years afterward she shed the broker role to take a job in a philanthropic foundation. After some time in the position, she dropped it in favor of developing her own antique business. At the age of fifty, Nancy now travels the world in search of bargains for her thriving business, and is simultaneously in the process of developing a bed-and-breakfast hotel and a lawn sculpture plant. "The career" is simply unfolded like a bedouin tent—possibly to vanish with the dawn.

The possibility of ersatz being has also encouraged the development of industries for *identity production*. Adult-education curricula, educational extension programs, technical schools, and home studies programs are by now unremarkable. More interesting is the mushrooming of personal packaging enterprises—organizations such as career-counseling firms, designed to construct one's identity in ways that are marketable. In the romantic period, by contrast, one was endowed with certain natural gifts or talents (genius, leadership, a fine voice, a strapping body) and the essential problem was to locate a niche in which to flourish or contribute. For the modernist, the individual was largely a machine production; the central problem was to gauge the product at an early age and, again, to locate a context in which it could produce. This mentality prompted the development of the various tests of skills and aptitudes, as a way to inform the young of the most promising career choice. With postmodernism, however, there is little in the way of an "essential person" for whom a niche is to be sought. There are niches, but the person is a constructed category, someone to be created in the form of a résumé or references. This attitude now pervades both high schools and universities. Students clamor for extracurricular activities, research assistantships, summer jobs, and the like not out of intrinsic interest (indeed the concept of "intrinsic" interest is virtually lost from view within modernism), but as the raw materials out of which applications and résumés can be constructed. For the more advanced, British bookstores now feature an elaborate series of *Bluffers' Guides*. The volumes furnish the reader with a quick glimpse of "insider's knowledge" for such domains as philosophy, mathematics, the theater, feminist ideas, wine, and even bluffing itself.

Of equal interest to the professional career is what Erving Goffman has called "the moral career."[6] As Goffman saw it, people are expected to pursue not only a professional career, but a social career as well, in which moral acceptability is the goal: They must appear to possess good character. Yet the concept of good character as a mark of identity—something truly defining one's inner being, traits, or deepest dispositions—is becoming an endangered species. Under postmodernism society comes to tolerate, if not anticipate, breaches in moral careers. No single act of deviance is "telling" of one's personality, because there is no personality to be told about. One's potentials are multiple, and circumstances being what they are, ersatz immorality is of no major consequence. John F. Kennedy could remain a hero even when White House assignations were widely discussed, Ted Kennedy's political career was only inconvenienced by Chappaquiddick, and Richard Nixon could be resuscitated as a figure of national prominence after being forced from the presidency in ignominy. There was little outrage when government officials such as Spiro Agnew, John Dean, Robert McFarlane, and Michael Deaver were found guilty of breaking laws. In the postmodern world such events are no longer indicators of "flawed character," but of unfortunate quirks, momentary slips in judgment, or complex situations.

Ersatz being also has interesting ramifications at the societal level. Of particular interest is the emergence of the *ersatz social movement*. Through broad media exposure to various forms of social protest, we incorporate the know how for membership in movements working for change. We know what it is to march for a cause, to be lost in the throes of "true belief," to create public havoc, and even to suffer beating and arrest. All of these "moves within the game" are within the repertoire of most members of the culture. Only the appropriate social conditions are necessary for the potential to be realized. The technologies of social saturation—telephones, news media, and copy services—enable millions of potential activists to be contacted quickly. Chinese students at Tiananmen Square, for example, used telephones, fax machines, and laptop computers to organize their protests, and video cameras and satellite relays to garner the immediate support of the international community. A new profession has sprung into being whose particular expertise is in creating social movements. Whether the nature of the cause is important to the success of such efforts remains unclear. It might well be argued that with effective media preparation, virtually any issue could be elevated to the level of public outcry. The streets, parks, and stadiums of any city may be filled at any time with chanting and exuberant demonstrators. Vocal opinion may be rendered instantly on nuclear disarmament, suffering farmers, AIDS victims, Nazism, environmental protection, homosexuals, Central America, Supreme Court nominations, nuclear energy, apartheid, abortion, housing . . .

To note the rapidity with which such movements are created is not to discredit the significance of the movements or the immediate commitment of the participants. The Live Aid concert of 1985 elicited support from millions of young people all over the United States and Europe, and generated millions of dollars for starving Ethiopians. A month before the concert, it is safe to say, only a small percent of the population was aware of famine in Ethiopia; one may doubt whether many had even heard of the country. And indeed, within weeks after the concert, Ethiopia disappeared into insignificance once again. Even if Live Aid was an immediate, one-time event, however, one should not doubt the emotional involvement of the participants. In the postmodern view, social outcry is not a matter of internal belief, basic morality, or deep-seated feelings; it is simply another form of performance. The question should not be whether the feelings are superficial or deep, but whether conditions favor the ritual of long-term commitment. A youth may join a march because it's a beautiful afternoon to be in the sun with his companions. If he is clubbed by the police for "no apparent reason," there are few options open in the ritual other than active resistance. If active resistance leads then to "more police abuse," a committed terrorist may be in the making. One knows how to do commitment; if it becomes the appropriate move in the dance of political protest it can scarcely be avoided.

At this point in the analysis, daily relations in the postmodern world seem highly problematic. Deep relations becomes an endangered species, the individual is fragmented over an array of partial and circumscribed relationships, and life is lived out as a series of incoherent posturings. As the constructed character of ersatz identities becomes increasingly evident, the self loses its credibility to both actor and audience. Daily life seems transformed into a game of superficial shamming, a scherzo of triviality. Yet, we must ask, is this a necessary conclusion? Is there any means of forestalling such a dolorous outlook on our condition? Perhaps. It should be apparent by now that this analysis, too, is constructed from the available shards of intelligibility washed up by cultural history. Such terms as "incoherent," "superficial," and "sham" gain their critical edge primarily from longstanding traditions of speech. Most immediately, they owe their rhetorical force to those aspects of romanticism and modernism that viewed persons as having fixed and substantial identities, and ideal relationships as a bonding of individual unities. Can we locate another form of analysis, one that may reconstruct these conditions in a more promising way and open new vistas for future action? The last chapter of this book will confront this question directly. In preparation, however, it is important to pass through the gates of the carnival.

INVITATION TO THE CARNIVAL

Diogenes was the first to recognize the danger embodied in . . . the artificial psychosis of "absolute knowledge" . . . and that the grandiose earnestness of idealistic discourse . . . stifles itself with its "cares," its "will to power," and its enemies, "with whom one cannot fool around."
—Peter Sloterdijk, *Critique of Cynical Reason*

Let us recall the analysis of language as outlined in chapter 4. We found that the traditional assumption that language can furnish us with maps or pictures of reality proves unintelligible. Truth as a correspondence between word and world lapses into nonsense. This is not to say, however, that all tellings are "false" or "mythological" either, for both of these concepts presuppose a possible condition of truth against which false or mythological statements could be compared. Rather, the entire concept of true and false, with respect to linguistic propositions, stands to be abandoned (or to be reconceptualized in some way other than its traditional form).

The same analysis may be made of our self-identifying actions. We have traditionally believed that our words and actions occur on the surface of the self, while the true reality of being lies beneath the surface. The surface may thus stand in a relationship of true or false to the underlying reality of self. But if this account of human action proves as unwieldy as the account of propositional truth (as the preceding chapters argue), then we may abandon the presumption that people's actions can authentically represent what they truly are. Terms such as *sham* and *pretense* in their traditional sense simply don't apply.

As many drawn by postmodern arguments conclude, however, it is insufficient to close off discourse at the loss of truth in language. Life goes on; we continue to talk; can we not go beyond cynicism in our attitude toward language? The answer to this question impinges, in turn, on our view of self and relations. Even if there is no inner self to which our actions should be true, life goes on; we continue to act. Is cynicism a necessary reaction to the loss of authenticity?

Certainly, cynicism is a tempting brew, clouding one's brain with the raptures of self-contented superiority. However, it is also a debilitating elixir, rendering one inactive and alienated. To avoid such an end, certain scholars speak of such reactions as "jubilation which results from new rules of the game" and an "emancipatory indulgence in irony." One is invited to "play the dandy," "let the signifiers frolic," and "piss against the wind."[7] Although the shadings differ, the various options share a strong ludic component: each invites one to reconceptualize language as a form of play. Yes, we continue to speak, to act as if our language tells the truth, and to furnish "authoritative insights," but we need not take such activities seriously. We needn't credit such linguistic activities with profundity,

In the postmodern mode, the way is opened to whimsy. Here the Paris-based designers Mattia Bonetti and Elizabeth Garouste display an arched set of drawers.

imbue them with deep significance, or set out to alter the world on their account. Rather, we might play with the truths of the day, shake them about, try them on like funny hats. Serious concerns are left at the carnival gate.

This attitude toward "true tellings" has a strong supporting rationale. Many of our major problems in society result from taking seriously such terms as *reality, authenticity, true, worthwhile, superior, essential, valid, ideal, correct,* and the like. None of these otherwise awesome distinctions possesses transcendent foundations; they are all constructions of particular language communities, used for pragmatic purposes at a particular moment in history. Yet when these traditional shibboleths are put into serious practice, they begin to establish divisions, hierarchies, insidious separations, oppression, and indeed mass liquidation. Every "reality" makes a fool of those who do not participate; every "valid" and "true" proposition creates a class of the deluded who do not share that language. For every "superior" position, those deemed "inferior" are pressed into silence. As Lyotard says, "The nineteenth and twentieth centuries have given us as much terror as we can take. We have paid a high enough price for the nostalgia of the whole and the one, for the reconciliation of the concept and the sensible, of the transparent and the communicable experience."[8]

Within the academic sphere, this line of reasoning now breeds fascinating new forms of scholarship. For the postmodern scholar all traditional forms of writing are suspect. Such writings purport to give objectively accurate accounts of what is the case. But in doing so they are but vain and possibly dangerous posturings. Precisely when the prose begs to be taken seriously one should resist, for it is at this point that new blinders are fastened to the sensibilities, and alternative voices are removed to the margins of awareness. The postmodern invitation is to play with the traditional forms. Avoid "saying it straight," using linear logic, and forming smooth, progressive narratives. One example of this new scholarly genre is worth quoting at length, not only because of its lively power, but because it nicely illustrates the various themes of doubt, self-reflection, and social construction that pervade postmodernism more generally. Consider the scene: A professor of anthropology at Rice University, Stephen Tyler, is asked to address a large gathering of scholars on the subject of anthropological research. They anticipate a coherent, suitably cautious, and rationally justified set of arguments—the standard expected of a high-ranking scholar. They are both shocked and mystified as Tyler begins:

> I'm of two minds about this. . . . Peras and aperion, boundary and the boundless, the unmoved one and the moving continuum, Apollo and Dionysus. . . . Peras in my Platonist mind—left hemisphere probably—the mind

as a book, the ur-form of the scribal hand, the capability of taking in hand, of out-of-hand-capability, emancipation (e-man-kap-), the hand that manipulates, a discipline of formulation that overcomes resistant material and engenders a contemplative attitude of craftsmanship, a passionate attention that assembles particulars and joins life and experience in an act of production/reproduction/creativity, a conceit that we call the concept (con-kap-) and thus note the role of Eros in the sexual act of conceiving the concept, the perfection of form, the nous, the fixed entity of the idea, the achieved whole of the inner psyche that makes the integrity of the private mind and repeats itself in the solitude of the book, in the trance-like stasis of reading and writing.

. . . my other mind . . . is Herculean, the mind of the word-processor/computer. . . . No craftsman's care here, no guiding hand, just a monkey-fingered poke at a key-mon-key-and the data base scrolls up before my eyes, the automatic outliner orders my thoughts into the algorithms of logic and procedures, and replaces the steadiness of contemplative formulation with an excess of dynamic possibilities, turning my private solitude into the public network, destroying my authorship by making a totalized textuality in which the text is only ancillary . . . yet i internalize it as calculative power, total manipulative control, abundant resource, speed, complete management of instantaneous processes as i zap from one frame to another or from text to picture, split screen, cursor through the menu, unwind dynamic sequences of images, rotating them, adding and deleting components, free-styling, flaming from one formulaic phrase to another, hypnotized by the phosphorescent glow of moving symbols. . . . power is mine! . . . i have the instantaneous and total knowledge of god and am ONE with the movement of thought. . . . I AM THE MOVING MATRIX!![9]

To be sure, there is a significant and coherent communication embedded within these introductory remarks, one that could be put into recognizable scholarly form. Tyler is distinguishing between two orientations toward scholarly writing itself—the one Platonic, craftsmanlike, and seemingly pure in its logic (modern in cast), and the other a spontaneous, rough-and-tumble frolic with language (leaning toward the postmodern). The first issues from a noble tradition of letters, the latter is a mongrel by-product of the personal computer. The very style in which the text is formed favors the latter; the rambunctious rambling itself serves as a critique of the noble tradition of letters. Further, by favoring a dream-world of associated phrases over linear logic, Tyler adds a range of rich laminations to the otherwise simple distinction. He brings to attention, for example, the goal of emancipation traditionally undergirding the former tradition, while simultaneously revealing its possible basis in conceit and erotic desire (with a self-gratifying end). At the same time, the favored orientation is given a self-reflexive tweak, as Tyler variously alludes to it as a primate's activity in which one banality is heaped upon another. By unseating the traditional form of writing, then, Tyler achieves a far more evocative and multihued account than the honored tradition would otherwise allow. And, in adopting a bumptious and self-mocking style, he also invites the audience to view the message itself as a form of jest.

This generalized jocosity reverberates through many traditionally serious professions. It first became evident in the pop artist's celebration of schlock. Consider, for example, Roy Lichtenstein's exaggerations of the comic strip, or Red Grooms, who invites the museum patron into a life-size mockup of a subway car, complete with graffiti, ghetto blasters, and grotesques of the common folk—including a flasher. Duane Hanson's statues depict lifelike museum guards and cleaning women; seeing such forms in museums, people frequently mistake them for real. Hanson is asking the patron to stop viewing art as either a mystical message from the artist's interior (the romantic view) or a presentation of the essentials of form (the modern view). Rather, we are told, the artist is part prankster, so relax and enjoy. (In the Philadelphia Academy of Fine Arts, one patron was so inspired by the invitation that for hours she adopted a frozen posture before a painting, giving other patrons the impression that she was a Hanson—life imitating art imitating life.) One locates the ludic component as well in much postmodern architecture. In many structures one finds the grandiose (romantic) and austere (modern) facades of the past now decorated in bright hues of pink, blue, and fuchsia.

Popular culture also shows many signs of entry to the carnival. Contrast the cinematic humor of the modernist era with that of today. In earlier times, humor often represented a force of good in the service of eradicating conventional evil. Thus, when comics such as Charlie Chaplin, Max Sennet, or Laurel and Hardy poked fun at others, their target was typically "the other." They were not the "good folks like us," but despots, egoists, the haughty, the crude, the mean, and the stingy. Comedy thus acted as a moral force, distinguishing between essentially good and evil persons. With postmodernism, the clarity in moral delineation begins to disappear. Early examples are furnished by the Beatles' films, which unceremoniously aped almost every traditional institution they touched. *Monty Python's Flying Circus* and a series of film spinoffs (*The Meaning of Life, Life of Brian*) extended the spirit of generalized satire. The popularity of such television shows as *Laugh-In, Saturday Night Live*, and *Not Necessarily the News* can largely be attributed to their irreverent spoofing of the traditionally sacrosanct. The same broad burlesque now characterizes the typical routine in the rapidly expanding number of comedy clubs. There is virtually no institution, office, or person remaining to claim

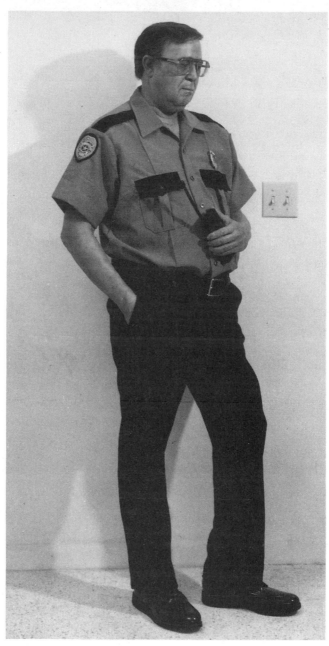

A security guard, or Duane Hanson's *Security Guard*: life or art, or is there a significant difference?

transcendent probity, superior virtue in a culture of the vile. The major difference between modernist comedy and postmodern is that we are all now "the other."

It is also in comedy that the implications of the carnival for the problem of self become most fully apparent. For as contemporary comedy warns, all actions are subject to satire from some perspective. All our attempts to do good works, to achieve, to improve, and to be responsible can be punctured with wit. The postmodern invitation is thus to carry the clown on one's shoulders—to always be ready to step out of "serious character" and locate its pretensions, to parody or ape oneself. Life itself may become a form of play, in which one transforms ventures into adventures, purpose into performance, and desire into drama.[10] Culture seems a carnival with a never-ending array of sideshows. It is in this way that we shall avoid the confining qualities of singular and ingurgitating realities. It is also in this way that we stand maximally open to the multiplicity of surrounding voices. For there is no need to defend one's reigning reality against the disagreeable clamor from without, to "persecute the infidels." Their realities, one sees, also possess an internal validity, and one may even be enriched by playing within their tents. And should one's preferred playings bring cries of pain from those outside one's tent, cries that may indeed be attributed to the playings themselves, one is optimally situated both to listen and to refashion. If one's business brings forth environmentalist animosity, one's club is attacked for its sexism, or one's actions are branded aggressive and exploitative, one need not be thrust into a defensive posture. If business, club life, and individual personality are all but sideshows at the carnival, then one may more easily modify their contours in light of their destructive effects on other realities.

TOWARD SERIOUS PLAY

This playfulness is the product of [the] shared ability to appreciate the power of redescribing, the power of language to make new and different things possible and important—an appreciation which becomes possible only when one's aim becomes an expanding repertoire of alternative descriptions rather than The One Right Description.
—Richard Rorty, *Contingency, Irony, and Solidarity*

An atmosphere of ironic drollery thus pervades postmodern consciousness, but many find this a difficult resting place. In particular, to unleash a culture of jesters and dandies seems both delimited and demeaning. It is delimited because it dramatically reduces the range of human activities in which one can satisfyingly participate. If all serious projects are reduced to satire, and one can only play, generate nonsense, or turn rituals into riot, then to be "serious" is self-deluding. All attempts at authenticity or earnest ends become empty—merely postures to be punctured by sophisticated self-consciousness. Yet, if there is nothing left to us but satire, we may be escaping one rut merely to tumble headlong into another, even if a merry one.

This outcome was brought home to me in a recent luncheon discussion. Around the table were a number of scholars drawn to various parts of the postmodern dialogue and anxious to pursue their broader implications. However, one of the participants was not only thinking about the topic; he was, like Stephen Tyler in the remarks quoted earlier, "living it." For him, every logically coherent proposal put forward by his companions was but a new toy. Each was a target for puns, wordplay, or ironic caricature. For a time the deconstructive antics were enjoyed by all. But slowly, as the luncheon bore on, it became clear that no "serious discussion" was possible. This customary form of pursuit, while fulfilling to many scholars, was "out of bounds." To underscore the postmodern dilemma most poignantly, it became apparent that should all participants "go postmodern" in this way, we would be reduced to an empty silence. The postmodern player exists, after all, in a symbiotic relationship with "serious culture." Without others to play the part of foolish fools, there are no opportunities for the heroic one.

It is also the derisive undertone of postmodern playfulness that many find objectionable. When all other projects are reduced to play, such projects are also demeaned. It is easy enough to join in the deconstruction of various forms of zealous puffery, to leave intellectual opponents stammering for justification, and to deride the transparent silliness of bourgeois culture. However, let us consider an alternative range of cultural concerns. How are we to respond, for example, to the death of a child, life in a cancer ward, crack houses in D.C., the condition of South African blacks, or the Holocaust? Does one wish in these instances to simply let the signifiers frolic and go piss in the wind? Even the most jaded postmodern would stop short of such a conclusion. Is some form of compromise possible, between the desire on the one hand to abandon the destructive potential of romanticist and modernist discourses, and on the other, to stop short of mirth turned sour?

Perhaps. For there is a forgotten theme in the melody of postmodern play: the theme of social interdependence. To play is admirable, but play that is simply deconstructive doesn't recognize the possible interconnections among us all. The ironic deconstruction of all meaningful discourse (and its related patterns of action) destroys the webs of interdependence on which social life so fragilely hangs. Such a stance is like a Pac-Man of social pattern, gobbling all that stands in its path. One feminist critic of the Stephen Tyler presentation quoted above likens unadulterated deconstructive play to macho masturbation. It is, she suggests, a celebration of self-serving autonomy. Compare Tyler's earlier passage with an excerpt from her critical rejoinder. In this performance paper a feminist Medusa is conversing with Post-Modern Man:

MEDUSA: Who are they trying to scare off? Full of Power and Manipulative Control, Abundant Resources, Speed, Complete Management. The New Army, complete with portable Zenises. Pulling the rug out from under the OLD GUARD. (Didn't we all want to run out of the stands and CHEER!!!?) Down with the OLD ORDER . . . Foundations, split into Gravity's Rainbow/Rules shredded ribbons adorning the May POLE, wavering in the Breeze of breathtaking words/ABSOLUTE-ly nothinged by the shock-ing PM troops/Wreaking CON-SENSE with NON-SENSE, PARADING, PANDERING, PARADOXING, PLAYING. What fun . . . London Bridge Is Falling Down. (DE-CONSTRUCTED) My Fair Lady. Where can we jump in? Shall we form a circle? Can we dance around the fire? the Pole? the falling bridges? Give us a hand? Give us a hand? Give us a hand . . .

PM MAN: (All they ever want are hand-outs . . . Give 'em an inch they'll take a mile. How many inches do they think we've got?) Besides can't you see we've got play to do? It's not easy just going off to play each day you know. It takes practice and dedication and grace. It's not something that you can just join in like that. We've got our ways. Can't you see you'll just muck it up? We're in the wrecking business. What busines is that of yours? "You make, we break": We can write it on the truck. Next thing you'll want us to settle down and play house. We've got to be movin' on. It's part of the code. Besides, John Wayne doesn't talk to girls, so adios. "Don't call us, we'll call you." . . . That's another thing. We don't make promises. Just another word for COMMITMENT (the really big C-word, the one that gets you behind bars, and I don't mean mixing martinis).

MEDUSA: Mick Jagger has a kid, maybe two.

PM MAN: Babies are phallic. If you need one, get one.

MEDUSA: But your phallus doesn't need bread.

PM MAN: Let 'em eat cake, as good ol' Marie put it. She had a feel for our rap. French of course . . . Post-modern life is, as Deleuze sez, nomadic. We are all homeless wanderers on the featureless, post-industrial steppe, tentless nomads, home packed up . . . Baby, the revolution has just begun. I mean the trashing is in dis-progress. Garbage cans full of rotten fruit, it is child's play. Disciplines to dismantle/Methods to maul/Truth to trample/Origins to emascu-late . . . We're a-dispersing . . .

MEDUSA: It's gonna be mighty COLD out there. . . .

PM MAN: Do you read me?? . . . Do you read me?

MEDUSA: You're fading, Major Tom.

SILENCE[11]

But if we agree on the undesirability of full-scale deconstruction, and on the necessity of interdependence, what then follows? At this point we may begin to envision the possibility of *serious play*. Gregory Bateson develops the following interchange between two avid conversationalists:

DAUGHTER: Daddy, are these conversations serious?

FATHER: Certainly they are.

DAUGHTER: They're not a sort of game that you play with me?

FATHER: God forbid . . . but they are a sort of game that we play together.

DAUGHTER: Then they're *not* serious.[12]

We engage in serious play when we enter into various relational forms—including linguistic constructions and associated actions—while at the same time treating the forms as contingent or contextually bounded. This means honoring the existing endeavors of human communities as pos-sessing an internal validity for the participants, but acknowledging that their validity lies wholly within their particular spheres. More concretely, one is invited to give oneself to the existing life-forms of various com-munities—to the rituals of parenthood, romance, friendship, religion, science, and the like. However, it also means sustaining the right of withdrawal, of throwing into relief one's participation by casting it in alternative frames. The postmodern emphasis on multiplicity, social con-struction, and self-reflexivity are not lost in the process of serious play; they remain ever-present reminders of the relative character of momen-tary commitments. But within the purview of serious play, commitments of a kind are possible. In the words of the French theorist Julia Kristeva, "This discovery . . . that I myself at the deepest levels of my wants and desires am unsure, centerless, and divided . . . does not eliminate my capacities for commitment and trust but makes them literally and in no other way *playable* (in the sense that a piece of music is playable)."[13]

Two metaphors give further dimension to the concept of serious play. First, on the concrete level, consider the athletic contest as paradigmatic.

Football, basketball, and baseball are all cultural contrivances. They are based on rules of human construction, and they are particular to certain cultures at certain times. Further, such games are preeminently social; one cannot play them alone. Finally, if one is to join in the social activity of the game, one must play by the rules. All this being so, when one is playing the game it becomes "all there is." Winning can furnish moments of great jubilation, and losing may rob Mudville of all joy. Yet in the end—sweaty, exhausted, and bruised—one can walk away and say, "It was only a game."

Such is the case with serious play. To pray, to feel remorse, to express gratitude, to conduct business, to make a scientific discovery are all forms of cultural ritual—constructed forms of activity particular to cultures in given times and places. And one may indulge in such activities fully, following their rules and thus relating to those making up such cultures. Without one's culture to define the games and places possible within it, there is simply no being to be. We owe our sense of existence, then, not to internal sources—passion, reason, observation, and the like—but to our participation in the communal forms. Or as Gadamer succinctly puts it, "all playing is a being-played."[14] At the same time, one should at all times be able to step back and see each of these rituals from the perspective of "other worlds." They are modes of life among many others.

And finally, with a slight variation on the metaphor, James Carse's volume *Finite and Infinite Games* adds an important dimension to the concept of serious play.[15] Carse proposes that one may distinguish between two kinds of games. The finite game is played for the purpose of winning, the infinite game for the purpose of continuing the play. The finite game will come to an end when someone has won; the infinite game can go on forever. Only a designated number of players may participate in a finite game; in the infinite game all may participate. The rules are different for each finite game; it is only by knowing the rules that one knows what the game is. However, in the infinite game the rules change in the course of play, when players agree that the play may be threatened by a finite outcome—a victory of some players and a defeat of others. In Carse's words, "Finite players play within boundaries; infinite players play with boundaries." And finally, "Finite players are serious; infinite players are playful."

In this way Carse recognizes the internal validity of life's serious quests, the conventional rituals by which we live most of our daily lives together. At the same time, he adds importantly to the concept of play. For, in Carse's terms, the form of play that recognizes the circumscribed character of the finite games is ultimately one that can unite all persons in the continuation of the human venture. Although the finite games of daily relatedness are essential, when their implications are fully extended they become exclusionary, hierarchical, and possibly deadly. It is when we rise above the finite game, open ourselves to the possibility of an infinitely changing array of rules—each opening ways for new participants—that the game of human existence finds greatest promise. We shall return to the broader social implications of this view in the final chapter.

EIGHT

Self-Renewal and Sincerity

"To thine own self be true"—with what a promise that phrase sings in our ears!
                                            —Lionel Trilling, *Sincerity and Authenticity*

Recurring images:

- Family members quietly bow their heads in prayer over the evening meal.
- Locked in rapturous embrace, a young couple pledges eternal love.
- A student drops out of college to find what she truly is and wishes to become.
- A chief executive thinks long and carefully about the future of his company, and announces his decisions to his vice-presidents.
- Scientists unlock further secrets of genetic coding.
- The president proposes a budget claimed to be "close to our economic realities."

Such scenes are scarcely unusual in contemporary life. Although rooted in romantic and modernist perspectives, these beliefs in a holy spirit, profound love, a core self, rational decision making, objective truth, and realistic conditions remain robust mainstays of Western culture. Furthermore, there are significant signs of renewed commitment to these beliefs, signs that people are becoming increasingly concerned about their spiritual well-being, their moral values, and their emotional capacities, and wish to locate a solid, objective basis for centering themselves and giving direction to the future. We detect groundswells of this desire in criticisms of higher education, new religious expressions, cultural preservation movements, movements on behalf of oppressed and needy minorities, city and community renewal programs, weekend self-enrichment workshops, the vigorous search for historical roots of ethnic identity, and movements for universal human rights.[1]

Does the prevalence of such activities not place substantial limits over the proposals of the preceding chapters? Need one be especially concerned with the possibilities of multiphrenia, or the demise of commitment, intrinsic values, truth, personal morality, emotion, and autobiography? Are the boundaries of the self truly so buffeted that the very category threatens to become submerged within the socius? Need one seek assurance in the replacement of individualism by more relational forms of life, or in the emergence of a more tolerant participation in the games of life? One might indeed say that the evidence for such shifts is meager; life in general goes on as usual. Even to the extent that there is a move in the postmodern direction, we also detect a consciousness of impending crisis and a concerted effort at cultural restoration.

To be sure, such doubts about my thesis are well advised. As I pointed out in the preface, I am not trying to document the societal norm. Rather, my hope is to isolate an emerging shift in perspective and related life patterns. The case is drawn from specially affected segments of the population—often the more urban, mobile, professional, affluent, and aspiring. Yet, as I have attempted to demonstrate, there is good reason to believe that what is taking place within these groups can be taken as a weathervane of future cultural life in general. For now, much remains normal; many subcultures are scarcely touched. In the longer run, though, the technologies giving rise to social saturation will be inescapable. And as they continue to expand and improve, so may the traditional mentalities and their related patterns of life slip silently away.

The primary purpose of this chapter is to explore the possibilities for retrenchment. If one scans the horizons and feels the cold shivers of impending loss, if one longs for a return to the true and the durable, can one "do something"? Surely the many attempts at self-renewal suggest that this may be so. People can generate a strong sense of solidarity, and with powerful repercussions. The reclaiming of national integrity among the East European nations and the thrust toward autonomy of ethnic groups within the Soviet Union are only two examples from recent times. Could broader and more sweeping movements effectively insulate Western culture against the intrusion of postmodern mores and mentalities? It is my view that in spite of their broad appeal, there is little reason to suspect that calls to defensive action will succeed. The necessary resources do not appear to be at hand. Why and whether this is so are the central concerns of what follows. In light of these considerations, we can turn in the final chapter to assessing the consequences.

RESISTANCE TO RETRENCHMENT

Through the rise of new communications technologies, other voices are increasingly incorporated into our own. Yes, there are robust remnants of past traditions. But what can prevent the proliferation of postmodern consciousness—a time when family members begin to feel that prayers are "merely ritual," lovers wonder whether words of profound devotion aren't a bit recherché, college students trade "finding oneself" for "networking," business executives wonder whether personal decisions are ever rational, scientists doubt the concept of "objective truth," and politicians recognize the term "realistic" to be a rhetorical device? One can scarcely imagine dismantling the technologies giving rise to the postmodern condition, and it seems we are far from reaching a plateau in terms of their diffusion or efficacy. If cultural retrenchment is to occur, the resources must be located elsewhere than in the world of technology. The chief alternative lies within the human realm—that is, the capabilities of human beings to organize themselves around purposes of significance. We must consider, in particular, the possibility of strong leadership, the inner resources of individuals, and the unification of communities against the emerging dissolution of self and related cultural forms.[?] As we shall find, the very technologies giving rise to the pluralism of postmodernism also serve to undermine the potential of these resources for solidifying cultural modes of understanding and action.

The Nostalgia for Leadership

The terrible power of [Reagan and Thatcher] has lain in their inability to decry any element of the ludicrous, fatuous, or fantastic in the constantly changing charades their image machines devise for them. They simply read the script, whatever it may say.
—Philip Norman, Faking the Present

I think they are more "showmen" than anything else, but I watch some of them anyway.   —Anonymous viewer of television evangelists

Many continue to hope for strong leaders, gifted individuals who can set high goals, steer a clear course, excite us to consistent and concerted effort, and thereby create worthy and enduring forms of cultural life. Yet can we, in the now-waning decades of the twentieth century, anticipate the emergence of inspiring leaders? American politics of recent decades has been a constant waiting game: "Is there a Democrat (or Republican) who can rise from the ranks to the stature of leader?" But is this hope not, in Beckett's terms, like "waiting for Godot"? To answer, it is first important to realize that beliefs in "strong leaders" can be traced to the romantic period. As we found, concepts of genius, deep character, inspiration, and profundity of insight were focal to the romantic consciousness. Such capacities were to be found only in a gifted few, who could be trusted as the true leaders. It is largely this heritage that prompts us to hope for the arrival of valiant leaders (even when we scarcely remember the meaning of the term *valiant*). For the romantic, *charisma* is a reality. It is this background that renders the culture vulnerable to gurus and Zen masters, evangelists, and mediums for reaching distant spiritual planes. And it is this background that prompts the hope that perhaps, just perhaps, the *next* president will lead us out of the quagmire of complexity.[3] As romanticism wanes, however, such feelings become little more than nostalgia.

But it is not simply the modernist skepticism of such concepts as genius, moral inspiration, and profound insight that engenders disbelief in the qualifications of the contenders. The overlay of modernist consciousness itself also places a low ceiling above those who would stand tall. In modernist perspective, characteristics of the deep interior are replaced by the virtues of rationality and objectivity. Thus, while we may still be vulnerable to talk of inspiration, destiny, or a glorious past, such language is usually limited to contexts of marginal status—ritual ceremonies, fundraisers, or Sunday morning services—far from the marketplace, halls of government, and other places where the "important decisions" are made. Where the stakes are "real," we want dispassionate rationality, objectivity, and productivity. Talk of "values," "rights," "justice," and the like, all of which are imbued with strong rhetorical force for the romanticist, are suspect, since they allow the passions through the door, and thus subvert the rationality of the decision maker. In effect, modernist language is incapable of "stirring the passions." The modernist image of those in high places is, in effect, the image of a good factory manager. For him or her to rely on the language of the romantic would be to lose credibility in this role.

To this composite, one must also add the forbidding image of perhaps the century's most powerful leader, Adolf Hitler. Hitler was a master of romantic rhetoric, his speeches brimming with passion and studded with words and phrases (spirit, destiny, purity) far removed from the merely material.[4] His public rituals were also suffused with evocative imagery from past religious and royal ceremonies. At the same time, Hitler's emphasis on military might, economic productivity, and geographic expansion appealed to the emerging modernism of the era. Hitler's state was to be the most powerful, efficient, and effective machine the world had ever known. So disastrous were the consequences, however, that the image of Hitler today shadows the path of anyone who aspires to be a giant among men. At a certain level, all forms of dramatic ascendancy now generate a sense of uneasiness. At base we cannot trust those very individuals whose images most fulfill the nostalgic hopes for strong leadership.

And now the very technologies that usher in the postmodern period also set in motion processes that ensure the role of strong leader will never be filled. To be sure, television, radio, and the press enable aspirants to develop enormous followings within relatively short periods. However, to become a trusted leader, one must be able to establish the reality of his or her identity. One must appear as an authentic being, whose persona is equivalent to his or her actual personality, who intrinsically possesses those qualities essential to superiority of position. Yet it is the achievement of authenticity that the technologies of social saturation serve to prevent.

Consider first the problem of *inauthentication by perfection,* or the disappearance of the "real" speaker through the perfection of the persona. Because of the great competition for media attention, it is essential for the aspiring leader to make maximal use of the time or space available. As a result, the aspirant's "natural ways of relating" will typically be replaced with "techniques of effective communication." He or she must suppress a local dialect, eradicate grammatical errors, eliminate unusual gestures, avoid controversial topics, dress in a broadly acceptable way, and communicate as effectively and succinctly as possible. These demands may entail special voice lessons, speechwriters, policy committees, makeup and costume experts, body-language advisers, and special groups to monitor and advise on media impact. In effect, as the media become essential to leadership roles, natural forms of communication are transformed into artificially fashioned performances.

As this transformation takes place, the credibility of the aspirant is demeaned. From both romantic and modern traditions we inherit a concept of authentic communication—a belief that a person's words should be an exterior expression of the core self. We wish to feel in contact with the person *behind* the mask—with his or her true feelings, intentions, and beliefs. As the natural habits of expression are replaced with demands for effective performance, however, the marks of sincere presence—fumbling for the correct word, colloquialisms, emotional disruptions, plain talk—are typically eradicated. The dress of "real people" is replaced with "proper attire," and signs of "natural age" are removed by makeup. Most important, ideas that should originate from "within" now appear to be the product of a committee or ghostwriter. It is not the individual who speaks, but the groups deliberating at one step removed. What previously appeared to be "authentic leadership" now approximates a puppet show. Or in Christopher Lasch's more acerbic terms, "The degeneration of politics into spectacle has . . . transformed policy making into publicity, debased political discourse, and turned elections into sporting events."

The media pose a second challenge as well to the candidate's sense of authenticity, namely *inauthentication by humanization*. As public attention toward the leader is increased, his or her personal life becomes a source of fascination in itself—partly because romantic beliefs in superhuman beings persist, and partly because modernist audiences hope to

"Let's run through this once more—and, remember, you choke up at Paragraph Three and brush away the tear at Paragraph Five."

Drawing by D. Reilly; © 1988 The New Yorker Magazine, Inc.

learn from the information how to achieve success for themselves. The media's efforts to "make the candidate known" are of special significance, for these efforts are influenced very strongly by the communication patterns of the aspiring leader. The aspirant typically adopts two postures toward the media. The positive presentation is designed to glorify and authenticate the individual's status as true leader. (War record, voting record, previous experience, heroic feats, self-sacrifice, and previous victories all serve in this capacity.) Information suppression removes from view any information suggesting flaws of character or odd habits. As we have seen, it is typical for the aspirant to adopt this posture—often by default—as all signs of an "unusual life-style" are laundered with care. The public performance is not personal.

This transformation of persons into spectacles threatens the very concept of the substantial or true self. If all that was substance in the romantic and modernist eras becomes style, then persons of substance cease to be believable. When "my personal opinion" is polished for public consumption, then it ceases to be personal; and if all is stylized there is nothing left over to count as "personal." The very category ceases to be meaningful. During George Bush's presidential campaign, *Newsweek* reported that, "While committed to the identical political end of making the president look good, the Bush media machine projects a less manipulative, less cynical, and ultimately more honest image than the Reagan stagecraft."[5] But if manipulation, cynicism, and honesty are constructions of the media, how is one to know what the candidate "truly" is? And if we cannot get behind the appearance, then the very idea of "truly" becomes superfluous. The literary critic Frederic Jameson suspects that precisely this outcome will occur in the arts: "The older models—Picasso, Proust, T. S. Eliot—do not work any more (or are possibly harmful), since nobody has that kind of unique private world and style to express any longer."[6] From the postmodern standpoint, the view of the unique, private world never did "work," in the sense of furnishing a legitimate portrait of the person. Rather, all claims to the kinds of personal qualities necessary for commanding leadership are largely exercises in rhetoric.

At the same time leaders are hollowed by their performances, the media are placed in a position of special significance. If they are to say anything "newsworthy," they must produce information that is outside the candidate's control—information that is either negative or hidden, information that will restore humanity to the aspirant. Yet it is precisely this kind of information that inauthenticates the aspirant's claim to "true leadership." What is more newsworthy than information contradicting the public image, or demonstrating at last that the "hero" is, after all, "just like us," or worse? Joyce Carol Oates has coined the term "pathography" to characterize the tendency to focus on the flaws, misdeeds, and short-comings of those in the public eye. The technologies responsible for social saturation enable the media to conduct their exposés with efficacy and dispatch. Information about virtually all aspects of the individual's life—from birth to the present—can be rapidly found. Friends, lovers, enemies, teachers, neighbors, secretaries—all are typically within phoning distance. Computerized records of school transcripts, bank statements, tax reports, traffic violations, criminal charges, and even video rental records all add to the efficacy of undermining. Photographs, letters, publications, tape cassettes, video recordings, all add "factual substance." The possibility of meteoric descent becomes ever-present, and thus the spiraling from view (at least temporarily) of Richard Nixon, Gary Hart, Michael Deaver, Jim and Tammy Bakker, Bess Myerson, Jim Wright, Pete Rose, Andreas Papandreou, Ben Johnson, Sosuke Uno, and Leona Helmsley.[7]

A thought experiment: Would the world be different today if Charles de Gaulle had faced a public that believed he didn't write a word he spoke, that all his views were controlled by a committee of advisers, that his clothing was selected by a costume designer and his manner of speaking by a language coach, that his university grades in economics were poor, that he disdained the common folk, that his alcohol consumption was inordinate, and that he had engaged in unusual sexual practices with prostitutes? If a de Gaulle were to surface today, such beliefs would form the hurdles he might face.

The Return to Inner Resources

Gone is the old legalistic sense of guilt and of cheated ideals when we tailor our ethical cloth to fit the back of each occasion.
—Joseph Fletcher, *Situation Ethics*

If new leadership is unlikely to galvanize resistance against dissolving traditions, a second resource is available: we ourselves, with our traditional sense of values and beliefs, and our innate capacity for sound reason. We sense the loss of valued traditions, and this very consciousness can serve as the impetus for cultural restoration. We must get back to basics, it is said, and the basics lie within our own character. We enter the present with a sack of history slung over our shoulders, and this weight shapes our posture. Each reader of this book, for example, brings a host of preferences, interests, and values that shape the way it is understood and accepted.

How powerful these personal resistances are, in the face of enormous alterations in the technological ethos, is difficult to gauge. It is clear that we are not speaking of absolute resistance. The question is not whether personal resources can sustain traditions forever, but rather how long and in which circumstances. At this point, the force of social saturation becomes keenly apparent. As the technologies of social saturation improve, we are also exposed to a multiplicity of voices. And when we learn that a deeply felt value is repudiated by the younger generation as "conservative and old-fashioned," condemned by those across town as "class bias," and excoriated by foreigners as "narrowly parochial"—where the search for an ultimate foundation leaves us finally with the apology, "I simply trepivalue it because I value it"—certainty of commitment becomes suspicious. When we profess love knowing that it might be sexual energy, codependency, a strategic ploy, or a ritual saying, it becomes difficult to use "love" as a standard for life decisions. And if what is obviously a "criminal act" in our own eyes is found by experts to be "a manifestation of unconscious forces," "a justifiable response to economic repression," or "commonly accepted behavior within that community," it becomes difficult to trust one's senses at all.

What of our capacity to reason, to sift the evidence, the competing perspectives, the probabilities, and to determine on a logical basis the soundest course of action? Does reason not enable us to hold fast to valued traditions and to steer a favorable course into the future? Again one faces the impending influences of social saturation. The national economic forecast takes a plunge, and the stock analyst makes a reasonable argument for selling; however, the press secretary convincingly demonstrates that the same plunge is a good sign for inflation and interest rates; a university economist reasons equally persuasively that the fluctuation is random variance. Reason "in general" leads only to chaos; only reasoning within a particular perspective lends itself to clarity. But whose perspective? Surely there are again several perspectives, each with its own compelling form of reason. One faces an infinite regress of reasons, each searching for its rationale.

Previous chapters have tried to show how such pluralism undermines the concept of truth, creates a consciousness of self-construction, and kindles doubt in any form of "internal essences" or resources. Can the Western tradition defend against such influences? On what inner resources can modernists and romanticists rely to steer clear of the shoals of uncertainty—including the incipient doubt in the very concept of inner resources? The critical difficulty in mounting a counteroffensive is that the two romanticist and modernist traditions are incapable of sustaining a defense, primarily because they are engaged in a mutual struggle that leaves both rhetorically impotent.

Romanticism both honored and rendered powerful a language of "ought." Values, moral sentiments, and a lifetime commitment to ideals sprang from the deep interior. They were "inalienable" because they were part of human nature itself, and the veil between human nature and divinity was thin. They were so self-evident that in 1903, G. E. Moore's *Principia Ethica* could declare "the good" to be an essential element of human makeup, directly available to intuition. Moral values were not ineffable hypotheticals, but palpable realities.

However, as modernism gained ascendancy, the language of "ought" was eviscerated. The modernist depended on reason and observation; moral values and sentiments had no rational justification; they were relativistic and "unreasonable" emotions. Belief in reason and observation granted both honor and credibility to the language of "is"; questions of "ought" were unanswerable and thus uninteresting. Observation was to furnish the senses with knowledge about what is the case; principles of logical reasoning would then lead to clear and ineluctable conclusions and even predictions. If the geological formation of a land mass is related to the frequency of earthquakes, and this knowledge enables us to predict future disasters, it matters not a whit whether you believe people "ought not" to suffer earthquakes. For the modernist, words that do not refer to real-world observables are obfuscating. Allowed free rein, sentiments or values would interfere with the processes of reason and observation.[8] Unleashed emotions are the enemy of species survival. Romanticism and modernism are thus set against each other, so that any thrust toward commitment to the one wars against the doubts generated by the other.

One may see the upheavals of the 1960s and 1970s as a renaissance of romanticism. As issues such as civil rights, atomic energy, the Vietnam war, feminism, gay rights, and freedom from oppression came to the fore, modernism seemed more and more morally vacuous. The sciences could build increasingly effective bombs, but were mute about whether they were to be dropped, and on whom. Governments could take miraculous strides in information processing, but the skills that improved technology were inapplicable to questions of oppression and surveillance. Scientific acumen could catapult a nation to power, but seemed irrelevant to the questions of domination and subjugation. There were no means by which the language of "is" could establish the grounds for "ought."

Yet once the roar of activist romanticism began to subside, the fatal question was posed. If moral values are necessary, how is one to choose

I KNOW WHAT YOU MEAN, MY DAUGHTER DOESN'T KNOW WHETHER TO GET MARRIED OR LIVE ALONE OR JUST MOVE IN WITH SOMEBODY OR TO QUIT SMOKING, EXCEPT FOR MARIJUANA, OR TO BECOME TOTALLY DRUG FREE. OR TO QUIT DRINKING ALTOGETHER OR TO HAVE A CHILD OR TO ADOPT OR JUST TO IGNORE SEX OR BECOME CELIBATE AND TAKE MORE SEDATIVES OR . . .

P. C. Vey

which values and what good? The romanticist of the nineteenth century did not need to ask this question. By and large the answers were self-evident. Once bitten by the gadfly of modernism, however, one can scarcely avoid scratching. Decisions on matters of values had to be reached on a *rational* basis. But alas, to invoke reason in search of value is once again to enter the labyrinth of modernism—the discourse of "is." And because logic itself is morally antiseptic, no viable solution to the dilemma of "ought" is forthcoming. In matters of inner resources, romanticism and modernism thus struggle to a standstill. Romanticism furnishes value without rationale; modernism provides logic without direction.

It is precisely this dilemma that makes Allan Bloom's best-seller *The Closing of the American Mind* so rousingly effective in its criticism, yet so frustratingly ineffectual in its response.[9] On the one side Bloom lends eloquence to modernist misgivings over the romanticist rebellion of the 1960s and 1970s. He decries campus agitators—blacks, left-wing radicals, feminists—for their injurious effects on higher education. He condemns the rampant egalitarianism that swept student culture because it denies the possibility that some positions are "true" and rationally "superior." He despises the moral indignation of these movements because, he says, "Indignation may be a most noble passion and necessary for fighting wars and righting wrongs. But of all the experiences of the soul, it is the most inimical to reason." Yet what case is then to be made for reason? How is it to be restored to its rightful place on the dais? Bloom's pace now falters, because he finds that when reason is turned free in the academy it goes despairingly astray. Thus Bloom laments the way scholars have questioned the rights established in the Declaration of Independence, the superiority of American principles, the sexism pervading the "great books" of the Western tradition, and the teachings of the Bible. For Bloom these are deplorable lines of argument. Yet one asks, Why is it that he is now chastising the exercise of reasoning powers? The answer lies in Bloom's commitment to values, the very resource that he found so debilitating in his initial thesis. In effect, it is the romanticist language of "ought" that inspires Bloom's lament: the natural rights of man, the moral presumptions of the Bible, the deep truths of the soul. Yet it is exactly the romanticist language of value that Bloom believes to be sapping the powers of higher education. Reason and value succeed in undoing each other. And undone, they are unable to resist the force of postmodern pluralism.

The Cementing of Community

This is a society in which the individual can only rarely and with difficulty understand himself and his activities as interrelated in morally meaningful ways with those of other, different Americans.
—Robert Bellah, *Habits of the Heart*

Not all modernists have wished to abandon concern with moral claims. Perhaps inspired by the romanticist renaissance of the 1960s, some sectors of the academy tried to build new moral foundations. These foundations were not to be built on the "emotivism" of the previous century, however, but on firm logic and good reasons. While intellectually exciting, such ventures have not elicited broad assent. In his celebrated volume *After Virtue*, Alasdair MacIntyre makes a strong case against attempts to rest moral claims on a rational basis.[10] Virtually echoing the pluralistic theme of postmodernism, MacIntyre points to the "interminable and unsettled character of so much contemporary moral debate [that] arises from the variety of heterogeneous and incommensurable concepts which inform the major premises from which the protagonists in such debates argue." MacIntyre's solution to the problem of "ought" is a return to the traditional communities from which judgments of good and evil spring organically from relations of interdependence. Moral commitment, MacIntyre proposes, is embedded in a "living tradition . . . an historically extended, socially embedded argument . . . of which the individual's life is a part."

Following MacIntyre, if strong leadership and inner resources are less and less able to sustain valued traditions, is there not reason to place hope in communities? Communities are more fundamental than either strong public leadership or private inner resources; indeed, without community there is neither leadership nor individual resources. Without the willing complicity of communities, leaders cannot lead; and one's inner values remain firm primarily because the community supports them. So is it not possible that communities of the like-minded could develop firm resistance to the relativisms of postmodern life? And isn't there good evidence of popular resistance in the various moral and conservative revitalization movements of recent years—in the Moral Majority, the Praise the Lord (PTL) Club, LePen's supporters in France, the rise of the Republican party in Germany, and the pro-life movement? Aren't these groups successfully bonding in the service of traditional values and beliefs?

Again the question is not whether communities of mutually supportive individuals can sustain a given tradition. Surely the endurance of most values and social patterns depends importantly on communal consensus. The small, face-to-face community, where coherence and consistency are staples of everyday life, galvanizes its members against extraneous and corrosive influences. We again find, however, that in spite of numerous pockets of effective resistance, technological drift does not favor strong and enduring communities of the traditional variety. In his *Nation of Strangers*, Vance Packard described how transportation technologies lend themselves to a high rate of social mobility—to families in continuous motion, moving from one environment or job setting to another.[11] A neighbor recently told me, "I lived in ten different homes before I was in my teens and went to six different schools."

More generally, the technology of social saturation works toward the dissolution of homogeneous, face-to-face communities, and toward the creation of a polymorphous perversity in social pattern. Both the character and the potentials of the community are transformed in substantial ways. Let us consider three separate but overlapping forms of emerging community, each of which diminishes people's capacity to sustain a given conception of reality and related standards of comportment.[12]

Perhaps the most common form of deterioration may be characterized as the *collage community*, a community in which homogeneity in life patterns gives way to a multiplicity of disjunctive modes of living. Collage communities are hardly a new addition to the landscape; they emerge wherever people migrate across the land. But their growth is hastened by all the modes of social saturation. And where they could once be singled out for their relative infrequency, they now tend to escape notice by virtue of their prevalence. Transportation systems can move households across continents on short notice; communication systems enable companies to spread across continents; broadly scattered social relationships allow people to seek employment in numerous locations; the potential for ersatz identity readies the individual for a multiplicity of career considerations. As mobility becomes increasingly easy, communities are set in perpetual motion. Statistics indicate that the average residence in most urban dwellings is less than four years.[13] As Bennis and Slater have said, "Nothing could be more revolutionary than a road."[14]

Central Florida is exemplary of the new wave of collage communities. A half-century ago the area was relatively homogeneous; traditional values and social patterns held. However, the Cape Canaveral installation brought with it new elements—government workers, scientists, and military personnel—and at the same time, businesses wishing to reduce operating costs found the climate favorable. Large companies such as Harcourt Brace Jovanovich imported a new culture of monied executives. Simultaneously, as the nation's elderly population grew in size, the southern warmth beckoned and the area became a center for retirement housing. Another cultural lamination was added. With the building of amusement centers, most notably Disney World, an army of young, educated employees arrived. And all this is to say nothing of the millions of tourists who are now a constant presence across central Florida. Relative homogeneity has given way to a mélange of disparate and often contradictory ways of life.[15]

In this and other collage communities, each group tends to exist within its own reality, sharing reasons, values, and customs. Yet to maintain their distinct traditions, members of each group must pick their way carefully through the streets, the institutions, the recreational locations of the collage community. Cross-group acquaintanceships and romances

must be discouraged, schools and places of worship separated, and political parties differentiated. Although major segments of the population
attempt to live behind these invisible walls, the divisions are inefficient
and hard to maintain. When the voice of "the other" continuously insinuates itself into one's radio, television, newspaper, magazines, novels,
films, and telephone receivers; when schools and churches strive to integrate the disparate forces; and when technology unites large numbers

of enthusiasts for rock concerts, professional sports events, political rallies, and so on, the enclaves are under threat. Everywhere the representations of the other are with us, searching to make themselves intelligible. And as the intelligibility is incorporated into our own, we are moved to reflect on the validity and superiority of our modes of life. As the strange views, values, and ways of life slowly become familiar, one's own traditional commitments gradually turn strange.

The second form of communal deterioration is represented in the *cardboard community*, a community in which all the trappings of face-to-face interdependence are maintained, but the participating bodies are absent. There are shopping areas, churches, community centers, and a fire department, but the houses and apartments are largely empty. Again, cardboard communities are not wholly new; commuting became a popular way of life as the technologies of rail and road were improved in the present century, removing much of the male population from the daily functioning of the face-to-face community. Rapid and low-cost transportation facilities have also expanded the population at vacation or weekend resort areas. From Maine to the Bahamas, from northern Minnesota to southern California, landscapes have changed dramatically to accommodate the vast numbers desiring vacation sites or retreats from their otherwise fractured lives. Local citizens in coastal communities of Spain, hill towns of France, and mountain villages of Switzerland are outnumbered by largely absentee landowners.

Within recent years, the cardboarding process has accelerated manifold. In particular, advances in low-cost air travel, long-distance phones, and electronic communication make it possible to work far from home, to work in several geographically distributed locations, or even to remain in continuous motion. For example, Karen and Karl, a young couple from Luxembourg, live together on weekends. During the week, however, Karen is a traveling consultant who receives instructions from an office in London; Karl travels in Scandinavia for a company in Frankfurt. Karen must also travel periodically to the United States for work with the home office of her company, run by a president whose directives typically emanate from the stern of a shark-fishing trawler in the Pacific. Everyone is somewhere else.

Finally, the deterioration of the traditional community is hastened by the emergence of *symbolic community*. Symbolic communities are linked primarily by the capacity of their members for symbolic exchange—of words, images, information—mostly through electronic means.[16] Physical immediacy and geographic closeness disappear as criteria of community. When loving support is squeezed from telephonic impulses, fascination is fired by "on-line" computer mates, ecstasy is procured for the price of an air ticket, and continuous entertainment is generated by the mere flick of a TV remote, who needs the tedious responsibility of a next-door neighbor? Most dramatic are those people who believe themselves to be part of a large, caring, and like-minded community whose members they scarcely know. Sports fans are but one example. It is said that the largest single public demonstration in the history of the Netherlands—eclipsing even the end of the Second World War—took place at the return of the country's World Cup–winning soccer club. Then there are electronic churches, religious communities whose primary interactions are carried out through the media (television, radio, and telephone). Faithful audiences of 10 to 20 million have been estimated for such programs as "Praise the Lord Club," "Old Time Gospel Hour," and "Hour of Prayer." The Christian Broadcasting Network (sponsor of the popular 700 Club) offers a full array of Christian entertainment, provides telephone counseling, and is backed up by a computerized direct-mail and fundraising operation.[17] Yet except for occasional attendance at the televised service retreat, there is virtually no face-to-face interaction among the membership.

In this context, it may be said that the technologies of social saturation actually contribute to the kind of social interdependence we call community. They enable new communities to form wherever communication links can be made—among truckers on CB radios, businessmen on electronic mail, hackers with home modems, and so on. New potentials for interdependence are a significant by-product of the socially saturated world.[18] At the same time, however, with each new potential for symbolic connection, the traditional face-to-face community loses its coherence and its significance in the life of its participants. For the participants are no longer possessions of the local community alone; their hopes, allegiances, and resources are propelled outward through the ether. Their sense of "belonging" is no longer only, or even primarily, rooted in the local soil. An acquaintance described communal history in a middle-class suburb of Minneapolis: "In the 1930s we were very close to our neighbors. Each house on the block had a front porch, and on summer evenings everyone would sit out, chatting across the yards, visiting for the evening on each other's porches. We didn't go away very often; gas was expensive and there weren't so many places to go. When radio became popular, we didn't sit out quite so much. Often our family would all go in and listen together to our radio. When TV came along things really got worse. We didn't see our neighbors so much; hardly ever did we spend a whole evening together. Things were more interesting inside. Then cars became cheaper to run, and you could even drive down to the Wisconsin Dells for the weekend. I go back to the neighborhood now, and there are mostly new people in those houses. From what they say, they don't even know the neighbors next door."

So in the end, what is to be said of the traditional community as a means of solidifying resistance against postmodern intrusions? As we find, communities are becoming increasingly less able to serve such a function. To do so, they would require the homogeneity of beliefs and the repetitive, face-to-face reinforcement that all the major technologies of the century are in the process of undermining. Indeed, the economic well-being of many traditional communities depends not only on this very technology, but on increasing its efficacy and proliferation. When the workers at Boeing or Rolls-Royce build a swifter airliner, when colleagues at Ford or Mercedes produce a more durable car, and when the neighbors of Silicon Valley invent new software, they are all contributing to the technology of social saturation. In effect, they hasten the breakup of whatever aspects of the traditional community still remain.

THE HALF-LIFE OF SINCERITY

KILROY: *Would you believe I am sincere . . . ?*
ESMERALDA: *I would believe that you believe that you are . . . For a while . . .*
KILROY: *Everything's for a while. For a while is the stuff that dreams are made of . . .* —Tennessee Williams, *Camino Real*

As we find, the technologies of social saturation weaken the capacity of leadership, personality, and community to sustain or rejuvenate the culture's tradition. Yet there is an additional tale to be told, one more subtle in its contours, but one relevant to any social encounter in which commitment is desired—whether among family members and friends or between government and the people. The concern here is with sincerity. Any successful attempt at cultural retrenchment must be suffused with a sense of sincerity. One must feel sincere in one's own commitments; otherwise there is little reason for sustaining them. By the same token, if others attempt to bolster our sagging beliefs, we demand they be sincere in doing so. If they are simply "having us on" for reasons of their own, we are scarcely compelled. To sustain the traditions in the face of corrosive influences thus demands that we perceive to be sincere both ourselves and those who support or lead us in the endeavor. Yet subtle forces at work not only reduce the generalized sense of sincerity, but even public trust in the concept itself.

The centrality of sincerity to social life can be most immediately traced to modernist assumptions of the self. As the seat of human action moved from the deep interior of romanticist days to the more conscious level of reason and observation, it became increasingly possible to speak of persons as knowable—by themselves or by others. For the modernist, that which was truly significant about a person—the essence of the self—lay slightly behind the eyeballs, reflecting the world and directing action. Intimacy was achieved not so much through a fathoming of souls as through an exchange of thoughts, beliefs, aspirations, and the like. Self-knowledge did not require a tortuous journey into an exotic interior region, but simply meant that one gained clarity about values, beliefs, or intentions. Thus where Freud, as a romantic, viewed self-knowledge as an arduous challenge, only possible with the aid of a skilled interpreter of the unconscious, his more modernist disciple Karen Horney proposed that people could undertake their own analysis. To the modernist, sincerity appeared both easy to achieve and essential to human relationships. To "speak your mind," "get it off your chest," or "tell it like it is" posed no special problem of fathoming the layers of the interior. One could, and should, be open and honest. Failing to reveal one's "true self" could lead to charges of insincerity: fakery, pretense, flattery, hypocrisy, dissimulation, affectation, theatricality, and so on. To "be sincere" was thus to define the reality of one's interior.

Yet as a critical component of social life, sincerity may be a dying swan. In part its demise was already prepared by the modernist context in which it flourished. While modernism placed a strong value on sincerity, it also contained elements that worked against sincerity's attainment. In the modernist period, the dominant image of the human was the machine (chapter 2). And if we are essentially machinelike, the strong inclination is to ask into the *function* of our actions—how do they operate, how efficient are they, what do they accomplish? Under modernist influences, such questions have now come to play a major role in society. Cost-benefit analyses are not confined simply to the world of business or government; it is wise, according to modernist wisdom, to assay all our actions in these terms. "What will I get from this relationship?" "what will this book do for me?" and "what is this favor going to cost me?" are the kind of questions that any sensible modernist should ask.[19] Yet to the extent that we ask ourselves what we gain and lose by our actions, what their functional value is, sincerity is in jeopardy.[20] Once viewed as an immediate and spontaneous expression of being, human action is now transformed into *instrumental* action—not a legitimate expression of self *sui generis*, but a means to some other end. Adults attending the funeral of a relative often become aware of the problem: considerations of inheritance creep into consciousness, disrupting the sense of sincere grief. Similarly, as one asks about the personal gains and losses of religious, political, or ethical participation, such commitments are redefined. By asking about the function of one's behavior ("What do I get from this?"), the actions are no longer defined as sincere expressions of self; the very question reconceptualizes them as a means to some other end. If my expressions of environmental concern are born of my concern in itself, I will sense their sincerity; if I believe they are means of soliciting your support for a political movement, their sincerity as self-expressions is undermined. What I am "truly" doing is attempting to secure your support. As modernism invites questions of instrumentality, it robs our actions of their face validity.

Under postmodern influences, the erosion of sincerity is taken to the limit. One comes to doubt the modernist assumption of a rational wellspring of action located in the brain, which authors our words, remembers, deceives, makes ethical decisions, and for present purposes, reflects or reports on its states of mind. Under postmodernism, suspicion attends such concepts as "true expressions" of self. If one is multiply populated, harboring myriad voices from culture and history, there is no expression that stands as the true. And for the postmodern, words do not "reflect" or "picture" states of mind. Words are not mirrors or pictures but integral parts of ongoing interchange. They construct the individual as this or that within continuous patterns of relationship. One may profess, "I am sincere," but such an expression is not so much a reflection of a mental state as a state of relatedness.

At this juncture I wish to place in focus several specific ways in which sincerity is undermined as a living reality. Each is derived from the technologies of saturation. These technologies, importantly responsible for the postmodern shift, also generate patterns of connection that significantly delimit or destroy the sense of sincerity. While the technology facilitates the growth of social movements in general, the technology is simultaneously set against their survival. As we shall see, concerted attempts at moral or political retrenchment may shorten the life of sincerity within the movements' ranks. Ironically, such attempts sow the seeds of their own demise.

FRACTIONATION AND COMPENSATION

One opens the circle a crack, opens it all the way, lets someone in, calls someone, or else goes out oneself, launches forth. . . . One launches forth, hazards an improvisation. But to improvise is to join with the World, to meld with it.

—Gilles Deleuze and Felix Guattari, A *Thousand Plateaus*

As we have seen, the technologies of social saturation lend themselves to a multiphrenic splitting of the individual into myriad, fractional relationships. Attempts to proceed effectively in such a complex world infect the modernist with an unsettling sense of manipulativeness. One may recoil against this condition, wishing to "simplify," "get back to roots," or focus on the "truly meaningful." One may wish to locate modes of sincere commitment, purposes and patterns that are deeply expressive of self. Once the process of saturation goes into high gear, however, such modes are discouraged. The process that generates the longing impedes its fulfillment.

How is one to determine if one is sincere in a given endeavor? One cannot simply "look inward" and know; what would one be looking at, what would sincerity look like, and how could one be sure the mind wasn't playing tricks? One is more likely to assess one's actions: "If I devote this many hours to the cause, I must be sincere" or "I wouldn't go to this much trouble if I weren't sincere."[21] Yet as the social world is increasingly saturated, each form of relationship demands its demonstration of allegiance. Thus each assessment of sincerity is made against a backdrop of multiple, competing alternatives. Each alternative that cries for attention will thereby drain the focal investment of seeming significance. Each comparison will inform one of the limits to his or her sincerity of commitment. Consider the lawyer in Wilton, Connecticut, who strongly desires to participate in a pro-choice demonstration in Washington, D.C.; she feels her commitment is sincere and her participation important. She can free herself from her caseload, but her son has an important soccer game that day in a nearby town. Her sister from Minneapolis will also be in New York City that week and wants her to come down. The evening before, an attractive attorney visiting from Britain unexpectedly asks her for a date the night of the demonstration. And this is to say nothing of the needs of her ailing father, who recently moved to the area, and her closest friend, who is in a deep depression over her divorce and needs her support. All represent significant investments, and when she decides she cannot attend, the importance of the cause is diminished and her sense of dedication thrown into question.

The problem is intensified in cases where one is a member of a face-to-face group of the committed. One's sincerity is then subject to evaluation by others: "Is she *really* one of us, or only a pretender?" When one's investments are multiple, the risk of being "found out" is always at hand: "just a bourgeois liberal," "a dilettante," "a Sunday Christian," "a dabbler." One is forced by suspicion to secrecy and compensatory action, hiding the alternative investments and making one's commitment especially strong. I am reminded here of an assistant professor who was strug-

gling to prove herself a serious intellectual in a male-dominated department of philosophy. However, she was also passionate about disco dancing. She feared that if her avocation were revealed to her colleagues, her
commitment to the realm of ideas would surely be discredited. Thus, late
at night, when all her worthy colleagues were in bed or buried in their
books, she would sneak off to the clubs in nearby towns and dance until
morning. Her problem mirrored many cases where one is supposed to
demonstrate commitment to transcendent values. The committed don't
disco—nor should they have a yen for stylish clothes, sexual adventures,
holiday cruises, Broadway musicals, gambling casinos, or cheap romance
novels. To display alternative investments is to become suspect in the
eyes of one's comrades, and thus to oneself.

With threats to sincerity pervasive, one is invited to intensify the level
of commitment. One must compensate for all the alternative investments
by demonstrating either how little they mean, or how central the cause
is to one's life. The "Christmas newsletter" is illustrative. One's closest
friends deserve a personal communication at this season of the year, one
that places them in a special position, above the crowd. Because one tends
to have so many "closest" friends, the Christmas letter is printed for broad
dissemination. Yet the very fact of its mass production destroys the value
of the communiqué as a symbol of sincere friendship. More broadly, the
enormous growth in the greeting-card industry owes some debt to this
search for sincerity. The multiplication of relations resulting from social
saturation demands some mass-produced means of declaring commitment. Yet the very impersonality of such cards undermines the attempt
to express significance and sincerity through this means. The buyer attempts to compensate by seeking better-than-average cards, or cards with
more personalized messages. Thus a market opens for specialty cards—
limited edition, or larger, or with more elegant or interesting designs,
and a higher price tag. As upscale cards become commonplace, newer
markets develop—cards with original artwork or hand-painted fabric.
(One recent visit to a card shop revealed a four-foot-tall birthday-card
figure designed to sit on the recipient's table.) Yet as the search for
sincerity spirals, the search loses its vitality. Trying to prove one's love
in the face of another's doubt is no longer loving in itself; rather it is a
tendering of proof. In the same way, *trying* to be sincere robs sincerity
of itself. If one must try, one is not doing it. And thus, as one seeks to
compensate against doubt, the sincerity of one's initial commitment is
obscured.

FROM PASSION TO PERFORMANCE

I've died so often, made love so much, I've lost touch of what's real.
  —From Alex Smith's cinematic silkscreen, *The Twentieth Century*

The civil-rights movement, SDS, the Yippies, the Weathermen, the Black Panthers, the Ashram at Puna, Crusaders for Christ, est training, Transcendental Meditation—such movements have filled the pages of cultural history over the past thirty years. All commanded enormous enthusiasm among their followings, but little more than memories remain. Why did interests wane and the movements dissolve? There are, of course, special stories to be told in each case, stories of internal strife, financial mismanagement, failings in leadership, outside competition, and the like. However, there is also a constant across these and other cases of evanescent movements. It is the presence of the technologies of social saturation: television and radio in particular, but also the modes of transportation that bring potential converts, audiences of onlookers, and potential expositors to the scene. These technologies lend enormous rhetorical power to such movements, and can swell their ranks manifold. (Indeed, terrorist movements depend for their very existence on media coverage. Isolated atrocities are of practically no political consequence; it is news about them that influences people and policy.) However, the very power furnished to the movements by the media simultaneously serves to undermine the sense of sincerity for their participants.

For participants in a movement, an audience, and particularly an audience on whose reactions may hinge the fate of the movement, transforms the purpose and definition of action. To sense that one's actions result from a belief, or an ideal held focally or passionately in mind, is to act sincerely. The belief is felt to be revealed immediately in action; the action is a transparent expression of self. However, to introduce an audience—whose numbers sometimes approach the millions—brings a host of new factors to the fore. One is inclined to ask, "How will our actions be perceived? Will they be persuasive? Will they be related in a positive way to others? Will the audience understand what is to be done?" And such broad concerns are eventually reproduced as questions of specific technique: "How are we to phrase our case? Who would be the most persuasive spokesperson? Should we add music? Should we alert the press? Would police violence increase or decrease public support?" Consideration of such questions yields a rational policy, and this policy is subsequently placed into action. Yet at this point the action is transformed. No longer is it a transparent reflection of a belief or ideal. Down to matters of facial expression and bodily posture, it is now a calculated, public performance—an attempt to *appear* sincere rather than sincerity itself. Or, in terms of the preceding discussion, it is now a *means* to an end rather than an end in itself. One is left only with the hope that beneath such actions still lie remnants of the grounding belief. If there is money or power to be acquired through such performances, these remnants may be lost entirely from view.

This loss of authenticity engendered by the creation of audience is not limited to the domain of social movements. The mass media must generate novelty in order to survive. Without the strange, the new, or the unknown, audiences would shrink substantially. An enormous demand is thus placed on the media to expose that which is otherwise hidden or little known. Very often this has meant ransacking the culture for pockets of subcultural variation. Life among the Cajuns, inner-city blacks, cabdrivers, Chinese-Americans, residents of Marin County, and so on all become subjects for media interest—serving both as the background for various dramas and as topics in themselves. Yet as those depicted by the media are exposed to these self-representations, their actions undergo a subtle change. That which was simply done unself-consciously for itself now becomes a matter of conscious concern. "How am I impressing others? What are they thinking of me now? Will this strengthen or weaken their stereotypes?" These questions insinuate themselves into daily life. That which was "simply me" is now co-opted by the cultural dramas created by the media; one becomes an actor in spite of oneself, and the culture slowly becomes a sham copy of itself.

This co-option of the subcultures is most severe in cases where media exposure may lead to economic gain. For such exposure often brings tourism, and without the continued evidence of difference, the tourist will be unsatisfied and the money unspent. Thus where the bonnets in the Dutch island of Marken, the beards and black hats in Pennsylvania Dutch country, and the kilts in Edinburgh were once unnoticed aspects of daily life, they are now essential to the economic well-being of the communities. No longer can they be considered authentic signatures of inner being for the wearer; they are now "costumes" within the dramas of local history. And without them the play ceases to go on. With the explosion in world tourism, much the same erosion in sincerity is now taking place in areas once remote from Western curiosity. As Westerners pay for the satisfaction of their curiosity, they turn convention into contrivance. When visiting in northern Thailand, I once asked for a guide to a village off the tourist track. The costumes worn in this village indeed proved worth the trip. When the villagers later put on a little sale of local artifacts for my benefit, however, the romance slowly turned leaden. The costumes were no longer possessions of the indigenous population; they were not unwitting expressions of self but commercial cunning.

MOVEMENTS AND METAPHORS

Even for stay-at-home [Britons], the American dream can be instantly assembled complete with baseball on TV, American six-packs, popcorn and "57 flavor" ice cream. There is apparently no Briton too incongruous or misshapen to sport a T-shirt proclaiming allegiance to Harvard, Yale or the Miami Dolphins. —Philip Norman, *Faking the Present*

There is an important sense in which each of us is a metaphor for those with whom we come in contact. They provide the images of what it is to be an authentic person, and as we incorporate others' modes of being— their mannerisms, their styles—we become their surrogates, metaphors of their reality. As we live long and comfortably within these metaphors, they turn literal; they take on the appearance of solidity, and seem sincere reflections of the truth within themselves. Indeed, the literal is simply metaphor grown complacent. In this light we can usefully draw contrasts between the attempts at committed action occurring in the traditional, face-to-face community and those typical of the broad movements of today. In the traditional context, the transition from metaphor to literal was more easily accomplished. With a restricted range of others from whom to draw, and a delimited set of opportunities within which to act, one could rapidly determine the metaphors of self and use them reliably and frequently. And with a restricted range of others consistently treating one's presen tation as literal, one could more easily concur. The sense of sincerity was achieved with facility. To "be saved" at the local Baptist church, for example, was virtually a natural act; the repeated actions of family, friends, and neighbors prepared one for it long in advance. One's "love of Christ" was a literal dimension of being.

Social saturation, by contrast, strews the route to a literal self with impediments. There are now teeming images from which to draw, often fleeting in duration, and the options for action are enormous. The audience for such actions is also complex; what plays with ease in one context may seem superficial in another. In effect, one's metaphors remain on the wing, and their constant hovering, soaring, and flapping encumbers one's stride toward the literal. At present the technologies saturate us with images of commitment—from Soweto to Tiananmen Square, Delhi to Prague. We see them overturn cars in Caracas, cover faces with handkerchiefs in Japan, fast in Ireland, and so on. Committed-isms whirl by as images in a vast social drama. Their semifictional character is signaled by their placement between prime-time drama and late-night comedy.[22] Within socially saturated society, committed activity does not grow congenially from the soil of well-worn local traditions, but from the accumulated hyperreality of the media. In this way, demonstrations in various parts of the world come to resemble each other. Black spirituals of protest are sung by white, upper-middle-class demonstrators; the Chinese in Tiananmen Square wear hippie headbands and bear a statue resembling the Statue of Liberty; candle-carrying anti-KGB demonstrators in Moscow are virtually indistinguishable from Take Back the Night demonstrators in American cities. And as one acquires the trappings of the form, one's actions lose the sense of spontaneity and sincerity. One's actions become a metaphor for the myriad exposures that have gone before, a continuation of the grand and glorious game, more like performances of commitment than commitment itself.

The effects of the media on sensed sincerity do not end here. As the images of commitment are made known to vaster audiences, they come to serve as icons from which other metaphors are derived. And as they are used in varying and multiple contexts, their significance is altered and destroyed. The raised fist, symbol of black power, is adapted and readapted so that years and contexts later Boris Becker can use it as a signal of his domination at Wimbledon. Blue jeans, signals of antimaterialist protest, are slowly transformed into designer items so expensive that only a materialist can afford them. Black leather accessories with metal studs, symbols of punk disgust with bourgeois culture, are retooled and reclaimed by the bourgeois as fashion items. The symbols of retrenchment and renewal thus function as authorless texts, to be interpreted and reinterpreted across time and culture. And as such diffusion takes place so are the original causes defused.

In a similar fashion, sincerity is also bled from the common, informal modes of cultural expression. The media expose society to a massive array of self-representations. Our manners of friendship, family relationships, romance, and animosity are documented, scrutinized, rhapsodized, and satirized. We see how the lips are pursed in moments of quiet anger, the fingers move to the mouth as expressions of serious thought, and the tongue flicks backward in moments of cautious reflection. As these images are exposed increasingly to the culture, they become the standards for expression, a subtle Miss Manners for the world of informal relations. They inform the culture, for example, as to how sadness is done—its duration, its modes of expression, and its proper intensity on various occasions. Indeed, in failing to meet these commonly recognized standards, one cannot properly define oneself as "being sad"—either to others or oneself. At the same time, however, as we approximate the representations of being, being itself slips from grasp. Our actions are suffused with the sense of metaphor, and we ourselves lose the ability to differentiate between their authenticity and their artifice. Is the kiss on the cheek a "true" signal of friendship or the way friends are supposed to be greeted? Is the father's sudden burst of temper a "true" burst or simply a hackneyed male ritual? Is the lover's moan of ecstasy a "true" expression of her inner state or her cinematic history brought to life? And if it becomes increasingly difficult to distinguish between sincerity and simulation, the distinction itself ceases to be viable. As Umberto Eco has summarized it, "The postmodern attitude is that of a man who loves a very cultivated woman and knows he cannot say to her, 'I love you madly,' because he knows that she knows (and that she knows that he knows) that these words have already been written by Barbara Cartland."[23]

We find, then, that important resources for sustaining and renewing longstanding cultural traditions seem to be losing their vitality. Strong leadership is a concept dependent on a romanticist worldview, now weakened by both the modern and postmodern turns. The technologies of social saturation also act to inauthenticate the candidates for leadership. The tried-and-true inner resources of the individual cannot be relied upon, for reason and moral sensibility are both undermined in the continued strife between romanticist and modernist discourses. Nor can community solidarity be depended on, for the stable, face-to-face community on which renewal might rest is rapidly eroding. In its place the technologies of social saturation are making possible an array of fragile, symbolic communities, tied together primarily by electronic impulse. And finally, the concept of sincerity, central to any attempt at cultural refurbishment, is also slipping from view. The fractionation of relationships brings into question the sincerity of any single commitment. Existing technologies transform sincere actions into calculated performances. And because we are saturated with images of commitment, attempts at renewal turn metaphoric. We arrive at a point at which the positive potentials of postmodernism must be unfolded.

NINE

Reckoning and Relativity

We move away from romanticism and modernism, not calmly and with reflection, but desperately and under siege.
—Robert Jay Lifton, personal communication

W hat are we to conclude about our emerging condition? How are we to evaluate the gains and losses in cultural life? My own evaluations of the postmodern turn have insinuated themselves throughout this book. I have pointed to numerous ways in which our traditions of understanding and action are being eroded. At the same time, I have been indulgent in my elaboration and reticent in my criticism of postmodern influences. Can we now press beyond this ambivalence, establish an evaluative posture, and clarify issues of significance? Of particular concern is the question of the future under postmodernism. If romanticist and modernist traditions are slipping away, is there a positive case to be made for the postmodern replacement? Are there ways in which selves and relationships stand to be enriched rather than impoverished? Are there positive lines of action that may be favored by the postmodern turn?

A CENTENNIAL DAMAGE REPORT

To see ourselves as others see us can be eye-opening. To see others as sharing a nature with ourselves is the merest decency. But it is [a] far more difficult achievement [to see] ourselves amongst others, as a local example of the forms human life has locally taken, a case among cases, a world among worlds.   —Clifford Geertz, *Local Knowledge*

I began this book with two central contentions: first, that we rely heavily on psychological language in making sense of ourselves and others, and second, that this language is built into many of our patterns of relationship. In effect, we speak of thoughts, intentions, feelings, hopes, dreams, fears, desires, beliefs, and values, and without such terms we could scarcely get on in either private or institutional life. A love affair would not be a love affair without the language of the emotions; a criminal trial could scarcely proceed without the discourse of intention; and many religious institutions would erode if bereft of the concept of the soul. I then proposed that Western discourse for understanding self and others is undergoing major transformation, and that as this language is altered, so are traditional patterns of cultural life.

In this context the initial concern was with the romanticist vocabulary of the person, largely inherited from nineteenth-century arts, letters, and cultural traditions. In the romanticist period the most significant ingredients of the individual were to be located in the deep interior of the person's being. It was thus possible to speak, for example, of passion, eternal love, the communion of souls, deep inspiration, wrenching grief, will, creativity, and true genius. Such terms also encouraged a variety of significant social patterns, including committed relationships, dedication to a life purpose, granting intrinsic worth or value to others, and trust in moral insight and leadership. Although they retain a significant presence in our lives, romanticist ways of speaking and acting have been substantially undermined in the twentieth century. Not only are romanticist concepts of the person fading from use (often they are reserved for specialized rituals or ceremonies), but in many circles they are viewed with skepticism or hostility.

The demise of romanticism can largely be attributed to the emergence of the modernist worldview. Modernism brought with it a return to the vocabulary of the Enlightenment, in which reason and observation reigned as the dominant figures in the human psyche. Through reason and observation, modernists believed, humans can discover the fundamental essences of the universe—including the essentials of human functioning. With the metaphor of the machine playing a dominant role, and the social sciences expanding and fortifying the modernist perspective, the fully functioning individual was said to be knowable (through observation), predictable, and subject to training by culture. Having acquired knowledge, values, and personality, the individual was said to be self-sustaining, capable of directing his or her actions on an autonomous basis. For many, such views seemed enormously optimistic. Genuine knowledge of self and others was within our grasp; sound decisions could be made for a promising future; if people were properly socialized they would be trustworthy, honest, and sincere; and with judicious planning the society could rid itself of its problems. Societies without war, crime, mental illness, drugs, prostitution, and suicide were within grasp.

Within the modernist frame, the deep interior became increasingly suspect. To posit a reality beyond the grasp of observation and reason seemed not only unjustified but unproductive—much like presuming the hand of the Devil in moving human affairs. Not only did such assumptions render the individual unknowable, but to believe that people were moved by strong passions, or commitments beyond time and circumstance, was to cast them in an anti-Darwinian mold. If this were indeed the nature of persons, it was reasoned, the species could not survive. Processes such as intention, inspiration, and creativity also became suspect, because they removed the individual from scientific understanding. If people are material creatures after all, and all material is subject to causal laws discoverable by science, then granting people the power to step outside causal forces by virtue of creative, inspirational, or intentional acts is to deny the efficacy of science. For the modernist, such concepts are as unrealistic as magical powers.

The social saturation brought about by the technologies of the twentieth century, and the accompanying immersion in multiple perspectives, have brought about a new consciousness: postmodernist. In its retrospective stance, it is skeptical, doubting the capacity of language to represent or inform us of what is the case. For if language is dominated by ideological investments, its usage governed by social convention, and its content guided by literary style, language does not reflect or mirror reality. And if language is not truth-bearing, then the very concept of objective reporting is rendered suspect. If this is so, there are no objective grounds for saying that people possess passion, intentionality, reason, personality traits, or any of the other ingredients of the romanticist or modernist worldviews. All such concepts are socially and historically contingent, the products of political and ideological forces, self-protective communities, and literary or aesthetic fashion. With the spread of postmodern consciousness, we see the demise of personal definition, reason, authority, commitment, trust, the sense of authenticity, sincerity, belief in leadership, depth of feeling, and faith in progress. In their stead, an open slate emerges on which persons may inscribe, erase, and rewrite their identities as the ever-shifting, ever-expanding, and incoherent network of relationships invites or permits.

At this point let us clamber toward higher ground and broaden our perspective. Situated above these three perspectives and their favored patterns of action, we can make two important observations. First, we find that in the three-way conflict of discourses, each simultaneously compels and repels. Romanticist discourse is inviting in its intimations of profound mysteries of the person, love, commitment, inspiration, and the like. At the same time, modernist discourse engenders a promising sense of security and optimism with its emphasis on the rational, reliable, knowable, and improvable aspects of the person. And the newly emerging postmodern perspective opens the way to a fascinating play of potentials and an increased sense of relational reality. Yet while each language defines a range of virtues, each finds flaws in the alternatives. For the romanticist, the rationality so praised by modernists is superficial and misleading; it is blind to the profundities of the human psyche, and deprives life of meaning and people of inherent value. Postmodernism seems to the romanticist little short of nihilism: All intrinsic properties of the human being, along with moral worth and personal commitment, are lost from view, leaving nothing to believe in. Similarly, the modernist reviles the romanticist for sentimentalism, head-in-the-sand impracticality, and the replacement of objective decision making by highfalutin morality, while decrying postmodernism's threats to truth and objectivity. To give up these virtues, the modernist maintains, is to revert to medievalism, to open the culture to the tyrannies of rhetoric, to deny us the optimistic sense of progress, and to reduce life to so many parlor games. Finally, as we have seen throughout the present volume, postmodernism undermines the validity of both the romanticist and the modernist projects, demonstrating their misleading and oppressive consequences. Each discourse is thus both promising and problematic.

In addition to the fundamental incompatibility of the perspectives, there is a second important point to be made: evaluation of these discourses can only take place from within a perspective. To favor one of these perspectives because it is "objectively true" presupposes that I have a perspective in which "objectively true" is an intelligible criterion of evaluation. If in my view "objective truth" is a misleading term, I can scarcely condemn a theory because it is objectively false. If I come to these discourses as a committed Christian, I can evaluate them in terms of the place they accord personal salvation. If souls do not exist in the world as I see it, salvation will play no role in my evaluation. Thus, for the romanticist, modernists are living empty and amoral lives. But this is so only if one accepts the reality of the deep interior. If the deep interior does not exist, as is true for the modernist, then romanticist criticisms lose their bite, and seem like so much idealistic prattle. Similarly, modernists must be committed to the importance of reason and observation in order to excoriate postmoderns for their rampant relativism. Postmodern skepticism follows from much of the reasoning laid out in earlier chapters of this book; neither romanticism nor modernism possesses the conceptual tools with which to question itself.

It becomes clear that one cannot mount what might be called a "pure" or "transcendent" evaluation of our emerging condition. That is, we cannot step outside a given perspective to ask about "gains" and "losses" in our vocabularies of understanding. We cannot ask whether the loss of romanticism is good or bad, for example, without having a perspective that makes certain criteria reasonable and important. If we are *inside* the romanticist perspective we shall find the loss of "inspiration," "passion," and "creativity" abhorrent, but if *outside*, good riddance to such folklore. Similarly, the passing of modernist views of the person is neither lamentable nor laudable except by virtue of adopting a perspective. Step inside modernism, and we despair the loss of objectivity, sincerity, and autonomy; abandon modernism and the disappearance of this vocabulary can be welcomed.

How are we then to proceed in the reckoning of this final chapter? I propose that to live in any culture is to absorb its perspectives and implicit evaluations. Thus, most of us have fallen heir to romanticist ways of talking and acting, and at the same time have been well schooled in the principles and practices of modernism. Further, because of my own immersion in the culture, these perspectives have subtly guided my choice of words and phrases in such a way as to champion romanticism and, perhaps to a lesser degree, modernism. The passings of these cultural modes have been viewed as "losses," and the very word implies their worth. Similarly, a dim view has often been taken of postmodernism—its multiphrenia, irrationality, and potential for superficiality. (Again, the very choice of such terms reveals my cultural roots.) I will thus attempt in the following pages to press beyond the familiar ground of romanticism and modernism, and to enter the postmodern perspective with a positive stance. If we give postmodern discourse an opportunity to expand, to make use of the available resources of the language, are there positive outcomes for the society in terms of practices and potentials? If we momentarily step outside our traditional perspectives, and test the waters of the postmodern alternative, is there reason for encouragement? There is, after all, good reason for making the attempt. For if the preceding analysis is correct, and the technologies of social saturation lead us ineluctably toward a postmodern consciousness, it may be wise to fathom the positive potentials. As I shall try to demonstrate, these potentials are substantial.

As a caveat, one should realize that these arguments do not necessarily follow from the postmodern context. Postmodernism has often been viewed as morally bankrupt (the romanticist argument), because it fails to profess any fundamental values or principles. More forcefully put, postmodernism fails to offer arguments against Nazism or other forms of cultural tyranny. While it is true that there are no necessary values favored by the postmodern turn, postmodernism does not thereby terminate all ethical and moral debate.[1] Further, there are certain preferences—moral, political, and social—that, while not demanded by postmodernist developments, are congenial with them. In the positive case that follows, these preferences will be given expression. In effect, it is possible to locate within the postmodern outlook a way of proceeding that has enormous potential for humankind—provided one is open to this view of potential. There are no foundations of value to be located here, no progressive program. But there are possibilities opened that may, within a given perspective, both enrich and sustain human life.

The promise of postmodernism is most effectively realized when contrasted with the problems inherent in the modernist worldview. Modernist assumptions of rationality, objectivity, and essentialism have been placed under attack in preceding chapters (especially 4 and 5). Yet even without a sustaining rationale, the modernist perspective continues to dominate Western culture. Thus we may usefully turn to three aspects of modernism—progress, individualism, and secure belief—the problems of which dramatically underscore the positive potential of the postmodern.

PROGRESS, PREGRESS, AND PLURALISM

But a storm is blowing from Paradise. . . . The storm irresistibly propels [us] into the future to which [history's] back is turned, while the pile of debris before [us] grows skyward. The storm is what we call progress.
—Walter Benjamin, *Illuminations*

The belief in human progress has long been a fixture of Western tradition. Often it has been linked to religious doctrines of the times, from the Homeric period, which held that people could become godlike, to later Christianity, in which people were encouraged to perfect their lives by living in God's will. With the rise of modernism in this century, spirituality has been in retreat. Because spiritual dimensions of human activity do not seem open to observation, they are generally consigned to the realm of mythology. However, modernism has retained a retooled concept of progress as its linchpin. The enchantment of modernism derives importantly from its promise of progress—the belief that, with proper application of reason and observation, the essences of the natural world may be made increasingly known, and that with such increments in knowledge the society may move steadily toward a utopian state. The sciences furnish a model of reason and observation operating at its most efficacious level. The burgeoning technologies of the age—in the domains of medicine, energy, transportation, communication, and so on—offer tangible proof of the capacity of science to progress. Thus, to think and act scientifically—whether in business, political decision making, or domestic life—is to move the society forward and upward.

What is to be made of the promise of progress from a postmodern perspective? We must first remove the taken-for-granted foundation from beneath the idol. The concept of progress is not derived from observation. It is a narrative form that organizes the way we understand what we observe—a rhetorical vehicle requiring the specification of goals, of events related to such goals, and of linear temporal sequence (see chapter 7). The narrative of progress is hardly universal, nor has it commanded univocal assent within the Western tradition.[2] It is one myth among many, and our very enchantment with it may operate as a form of cultural blindness. What alternative stories are removed from view? asks the postmodern; what may they tell us about life's possibilities and potentials? We must consider whose voices are raised on behalf of progress and who gains (and loses) by accepting such a view.

In this light, let us allow alternative voices room for expression, not only to determine possible deficits in our current romance with progress, but to provide a rationale for other options of action. At the outset, one can raise a voice in protest even within the modernist framework itself. Adopting the modernist view that we can indeed observe and measure our progress toward mutually acceptable goals, we may find that the case for progress is not only poor but indeed tragic in its implications. There are compelling reasons to believe that all that has passed for progress within the modernist conception is actually carrying the culture *in reverse*.

Consider first the systematic blinding required in order to label a given outcome an "improvement" or a "sign of progress." In order to lend validity to such labels, we must remove from view everything outside the outcomes in question. Thus, it is possible to say that Johnny's grade improvement, Peggy's raise in salary, or the nation's stronger defensive capability are signs of progress, but only so long as we focus on the specific dimensions in question (grades, income, arsenals). In order for such events to stand as progress, we cannot go about searching for simultaneous deteriorations in Johnny's sense of well-being (along with that of his classmates), Peggy's relationship with her children or her competitors, or national programs of disease prevention or social welfare. Deficits and deterioration within these parallel realms challenge the validity of the presumption of progress. (For example, pride in Johnny's academic progress goes flat when he is rendered cheerless, listless, and friendless.) Let us press the case further.

In a number of celebrated cases, assessments of the ancillary losses are found to outweigh by far the gains made in the selected domain of progress. The Nobel Prize–winning discovery of the insecticide DDT in 1939 was heralded as a major step forward in increasing agricultural productivity and saving people from malaria. Progress became possible in two important domains. By 1950 it became clear, however, that DDT was toxic to many animals, and species dependent on insects for survival were being exterminated: fish-eating and carnivorous birds were also threatened. Further, the availability of the additional foodstuffs made possible by DDT enabled human populations to expand to record, potentially calamitous highs. Rachel Carson's *Silent Spring* brought public attention to these and other side effects of progress, and by 1970 DDT was placed under strict control.[3] As the recent discovery of significant amounts of DDT in the penguins of Antarctica makes clear, however, the effects of the chemical continue to reverberate throughout the environment.

This of course is but a single example among many that could be selected. There is reason to believe, however, that any case examined with care will reveal a similar accumulation of negative repercussions. Those claims to "genuine progress" that remain do so only because the requisite research has not been undertaken to demonstrate otherwise. On what grounds can this be argued? Consider the possibility that for every event called "progress" there are multiple reverberations or side effects unrelated to the dimension of focal concern. No "advances" occur in a social or ecological vacuum. Further, each of these effects necessarily upsets the status quo in these ancillary domains. And, because the existing situation in most of these domains is, in certain respects, "livable," "satisfactory," or just "ordinary life," these side effects are typically untoward, unwelcome, or disruptive. Thus the modal condition is one in which progress in one domain actually moves the culture backward, in a multitude of related domains.

Yet the problem only begins at this point. For if a culture is committed to progress, then each unanticipated disruption calls for remedial action. Improvements in these various domains must be made to offset the worsening conditions. These improvements set in motion an additional wave of disruptive reverberations in still other domains, which again call for compensatory improvement, and still further side effects. The waves of disruption broaden and accelerate. More summarily, every action undertaken in the name of progress may set in motion a process of *pregression,* that is, an accelerating or progressive regression.

To appreciate the potentials of pregression, consider the simple case of fertilizer. Attempts are frequently made to improve crop production through fertilizer, an unremarkable but measurably effective means of achieving progress in the production of foodstuffs. However, the process of pregression now commences. Greater crop production means, at least temporarily, increased income across a broad spectrum of the population. Thus, people are free to buy more and larger cars. A new problem now results: overcrowded highways. The problem is solved by building new and larger roads, reducing nature to concrete ("Take paradise and put up a parking lot"). This move reduces the amount of arable land and the quantity of oxygen produced through photosynthesis. More problems to be solved. At the same time, the increase in automobiles pollutes the air, spoiling the quality of life, reducing property values, and killing off forests (as in Germany's Black Forest). These new problems can be partially solved by greater emission controls. This in turn increases the demand for fuel oil, reducing the nation's balance of payments . . .

The increased income also sparks a demand for higher-quality food, including fresh meat. This problem is solved by increasing the number

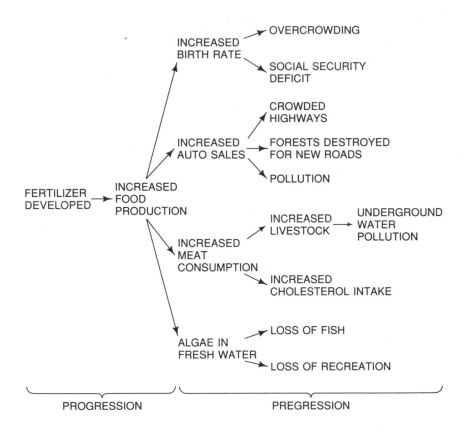

of pigs and cows. As the waste products of the livestock seep into the underground water, the culture's water resources become contaminated (a "new problem" now confronting both the Germans and the Dutch). Simultaneously, the new sources of wealth enable people to have more children and to live longer. This moves the population toward overcrowding (a new problem to be solved through birth control), and new stresses are placed on future social-security resources. And all this is to say nothing of the effects of fertilizers on increasing the growth of algae in lakes and canals (consider the catastrophe in Venice).[4]

Chaos theorists now speak of a "butterfly effect," the enormous reverberating effect generated by a tiny perturbation in one sector of a system. As it is said, the movements of a butterfly in Hong Kong may, through a series of concatenated events, launch a tornado in Texas. And so it is in the case of pregression. How often is "progress" not the attempt to overcome the repercussions of long-removed impulses toward betterment? Pregression may be the rule rather than the exception.

As we find, the case for progress is insubstantial even within the modernist framework. As we shift to the postmodern perspective, new and different shortcomings become focal. From this perspective, to call a given set of events "progress" is to adopt a linguistic pose, with no other foundation than the assent of others to the meaning system in use at the time. The set of events may just as easily be construed in many other ways, and these alternative constructions, which may represent subcultures otherwise marginalized by the "voice of progress," can lead to substantially different evaluations of the events.

To illustrate: From her research on middle-class culture, Barbara Ehrenreich concludes that the leitmotif of middle-class life is an incipient fear of failure, "of growing soft, of failing to strive, of losing discipline . . . and always . . . of falling."[5] Ehrenreich is acutely sensitive to the life-themes of the middle class, but her analysis underestimates the extent to which issues of gains and losses, success and failure, upward and downward pervade Western culture more generally. Further, the very quest for progress contributes to the widespread fear of falling. As we have seen, the narrative of progress depends on establishing some form of "good"—a value or a goal. Establishing the goal lays the foundation for a social hierarchy in which each individual may be ranked in terms of his or her proximity to the goal. Such comparisons are made at the national level (How is our nation faring in terms of GNP, number of atomic warheads, health standards, math ability?), the community level (Is our community better than others in quality-of-life ratings, crime rate, winning teams?), and the individual level (Am I improving in income, education, weight, sports ability?). The games themselves are most often favored by those in a position to win them. Thus, the system of economic competition is preferred by the wealthy; educational attainment is positively endorsed by families who are educated; arms races are most fully pursued by nations equipped to purchase large numbers of weapons. And, with only a single slot available for number one, the vast majority of people who take the games for granted step into a system they are destined to lose. Consider the many whose lives are wracked daily by the fear of failing on the one hand and the frustration of slow movement forward on the other. The promise of progress thrusts them into a lifetime struggle toward a summit never to be attained, evoking in the end a sense of failure, of having been unable to realize "what I could have been," "should have been," or "wanted to be." For many others, who sense the futility of a game stacked against them, the preferred course may be a life of alcohol, drugs, sleeping in doorways, or crime (a different game in which success is more likely).

This account is, however, only one alternative to the modernist characterization of progress. There are others; progress may also be seen as a form of secular religion, as a societal addiction, or as a rationalization for exploitation. And each of these accounts has alternative implications for social policy and individual life patterns. This is not to say that postmodernism is pitted against all efforts "to progress" or "to improve" selves or relationships. However, the postmodern tactic of deconstruction and reconstruction does have the capacity to emancipate the culture from the blinding and deeply problematic effects of this grand modernist narrative. The virtually unquestioned cry for "progress" is reduced to a rhetorical exhortation, thereby opening spaces for intelligible alternatives. When actions are then justified in the name of excellence, improvement, betterment, getting ahead, and the like, one should be neither awed nor aroused. For this is but the preferred language of a particular community, one among many. A more propitious reaction to such exhortations might be to reflect on the following: Are there other ways of viewing the proposal? Who benefits and who loses from this particular way of defining the goals? For example:

- Should children's participation in sports, dance, ice skating, playing musical instruments, drawing, and writing be channeled toward formal competitions in which hierarchies of the good prevail? Should the athletically gifted adolescent be encouraged to train for an Olympic gold medal? What are the pregressive repercussions of such competitions— for self-esteem, family life, and neighborhood friendships?
- Should the striving professor press on to produce another book? Computer technology now makes it possible to generate a completed man-

uscript in half the time required ten years ago, and perhaps a tenth of the time required a century ago. The scholar whose lifetime output was three books in 1970 can now produce six books. Does the world now need twice as many scholarly books, twice as many trees reduced to inert forms in dark stacks whose primary contact with human beings is the occasional duster?

· Must permits be given for the building of new houses or housing developments? With the population of the West now beginning to level, why is it progress for people to strive for new and better houses? Is the driving metaphor a medieval vision of *Every man a king in his own castle*? Is the upward limit to emulate Leona Helmsley, with an $11 million palace? Who and what is laid to waste in the desire for a marble swimming pool and chandeliers of gold? Would humankind not be better off by trading the metaphor of the castle for that of the nest?

· Must personal incomes continue to rise steadily throughout life? "Cost-of-living" figures may indeed increase annually, but such figures are threatening to security only if one presumes a constancy of need across the lifespan. If one owns furniture, it need not be purchased again at a higher rate. If one makes a down payment on a house in 1970, one continues to pay a 1970 price for the house in 1990. And is the relationship between income and life quality linear, such that those with the highest incomes live more fulfilling lives? In 1989 Michael Milken made a million dollars an hour, twenty-four hours a day. Was his sleep more peaceful or his breakfast more nourishing than the average farmer's? The hierarchy of income has no summit, so why do we presume that it is worth the climb?

· Must the United States race ahead to place a human being on Mars? Is there really a "space race"? Who else is competing? And for what prize? How much uranium are we now mining on the moon? To what extent is the "exploration" of space a means toward the "exploitation" of space—toward more dominating weaponry, under another name?

These are only a handful of the kind of irreverent questions that seem increasingly imperative. With the conversion of cultures to hierarchies in which upward scrambling becomes the meaning of life, the planet is being laid waste. It is now hardly newsworthy that petroleum reserves are being depleted, lakes and rivers are polluted or drying up, the ozone layer is growing thin, forests are disappearing, underground water supplies are becoming undrinkable, air unbreathable, beaches unswimmable, noise levels unendurable, fish and animal species extinct, and so on. Pity the primitive with only a handful of concerns; in the service of progress we moderns can now produce them by the hundreds. Would we not be more suited to our world with less progress and more carnival?

In addition to the alteration in attitude it favors, postmodernism also holds implications for practical decision making. The case for progress, or improvement, is typically made within a relatively circumscribed social domain: a domain of people to whom the case is fully intelligible. Progress in weaponry, for example, is a concept central to Pentagon officials, which over time takes on significance within other sectors of government. Progress in medicine is largely a matter for the medical profession, with ancillary concern developing in a limited number of other areas. Likewise, progress in one's career may be a matter settled primarily within one's occupational setting. However, if each thrust toward improvement generates an array of regressive reverberations across broad and disparate domains, and if each definition of progress can be countered by significant alternatives within these domains, then circumscribed decision making may have disastrous consequences. Or to put it conversely, the greater the array of perspectives brought to bear on proposals for progress and their repercussions, the more congenial the outcome to society (and the environment) at large. Postmodernism thus invites a dramatic increase in the parties given voice in making decisions for improvement. How are "weapons improvements" viewed by other nations, various religious groups, communities where stockpiling is to occur? How are improvements in medicine likely to affect hospital costs, population growth, the social-security system? What effects are career advancement likely to have on one's children, one's friendships, and the quality of life within the community? By expanding the number of perspectives, the issue does indeed grow in complexity. Without addressing this complexity, however, the claim to progress is but a charade.

The same technology that sensitizes us to the plurality of perspectives can facilitate this broadening colloquy. With the enormous increases in linkages of communication, the means are in place for far more extended and inclusionary decision making than was ever possible before. To create an effective pluralism, we must (1) open the decision processes to a far more extended audience, (2) substantially increase the number of individuals who could translate proposals of one group into the frameworks of others (how do "medical advances," for example, affect the black population, the holders of medical insurance policies, the aged, etc.?), and (3) open the channels for feedback. Consider the case of representative government in the United States. After election to Congress, the representative virtually disappears from local view. Scant information is available concerning most of the issues at stake, and the representative's position is rarely made clear. When local issues receive publicity their definition is limited to either the representative's account or that of news reporters. Public input to the representative is generally limited to either mail or telegraph, or to voting some years later. In effect, the system of representation continues to operate according to a nineteenth-century communications system and a modernist conception of a single truth. We must find means of furnishing continuous information to the public, enabling partisan interpretations to be made of the situation, and facilitating rapid reactions from the public. All of these ends might be accomplished, for example, with the addition of UHF television channels and an array of 800 telephone numbers or interactive television devices. In effect, we possess the means by which our systems of representation may finally be brought into sync with the ideals of pluralist decision making.[6]

FROM INDIVIDUALISM
TO RELATIONAL REALITIES

[If we] can include everything coherently and harmoniously in an overall whole that is undivided, unbroken, and without a border, then . . . from this will flow orderly action within the whole.
—David Bohm, *Wholeness and the Implicate Order*

One ponders, "How should I live my life?" and considers the "desire for fulfilling work," "needs for loving relationships," "hopes for children," or "wants for financial security." One pauses to consider how the day or the evening should be spent, and again account is taken of one's wishes, needs, hopes, and fears. Such contemplations are commonplace. Yet consider some contrasting possibilities. How often do we ask, for example, "I wonder what my family will do with its life?" "What will my community do this month?" or "How will my marriage fare today?" We find it "only natural" to contemplate our own personal desires, needs, wants, and fears and to direct our lives accordingly. It is awkward and confusing to lay the self aside and to focus on broader units of being. Relationships come and go, we believe, but self remains till death. The individual self is the center of society; relationships are but artificial by-products of interacting individuals.

Yet what seems so natural and self-evident in daily life is both peculiarly Western and historically perishable. For many Asians, matters of self seem puny compared to concern for family; in Southeast Asia, the fate of community may far outweigh considerations of individual trajectory. Even within much of Western culture, not until the Enlightenment did individual worth and capabilities achieve hegemony over and against the more holistic units of clan and community. At present, the concept of the individual psyche as the wellspring of human action insinuates itself into virtually every aspect of cultural life. The economic system is based on the concept of the individual decision maker. Individuals have a right to choose what they buy and sell (including their labor), and when these rights are properly exercised, it is said, the result is prosperity for all. The democratic system of government similarly relies on the concept of the individual voter. Again, it is believed, if each individual exercises his or her powers of reason and estimates of value, the result will be a common good. Both the system of justice and informal codes of morality are similarly focused on the individual, whose private intentions are base or honorable, and who must stand responsible for his or her actions. And, too, the vast majority of existing hierarchies—in systems of education, business, government, athletics, and so on—are based on the assumption of individual skills or achievements.

Both the romantic and modernist conceptions of the person have contributed strongly to the individualistic perspective and its related institutions. For the romantic, relationships such as marriage and friendship were surely significant—even sacred. However, their significance depended on their links to the deep interior. A relationship that united souls was profound; one bereft of such communion was merely profane. Similarly, modernism reasserted the importance of individual reason and observation for human action; one should listen not to authorities or groups but to the evidence of one's own reason and senses. The ideal human being under modernism was self-reliant, self-motivated, and self-directing.

Although such terms as "individual rights," "democracy," "moral integrity," "autonomy," and "personal worth" have enormous rhetorical power, their very appeal acts as a barrier to critical scrutiny. Within recent years, however, increasing numbers of scholars have pressed on to inquire into the problems of individualism. What is the downside to the tradition of individualism? Are there viable alternatives? In his widely discussed volume *The Culture of Narcissism*, Christopher Lasch argues that the individualistic orientation favors a "me-first" pursuit of self-gratification.[7] This pursuit trivializes emotional relationships, sexual intimacy, scholarly research, and political life, as each becomes an arena for "getting one's own." In *Habits of the Heart*, the Berkeley sociologist Robert Bellah and his colleagues conclude that individualist ideology interferes with the development of commitment at every level of society, from marriage and community to participation in national politics.[8] When the individual rationalizes his or her actions in terms of gains and losses to self, the conception of broader, public goods recedes from view. Such conceptions are distinctly lacking from the culture, they argue; people fail to remain in relationships any longer than they can justify in terms of their own interest. Richard Sennett's *The Fall of Public Man* compares the character of public life in earlier and less individualistic centuries with that of today.[9] He finds that our individualistic preoccupation with self, and concomitant fear of sincerity and self-revelation, militate against the kind of public life in which people mingle freely on the streets, in parks, or at public gatherings and speak with civil constraint, without embarrassment, and with a sense of the common good. As he sees it, public life has given way to privatized, claustrophobic, and defensive modes of living.

Others write of how individualism lends itself to a sense of isolation, loneliness, and anomie; promotes forms of economic exploitation; champions a competitive as opposed to a cooperative view of international relations; and leads to a relentless plundering of natural resources in the service of competition and self-gratification. As individualism gains ascendance, social life begins to approximate a Hobbesian condition of all against all.

Such criticisms have sparked wide debate in recent years. Postmodern thought adds important new dimensions to the arguments, for it brings the ontological fundamentals of individualism into question. As we have seen, under postmodernism, processes of individual reason, intention, moral decision making, and the like—all central to the ideology of individualism—lose their status as realities. The boundaries of the individual as a unit of reality blur; individuals are viewed as the product of social

Sidney Goodman's neo-realist work *Figures in a Landscape* adds visual dimension to the growing discontent with individualist ways of life.

construction. Yet despite having deconstructed the reality of the individual actor, we continue to speak of reason, emotion, memory, and the like, and we must do it for some reason other than giving expression to inward impulses. From Wittgenstein to contemporary literary theory, scholars have concluded that the language of mental life gains its significance or meaning from its use in social life. The meanings of "good reasoning," "bad intentions," "accurate memory," and the like are determined by the way such words are used in carrying out relationships.

The implications of this latter conclusion are of no small consequence, for as I suggested in chapter 6, they replace the individual as the center of human action with the relationship. Individuals themselves cannot "mean" anything; their actions are nonsensical until coordinated with the actions of others. If I extend my hand and smile, the gesture hovers at the edge of absurdity until reciprocated by another. My words don't become "communication" until they are treated by others as intelligible. And as so deftly portrayed in Jerzy Kosinski's *Being There*, even the language of an idiot can be profound in consequence if others treat it thusly. In effect, when postmodern arguments are extended, we find it possible to replace an individualistic worldview—in which individual minds are critical to human functioning—with a relational reality. We can replace the Cartesian dictum *cogito ergo sum* with *communicamus ergo sum*, for without coordinated acts of communication, there is simply no "I" to be articulated.[10]

The postmodern turn thus not only de-objectifies the individual self but points the way to a new vocabulary of being. The ground of debate shifts significantly; no longer need we be concerned with the tyranny of what David Riesman called "groupness," in which private needs and desires are compromised by group demands.[11] If individuals are by definition elements within relationships, they can neither stand apart from the social world nor be pushed and pulled by it, any more than the movements of a wave can be separated from or determined by the ocean. The sense of being threatened by the oppressive group becomes not a case of "me against the group," but of the conflict between one form of relatedness and another.

Similarly, as reality shifts toward relatedness, marriage and other forms of commitment are also altered. If committed intimacy proves arduous, the alternative is not one of "freedom" from burdening responsibilities. One chooses not between relationship and individual autonomy, but between varying forms of interdependence—between face-to-face connection and symbolic community, or cross-time coherence and multiphrenic embeddedness. Those who live alone need not be pitied, however, for from the present view, we are never alone, even if isolated from others' physical presence. So long as our actions are intelligible, they are intelligible within a system of meaning. And meaning, as we have seen, is not the product of individual minds but of relationships. To act before witnesses does not render such actions more social. Living alone is simply one form of relatedness among others, with certain advantages and liabilities depending on one's perspective and patterns of ongoing interchange. Similarly, it is not the isolated individual who is born and who dies; one is born into relatedness, both defined by it and defining of it. Upon one's death, it is a pattern of relationships that perishes.

These insights are unsteady and imperfectly developed, because the discourse of relationship has scarcely been unfolded. A vast potential looms, but we cannot leap headlong into new vocabularies of being any more than we can speak a foreign language we have never heard. New vocabularies and related patterns of action must inevitably spring from what exists; they must gain strength and intelligibility from the patterns of interdependency in which we are already entwined. Chapter 6 explored several ways in which individual concepts of mind are currently being redefined in relational form. Autobiography, emotion, and moral decision making were "taken out of the head" and placed into the socius—reconstructed as achievements of relationship rather than of single individuals. In this way the traditional terms are retained, but the implications—both for language and for related action—are altered. Similar kinds of reconstructions are now being invited across a broad spectrum. How can practices and institutions traditionally expressed individualistically be reconceptualized as forms of relatedness? And what new alternatives for action result? Let us briefly consider two possibilities: the stock market and the judicial system.

The stock market, the heart of the capitalist process, is traditionally understood in individualistic terms. The behavior of the market is essentially reducible to the rational decision-making processes of each participant. Each individual operates to maximize gains and minimize losses, and the sum total of transactions constitutes the market outcome. Yet if "rational decision making" is not, as ventured in preceding chapters, a process within the mind, we can view the stock market as a pattern of interdependent relationships. In this context the market becomes intriguing indeed. For in the society at large, the reality of money is fixed. There is such unequivocal agreement that a dollar is a dollar, a mark a mark, and so on, that the common reality is for all practical purposes objective. Yet the stock market is a critical arena in which this common reality is suspended, is indeed opened for continuous renegotiation. The value of a given stock can be redefined either upward or downward. No inherent rules govern what form of intelligibility may enter the arena of negotiated reality; no rational principles constrain the meanings that may be placed on cultural events.

Having recast the stock market as a relational arena, we can confront a critical problem within the system. As brokers and their colleagues share speculations, doubts, and hopes about presidential promises, the effects of mergers, threats of war, popular sentiments, and so on, the market is subjected to radical, unsystematic fluctuation. Its ups and downs depend on the shifting mélange of conjectures and interpretations exchanged by its participants, over which there appears to be limited constraint. In this sense the economic well-being of the nation (and indeed the world) is built on an array of fragile and ever-shifting meanings. On any given day, a sudden scare in the Japanese market, opinion perturbations in the White House, or a shift in Arab oil policies could send the American economy into a brutal recession. If enormous swings in the market are to be avoided, if the economy is to be insulated against sudden catastrophe, the local reality of the stock market must be opened to other voices. Communication linkages and feedback devices could provide constant input from the government, large corporations, economic theorists, and experts in other fields—politics, sociology, psychology. The effects of market realities are too far-reaching to be left to the informal, impulsive, and frenetic negotiations of a small and singularly preoccupied group of persons.

Relational analyses can also be extended to the institution of justice. Postmodernism brings the concept of "voluntary decision making" into critical focus. As the justification for such a belief deteriorates, the concept of the individual who chooses "wrong" loses tenability. To be sure, individuals break the law, but from the postmodern perspective, such actions should be attributed not to the individual alone but to the array of relationships in which he or she is a part. The crime is but a manifestation of these relationships—the ordinary complicities of daily life. (See the discussion of lying in chapter 6.) This perspective is slowly beginning to enter contemporary legal practice. For example, in suburban Philadelphia a woman in army fatigues entered a shopping mall and began firing at the customers, killing and wounding several before being apprehended. From the individualistic standpoint, she alone was responsible for her actions. With more relational considerations at hand, however, lawyers have broadly extended the network of responsibility, bringing suit against mental-health officials who knew of her distraught condition, the local police department which was also aware of the potential danger she posed, the shopping mall for its poor security measures, the shop that sold her a weapon, and so on. This mode of justice is strongly favored by the relational stance, and could usefully be expanded throughout jurisprudence.[12] As the traditional concept of "immoral decisions" becomes moot, the issue is not to extend the boundaries of guilt. Rather, it is to reduce the myopia of "every man for himself" and to vitally expand sensitivity to the network of relations in which we participate. As the theologian Catherine Keller writes, "Only a self forged in the image of an inner hardness, mistaken for integrity, could separate itself from the matrix of all life."[13]

TOTALIZING DISCOURSE VS. THE FREE PLAY OF BEING

Reality was once a primitive method of crowd control that got out of hand. In my view, it's absurdity dressed up in a three-piece business suit. . . . I can take it in small doses, but as a lifestyle I find it too confining.
——Jane Wagner, *The Search for Signs of Intelligent Life in the Universe*

Consider the object in your hand—obviously a book. And if it is a book, it is primarily there to be read. But how else could it be defined? It could also be used as fuel for a fire, a paperweight, a doorstop, a gavel (rapped to gain attention), an instrument of aggression (when hurled across the room), and poor-quality toilet paper (oh no, not my book!). Let us press still further. In what sense is this object a crocodile (attempting to devour one's mind), a seducer (luring the reader into its keep), a river (of flowing words), or a battle cry (stirring one to arms against old rhetoric)? If we remain in the modernist tradition, simply "telling it like it is," these alternatives are suppressed. As a result, so are the actions invited by the alternative definition. If this is *truly* a book, there is little more than reading to be done with it. Expand the vocabulary, and its capacities are multiplied. Press the vocabulary into the realm of metaphor, and the envelope of limitations begins to vanish. And what but social convention favors its existence as a book?

And so it is with conceptions of the person. If our vocabulary of understanding self and others is constrained, so is the range of intelligible actions. Consider the romantic and modernist views of the person. Such views approximate closed systems, sets of propositions that cohere within themselves, but that deny alternative accounts of reality. They define the person in certain ways, but fail to recognize other possibilities. To a point, they are totalizing—complete within themselves, insulated from self-criticism. And, because they admit only a specialized vocabulary of understanding, they place important limits over human action. For example, the committed romanticist may avoid "obviously rational" options because they do not "feel right," or resonate with intuition or spirit. Personal losses may throw the romanticist into long and painful periods of grief, remorse, or thoughts of suicide. The romanticist fails to appreciate the beauty of the rational plan, the simple but functional architectural line, the impact of a single-hued canvas, or the sensuality of musical sounds for their own sake. And the romanticist cannot easily devote time and energy to his or her children with confidence in a lasting outcome, or participate in a community of scientists with the satisfying sense that the future can be controlled. The romanticist may view with antipathy those who hold fast to a job for the sake of security, who strive to accumulate wealth, who dress for success, who advise and consent, and whose friendships are used as "connections."

At the same time, the modernist is locked within a conceptual world in which there is little possibility of being swept away in a tide of blissful enchantment ("immature, unreasonable . . . and dangerous"). A jaundiced eye is similarly turned toward spiritual experiences, mysticism, and a sense of bonded unity with nature. Impetuous actions, defiance of the normal, Dionysian revelry—all are subverted by the modernist quest. Further, the sense of loyalty or deep commitment—either to persons or to ideals—is lacking from the modernist approach. The modernist will avoid close contact with the devoutly religious, eccentrics, and the mentally ill, all of whom seem moved by forces beyond reason. And, while paying special attention to the young and "unformed," the modernist scorns the elderly and the infirm (they do not serve a useful function). As Paul Ricoeur has concluded, each form of universalization "constitutes a sort of subtle destruction, not only of traditional cultures . . . but also of . . . the creative nucleus of great cultures, that nucleus on the basis of which we interpret life . . . the ethical and mythical nucleus of mankind."[14]

In *The Battle for Human Nature*, Barry Schwartz describes how modernist conceptions of social science are obliterating the traditional language of morality.[15] For example, modernist economic theory is largely based on a view of rational man, busily maximizing gains and minimizing losses. Similarly, behaviorist theory in psychology holds that people act primarily to achieve rewards and avoid punishment, and evolutionary biology proposes that human beings act in ways that sustain and proliferate their own genes, insuring the survival of the next generation. These influential theories work in harmony, proposes Schwartz, each painting a picture of "natural man" as fundamentally greedy and self-centered. As these intelligibilities become accepted truth within society, they justify certain ways of life. People learn that self-centered actions are "only natural"; altruistic activity is against nature. The language of morality—largely romanticist—simultaneously falls into disuse. If people are *just naturally* self-centered, then there is little reason to argue that they should not be. This would be similar to arguing that it is immoral for people to breathe. A modernist might search for technical means of curbing natural greed (increased surveillance, police protection). However, to resort to a language of moral good, a discourse concerning what is just and good in human action, is simply a waste of effort—equivalent to discussing the nature of heaven. In the hands of modernist discourse, moral deliberation is increasingly forced to life's margins.[16]

In this context, the postmodern turn is instructive. From the postmodern perspective both the romantic and modern realities are relativized. Convictions that people do (or do not) possess an unconscious mind, soul, intrinsic worth, inherent rationality, sincerity, personality traits, and so on, turn strange. These are, after all, ways of talking, not reflections of the actual nature of persons. In contrast to the narrow range of options and the oppressive restraints favored by totalizing systems of understanding, postmodernism opens the way to the full expression of all discourses, to a free play of discourses. The Russian literary theorist Mikhail Bakhtin used the term *heteroglossia* to refer to the multiplex nature of language within a culture.[17] The existing language of any culture bears the remnants and admixtures of languages from various subcultures and historical eras. In this sense, postmodernism invites a heteroglossia of being, a living out of the multiplicity of voices within the sphere of human possibility. For the postmodern, the vocabularies of personhood are less mirrors of truth than they are means of relating. There is little reason to suppress any voice. Rather, with each new vocabulary or form of expression, one appropriates the world in a different way, sensing aspects of existence in one that are hidden or absent in another, opening capacities for relatedness in one modality that are otherwise hindered.

In this respect, neither the romantic nor the modern traditions need be lost from the culture. Modernist attributes of the person such as rationality, sincerity, and perfectibility need not be abandoned, nor must modernist forms of relationship—investing in children, building hierarchies, conducting science, building for the future—be ultimately condemned. Rather than viewing such concepts and actions as true, final, and superior, however, we can see them as potentials. To draw from the discussion in chapter 7, they are serious games, cultural life-forms that possess internal coherence and a local validity. In the same way, the postmodernist perspective invites a resuscitation of romanticism. A person need not be embarrassed to speak of his or her soul, passion, or communion with nature. Further, we are invited to reinvigorate the language of morality, not because moral principles furnish solutions to life's problems but because moral discourse is embedded within and serves to sustain particular cultural patterns.[18] Through postmodernism, then, both modernism and romanticism are revitalized, but neither to the exclusion of the other. They take their places as significant and substantial entries into the array of serious games developed and elaborated by the culture over the centuries.

It is also apparent that the process of enriching the discourse of the self only begins with the romantic and modern motifs. From the postmodern perspective, we are invited to inquire into eras long past as well. How might our capacities for relating be expanded through exploring the mystery of Mithraic cults, rekindling the Dionysian impulse, reestablishing courtly manners, or mastering the possibilities of asceticism? All are cultural patterns—languages and forms of relationship—that have grown into disuse, and yet, like Greek statues or Renaissance paintings, they can still activate our potentials. Consider the concept of *sophrosyne*, focally important for Homeric Greeks, but now largely lost from usage.[19] As we might now appropriate the concept, it would refer to a special virtue: the harmonious blending of intense passion and perfect control. For the Greeks, sophrosyne was symbolized by the image of a charioteer, gracefully guiding and holding in check his spirited horses. Could such an image not be incorporated into contemporary activities—replacing victory, for example, as the goal of athletic training, or profit as the chief aim of executive life?[20]

Further, we are invited to expand outward, to incorporate the possibilities inherent in other cultural forms—borrowing and integrating intelligibilities from Asian, Polynesian, Arab, Indian, and African cultures. Consider, for example, the concept of *amae*, central to relationships in Japan but for which there is no exact translation in English. Amae is akin to our concept of dependency, but it also implies that the dependent one may coax and play, and seek another's indulgence with sweet and loving innocence. Amae may characterize the relationship between parents and children, or between adults.[21] The creative development and expansion of this discourse (and related patterns of action) might serve as an invaluable alternative in the West to the emphasis placed on autonomy and personal control. At a time when the evils of "codependency" are so broadly assailed by mental-health professionals, a linguistic space is much needed for positive ways of viewing bonded relationships.

This openness to multiplicity has much in common with Robert Jay Lifton's concept of the *protean life-style*.[22] He proposes that the image of Proteus, the sea god of Greek mythology—who could change his shape from wild boar to dragon to fire or flood—is reflected increasingly in

The British artists Gilbert and George represent their work as an outcome not of the single creative mind, but of their relationship. They also find within the postmodern context a means of revitalizing a spiritual language.

contemporary life-styles. The protean style is characterized by a continuous flow of being, without obvious coherence through time. As a protean being, one "holds in one's head, and does frequently and in a great variety of ways, images that are contradictory and seem to take one in opposite directions simultaneously." Experimentation with being, risk, and absurdity is characteristic of the style. David Miller is similarly sensitive to this emerging orientation in his description of the *new polytheism*.[23] As Miller describes it, this emerging pattern is "a matter of the radical experience of equally real, but mutually exclusive aspects of the self. Personal identity cannot seem to be fixed. . . . The person experiences himself as many selves, each of which is felt to have . . . a life of its own, coming and going without regard to the centered will of a single ego."[24] And, "surprisingly, the experience is not sensed as pathology."[25] Miller views such an orientation as vastly liberating. In this sensitivity to multiple forms of spirituality, he sees the possibility for a person to "move meaningfully through a pluralistic universe."

By contrast, to strive for singular truths, superior reasons, foundational moralities, or standardized modes of comportment within a culture is to reduce the options for relating—both within the culture and in relationships outside it. As the topspin and the slice expand the vocabulary of a neophyte tennis player, so opening the culture to the influence of alternative intelligibilities increases its potential for getting on in its games. If we view anger, for example, as a biological urge, triggered by frustrating circumstances and largely beyond conscious control, we come to take bursts of hostility to be normal and wife-battering and child abuse to be unfortunate by-products of the human constitution. If the concept of anger is successfully reconceptualized as a form of cultural performance—sustained by cultural models and built into patterns of relationship—new attitudes, treatments, and legal procedures are opened for experimentation.

For the more practically minded, such expansion has enormous implications. Each cultural form—each language of understanding—offers only a limited range of solutions to the problems confronting a culture. To break the bonds of any "given"—in government, business, education, and so on—is to open the way to new solutions. Consider education. Traditional educational practices are built around improving the minds of single individuals. Sustained by modernist assumptions, teachers and professors take the role of authorities in a given subject, their task to fill the students' minds with knowledge of their specialty. The postmodernist, however, would view academic subjects as forms of discourse peculiar to communities (biologists, economists, etc.) engaged in different activities. Students themselves are experts within the discourses of their own particular subcultures—languages that help them to maintain their life-styles and adapt to the world as they construct it. Thus, education should not be a matter of replacing "poor" with "superior" knowledge, but should be a dialogue, in which all subcultures may benefit from the discourses of their neighbors. Teachers would invite students into modes of dialogue as participants rather than pawns, as collaborative interlocutors instead of slates to be filled. Ideally, the circumscribed discourse of "the disciplines" should also be rendered vulnerable—opened to extension, elaboration, and enrichment through the commingling of languages. Experiments with this kind of interactive education are taking place with increasing frequency. Postmodernist writings furnish such experiments with a supportive context.[26]

In the world of business, the implications are again substantial. The modernist organization was established around a guiding rationale—a "theory of the firm"—to be carried out under the guidance of corporate managers. From the postmodern standpoint, however, leaders lose their credibility as "superior knowers," and guiding rationales prove empty. The very possibility of a single individual, or a small group, determining the actions of the whole is challenged, for this small minority can see the world in only a circumscribed way, and can contemplate but poorly the myriad forms of relationship in which their colleagues are engaged. Postmodernism thus replaces the emphasis on the rational and superior leader with a sharing of realities across the subcultures of the organization. The organization must be open to the shared realities outside its boundaries, not only in order to increase its own argots for action, but so as to become more intelligible and integrated into the culture at large.[27] As many organizations are now finding, it is useful to loosen ties with various subunits—with research wings, marketing departments, personnel training, and the like—and to encourage these groups to furnish services to other firms. Working in this semiautonomous way, such units thus take on functions within multiple organizations. They play a common role within a variety of different settings, "flexible specialists" whose ever-expanding stock of "local knowledges" render them effective.

Finally, consider the therapeutic implications of postmodernism. Traditional practices of therapy, guided by both romanticism and modernism, place the therapist in the role of the expert who goes about assessing the problem of the individual mind, locating repressions, conflicts, misconceptions, or cognitive aberrations, and correcting such deficits through therapy. Under postmodernism, not only is the therapist's expertise in mental matters thrown into jeopardy, but the very reality of a "patient" with a "mind to be known and corrected" loses credibility. Rather, the individual is viewed as a participant in multiple relationships, with "the problem" only a problem because of the way it is constructed in certain of these relations. The challenge to the therapist is thus to facilitate renegotiation of the meaning system within which "the problem" exists. The therapist actively enters dialogue with those who maintain the problem definition, not as a clairvoyant, but as a coparticipant in the construction of new realities.[28] The emphasis may be placed on new narratives and metaphors for understanding one's life and improving skills for negotiating meaning.

The advantages of opening the door to multiple realities are slowly being realized within the culture more generally. With the waning of modernist demands for singular truths, societies as organized machines, and a singular narrative of progress, appreciation grows for local cultures, deviant truths, and exotic traditions. In Lyotard's terms, we are invited to "gaze in wonderment at the possible diversity"[29] of human patterning. In architecture this consciousness is manifest in the trend toward *regionalism*, or making use of the local traditions of design (as opposed to the International Style favored by modernism). In the performing arts we find a trend toward *tribalism*, an increased valuing of ethnic and racial traditions as they may fill out possibilities for aesthetic or dramatic expression.[30] In the political arena we find strong moves toward *localism*. Cities and small towns increasingly remove themselves from state and national dependency, as they locate linkages (through technology) to those who more directly share in their concerns.[31] To be sure, these celebrations of variation are not without cost. The same technologies that undermine the dreams of "one great truth" also bring these voices into contact, and thus conflict.

CONFLICT AND CONVERGENCE

I had grown inside me a list of over two hundred things that I had to tell my mother so that she would know the true things about me and to stop the pain in my throat. . . . There were my fights at Chinese school. And the nuns who kept stopping us in the park . . . to tell us that if we didn't get baptized we'd go to a hell like one of the nine Taoist hells forever. . . . And the Mexican and Filipino girls at school who went to "confession," and how I envied them their white dresses and their chance each Saturday to tell even thoughts that were sinful. If only I could let my mother know the list, she—and the world—would become more like me, and I would never be alone again.
—Maxine Hong Kingston, *The Woman Warrior*

Totalizing discourses have a final deficit. Not only do such systems truncate, oppress, and obliterate alternative forms of social life; they also set the stage for schism. To be convinced of the "truth" of a discourse is to find the alternatives foolish or fatuous—to slander or silence the outside. Warring camps are developed that speak only to themselves, and that seek means of destroying others' credibility and influence (and life), all with an abiding sense of righteousness. As modernism gained hegemony, for example, religion was forced out of college curricula and replaced by science, the eloquent were replaced by the efficient, school prayer was replaced by guidance counseling, organizational loyalty by systems analysis, and psychoanalysis by cognitive therapy. As such transitions occur, subcultures form of "fools and knaves"—those who, from one standpoint or another, "don't know what they are talking about," "are deluded" or "absurd," or "immoral." At the same time, the oppressed countercultures strive—heroically, from their standpoint—to return society to a right-minded path. When convinced of the truth or right of a given worldview, a culture has only two significant options: totalitarian control of the opposition or annihilation of it.

Totalitarianism is no longer a viable option, for as modernists put the case, democracy is now victorious; there remain no viable competitors within the major nations of the world. To the extent that the term *democracy* refers to a pluralism of expressions, the modernists may be correct. One should not thereby draw the conclusion, however, that "democracy" (however defined) is now proven superior to all other forms of social organization. The present pluralism of expression seems most appropriately attributed to the century's explosion of the technologies of social saturation. As these technologies have seeped into the practices of everyday life, patterns of information exchange have become relatively uncontrollable. Citizens exposed to an ever-expanding array of perspectives may on short notice join in symbolic communities with others from around the globe (see chapters 7 and 8). Totalitarian forms of governance cannot easily function because they simply do not have the tools to subvert such processes. It could not happen in the Soviet Union and China, and it will become increasingly difficult for any future regime.

In Western culture, then, we find ourselves confronting a potential chaos of conflict. Each symbolically related subculture becomes increasingly free to claim the right of its rationality, its forms of value, and its patterns of action. How can the resulting chaos be resolved? It is to this criticism that postmodernism is most vulnerable. For the postmodern there is no transcendent reality, rationality, or value system with which to rule between competitors. Or, in MacIntyre's terms, "There is no other way to engage in the formulation, elaboration, rational justification, and criticism of accounts of practical rationality and justice except from within some particular tradition."[32] To romanticists and modernists, this conclusion seems nothing short of a monstrous relativism. Romanticists decry postmodernism's *moral* relativism; for them, to abandon moral principles, and thus withdraw from the decision-making process, is itself a form of immorality. For modernists, moral commitments are merely irrational matters of the heart; they chastise postmodernists' *ontological* relativism, or inability to rule between competing accounts to find what is objectively the case. Postmodernism fails to give any credence to the possibility of adjudication by virtue of good reason, which modernists fear will cause society to revert to a process of "might makes right."

Such critics are correct in attributing a certain degree of moral and ontological relativism to postmodernism. Postmodernist arguments challenge the possibility of transcendentally right or wrong answers—based on either moral or rational standards. What the critics fail to recognize, however, is that the major schisms within or between cultures derive not from relativism, but from the very forms of totalization that the critics themselves encourage. It is the commitment to an "ethically" or "rationally" superior standpoint that sets the stage for the kind of separatism, name-calling, and defamation that breeds civil strife. "Principled solutions" will inevitably favor one side or another; adherence to such solutions is only mystified by the claim to clairvoyance on moral or rational grounds. Thus, the kinds of principles favored by romanticists and modernists do less to solve conflicts than to fertilize the absolutist soil from which they spring. With the full flowering of postmodernism, the very concept of "foundational conflicts" between good and evil, true and false, rational and irrational would dwindle into obscurity. To silence, incarcerate, or kill adherents of differing political, religious, economic, or ethical discourses (and their related practices) would cease to make sense. Such actions would be akin to Wagner-lovers burning the works of Verdi, baseball fans setting terrorist bombs in football stadiums, or Chinese gourmands sending freedom fighters to liberate the guests at French restaurants.

Is there any reason to anticipate the emergence of such tolerance and integration of perspectives? It is on this point that the technologies of social saturation, and the accompanying alteration in self-definition, are most optimistic. For as such technologies become increasingly effective, we become increasingly populated with the identities of others, and come increasingly to recognize the extent of our relational embeddedness. As this occurs, the separation between self and other becomes diminished, and warfare becomes a nonsensical proposition.

The globalizing of business perhaps contributes most to the growing consciousness of relatedness. Since the 1960s, the growth of transnational businesses has been little short of phenomenal. Every ten years the average multinational enterprise has added subsidiaries in seven new countries, with many companies now reaching a global limit.[33] In 1989 U.S. companies increased their investments in Western Europe alone by $19 billion, compared with a little over $3 billion in 1988.[34] Any transnational with a home base in a given nation is now dependent on the actions of participants—both personnel and customers—throughout the world. For such companies as Exxon, IBM, Kodak, and Coca-Cola, among many others, over 60 percent of the profits are from the "foreign" sector.[35]

Because the size of many transnational businesses eclipses the gross national product of many nations, government policies are also influenced by business investments. As the transnationals move toward interdependence, governmental policies must become increasingly sensitive to the collective linkage of fates. The very idea of independent or sovereign nations is thrown into question.[36] For many businesspeople, the impetus toward national sovereignty interferes with economic transactions across cultures, and is thus to be discredited. It is in this climate that the nation-states of Europe are giving up much of their autonomy to form the European Community. As consciousness of interdependence expands, so withers the distinction between self and other, mine and yours.

The breakdown in the sense of self vs. other is also facilitated by the complicated financial and investment patterns fostered by transnational business. It is increasingly difficult to determine the national or even local point of origin of a company—where it "belongs," or with what people it is to be identified. For example, Americans think of British Petroleum as essentially British—despite its being multinational. In fact, as Robert Horton, top executive at BP, announced, "Fifty-five percent of BP's assets are in the United States. We're much more American than we are British!"[37] Similarly, if we look more closely we find that Columbia Pictures and CBS Records—both so quintessentially American—are owned by Sony. RCA Records and Doubleday books are owned by the German firm of Bertelsmann A.G.; the Manhattan Savings Bank is owned by the Lebanese Edmond Safra; and England's Grand Metropolitan Ltd. owns both Pillsbury and Burger King. The picture grows even more complex when we consider the growing pattern of multiple investments. For example, the People's drugstore and Roy Rogers chains seem "down-home" American, yet both are subsidiaries of the Canadian firm Imasco Ltd. However, because of its heavy investments in Canada, England's B.A.T. lists Imasco as its subsidiary.[38]

Coupled with the international expansion of business is the continuous exchange of culture. In the final analysis, it is not simply "economic commodities" that are moving about the globe, but cultural artifacts. Embodied in the imported automobiles, clothing, foodstuffs, entertainments, pharmaceuticals, and computers are values, tastes, and desires. As the products insinuate themselves into cultural patterns, the coherence of the traditions begins to erode. As Westerners incorporate Zen meditation, aikido, Toyota, Kurosawa, and sushi into their life-styles, and as Japanese buy Springsteen records, hamburgers, Picassos, and Times Square, the cultures incorporate fragments of each other's identities. That which was alien is now within.

Transnational businesses have developed largely in response to economic incentives. But a second movement deserves attention—less visible perhaps, but empowered by the kinds of ideals that fire one's fantasies. On the grassroots level, the technologies of saturation have facilitated the development of some 20,000 transnational organizations—most of them emerging since 1950—devoted to social change. The Hunger Project, the World Health Assembly, the International Physicians for the Prevention of Nuclear War, the Nature Conservancy, Greenpeace, and the International Foundation for the Survival and Development of

Humanity are illustrative of the kinds of global social change organizations (GSCOs) that are springing into existence. Significantly, all these organizations cut across national boundaries, exist as entities outside the nation-state, and bring together peoples who have otherwise existed in a state of mutual indifference or antagonism. Further, there are indications that such organizations can be effective. For example, the World Health Assembly declared in 1980 that smallpox had been eradicated from the planet. It was the first global problem in human history to be solved by organized action on a world scale. As the technologies become more effective, the potentials of such organizations are enhanced.[39]

At this point, one can also appreciate more fully the postmodern emphasis on self-reflexivity, irony, and play (as discussed in chapters 5 and 7). As we become aware that our sayings lack foundation in either passion or reason, and as our commitments slowly reveal themselves as postures, we can scarcely avoid a sense of deep humility.[40] We can hardly advocate our own beliefs, reasons, and passions above all others, for the very effort attests to the hollowness of their bases. And we are thus invited to defuse the hegemonic explosive—to remove the detonators of "ultimate significance" and "greatest good." At least one commentator, Mark Taylor, locates in the postmodern deconstruction of the self the potentiality for a new theology—or, in his term, *a/theology*—in which the "free play of carnival and comedy overturns every form of repressive transcendence."[41] The endless wandering in the maze of meaning, the breaking down of oppositions, and the inability to fix finally the good and the real engenders, for Taylor (quoting Altizer), a state of *mazing grace*, "a way of totally loving the world and a way (writing) of love itself in a time and world in which God is dead."[42]

It would be a mistake to paint the picture of postmodern conflict resolution *tout en rose*. Full integration of identities and interests across cultural groups is far from apparent, and the available technologies enable new social movements to flower at any time.[43] We confront lethal conflicts between pro-life and pro-choice groups; Irish Catholics and Protestants; Israelis and Palestinians; Castilian and Basque separatists: and South African white supremacists and black nationalists. Further, because systems of belief and action often impinge on each other, threatening mutual destruction, agonies of contradiction will always be present. Neo-Nazis, drug dealers, the KKK, and the Mafia all represent ways of life that are coherent, intelligible, and even moral for the participants. However, in posing such a lethal threat to neighboring peoples, such forms of life pose significant problems indeed.

I can see no simple solutions to such conflicts; some are embedded so deeply within cultural traditions that centuries of strife may be necessary before they abate. However, the postmodern perspective does invite certain modes of easing the intensity of such antagonisms.[44] Three of these are particularly worthy of comment.

The first is to shift the major focus *from principles to participants*. It is traditional in Western culture to respond to conflict by locating an abstract system of justification, rules, principles, or laws that can save us from our differences. In medieval times, people looked to biblical scripture for solutions; romanticists sought moral principles; modernists relied on sound reason. From the postmodern perspective, however, principled solutions are futile and misleading. None are nonpartisan; each proposes a specific worldview and thus favors those positions and persons consistent with it (so that solving a problem by "logical means" will derogate those for whom emotional truths prevail). And no system of language allows derivations to specific realities; nothing about the concept of "justice" tells us where it should be applied. Whether a rule or criterion applies in a given situation depends on a local process of negotiation; and any abstraction (moral injunction or rational principle) may be applied anywhere if the participants have the negotiating skills.

Rather than permitting us to take misguided comfort in transcendent principles, postmodernism confronts us with the immediacy of interdependence. We are discouraged from seeking refuge in systems of language believed to be outside and above us, there (like God or the Constitution) to guide us in times of crisis. Rather, we are alone together in our strife. By resorting to abstract systems of justice, laws, and moral codes, we succeed primarily in lending virtue to our own position, fortifying our sense of righteous purpose, and further denigrating the opposition. Postmodernism urges us to abandon such activities in favor of direct interchange with the other. What is the worldview within which their actions are intelligible and good? What place do we hold in that worldview? How do they perceive our view and their place within it? Rather than shutting out the voices of drug dealers, Mafiosi, and the KKK from the public forum, it is important to expand the possibilities for dialogue. For most of society such persons are "the other," alien and despised; for most participants in such groups society at large occupies a similar position. With the enormous expansion in the technologies of human connection, means are now available for overcoming these barriers.

Second, we should recognize that those we call enemies are enemies only by virtue of our own perspectives; were there no systems of belief, there would be no antagonists. We ourselves create the conditions for antagonism. Instead, forms of dialogue should be encouraged that *free the signifiers*—that break down existing structures of language and enable disparate discourses to commingle. As genres blur, we are able to see how antitheses develop from the use of language itself, and how the signifiers of one belief system derive their meaning from those of the other. We also need conditions that can foster new metaphors for reshaping the understanding of given positions, or reduce the differences among antagonists. New historical narratives may be required that bring causes closer together, or demonstrate similarities of heritage. Hopefully, as the signifiers begin to mingle and the boundary between intelligibilities deteriorate, so will antagonisms in word and action recede. Pro-life and pro-choice advocates, for example, seldom perceive the "lived realities" of the opposition. There are other possible metaphors around which the definition of "human being" may be constructed than those now separating such groups. And both share a common history of values, the very commonality of which forms the basis for the antagonism. With less resort to laws and abstract rights, and greater emphasis on open and creative dialogue about people's daily lives, there is hope for a grafting of mutually incorporating intelligibilities.[45]

Finally, the resolution of existing conflicts must *press beyond dialogue*. Wittgenstein once pointed out that although a committed realist and an enthusiastic idealist might disagree philosophically on the nature of reality, when it came time to raising their children, they would both speak about the world in roughly the same way. Each will "teach his children the word 'chair' after all, for of course, he wants to teach them to do this and that, e.g., to fetch a chair." Then, Wittgenstein asks, "Where will be the difference between what the idealist-educated children say and the realist ones? Won't the difference only be one of the battle cry?"[46] The point has important implications for the reduction of conflict. First, many conflicts may be primarily a matter of battle cries. Differences in religious or political beliefs, for example, may have little important bearing on more general styles of life. These beliefs are essentially forms of discourse, and to do battle over one way of talking as opposed to another is gratuitous indeed. Again the postmodern warning against the objectification of discourse is apposite. Second, and most important for present purposes, we confront in this instance the limits of linguistic interchange. For in many cases, there may be significant conflict in ways of life— patterns of education, cleanliness, intimacy, economic activity. And even if means could be located of reconciling disparate realities, these conflicts would remain. Attention may usefully shift, then, from the linguistic negotiation of reality to the coordination of actions in everyday life. Putting belief systems aside, can persons locate means of integrating disparate life-styles? There are promising examples: the way athletes and musicians from all walks of life generate smooth and effective teams or musical groups, and the ways business executives and scientists from conflicting cultural backgrounds work together to generate multinational corporations and cooperative research undertakings. Similar undertakings are required for successful bridging of life-styles.

Although each of these options is invited by a postmodern posture, postmodern thought does not in itself opt for the abolition of conflict. When conflicts are untenable, postmodernism opens the way to means of melding; from the postmodern perspective, however, a certain degree of conflict in society is both unavoidable and desirable. It is unavoidable, for to speak within a discourse at all is to take a certain moral or political stand against others. "Every discourse, by operating under certain assumptions, necessarily excludes other assumptions. Above all, our discourses exclude those others who might disrupt the established hierarchies or challenge the prevailing hegemony of power," says David Tracy.[47] Thus, there will always be a tension between those within a discourse and those marginalized by it. And, if deep and destructive schisms are to be avoided, there is reason for setting the signifiers free, generating oppositional realities, and breaking down the internal logics of the dominant discourses.[48]

This is a good point to end this book. The text now speaks of flowering forms of relatedness, a growing consciousness of global interdependence, an organic relationship to our planet, and the withering of lethal conflict—all so hopeful in implication. But is this not to indulge once again in romanticist dreams of the good society, and to invoke the great modernist narrative of progress? Are we not, at last, merely giving way to the traditional pleasures of the text? Reflexive reconsideration is required: can we now blend these richly elaborated discourses into new forms of serious games that can take us beyond text and into life? And can we do so without losing sight of context and contingency, without making fast the language, or formulating final solutions? We move now beyond the speakable to action.

Notes

Chapter 1: The Self Under Siege

1 David Nicholson-Lord, "Death by Tourism," *The Independent*, 5 Aug. 1990.

2 Ludwig Wittgenstein, *Tractatus Logico-Philosophicus*, trans. D. F. Pears and B. F. McGuinness (London: Routledge and Kegan Paul, 1922).

3 As argued by James Deese in *American Freedom and the Social Sciences* (New York: Columbia University Press, 1985), for example, the concept of free choice, critical to the concept of democracy, is threatened by the attempt of the social sciences to define human action as environmentally determined.

4 Clifford Geertz, *The Interpretation of Cultures* (New York: Basic Books, 1973).

5 Ibid., p. 390.

6 Other interesting examples of nonindividualist conceptions of self can be found in Lawrence Rosen's description of Muslim life, *Bargaining for Reality* (Chicago: University of Chicago Press, 1984) and John Kirkpatrick's account of the Marquesas islanders in G. White and J. Kirkpatrick, eds., *Person, Self, and Experience: Exploring Pacific Ethnopsychologies* (Berkeley: University of California Press, 1985). For more general accounts of alternative conceptions of mental functioning, see Dorothy Holland and Naomi Quinn, eds., *Cultural Models in Language and Thought* (Cambridge: Cambridge University Press, 1987); Dorothy Lee, *Freedom and Culture* (New York: Prentice-Hall, 1959); Anthony Marsella, George Devos, and Francis Hsu, *Culture and Self: Asian and Western Perspectives* (New York: Tavistock, 1985); and Paul Heelas and Andrew Locke, eds., *Indigenous Psychologies* (London: Academic Press, 1981).

7 For example, Robert Plutchik's attempt at an exhaustive review concludes with a list of eight "fundamental" emotions: fear, anger, joy, sadness, acceptance, disgust, expectation, and surprise. In Robert Plutchik and Henry Kellerman, eds., *Emotion, Theory, Research and Experience*, vol. 1 (New York: Academic Press, 1980).

8 See, for example, Catherine Lutz, *Unnatural Emotions* (Chicago: University of Chicago Press, 1988).

9 Michelle Z. Rosaldo, *Knowledge and Passion* (Cambridge: Cambridge University Press, 1980).

10 One of the most complete analyses of self-conception throughout history is Charles Taylor's *Sources of the Self* (Cambridge, Mass.: Harvard University Press, 1989). For Taylor, however, the aim of historical work is not so much to question contemporary assumptions but to enrich them by reactivating the historical legacy.

11 John O. Lyons, *The Invention of the Self* (Carbondale: Southern Illinois University Press, 1978). Debate still rages, however, concerning the origins of the individualized self in Western culture. R. B. Onians, in *The Origins of European Thought* (Cambridge: Cambridge University Press, 1951), traces beliefs in a form of life-soul, dwelling within the head, to Homeric times; Mark Taylor, in *Erring: A Postmodern A/Theology* (Chicago: University of Chicago Press, 1984), finds important roots in Augustine's confessions, which marked the beginning of a literary genre in which the unfolding of personal subjectivity serves as the major subject; Marxist theorists are more likely to emphasize the concept as an ideological objectification of capitalist economics. As Lyons properly discerns, "the invention of the self cannot be dated from a cry of 'Eureka' from a bathtub, for it was made up of parts and accretions" (p. 8).

12 Lyons, *The Invention of the Self*, p. 157.

13 Kenneth J. Gergen, Gabriel Gloger-Tippelt, and Peter Glickman, "Everyday Conceptions of the Developing Child," in Gun Semin and Kenneth Gergen, eds., *Everyday Understanding: Social and Scientific Implications* (London: Sage, 1990). Also apposite is William Kessen's article, "The American Child and Other Cultural Inventions," *American Psychologist* 34 (1975): 815–20.

14 Philippe Aries, *Centuries of Childhood* (New York: Random House, 1962).

15 J. H. van den Berg, *The Changing Nature of Man* (New York: Delta, 1961)

16 Quoted in ibid., p. 21.

17 Quoted in ibid., p. 22.

18 Elisabeth Badinter, *Mother Love: Myth and Reality* (New York: Macmillan, 1981).

19 Quoted in ibid., p. 62.

20 For a more extended account of the process, see Kenneth Gergen, "Therapeutic Professions and the Diffusion of Deficit," *Journal of Mind and Behavior* 11 (Autumn 1991): 353–368. For a related critique see Martin Gross, *The Psychological Society* (New York: Random House, 1987), and Nikolas Rose, *The Psychological Complex* (London: Routledge and Kegan Paul, 1985).

Chapter 2· From the Romantic to the Modern Vision of Self

1 It is perhaps an overstatement to call the romanticist conception of self "new," as romanticism draws importantly from earlier classical and Christian traditions. Useful resources for locating the romanticist view of self include M. H. Abrams, *Natural Supernaturalism: Tradition and Revolution in Romantic Literature* (New York: Norton, 1971); Lorenz Eitner, *Neoclassicism and Romanticism, 1750–1850* (Englewood Cliffs, N.J.: Prentice-Hall, 1970); Lillian R. Furst, *Romanticism in Perspective* (London: Methuen, 1969); Robert F. Gleckner and Gerald E. Enscoe, *Romanticism: Points of View* (Detroit: Wayne State University Press, 1975); Leslie A. Marchand, *"Alas! the Love of Women!": Byron's Letters and Journals* (Cambridge, Mass.: Harvard University Press, 1974); Henri Peyre, *What Is Romanticism?* trans. R. Roberts (Mobile: University of Alabama Press, 1977); and H. G. Schenk, *The Mind of the European Romantics* (London: Constable, 1966).

2 Morton M. Hunt, *The Natural History of Love* (New York: Knopf, 1959).

3 Ibid., pp. 257–58.

4 Percy Bysshe Shelley, "On Love," in *Shelley's Literary and Philosophical Criticism*, ed. John Shawcross (London: Henry Frowde, 1976), p. 43.

5 Friedrich Schiller, *Poems of Schiller* (Boston: Cassino, 1884), p. 18.

6 John Keats, *Complete Poems and Selected Letters*, ed. Clarence DeWitt Thorpe (New York: Odyssey, 1935), p. 523.

7 Schiller, *Poems*, pp. 35–36.

8 Paul Rosenblatt, *Bitter, Bitter Tears: Nineteenth-Century Diarists and Twentieth-Century Grief Theories* (Minneapolis: University of Minnesota Press, 1983).

9 Johann Wolfgang von Goethe, *The Sufferings of Young Werther*, trans. D. E. Wellbery (New York: Suhrkamp, 1988), p. 27.

10 Ibid., p. 60.

11 Ibid., p. 33.

12 For elucidations of the importance of imagination in the romantic conception of the person see especially Abrams, *Natural Supernaturalism*, and Peyre, *What Is Romanticism?*

13 William Blake, *Complete Writings*, ed. Geoffrey Keynes (London: Oxford University Press, 1972).

14 Keats, *Complete Poems*, p. 178. Useful discussions of the romantic conception of imagination may be found in Furst, *Romanticism in Perspective*, pp. 117–210, and Peyre, *What Is Romanticism?* pp. 128–48.

15 Schiller, *Poems*, p. 271.

16 Friedrich Nietzsche, *Thus Spake Zarathustra*, trans. R. J. Hollingdale (Harmondsworth: Penguin, 1961).

17 Eugène Delacroix, *The Journal of Eugène Delacroix*, trans. W. Pach (New York: Covici-Friede, 1937), p. 82.

18 See discussions in Peyre, *What Is Romanticism?* pp. 71–87 and Schenk, *The Mind of the European Romantics*, pp. 49–57.

19 Delacroix, *Journal*, p. 93.

20 For an excellent account of the realization of the romanticist conception of self in art see Wylie Sypher, *Loss of the Self in Modern Art and Literature* (New York: Random House, 1962).

21 Carl Dahlhaus, *Between Romanticism and Modernism*, trans. Mary Whitall (Berkeley: University of California Press, 1980).

22 Shelley, *Criticism*, p. 79. In his absorbing work *On Moral Personhood* (Chicago: University of Chicago Press, 1989), Richard Eldridge also demonstrates a social (as opposed to an individualistic) element in certain romanticist views of morality. In particular, one finds in Wordsworth's work that moral being can only be achieved through cooperative relations within communities.

23 Quoted in Peyre, *What Is Romanticism?* p. 124.

24 See especially Abrams, *Natural Supernaturalism*.

25 For an account of other antecedents to Freudian theory see Lancelot Whyte, *The Unconscious Before Freud* (New York: Basic Books, 1960). At least one commentator has pointed out that the view of humans as limited in their capacities can be traced to classicism, and in this respect the argument is made that Freud is also classicist in his view of human frailty: Carlos Strenger, "The Classic and Romantic Vision in Psychoanalysis," *International Journal of Psychoanalysis* 70 (1989): 593–610.

26 Useful discussions of modernism include John Herman Randall, Jr., *The Making of the Modern Mind* (Boston: Houghton Mifflin, 1940); Marshall Berman, *All That's Solid Melts Into Air: The Experience of Modernity* (New York: Simon and Schuster, 1982); Michael Levenson, *A Genealogy of Modernism* (Cambridge: Cambridge University Press, 1984); J. Mordaunt Crook, *The Dilemma of Style* (Oxford: Oxford University Press, 1987); John Russell, *The Meanings of Modern Art* (New York: Harper & Row, 1974); David Frisby, *Fragments of Modernity* (Cambridge: Polity Press, 1985); and Francis Frascina and Charles Harrison, eds., *Modern Art and Modernism* (London: Open University, 1982).

27 Bertrand Russell, *Our Knowledge of the External World* (New York: Menton, 1956).

28 Ricardo Quinones's *Mapping Literary Modernism* (Princeton: Princeton University Press, 1985) demonstrates the affinity of much modern literature with scientific aims of prediction and control. Recognizing the shortcomings of any univocal view of period, however, Quinones simultaneously points to important opposing (intuitionist) tendencies in modernist literature.

29 See also Peter T. Manicas's useful discussion in *A History and Philosophy of the Social Sciences* (Oxford: Blackwell, 1987).

30 For further discussion of Enlightenment influences on twentieth-century beliefs in progress, see Ernst Cassirer, *The Philosophy of the Enlightenment* (Princeton: Princeton University Press, 1959) and John Passmore, *The Perfectibility of Man* (New York: Scribner's, 1970). For a discussion of the way such utopian thinking pervaded twentieth-century psychological writings, see J. G. Morawski, "Not Quite New Worlds: Psychologists' Conceptions of the Ideal Family in the Twenties," in Miriam Lewin, ed., *In the Shadow of the Past: Psychology Portrays the Sexes* (New York: Columbia University Press, 1984).

31 Quoted in Crook, *Dilemma of Style*, p. 235.

32 See Marcel Franciscono, *Walter Gropius and the Creation of the Bauhaus in Weimar: The Ideals and Artistic Theories of Its Founding Years* (Urbana: University of Illinois Press, 1971). However, to emphasize once again the lack of a univocal worldview in what I am terming the "romanticist" and "modernist" periods, note should also be taken of the strong spiritual elements that entered into Bauhaus thinking. To Johannes Itten, responsible for foundational courses at the Bauhaus, for example, the work of art was the realization of a "spiritually emotional vibratory power."

33 For a useful discussion of the relationship between the New Criticism and modernist science, see Art Berman, *From the New Criticism to Deconstruction* (Urbana: University of Illinois Press, 1988).

34 Arnold Schönberg, *Style and Idea* (New York: Philosophical Library, 1950), p. 415.

35 Quoted in Marshall Berman, *All That's Solid*, p. 331.

36 Ibid.

37 For a similar view of modern dance see Daniel Michael Levin, "Postmodernism in Dance: Dance, Discourse, Democracy," in H. J. Silverman, ed., *Postmodernism: Philosophy and the Arts* (New York: Routledge, 1990).

38 Clement Greenberg, "Modernist Painting," *Art and Literature* 25 (Spring 1965): 193–201. It is the search for essences that later gives force to both minimalist and conceptual art, the first manifesting a purity of aesthetic denotation (e.g., Barnett Newman's *Stations of the Cross*) and the second a purity of the rational idea. See Gregory Battcock, ed., *Minimal Art* (New York: Dutton, 1968).

39 Ernest Hemingway, *The Sun Also Rises* (1926; reprint ed., New York: Collier, 1986), p. 56.

40 Hemingway's work follows from a particular strand of literary modernism, often called "realist." For other examples, see George J. Becker, ed., *Documents of Modern Literary Realism* (Princeton: Princeton University Press, 1963). This tradition was largely repudiated by modernists working toward more hermetically pure literary forms. Much of this latter work may seem to contradict the present emphasis on an "essential self," a matter addressed in note 45 below.

41 For a discussion of the machine metaphor in modern literature and poetry see Hugh Kenner, *The Mechanical Muse* (Oxford: Oxford University Press, 1987).

42 See Crook, *Dilemma of Style*, p. 227.

43 C. R. Ashbee, *Craftsmanship in Competitive Industry* (London: Campden, 1908), p. 9.

44 Le Corbusier, *Towards a New Architecture*, trans. Frederick Etchells (London: John Rodker, 1931).

45 Literary scholars identify a strong countercurrent within modernist literature, one that emphasized the fragmentation or disintegration of the fundamental or true self. Works of Conrad, Eliot, Joyce, Musil, Proust, and Woolf are among those frequently cited as examples of this tendency. See, for example, Dennis Brown, *The Modernist Self* (London: Macmillan, 1989); Robert Langbaum, *The Mysteries of Identity: A Theme in Modern Literature* (Chicago: University of Chicago Press, 1977); and Wylie Sypher, *Loss of the Self* (New York: Random House, 1962). These scholars argue from a variety of different perspectives, but in my view, most of them ultimately reinforce my position that modernists generally believed in a true or deep sense of identity. For example, it

is proposed by some scholars that as Freudian thinking entered the literary realm, writers increasingly gave expression to a sense of alienation from an unknown inner self. Yet as we have seen, this inner region is the "true self" of the romantic era. The sense of alienation functions as a tribute to the importance of such a deep self. Other scholars trace the breakdown of the self to writers' attempts to transcend the literary conventions of rational order and to give expression to ongoing conscious experience. Thus in the case of Proust and Joyce (and to some degree Eliot), for example, cross-time coherence in perspective or point of view is often lacking. One senses a transiency, contingency, or lack of rational center. Yet in all this work there is an accompanying sense that the rationally coherent aspect of self is an artificial and possibly rhetorical imposition, and that a transcendent consciousness (the author) lies behind as the true center. In still other cases, scholars trace the loss or fragmentation of self to social, technological, or economic conditions. Yet in these instances one typically senses a lament at loss. Even in the late modernist works of Samuel Beckett, whose anguish over the void of contemporary life is extreme, much of the drama lies in the work's implicit critique of the contemporary erosion of meaning. The unspoken invitation to the audience is for a reaffirmation of value or meaning—in effect, the reinstigation of a committed self.

46 Kurt W. Back, "Thriller: The Self in Modern Society," in John Shotter and Kenneth Gergen, eds., *Texts of Identity* (London: Sage, 1989).

47 The mechanical metaphor of the self is not new to the present century. As Michael Kearns demonstrates in *Metaphors of the Mind* (Lexington: University of Kentucky Press, 1987), such metaphors can be found even in eighteenth-century writings. It is the dominance of the metaphor in the present century that is most significant.

48 Ulrich Neisser, *Cognition and Reality* (San Francisco: W.H. Freeman, 1976). For a contemporary expression of the same mechanistic view see Philip N. Johnson-Laird, *The Computer and the Mind* (Cambridge, Mass.: Harvard University Press, 1988).

49 See also Bernard Doray's *From Taylorism to Fordism: A Rational Madness* (London: Free Association Books, 1988) for an account of the way in which the modernist conceptualization of the body as a machine lent itself to the logic of the industrial assembly line. From this perspective the body could simply function as a unit within a larger machinelike process.

50 George A. Kelly, *A Theory of Personality* (New York: Norton, 1963), p. 4. Whether Kelly or any other individual discussed here is truly a "modernist" depends significantly on the focus of attention. As Sandra Bem demonstrates, in Kelly's emphasis on the unique character of each individual and the possibility that the self could construct the world from within, he demonstrated romanticist leanings. See Bem's "Gender Schema and the Romantic Tradition," in Philip Shaver and Clyde Hendrick, eds., *Sex and Gender* (Newbury Park, Calif.: Sage, 1987). As I outlined in "Cognitive Theory and the Return of Romanticism" (paper presented in the 1990 meetings of the American Psychological Association), if stress is laid on what are called "top-down" processes in information processing, one begins to detect a return to certain romanticist tenets. This reinstatement of romanticism operates so as to undermine the very scientific foundation upon which cognitive science is based.

51 As a contemporary extension of Kelly's views, see Aaron Beck, *Love Is Never Enough* (New York: Harper & Row, 1988), in which it is argued that problems in marital relationships are not primarily solved through mutual love. Rather, specifically "cognitive" techniques are required to bring about satisfying intimacy. Authoritative treatments of love continue to reiterate the romanticist and modernist conceptions. Contrast, for example, the modernist spin given to love by Robert J. Sternberg and Michael L. Barnes in *The Psychology of Love* (New Haven: Yale University Press, 1989) with the revitalized romanticism found in Ethel Spector Parsons's *Dreams of Love and Fateful Encounters* (New York: Norton, 1989).

52 Erik H. Erikson, *Identity, Youth, and Crisis* (New York: Norton, 1968).

53 Carl R. Rogers, *On Becoming a Person* (Boston: Houghton Mifflin, 1961).

54 Mark Taylor's *Journeys to Selfhood: Hegel and Kierkegaard* (Berkeley: University of California Press, 1980) adds an important dimension to this discussion. As he argues, the search for an inner or core self may be traced to early Christian mythology. In effect, both romanticism and modernism carry reverberations of cultural forms long removed.

55 Martin E. Seligman, *Learned Helplessness* (San Francisco: W.H. Freeman, 1975).

56 An excellent review is furnished by Albert Bandura, *Principles of Behavior Modification* (New York: Holt, Rinehart and Winston, 1969).

57 John B. Watson, *Psychological Care of the Infant and the Child* (New York: Norton, 1928), pp. 46–47.

58 Frederick W. Taylor, *Principles of Scientific Management* (New York: Harper & Row, 1911).

59 Jacob Azerrad, *Anyone Can Have a Happy Child* (New York: Warner, 1980), p. 18.

60 See Nikolas Rose's *The Psychological Complex* (London: Routledge and Kegan Paul, 1985), for an acute analysis of the way in which scientific prediction and control in psychology was wedded to the grand designs of modernist institutions (government, schools, prisons, etc.) for the systematic management of peoples.

61 David Riesman, *The Lonely Crowd* (New Haven: Yale University Press, 1950), p. 15.

62 Ibid., p. 16.

63 Ibid., p. 22.

64 Solomon E. Asch, "Forming Impressions of Personality," *Journal of Abnormal and Social Psychology* 41 (1946): 258–90.

65 Carl I. Hovland, Irving L. Janis, and Harold Kelley, *Communication and Persuasion* (New Haven: Yale University Press, 1953).

66 See, for example, Carl I. Hovland and Irving L. Janis, eds., *Personality and Persuasibility* (New Haven: Yale University Press, 1953).

67 William J. McGuire, "The Nature of Attitudes and Attitude Change," in Gardner Lindzey and Elliot Aronson, eds., *The Handbook of Social Psychology* (Reading, Mass.: Addison-Wesley, 1968).

68 Theodor Adorno et al., *The Authoritarian Personality* (New York: Harper and Row, 1950)

69 David C. McClelland and David G. Winter, *Motivating Economic Achievement* (New York: Free Press, 1969).

Chapter 3: Social Saturation and the Populated Self

1 Although rail transportation in the United States accounts for a smaller proportion of public travel, the number of rail passengers continues to mount. The U.S. Department of Transportation's *15th Annual Report, Fiscal Year 1981* (Washington: U.S. Government Printing Office, 1981) reports that from 1972 to 1981, the number of passengers increased from 13.7 million to 20.6 million. See also F. D. Hobbs, "Transportation," in *Encyclopaedia Britannica* (1988).

2 *International Herald Tribune*, 15 May 1990.

3 See Andrew C. Brix, "Postal Systems," in *Encyclopaedia Britannica* (1988). The *Annual Report of the Postmaster General, 1986* (Washington: U.S. Government Printing Office, 1986) says that the annual volume of mail continues to increase at a steady and substantial rate for all classes, including priority, express, second-class, and third-class. The volume within the latter two classes jumped from a total of 45 billion in 1982 to 65 billion by 1986.

4 John B. Rae, *The American Automobile Industry* (Boston: Twayne, 1984).

5 *U.S. News and World Report*, 23 July 1990.

6 Hobbs, "Transportation."

7 Ivan Stoddard Coggeshall et al., "Telecommunications Systems," *Encyclopaedia Britannica* (1988). Calvin Sims, "U.S. Phone Companies Prospering as Costs Fall," *Inter-*

national Herald Tribune, 23 May 1989, reports that long-distance services are expected to be "the growth industry of the 1990s."

8 *Statistical Abstracts of the United States, 1987* (Washington: U.S. Government Printing Office, 1987).

9 Coggeshall et al., "Telecommunications."

10 For a detailed account, see Tino Balio, ed., *The American Film Industry* (Madison: University of Wisconsin Press, 1985). Also see Elizabeth Weis et al., "Motion Pictures," *Encyclopaedia Britannica* (1988).

11 Philip S. Unwin, George Unwin, and Hans Georg Artur Viktor, "Publishing," *Encyclopaedia Britannica* (1988).

12 *UNESCO Statistical Yearbook,* 1989, and R.R. Bowker Data Services, New York.

13 *Air Transport 1987* (Washington: Air Transport Association of America, 1987). See also F. D. Hobbs, "Transportation."

14 *Statistical Abstracts*; also see Robert Bailey, "Industry Rides Wave of Expansion," *International Herald Tribune,* 11 June 1989.

15 Mark Frankel, "Jets of the Future," *Newsweek,* 3 July 1989, 38–39.

16 Cobbet Steinberg, *TV Facts* (New York: Facts On File, 1985).

17 See, for example, G. Comstock et al., *Television and Human Behavior* (New York: Columbia University Press, 1978) and L. D. Eron, "Prescription for Reduction of Aggression," *American Psychologist* 35 (1980): 244–52.

18 Richard Schickel, *Intimate Strangers: The Culture of Celebrity* (New York: Doubleday, 1985).

19 Cynthia Heimel, *Village Voice,* 2 Jan. 1990.

20 Glenn D. Bradley, *The Story of the Pony Express* (Chicago: McClurg, 1913).

21 Tom Forester, *High-Tech Society* (Cambridge, Mass.: MIT Press, 1987).

22 *USA Today,* 4 May 1989.

23 Stewart Brand, *The Media Lab: Inventing the Future at MIT* (New York: Viking, 1987), p. 24.

24 Ibid., pp. 36–39.

25 The capacity for digitizing information enables TV cameramen to shoot video in Tiananmen Square, for example, and (via live satellite transmission) have it readied for viewing in the U.S. within five minutes.

26 Brand, *The Media Lab.*

27 Joe Bernard, "Tomorrow's Edition," *TWA Ambassador* (July 1990): 38–40.

28 A useful description of communication in the traditional or "monocultural" community is furnished by W. Barnett Pearce in *Communication and the Human Condition* (Carbondale: University of Northern Illinois Press, 1989).

29 Joshua Meyrowitz, *No Sense of Place* (New York: Oxford University Press, 1985). A similar thesis is developed by Neil Postman in *The Disappearance of Childhood* (New York: Delacorte, 1982).

30 Shoshana Zuboff, *In the Age of the Smart Machine* (New York: Basic Books, 1988).

31 Bruce Wilshire describes the process by which humans come to imitate each other as *mimetic engulfment.* See his "Mimetic Engulfment and Self-Deception," in Amelie Rorty, ed., *Self-Deception* (Berkeley: University of California Press, 1988). Many social scientists believe that such tendencies are innate, appearing as early as the first two weeks of life.

32 Mary Watkins, *Invisible Guests: The Development of Imaginal Dialogues* (Hillsdale, N.J.: Analytic Press, 1986); Eric Klinger, "The Central Place of Imagery in Human Functioning," in Eric Klinger, ed., *Imagery, Volume 2: Concepts, Results, and Applications* (New York: Plenum, 1981); Mary Gergen, "Social Ghosts, Our Imaginal Dialogues with Others" (paper presented at American Psychological Association Meetings, New York, August 1987). See also Mark W. Baldwin and John G. Holmes, "Private Audiences and Awareness of the Self," *Journal of Personality and Social Psychology* 52 (1987): 1087–1198.

33 Hazel Markus and Paula Nurius, "Possible Selves," *American Psychologist* 41 (1986):

954–69. Closely related is Barbara König's fascinating novel, *Personen-Person* (Frankfurt: Carl Hanser Verlag, 1981). The narrator realizes that she may be soon meeting an attractive man. The entire volume is then composed of a dialogue among her many inner voices—the residuals of all her past relations.

34 Paul C. Rosenblatt and Sara E. Wright, "Shadow Realities in Close Relationships," *American Journal of Family Therapy* 12 (1984): 45–54.

35 Michael Billig et al., *Ideological Dilemmas* (London: Sage, 1988).

36 See Peter Berger, Brigitte Berger, and Hansfried Kellner, *The Homeless Mind* (New York: Random House, 1973), for a precursor to the present discussion.

37 T. S. Eliot, "The Love Song of J. Alfred Prufrock," in *The Waste Land and Other Poems* (New York: Harvest, 1930).

Chapter 4: Truth in Trouble

1 *Chronicle of Higher Education*, 28 March 1990.

2 For a critical analysis of this fragmentation in disciplines, see Edward Said's "Opponents, Audiences, Constituencies, and Community," in W. J. T. Mitchell, ed., *The Politics of Interpretation* (Chicago: University of Chicago Press, 1983).

3 For a more thorough account of the relationship between modernism and the fragmentation of experience, see David Frisby, *Fragments of Modernity* (London: Polity Press, 1985).

4 Jean-François Lyotard, *The Postmodern Condition: A Report on Knowledge* (Minneapolis: University of Minnesota Press, 1979), p. 29.

5 In his *Disappearing Through the Skylight* (New York: Viking, 1989), O. B. Hardison, Jr., adds an interesting and important dimension to the present analysis. He argues that the technologies and rational systems of analysis introduced in the modernist phase moved reality from the realm of the immediately accessible, or the realm of the senses, and placed it in forms available only to technological instruments. Reality is thus displaced into an anterior or hypothetical realm.

6 Thomas S. Kuhn, *The Structure of Scientific Revolutions*, 2nd rev. ed. (Chicago: University of Chicago Press, 1970).

7 Although a host of scholars fastened on and extended Kuhn's thesis as described here, Kuhn himself subsequently withdrew from its radical implications. In *The Essential Tension* (Chicago: University of Chicago Press, 1977) he attempts to restore a form of foundational order to science by converting what were previously viewed as rational imperatives into "epistemic values."

8 Paul K. Feyerabend, *Against Method* (New York: Humanities Press, 1976).

9 Norbert R. Hanson, *Patterns of Discovery* (London: Cambridge University Press, 1958).

10 Ibid., p. 17.

11 Harold Garfinkel, *Studies in Ethnomethodology* (Englewood Cliffs, N.J.: Prentice-Hall, 1967).

12 Bruno Latour and Stephen Woolgar, *Laboratory Life: The Social Construction of Scientific Facts* (Beverly Hills: Sage, 1979).

13 Significant works in this domain include Barry Barnes, *Scientific Knowledge and Sociological Theory* (London: Routledge and Kegan Paul, 1974); Karen Knorr-Cetina, *The Manufacture of Knowledge* (Oxford: Pergamon, 1981); Everett Mendelsohn, "The Social Construction of Scientific Knowledge," in Everett Mendelsohn and P. Weingert, eds., *The Social Production of Scientific Knowledge* (Dordrecht: Reidel, 1977); and H. M. Collins, *Changing Order* (Beverly Hills: Sage, 1985).

14 Mary Hawksworth, "Knower, Knowing, and Known: Feminist Theory and Claims of Truth," *Signs* 14 (Spring 1989): 550.

15 This line of argument has precipitated lively debate in philosophy and related areas between those favoring pluralism or perspectivism and those attempting to defend Enlightenment views of a singular, knowable, and describable world. See, for example,

Jerald R. Aronson, *A Realist Philosophy of Science* (London: Macmillan, 1984); Nelson Goodman, *Ways of Worldmaking* (Indianapolis: Hackett, 1981); Rom Harré, *Varieties of Realism* (Oxford: Blackwell, 1986); Martin Hollis and Steven Lukes, eds., *Rationality and Relativism* (Cambridge, Mass.: MIT Press, 1982); David Lewis, *On the Plurality of Worlds* (Oxford: Blackwell, 1986); and David Papineau, *Reality and Representation* (Oxford: Blackwell, 1987).

16 See, for example, Naomi Weisstein, "Psychology Constructs the Female," in Vivian Bornick and Barbara K. Moran, eds., *Women in Sexist Society* (New York: Basic Books, 1971); Mary Gergen, ed., *Feminist Thought and the Structure of Knowledge* (New York: New York University Press, 1988); Sandra Harding, *The Science Question in Feminism* (Ithaca: Cornell University Press, 1986); Ruth Bleier, *Science and Gender: A Critique of Biology and Its Theories on Women* (New York: Pergamon, 1984); and Andrea Jaeger, *Feminist Politics and Human Nature* (New York: Rowman and Allanheld, 1983).

17 Emily Martin, *The Woman in the Body* (Boston: Beacon, 1987).

18 Quoted in ibid.

19 Edward E. Sampson, "Psychology as an American Ideal," *Journal of Personality and Social Psychology* 36 (1978): 1332–43, and "Cognitive Psychology as Ideology," *American Psychologist* 36 (1981): 730–43.

20 This problem has returned in full force in recent years to many influenced by the works of Gregory Bateson and Humberto Maturana. See, for example, Paul Watzlawick's *How Real Is Real?* (New York: Random House, 1976) and *The Invented Reality* (New York: Norton, 1984). Also see Frederick Steier, ed., *Research and Reflexivity* (London: Sage, 1991).

21 Ludwig Wittgenstein, *Philosophical Investigations*, trans. G. Anscombe (New York: Macmillan, 1963).

22 Ibid., fragment 154.

23 Richard Rorty, *Philosophy and the Mirror of Nature* (Princeton: Princeton University Press, 1979), p. 7.

24 Hans-Georg Gadamer, *Philosophical Hermeneutics*, trans. D. E. Linge (Berkeley: University of California Press, 1976).

25 Gadamer himself believed that in spite of the power of the existing forestructure of understanding, it was possible to suspend one's biases and let the text pose its own questions. Thus, the text had the power to extend one's current horizons of understanding. In the end one reached a "fusion of horizons," which do not represent an understanding of the text in itself so much as a dialogically derived amalgam of text and forestructure. No compelling account of how such a fusion could take place has been offered.

26 Stanley Fish, *Is There a Text in This Class?* (Cambridge, Mass.: Harvard University Press, 1980). For related arguments also see Susan R. Suleiman and Inge Crosman, *The Reader in the Text* (Princeton: Princeton University Press, 1980).

27 Quoted in David Lodge, *Small World: An Academic Romance* (London: Secker and Warburg, 1984), p. 29.

28 A similar line of thinking is creating intense discussion in contemporary anthropology, where many argue that ethnographic accounts create images of "the other" that serve primarily to sustain Western values and to promote a sense of Western superiority. Edward W. Said argues in *Orientalism* (London: Routledge and Kegan Paul, 1978) that writings about oriental cultures are part of a "Western style for dominating, restructuring, and having authority over the orient (p. 3)." See also Johannes Fabian, *Time and the Other: How Anthropology Makes Its Object* (New York: Columbia University Press, 1983), and George Marcus and Michael Fischer, *Anthropology as Cultural Critique* (Chicago: University of Chicago Press, 1986).

29 Roland Barthes, *Image, Music, Text*, trans. Steve Heath (New York: Hill and Wang, 1977), p. 146.

30 Michel Foucault, "What Is an Author?" in Josue V. Harari, ed., *Textual Strategies* (Ithaca: Cornell University Press, 1979). Careful historical work on the emerging concept

of authors as personal owners of their words can be found in Mark Rose, "The Author as Proprietor: Donaldson v. Becket and the Genealogy of Modern Authorship," *Representations* 23 (1988): 51–85.

31 See especially Jacques Derrida, *Of Grammatology*, trans. Gayatri Chakravorty Spivak (Baltimore: Johns Hopkins University Press, 1977); also see Derrida's *Writing and Difference*, trans. A. Bass (Chicago: University of Chicago Press, 1978).

32 Hayden White, *Tropics of Discourse* (Baltimore: Johns Hopkins University Press, 1978). For additional treatments of the way the demands of discourse dominate existing accounts of the social and natural sciences, see Herbert Simons, *Rhetoric in the Human Sciences* (London: Sage, 1989); John Nelson, Allan Mcgill, and Donald McCloskey, eds., *The Rhetoric of the Human Sciences* (Madison: University of Wisconsin Press, 1987); Donald McCloskey, *The Rhetoric of Economics* (Madison: University of Wisconsin Press, 1985); Charles Bazerman, *Shaping Written Knowledge* (Madison: University of Wisconsin Press, 1988); and David E. Leary, *Metaphors in the History of Psychology* (Cambridge: Cambridge University Press, 1990).

33 White, *Tropics of Discourse*, p. 125.

34 For one elaboration of this position, see Bronwyn Davies and Rom Harré, "Positioning: The Discursive Production of Selves," *Journal for the Theory of Social Behaviour* 20 (1990): 43–64.

Chapter 5: The Emergence of Postmodern Culture

1 Useful analyses of the postmodern turn include Hans Bertens and Douwe Fokkema, eds., *Approaching Postmodernism* (Amsterdam: John Benjamins, 1986); Steven Conner, *Postmodernist Culture* (Oxford: Blackwell, 1989); Arthur Kroker and David Cook, *The Postmodern Scene* (New York: St. Martin's Press, 1988); Mike Featherstone, ed., "Post Modernism," *Theory, Culture & Society* 5 (1988); Linda Hutcheon, *A Poetics of Postmodernism: History, Theory, Fiction* (London: Routledge, 1988); Hal Foster, ed., *The Anti-Aesthetic: Essays on Postmodern Culture* (Port Townsend, Wash.: Bay Press, 1983); Alan Wilde, *Horizons of Assent: Modernism, Postmodernism, and the Ironic Imagination* (Baltimore: Johns Hopkins University Press, 1981); Hugh J. Silverman, ed., *Postmodernism: Philosophy and the Arts* (New York: Routledge, 1990); and Bryan S. Turner, ed., *Theories of Modernity and Postmodernity* (London: Sage, 1990).

2 Clifford Geertz, *Local Knowledge: Further Essays in Interpretive Anthropology* (New York: Basic Books, 1983).

3 Mark Wigley, "Deconstructivist Architecture," in Philip Johnson and Mark Wigley, *Deconstructivist Architecture* (New York: Museum of Modern Art, 1988).

4 Mario Botta, "Banken Lieben Botta," *Bilanz* (1988): 117–21 (my translation).

5 Johnson, preface to *Deconstructivist Architecture*, p. 8.

6 For a discussion of double coding, see Charles A. Jencks, *The Language of Post-Modern Architecture* (London: Academy, 1984).

7 Robert Venturi, *Complexity and Contradiction* (New York: Museum of Modern Art, 1977), p. 17.

8 Robert Venturi, Denise Scott Brown, and Steven Izenour, *Learning from Las Vegas* (New York: Rizzoli, 1984).

9 For a more extensive discussion of the breakdown of traditional boundaries among literary genres, see Hutcheon, *A Poetics of Postmodernism*. Also relevant are Patricia Meyer Spacks's observations on twentieth-century autobiographies, which she says "deliberately adopt the technique of novels. Twentieth-century novelists write thinly veiled autobiography, call it a novel, then complain if readers suspect some direct self-revelation. Or they write real novels and complain; readers still believe them to be autobiography. The multiplying confusions of genre are encouraged and publicized, becoming part of the general confusion of our time." From *In Imagining a Self* (Cambridge: Harvard University Press, 1976), p. 300.

10 Contemporary South and Central American writing (for example, the work of Mario Vargas Llosa, Gabriel García Márquez, Abel Posse) is especially noteworthy for its mixing of historical and fictional genres—"the historicizing of fiction and the fictionalizing of history."

11 Bruce Crowther has used this term in describing the mixing of reality and myth in historical films. See his *Hollywood Faction: Reality and Myth in the Movies* (London: Columbus, 1984). Luiz Costa Lima's *Control of the Imaginary* (Minneapolis: University of Minnesota Press, 1988) also provides an absorbing account of how the distinction between truth and fiction developed, and with it a suspicion of fiction's power.

12 Georges Perec, *W: Or the Memory of Childhood*, trans. D. Bellos (Boston: Godine, 1988).

13 Interview in the *International Herald Tribune*, 9 May 1989.

14 Even more extreme is the work of the young composer John Moran, whose musical *The Manson Family* re-creates a brutal historical event as slapstick comedy. Minimalist music is mixed with idioms from *Hawaii Five-O*, back-projected film, and dance.

15 For a discussion of postmodernism and rock music, see Steven Connor's *Postmodernist Culture* (Oxford: Blackwell, 1989).

16 Daniel Boorstin, *The Image: A Guide to Pseudo-Events in America* (New York: Harper and Row, 1964).

17 Susan Sontag, *Illness as Metaphor* (New York: Vintage, 1979).

18 Quoted in David L. Altheide, *Creating Reality: How TV News Distorts Events* (Beverly Hills: Sage, 1976).

19 Ed Joyce, *Prime Times and Bad Times* (New York: Doubleday, 1988).

20 For additional accounts of ways "reality" is constructed by the news media, see David Morrison and Howard Tumber, *Journalists at War* (Beverly Hills. Sage, 1988); Shanto Iyengar and Donald Kinder, *News That Matters* (Chicago: University of Chicago Press, 1987); Horace Newcomb, *TV: The Most Popular Art* (Garden City, N.Y.: Anchor, 1974); and Herbert Gans, *Deciding What's News* (New York: Vintage, 1979).

21 Murray Edelman, *Constructing the Political Spectacle* (Chicago: University of Chicago Press, 1988).

22 As *New York* magazine reports (28 March 1988) it is largely for this reason that many subcultures—religious sects, black Americans, Asian Americans, Hispanics—now develop their own news media. They feel they cannot trust "the common news."

23 Jean Baudrillard, *The Evil Demon of Images* (Sydney, Australia: Power Institute of Fine Arts, 1987).

24 The term *hyperreality* has also been used by the postmodern semiologist and novelist Umberto Eco to refer to cases in which people's imagination demands "the real thing," but in order to attain it, they must generate fakes. Over time the fakes come to substitute for the real; they become the real. See his *Travels in Hyperreality* (Orlando: Harcourt Brace Jovanovich, 1986). Fascinating in this respect are modern instances of electronic realities competing on a par with those commonly accepted as normal. For example, in electronic variations on role-playing games such as Dungeons and Dragons, thousands of young computer buffs enter a game world in which they acquire identities, travel from place to place, relate to others, confront life and death, and so on. Such games can absorb hundreds of hours, and many players report them to be more fascinating than their "normal" relationships. In a related sector, computer technologists are perfecting systems of "virtual reality," in which individuals don a pair of goggles that transmits images to them in three dimensions; through the use of electronic gloves they can also participate in the world before them. They can manipulate "objects" in the virtual world, travel from place to place, see the world from multiple perspectives, and carry on relationships with other participants in the same program.

25 For additional accounts of constructed realities, see Arthur Kleinman, *The Illness Narratives* (New York: Basic Books, 1988); Arthur Caplan, H. Tristram Engelhardt, and James McCartney, eds., *Concepts of Health and Disease* (Reading, Mass.: Addison-Wesley, 1981); James Clifford and George Marcus, *Writing Culture* (Berkeley: Uni-

versity of California Press, 1986); Paul Watzlawick, *The Invented Reality* (New York: Norton, 1984); Michael Mulkay, *The Word and the World* (Hempstead: George Allen and Unwin, 1985); and Alain Corbin, *The Foul and the Fragrant* (Cambridge, Mass.: Harvard University Press, 1986).

26 Family researchers also report what they see as a postmodern breakdown in the traditional lines of family authority. Not only are parental perspectives losing much of their traditional power in family life, but the children's voice in family policy is also being augmented by community inputs. Much of the energy behind community ecology movements, for example, is reported to be that of children (*USA Today*, 20 Aug. 1990). See also Kurt Luscher, Franz Schultheis, and Michael Wehrspaun, eds., *Die Postmoderne Familie* (Konstanz: Universitats Verlag, 1990).

27 For a review of these and related arguments, see Robert Gordon, "Critical Legal Histories," *Stanford Law Review* 36 (1984): 101–30; Roberto Unger, *The Critical Legal Studies Movement* (Cambridge, Mass.: Harvard University Press, 1986); and Sanford Levinson, "Law as Literature," *Texas Law Review* 60 (1982): 391–92. Even the more conservative legal thinker Richard A. Posner concludes in his recent work *The Problems of Jurisprudence* (Cambridge, Mass.: Harvard University Press, 1990) that legal principles have no rational foundations, and that legal decisions are strongly dependent on the personal tastes and values of the judiciary.

28 Quoted in Grace Glueck, "Clashing Views Reshape Art History," *New York Times*, 20 Dec. 1987.

29 For the full critical account of the works in this exhibit, see Gill Saunders, *The Nude: A New Perspective* (London: Herbert, 1989).

30 *The New York Times Book Review*, 26 Feb. 1989.

31 Quoted in James Atlas, "Ferment in Higher Education," *Dialogue* 2 (1989): 21–27.

32 Bruno Latour, *Science in Action* (Cambridge, Mass.: Harvard University Press, 1987), p. 185.

33 Paul K. Feyerabend, *Against Method* (New York: Humanities, 1976).

34 For Feyerabend's extension of his views of relativity in science to social pluralism see his *Science in a Free Society* (London: Verso, 1982).

35 Alain Robbe-Grillet, *L'Année Dernier à Marienbad* (Paris: Editions de Minuit, 1961).

36 Milan Kundera, *The Unbearable Lightness of Being* (New York: Harper & Row, 1984).

37 Kundera is only one of a large number of writers working within or close to a postmodern vein. Illustrating the postmodern breakdown in narrative rationality even more fully are the works of Thomas Pynchon (*Gravity's Rainbow*), Italo Calvino (*If on a winter's night a traveler*), and D. M. Thomas (*The White Hotel*). For further accounts of the shifting perspectives of the postmodern novel and the breakdown of conventional rationality, see Brian McHale, *Postmodernist Fiction* (New York: Methuen, 1987); Elizabeth Dipple, *The Unresolvable Plot* (London: Routledge, Chapman, and Hall, 1988); and Hutcheon, *A Poetics of Postmodernism*.

38 Suzi Gablik, *Has Modernism Failed?* (New York: Thames and Hudson, 1984).

39 For an elucidating discussion of Rauschenberg and postmodernism, see Douglas Crimp, "On the Museum's Ruins," in Hal Foster, ed., *The Anti-Aesthetic* (Port Townsend, Wash.: Bay Press, 1983). See also Rosalind Kraus, "The Originality of the Avant-Garde: A Postmodernist Repetition," *October* 18 (Fall 1981): 47–66, for a discussion of the disappearance of the self as the origin of artistic works. Especially illuminating is her discussion of Sherrie Levine's "photo-piracy." Levine takes photographs of recognized works of art, and signs them in her own hand. In this way she produces an "original" that is at the same time a copy; the originality of the recognized original is simultaneously thrown into doubt.

40 Charles Jencks, ed., *The Post-Avant-Garde: Painting in the Eighties* (London: Academy, 1987).

41 For further discussion of multiple narrative forms in contemporary soap opera, see Ien Ang, *Watching Dallas* (Amsterdam: Methuen, 1982). See also Muriel G. Cantor and Suzanne Pingree, *The Soap Opera* (Beverly Hills: Sage, 1983).

NOTES

42 Consistent with the view that the soaps reflect the social saturation of the postmodern life, Ang *(Watching Dallas)* writes of *Dallas,* "Viewers cannot simply identify with one character in order to understand and judge all the developments from that character's point of view, as is mostly the case in an adventure story. . . . Characters are sometimes particularly inconsistent in their behaviour and within a short period can completely change their attitude" (p. 76). Sarah Ruth Kozloff contends that the use of the same protagonist as a leading player in multiple storylines is a major means by which television compensates for the lack of suspense within any single story. In "Narrative Theory and Television," in Robert C. Allen, ed., *Channels of Discourse* (Chapel Hill: University of North Carolina Press, 1987).

43 E. Ann Kaplan, *Rocking Around the Clock* (New York: Methuen, 1987).

44 The values advocated by different MTV clips vary dramatically. Kaplan identifies five major types of video, among them the socially conscious, the nihilist, and the traditionally classic and romantic.

45 Ibid., p. 34.

46 Hilary Lawson, *Reflexivity: Problems of Modern European Thought* (London: Anchor, 1985).

47 It should be noted that many scholars believe the tendency toward self-reflexivity to be primarily a product of modernism. As modernism tended toward a fragmentation of perspectives (see chapter 2), it is argued, people were cut away from a secure sense of centeredness. Thus, as psychologist Louis Sass proposes, modernism gave rise to the kind of hyperreflexivity characteristic of schizophrenia. See his "Introspection, Schizophrenia and the Fragmentation of the Self," *Representations* 19 (1987): 1–34. The major difference between the kind of fragmentation said to characterize modernist writings and that found in the postmodern lies, I believe, in the modernist lament over loss. For the modernist, one *should* possess a unified identity. As I am proposing, however, with the enormous effects of technological change and the consequent suspicion of cultural traditions, the value of a unified self became increasingly difficult to sustain. For the postmodernist the supposition of a unified identity ceases to be compelling. There is little lament, anxiety, or dread at aimless fragmentation, which simply becomes a way of life without strongly negative connotations.

48 Roland Barthes, *A Lover's Discourse* (New York: Hill and Wang, 1987), p. 146.

Chapter 6: From Self to Relationship

1 An absorbing account of self-definition in cases of sickness and approaching death is contained in Arnold R. Beisser, *A Graceful Passage* (New York: Doubleday, 1990). A spate of recent philosophical work has also centered on the problem of identifying what it is to be a self, or the fundamental definition of being human. See, for example, Jon Elster, *The Multiple Self* (London: Cambridge University Press, 1986); Adam Morton, *Frames of Mind* (Oxford: Oxford University Press, 1980); Richard Eldridge, *On Moral Personhood* (Chicago: University of Chicago Press, 1989); Kathleen V. Wilkes, *Real People* (Oxford: Clarendon, 1988); and Bernard Williams, *Problems of the Self* (Cambridge: Cambridge University Press, 1973). One of the most interesting aspects of this work is that it exists at all, for only under particular cultural conditions would the question be considered worthy of such attention.

2 See also James Clifford, *The Predicament of Culture* (Cambridge, Mass.: Harvard University Press, 1988), for a discussion of twentieth-century threats to the conception of "pure cultures" and emerging issues in the "politics of identity," or the challenges placed on persons to seem pure in their cultural identities.

3 I argue that the chief source of gender breakdown is the technologies of social saturation and the resulting pluralism of definition. However, this does not at all rule out additional processes having the same effect. For example, as German sociologists Ulrich Beck and Elisabeth Beck-Gernsheim propose in their volume *Das Ganz Normale Chaos der Liebe*

(Frankfurt: Surkamp Verlag, 1990), the progressive individualizing of Western culture achieves much the same erosion of gender lines. With women joining the workforce, and marriage postponed, both men and women are adding to their traditional roles those assigned to the opposite sex.

4 John Money, *Man and Woman* (Baltimore: Johns Hopkins University Press, 1972). See also his *Sex Errors of the Body: Dilemmas, Education, Counseling* (Baltimore: Johns Hopkins University Press, 1968) and *Gay, Straight, and In-Between* (New York: Oxford University Press, 1988).

5 Suzanne Kessler and Wendy McKenna, *Gender: An Ethnomethodological Approach* (New York: Wiley, 1978). See also Sherry Ortner and Harriet Whitehead, *Sexual Meanings: The Cultural Construction of Gender and Sexuality* (Cambridge: Cambridge University Press, 1981).

6 Social scientists have taken a keen interest in the processes by which people are socially constructed, the forms of this construction, and the consequences. See, for example, James Averill, *Anger and Aggression: An Essay on Emotion* (New York: Springer, 1983); Jeff Coulter, *The Social Construction of the Mind* (New York: Macmillan, 1979); Theodore R. Sarbin and J. C. Mancuso, *Schizophrenia: Medical Diagnosis or Moral Verdict?* (New York: Pergamon, 1980); Michael Carrithers, Steven Collins, and Steven Lukes, *The Category of the Person* (Cambridge: Cambridge University Press, 1985); Peter L. Berger and Thomas Luckmann, *The Social Construction of Reality* (Garden City, N.Y.: Doubleday, 1966); Kenneth Gergen and Keith Davis, eds., *The Social Construction of the Person* (New York: Springer, 1985); Rom Harré, ed., *The Social Construction of Emotion* (Oxford: Blackwell, 1986); Judith Lorber and Susan A. Farrell, *The Social Construction of Gender* (Newbury Park, Calif.: Sage, 1990); Jan Smedslund, *Psycho Logic* (Berlin: Springer, 1988); John Shotter, *Social Accountability and Selfhood* (Oxford: Blackwell, 1983); and David F. Greenberg. *The Construction of Homosexuality* (Chicago: University of Chicago Press, 1988).

7 Arlie Russell Hochschild, *The Managed Heart* (Berkeley: University of California Press, 1983), p. 13.

8 Erving Goffman, *The Presentation of Self in Everyday Life* (Garden City, N.Y.: Doubleday, 1959); *Strategic Interaction* (Philadelphia: University of Pennsylvania Press, 1969); *Stigma* (Englewood Cliffs, N.J.: Prentice-Hall, 1963).

9 William Sansom, *The Perfect Gentleman* (London: Heath, 1956), pp. 230–31.

10 Joe McGinniss, *The Selling of the President* (New York: Trident, 1968).

11 Mark L. Snyder, "Self-Monitoring Processes," in Leonard Berkowitz, ed., *Advances in Experimental Social Psychology*, vol. 12 (New York: Academic Press, 1979).

12 David Riesman, *The Lonely Crowd* (New Haven: Yale University Press, 1950).

13 Snyder, "Self-Monitoring Processes," p. 134.

14 Louis A. Zurcher, Jr., *The Mutable Self* (Beverly Hills: Sage, 1977).

15 Michael Wood and Louis A. Zurcher, Jr., *The Development of Postmodern Self* (New York: Greenwood, 1988), p. 35.

16 In her interesting volume *Positive Illusions: Creative Self-Deception and the Healthy Mind* (New York: Basic Books, 1989), Shelley Taylor unfolds an argument that lends further support to the pastiche personality. She proposes that successful coping in contemporary society requires one to construct a positive picture of the self. However, the analysis remains modernist in its view of these self-constructions as "illusions."

17 As Stuart Ewen demonstrates in *All Consuming Images* (New York: Basic Books, 1988), the emphasis on style within the middle class has steadily increased since the industrial revolution, due to the availability of cheap commodities through which the upper class could be aped. The present argument does not deny the multiple forces at play in producing style consciousness within the present century. I do argue, however, that the modernist consciousness was not favorable to high style, and that social saturation and the resulting demands for multiple presentations are now intensifying consciousness of style.

18 Many decry the increasing emphasis on style on the grounds that it alienates people

from their essential selves, natural feelings, sense of identity, and self-knowledge. Such a critique can be found not only in Ewen's *All Consuming Images* but also in Hochschild's *The Managed Heart*. From the present standpoint, however, such critiques reflect both romanticist and modernist assumptions of an essential, true, or unacculturated self. As one moves in the postmodern direction, one comes to view the sense of a true and essential self as a style to which one has become accustomed; "being" is well-practiced "seeming." In *The Culture of Narcissism* (New York: Norton, 1979), Christopher Lasch gives voice to another common sentiment, namely that the pursuit of style is self-indulgent. Yet from the present standpoint, self-styling is antithetical to narcissism; rather, style is a form of language, and thus essentially *for others*. Style is built into forms of relationship, and without others to "read the language" it would fail to motivate. See Dick Hebdige, *Subculture: The Meaning of Style* (London: Methuen, 1979).

19 Quoted in L. Baier, *Gleichheitzeichen: Streitschriften über Abwerichung und Identität* (Berlin: Wagenbach, 1985), p. 19.

20 See also Christine Brooke-Rose's essay, "The Dissolution of Character in the Contemporary Novel," in Thomas Heller, Morton Sosna, and David Wellbery, eds., *Reconstructing Individualism* (Stanford: Stanford University Press, 1986), pp. 184–96.

21 Jean Baudrillard, *The Ecstasy of Communication* (New York: Autonomedia, 1987), p. 10.

22 For a review of organizational culture, see Gareth Morgan, *Images of Organization* (Beverly Hills: Sage, 1986).

23 For a review, see Lynn Hoffman, *Foundations of Family Therapy* (New York: Basic Books, 1981).

24 Perhaps women will play a leading role in fashioning the relational reality. As M. Brinton Lykes concludes from his extensive interviewing, women are less invested in concepts of autonomy, independence, and separation than men, and are more likely to see themselves as embedded within relationships. "Gender and Individualistic vs. Collectivist Bases for Notions about the Self," *Journal of Personality* 53 (1985): 356–81.

25 For additional accounts of ways in which concepts of the individual person can be refigured within a relational form, see David Middleton and Derek Edwards, *Collective Remembering* (London: Sage, 1990); Karen Burke LeFevre, *Invention as a Social Act* (Carbondale: Southern Illinois University Press, 1987); Kenneth J. Gergen, "Social Understanding and the Inscription of Self," in J. Stigler, R. Shweder, and G. Herdt, eds., *Cultural Psychology: Essays on Comparative Human Development* (Cambridge: Cambridge University Press, 1989); and E. E. Sampson, "Deconstructing Psychology's Subject," *Journal of Mind and Behavior* 4 (1983): 135–64.

26 For a lively account of the stylistic or rhetorical bases of effective autobiography, see Herbert Leibowitz, *Fabricating Lives: Explorations in American Autobiography* (New York: Knopf, 1989).

27 For a more detailed account of narrative forms and their construction see Kenneth J. Gergen and Mary M. Gergen, "Narrative and the Self and Relationship," in Leonard Berkowitz, ed., *Advances in Experimental Social Psychology*, vol. 21 (New York: Academic Press, 1979). Also relevant are discussions by Donald Polkinghorne, *Narrative Knowing and the Human Sciences* (Albany: State University of New York Press, 1988), and Theodore R. Sarbin, ed., *Narrative Psychology* (New York: Praeger, 1986). For a discussion of the way the media generate narrative forms for public consumption, see James Carey, *Media, Myths, and Narratives* (Beverly Hills: Sage, 1988). For a discussion of the way personal lives become saturated with textuality, see John Shotter and Kenneth Gergen, eds., *Texts of Identity* (London: Sage, 1989).

28 See Elizabeth F. Loftus, *Eyewitness Testimony* (Cambridge, Mass.: Harvard University Press, 1979).

29 Middleton and Edwards, *Collective Remembering*.

30 Donald Spence, *Narrative Truth and Historical Truth* (New York: Norton, 1982).

31 Stanley Schachter, "The Interaction of Cognitive and Physiological Determinants of

Emotional State," in L. Berkowitz, ed., *Advances in Experimental Social Psychology,* vol. 1 (New York: Academic Press, 1964).

32 Catherine A. Lutz, *Unnatural Emotions* (Chicago: University of Chicago Press, 1988).

33 James R. Averill, *Anger and Aggression* (New York: Springer, 1982). See also Carol Tavris, *Anger: The Misunderstood Emotion* (New York: Simon and Schuster, 1981); Rom Harré, ed., *The Social Construction of Emotions* (Oxford: Blackwell, 1983); and F. G. Bailey, *The Tactical Uses of Passion* (Ithaca: Cornell University Press, 1983).

34 See Gergen and Gergen, "Narrative and the Self," for a more detailed discussion of emotional scenarios.

35 Lawrence Kohlberg, "Stages and Sequences: The Cognitive-Developmental Approach to Socialization," in David A. Goslin, ed., *Handbook of Socialization Theory and Research* (Chicago: Rand McNally, 1969).

36 Carol Gilligan, *In a Different Voice* (Cambridge, Mass.: Harvard University Press, 1982). For an extension of this position into the realm of thought processes, see the discussion of Mary Field Belenky et al. on constructed knowledge as an integration of voices in *Women's Ways of Knowing* (New York: Basic Books, 1986).

37 Gilligan, *In a Different Voice,* p. 138.

38 Richard Rorty reaches much the same conclusion in his essay "Postmodernist Bourgeois Liberalism," *Journal of Philosophy* 80 (1983): 583–89.

39 Serving as a useful prolegomenon to such an account is Michael J. Sandel's *Liberalism and the Limits of Justice* (Cambridge: Cambridge University Press, 1982). Here Sandel provides a telling critique of the traditional, individual-centered view of justice, in which autonomous individuals determine the nature of the good, deliberate, and choose their actions in accord with the dictates of their conscience.

40 For a more detailed account of the problem of deceit, see Kenneth J. Gergen, "Invitciones al engano: an analisis micro-social," *Buletin de Psicologia* 22 (1989): 7–40.

Chapter 7: A Collage of Postmodern Life

1 The present account is indebted to Anthony Giddens's discussion of "structuration" in his *New Rules of Sociological Method* (New York: Basic Books, 1976). Giddens proposes that the culture molds the behavior of the individual, and that the individual thereafter serves to perpetuate the existing forms of culture. However, this kind of formulation confronts the problem of mutually exclusive ontologies. That is, if all that is culture is subtracted from the world, there is nothing left over to serve as an individual; if all individuals are deleted, no culture remains. The terms "culture" and "individual" thus appear as two different ways of labeling the same reality. To speak of them as *acting upon* each other becomes problematic.

2 For a review of modernist research on love, see Clyde Hendrick and Susan Hendrick, *Liking, Loving, and Relating* (Monterey: Brooks Cole, 1983).

3 The frequency with which commitments are broken in contemporary society is nicely evidenced by the publication of Helen Rose Fuchs Ebaugh's *Becoming an Ex: The Process of Role Exit* (Chicago: University of Chicago Press, 1988).

4 See Vance Packard, *A Nation of Strangers* (New York: David McKay, 1972).

5 For an analysis of the contemporary breakdown in conventional life patterns, see Marlis Buchmann, *The Script of Life in Modern Society: Entry into Adulthood in a Changing World* (Chicago: University of Chicago Press, 1989).

6 Erving Goffman, *Asylums* (New York: Doubleday, 1961).

7 This last metaphor for the postmodern attitude is that of Peter Sloterdijk, from *Critique of Cynical Reason* (Minneapolis: University of Minnesota Press, 1987).

8 Jean-François Lyotard, *The Postmodern Condition: A Report on Knowledge* (Minneapolis: University of Minnesota Press, 1984).

9 Stephen Tyler, "A Postmodern for Instance," in Lorraine Nencel and Peter Pels, eds., *Identity and Ideology in Social Science Knowledge* (London: Sage, 1991).

10 See also Robert Jay Lifton's relevant discussion of irony and the protean personality configuration in *The Future of Immortality* (New York: Basic Books, 1987), pp. 20–21.

11 Mary M. Gergen, "From Mod Masculinity to Post-Mod Macho: A Feminist Re-Play," *Humanistic Psychologist* 1 (1990): 95–104.

12 Gregory Bateson, *Steps to an Ecology of Mind* (New York: Ballantine, 1972).

13 Julia Kristeva, *In the Beginning Was Love* (New York: Columbia University Press, 1987), pp. 7–8.

14 Hans-Georg Gadamer, *Truth and Method* (New York: Seabury, 1975).

15 James P. Carse, *Finite and Infinite Games* (New York: Macmillan, 1986).

Chapter 8: Self-Renewal and Sincerity

1 So profound has the religious ferment of the past thirty years been that historian William McLoughlin, in *Revivals, Awakenings, and Reform* (Chicago: University of Chicago Press, 1978), has labeled the period America's "Fourth Great Awakening."

2 I am not including here a discussion of cultural traditions as a force of resistance, primarily because I am proposing more generally that under the influence of the technologies of saturation the traditions are rapidly breaking down. However, as argued by Walter Anderson in *Reality Isn't What It Used to Be* (New York: Harper and Row, 1990), in the United States, in any case, there is no univocal view of what the traditions are. Some claim the traditions favor the conservative right, others that they give precedence to a revolutionary left, and so on. Tradition itself becomes a construction of the present.

3 See Roy Wallis, *Elementary Forms of the New Religious Life* (London: Routledge and Kegan Paul, 1984), for a discussion of the instability of charismatic leadership in contemporary religion. See also Kenneth A. Bruffee's volume, *Elegiac Romance: Cultural Change and the Loss of the Hero in Modern Fiction* (Ithaca: Cornell University Press, 1983), for an analysis of the disappearance of the hero from the modern novel. In place of heroic novels, argues Bruffee, there is now the elegiac romance, in which the major protagonist outgrows the delusion that there are "real heroes."

4 Using both romanticist and modernist images, Hitler spoke of the National Socialist Party as "our campaign of the spirit and reason." See Paulo Valesia's essay, "The Beautiful Lie: Heroic Individuality and Fascism," in Thomas Heller, Morton Sosna, and David Wellbery, eds., *Reconstructing Individualism* (Stanford: Stanford University Press, 1986).

5 Thomas M. DeFrank, "Playing the Media Game," *Newsweek*, international edition, 17 April 1989. For a more general treatment of the "sham" identities created by the media during elections, see Jack W. Germond and Jules Witcover, *Whose Broad Stripes and Bright Stars?* (New York: Warner, 1988). For an analysis of the fashioning of the presidential image in the communications media, see Roderick P. Hart, *The Sound of Leadership: Presidential Communication in the Modern Age* (Chicago: University of Chicago Press, 1987).

6 Frederic Jameson, "Postmodernism and Consumer Society," in Hal Foster, ed., *The Anti-Aesthetic, Essays on Postmodern Culture* (Port Townsend, Wash.: Bay Press, 1983), p. 115.

7 Also relevant is Richard D. Altick's *Lives and Letters: A History of Literary Biography in England and America* (New York: Knopf, 1965), in which he describes how twentieth-century biography has shifted from a valuing of the subject to an exposure of his or her dark underside.

8 See Alan Gewirth's *Reason and Morality* (Chicago: University of Chicago Press, 1978) for a "modernist" attempt to solve problems of morality on a rational basis.

9 Allan Bloom, *The Closing of the American Mind* (New York: Simon and Schuster, 1987).

10 Alasdair MacIntyre, *After Virtue* (Notre Dame: University of Notre Dame Press, 1981).

11 Vance Packard, *A Nation of Strangers* (New York: David McKay, 1972).

12 The breakdown of the traditional face-to-face community was already in progress, owing much to industrialization and the consequent dislocation of large populations of workers. In this sense Ferdinand Tonnies's famous distinction between the *Gemeinschaft* (the society in which close, interpersonal relationships form the base) and the *Gesellschaft* (in which people are recognized largely by the functions they serve) captures not two types of community, but social patterns in historical transition. Robert Park and other participants in the Chicago school of urban sociology also go on to describe the breakdown in face-to-face neighborhoods produced by the modern city's demands for large organizations and the opportunities for upward mobility.

13 Alvin Toffler, *Future Shock* (New York: Bantam, 1970).

14 Warren G. Bennis and Philip E. Slater, *The Temporary Society* (New York: Harper and Row, 1964).

15 For detailed description of the kinds of pastiche communities facilitated by the technologies of saturation, see Richard Louv, *America II* (Los Angeles: Tarcher, 1983).

16 As Benedict Anderson demonstrates in his *Imagined Communities* (London: Verso, 1983), the very idea of a nation-state (an "official nationalism" to which individuals commit their lives) as opposed to a dynasty or kingdom, for example, depended importantly on the development of printing and technologies that could construct a sense of shared communality over a broad spectrum. At this point in time, however, so many and so diverse are the technologies unifying persons under some cause that the "nation-state" stands as simply one more competitor for affiliation. One confronts the not-unlikely situation of finding one's affiliation with the nation opposed to that with one's business, religion, political grouping, ethnic community, and friendships with people of other nations.

17 See Stewart M. Hoover, *Mass Media Religion* (Beverly Hills: Sage, 1988).

18 Interestingly, analysts such as Anthony Cohen, in *The Symbolic Construction of Community* (London: Tavistock, 1985), propose that the view of communities as geographically and behaviorally circumscribed is now a form of myth. Communities are now based on nothing more than symbolic relations.

19 For a discussion of the ways in which modernist psychology has universalized these questions, adding weight to their "reasonableness," see Kenneth J. Gergen, *The Psychology of Behavior Exchange* (Reading, Mass.: Addison-Wesley, 1969).

20 For a discussion of the commercialization or "selling of the movement," see Thomas Robbins, *Cults, Converts, and Charisma* (London: Sage, 1988).

21 For a psychologist's account of such practices, see Daryl J. Bem, "Self-perception Theory," in Leonard Berkowitz, ed., *Advances in Experimental Social Psychology*, vol. 6 (New York: Academic Press, 1972).

22 For an analysis of political events as forms of social drama, see Robin Wagner-Pacifici, *The Moro Morality Play: Terrorism as Social Drama* (Chicago: University of Chicago Press, 1986).

23 Umberto Eco, *Postscript to the Name of the Rose* (San Diego: Harcourt Brace Jovanovich, 1983), p. 67.

Chapter 9: Reckoning and Relativity

1 Among the most vociferous critics of the moral and political emptiness of postmodernism are neo-Marxist critics. In *Against the Grain* (London: Verso, 1986), Terry Eagleton captures one of the central themes of the present book in the following criticism: "The depthless, styleless, dehistoricized, decathected surfaces of postmodernist culture are not meant to signify an alienation, for the very concept of alienation must secretly posit

a dream of authenticity which postmodernism finds quite unintelligible. Those flattened surfaces and hollowed interiors are not 'alienated' because there is no longer any subject to be alienated and nothing to be alienated from, 'authenticity' having been less rejected than merely forgotten" (p. 132). See Fredric Jameson, "Postmodernism, or the Cultural Logic of Late Capitalism," *New Left Review* 146 (1984), and Arthur Kroker and David Cook, eds., *The Postmodern Scene, Excremental Culture and Hyper-Aesthetics* (New York: St. Martin's, 1986), for additional critiques. Postmodernist thinkers have not been univocally content with either the neo-Marxist view of postmodernism or a single-minded negativity. As John Fekete argues in *Life After Postmodernism* (London: Macmillan, 1988, p. iii), "the postmodern paradigm shift may place value-theoretical interventions into positions of far greater esteem" than in the preceding century. More positively, recent theological writing has begun to find in postmodern work a new opening to a conception of God and to more promising forms of human relatedness. See, for example, Mark Taylor, *Erring: A Postmodern A/theology* (Chicago: University of Chicago Press, 1981), and David Tracy, *Plurality and Ambiguity* (San Francisco: Harper and Row, 1987). In contrast to these more positive views, Mark Edmundson ("Prophet of a New Postmodernism," *Harper's* Dec. 1989) distinguishes between a negative and a positive phase of postmodernism. As he sees it, writers of the initial (negative) phase—such as Samuel Beckett, Thomas Pynchon, and John Ashbery—tended to dwell on the destruction of meaning, truth, authority, and reason, whereas later postmoderns like Salman Rushdie, Richard Rorty, and Milan Kundera see in this destruction the possibility for creative metamorphosis. Here I am attempting to press forward in the latter direction.

2 For accounts of the close relationship between the concept of progress and Enlightenment foundations of modernism and of science, see David Marcell, *Progress and Pragmatism* (Westport, Conn.: Greenwood, 1974), John Passmore, *The Perfectibility of Man* (New York: Scribner's, 1970), and John Randall, Jr., *The Making of the Modern Mind* (Cambridge, Mass.: Riverside, 1940). As these analyses make clear, however, romanticist thought also entertained positive accounts of progress, and the concept can be traced at least as far back as early Greek and Christian writings.

3 Rachel Carson, *Silent Spring* (Boston: Houghton Mifflin, 1962).

4 For a thoughtful critique of the negative social effects of the unbridled pursuit of medical progress, see Daniel Callahan, *What Kind of Life: The Limits of Medical Progress* (New York: Simon and Schuster, 1989).

5 Barbara Ehrenreich, *Fear of Falling: The Inner Life of the Middle Class* (New York: Pantheon, 1989).

6 Recent organizational theory also criticizes the traditional belief in top-down leadership, and argues that the viability of the contemporary organization depends on its susceptibility to multiplicity of voice—its capacity to participate simultaneously in multiple dialogues within and outside its physical confines. See Kenneth J. Gergen, "Organizational Theory in Postmodern Culture," in Michael Reed and Michael Hughes, eds., *Rethinking Organization* (London: Sage, forthcoming). See also Shoshana Zuboff's discussion of "concentric organizational structure" in *The Age of the Smart Machine* (New York: Basic Books, 1984).

7 Christopher Lasch, *The Culture of Narcissism* (New York: Norton, 1979).

8 Robert N. Bellah et al., *Habits of the Heart* (Berkeley: University of California Press, 1985).

9 Richard Sennett, *The Fall of Public Man* (New York: Knopf, 1977).

10 As the Soviet literary theorist Mikhail Bakhtin writes, "The very being of man (both internal and external) is a *profound communication*. To *be* means to *communicate*." In *Problems of Dostoevsky's Poetics,* trans. Caryl Emerson (Minneapolis: University of Minnesota Press, 1984), p. 287.

11 David Riesman, *Individualism Reconsidered* (New York: Free Press, 1954).

12 Promising in this respect is a new state law in California that holds parents responsible

for unlawful activity on the part of their children. A thirty-seven-year-old mother was recently charged, for example, for "failure to exercise reasonable control," when her seventeen-year-old son was convicted of rape.

13 Catherine Keller, *From a Broken Web* (Boston: Beacon, 1986), p. 248.

14 Paul Ricoeur, *History and Truth*, trans. C. A. Kelbley (Evanston: Northwestern University Press, 1965), p. 276.

15 Barry Schwartz, *The Battle for Human Nature* (New York: Norton, 1986).

16 See Page Smith's *Killing of the Spirit* (New York: Viking, 1990) for an analysis of the way in which social science education marginalizes and suppresses the language of the soul and the emotions.

17 Mikhail Bakhtin, *The Dialogic Imagination* (Austin: University of Texas Press, 1981).

18 An outstanding attempt to reinvigorate historical contributions to moral discourse is Charles Taylor's *Sources of the Self* (Cambridge, Mass.: Harvard University Press, 1989).

19 Helen North, *Sophrosyne* (Ithaca: Cornell University Press, 1966).

20 Roland Barthes is interesting in this context, for in *A Lover's Discourse* (New York: Hill and Wang, 1978), he attempts to resuscitate and enrich a language he feels has become "unreal" and "exiled" from the surrounding languages.

21 Takeo Doi, *The Anatomy of Dependence*, trans. J. Bester (Tokyo: Kodansha, 1973).

22 Robert Jay Lifton, *The Future of Immortality* (New York: Basic Books, 1987).

23 David Miller, *The New Polytheism* (New York: Harper and Row, 1974).

24 Ibid., p. 193.

25 Ibid., p. 78.

26 For relevant discussions, see Roland G. Tharp and Ronald Gallimore, *Rousing Minds to Life* (Cambridge: Cambridge University Press, 1988), and Allan Collins, "Cognitive Apprenticeship: Teaching Students the Craft of Reading, Writing, and Mathematics," in L. B. Resnick, ed., *Cognition and Instruction: Issues and Agendas* (Hillsdale, N.J.: Erlbaum, forthcoming).

27 Illustrative of the emerging orientation are David Cooperrider and Suresh Srivastva, "Appreciative Inquiry into Organization Life," *Research in Organizational Change and Development* 1 (1987): 129–69; Robert Cooper and Gibson Burrell, "Modernism, Postmodernism, and Organizational Analysis: An Introduction," *Organizational Studies* 1 (1988): 91–112; W. Pasmore and F. Friedlander, "An Action Research Program for Increasing Employee Involvement in Problem Solving," *Administrative Science Quarterly* 27 (1982): 343–62. See also Gergen, "Organizational Theory in the Postmodern Era," and Zuboff, *Age of the Smart Machine*.

28 For examples of this orientation see Bill O'Hanlon and James Wilk, *Shifting Contexts* (New York: Guilford, 1987); Lynn Hoffman, "Constructing Realities: An Art of Lenses," *Family Process* 1 (1990); Harold Goolishian, Harlene Anderson, and Lee Winderman, "Problem Determined Systems: Transformation in Family Therapy," *Journal of Strategic and Systemic Therapies* 5 (1986); and Jay S. Efran et al., *Language Structure and Change: Frameworks of Meaning in Psychotherapy* (New York: Norton, 1990).

29 Jean-François Lyotard, *The Postmodern Condition: A Report on Knowledge* (Minneapolis: University of Minnesota Press, 1984), p. 26.

30 See, for example, Richard Bernstein, "The Arts Catch Up with a Society in Disarray," *The New York Times*, 2 Sept. 1990.

31 Beatrix Campbell, "New Times Towns," in Stuart Hall and Martin Jacques, eds., *New Times: The Changing Face of Politics in the 1990s* (London: Lawrence and Wishart, 1989).

32 Alasdair MacIntyre, *Whose Justice? Which Reality?* (Notre Dame: University of Notre Dame Press, 1988).

33 Majid F. Tehranian et al., *Communications Policy for National Development: A Comparative Project* (London: Routledge and Kegan Paul, 1977).

34 *Forbes*, 23 July 1990.

35 Ibid.

36 Herbert I. Schiller, "The Erosion of National Sovereignty by the World Business Sys-

tem," in Michael Traber, ed., *The Myth of the Information Revolution* (London: Sage, 1986). See also David Held, "The Decline of the Nation State," in Hall and Jacques, eds., *New Times: The Changing Face of Politics in the 1990s*.

37 *International Herald Tribune*, 10 Feb. 1990.

38 *Forbes*, 23 July 1990.

39 For further discussions of this movement, see the special issue of *Human Relations* (Fall 1990), edited by David A. Cooperrider and William A. Pasmore.

40 Richard H. Brown, *Society as Text* (Chicago: University of Chicago Press, 1987).

41 Taylor, *Erring*, p. 168.

42 Thomas J. J. Altizer, "Eternal Recurrence and the Kingdom of God," in D. B. Allison, ed., *The New Nietzsche* (Cambridge, Mass.: MIT Press, 1985), p. 245.

43 For a summary of the critique of postmodernism's pluralist emphasis, see Steven Connor, *Postmodernist Culture* (Oxford: Blackwell, 1989).

44 For an analysis of world politics as a confrontation of meaning systems, see Michael J. Shapiro, "Textualizing Global Politics," in James Derian and Michael J. Shapiro, eds., *Interactional/Intertextual Relations* (Lexington, Mass.: Lexington, 1989).

45 As Michael Schrage argues in his recent volume, *Shared Minds: The New Technologies of Collaboration* (New York: Random House, 1990), the technologies of social saturation offer almost unlimited possibilities for global collaboration and negotiation.

46 Ludwig Wittgenstein, *Philosophical Investigations* (New York: Macmillan, 1963), p. 64E.

47 Tracy, *Plurality and Ambiguity*.

48 For discussions of the necessity for disturbing the institutionalized order, see Samuel Weber, *Institution and Interpretation* (Minneapolis: University of Minnesota Press, 1987), and Michel De Certeau, *Heterologies* (Minneapolis: University of Minnesota Press, 1986). See also Kenneth J. Gergen, "Toward Generative Theory," *Journal of Personality and Social Psychology* 36 (1978): 1344–60.

Index

Authoritarianism, 13, 45
Authority, 45, 271n26; erosion of, 16, 123–26, 134, 140; voice of, and power structures, 96
Authorship, 130; and deconstructionism, 109; notion of, 106
Autobiography, 116, 170, 243, 269n9; and personal histories, 161, 164
Automobiles, 50–51, 234
Autonomy, 147, 156, 230, 240; and morality, 168; self-serving, 195
Averill, James, 165
Ayckborn, Alan, 135
Azerrad, Jacob, 43

Back, Kurt W., 39, 140
Bacon, Francis, 29, 141
Badinter, Elisabeth, 12–13
Bailey, Benjamin, 21
Bakhtin, Mikhail, 247
Bali, 8–9
Balwin, Bruce A., 74
Banking, 59, 243
Barnes, William, 22
Barthes, Roland, 106, 135
Bateson, Mary C., 171
Batman (film), 56
Battle for Human Nature (Schwartz), 246
Baudelaire, Charles-Pierre, 20, 27
Baudrillard, Jean, 63, 121–22
Bauhaus school, 31, 33, 37, 263n32
Bear, The (Faulkner), 39
Becker, Boris, 53, 166, 224
Beckett, Samuel, 202, 263n45
Behaviorism, 39, 42–43, 246
Behavior of Organisms, The (Skinner), 39
Bell, Clive, 32
Bellah, Robert, 210, 240
Benjamin, Walter, 231
Bennett, William J., 125–26
Bennis, Warren G., 182, 212
Benny, Jack, 39
Berg, J. H. van den, 12
Berger, Brigitte, 73
Berger, Peter L., 73, 119
Berman, Marshall, 32
Bertolucci, Bernardo, 178
Beuys, Joseph, 113
Bible, 12, 44, 103, 104, 210
Billig, Michael, 72–73
Biology, 87, 91, 94, 118, 246; conception of human behavior, 96; and emotions, 165; and gender, 144, 145

Blacks, 86, 96, 194, 210, 222, 224, 256
Blake, William, 23
Blanchard, Doc, 39
Bloom, Allan, 85, 210
Bluffing, 185
Body, 96–97, 141–45; and emotion, 164, 165; and gender, 143–45; posture of, as calculated, 221–22; and strategic manipulation, 149; and techniques of communication, 203
Bohm, David, 4, 239
Boorstin, Daniel, 119–20
Boswell, James, 11
Botta, Mario, 113–14
Bourdillon, Francis W., 20
Bourgeois culture, 78, 224
Brando, Marlon, 178
Breathing, 34
Britain, 12, 50, 51, 52, 255
British Petroleum (BP), 255
Brooks, Cleanth, 31
Buddhism, 56, 74, 179, 202, 255
Bulimia, 13, 15
Bulletin-board services, 58–59
Burma, 51
Bush, George, 205
Business, 217, 250–51; and electronic mail, and employee relations, 64; and global expansion, 53, 254–55; and individualism, 240; and patriarchy, 96; and the relational self, 158

Cage, John, 34, 117
Canada, 52
Cancer, 120, 194
Cannibal in Manhattan, A (Janowitz), 116
Cape Canaveral, 212
Capitalism, 31
Careers, 11, 183–85, 238
Carnival, 187–93, 238, 256
Carse, James, 197
Carson, Rachel, 233
Cat on a Hot Tin Roof (Williams), 39
CBS Records, 255
Celebrities, 55–56, 71–72, 143–44, 120
Cézanne, Paul, 34
Charisma, 202
Chicago, Judy, 132
Child abuse, 250
Child development, 69, 87, 146, 168
Childhood, 11–13, 163–64
Child rearing, 18–19, 42, 43–44, 179–80; and achievement motivation, 46; and gen-

der, 145; and morality, 83–84, 168; and television, 64
China, 50, 185, 223, 224, 252, 254
Christian Broadcasting Network, 215
Christianity, 20, 72, 167, 223, 229, 231
Christmas letters, 220
Chung, Connie, 71
Churchill, Winston, 39
City of Tomorrow, The (Le Corbusier), 31–32
Civil rights, 208, 221
Clark, Joe, 123
Cleese, John, 136
Closing of the American Mind, The (Bloom), 210
Coding, multiple (double coding), 114–15
Cognition, 40, 46, 99
Columbia Pictures, 255
Comedy, 191–93, 224, 256
Commitment, 15, 17, 27, 174; crisis in, 175–77, 181; and modernism, 146; and romanticism, 227; sincerity of, 221, 225
Communism, 31, 224
Community: cardboard, 211, 214; and celebrities, 56; cementing of, 210–16; collage, 212; face-to-face, 61–64, 66–67, 212, 214–16, 223, 225, 242, 277n12; and quality-of-life ratings, 235; symbolic, 214–15, 242
Compensation, 218–20
CompuServe, 59
Computer(s), 2, 40, 58, 59, 60; music, composition of, 34; personal, 190
Comte, Auguste, 20
Conflict, 252–59
Conformity, social, 44–45
Congress, 238
Constitution, 105, 257
Contemplation (Amberg), 26
Contest of Ladies (Sansom), 149
Cooking, 118
Copernicus, Nicolaus, 90
Cosmos, theory of, 90
Cost-benefit analyses, 217
Courtship, 62–63, 64, 65, 182. *See also* Love; Romance
Creationism, 95
Creativity, 6, 23, 106, 227; and modernism, 228; personality tests for, 46; and romanticism, 229
Crime, 227, 228, 235, 236, 244
Criteria, for the self, 77, 148–49, 150
Cronkite, Walter, 56
Crosby, Bing, 39
Cubism, 36

Cultural studies, 85, 86
Cunningham, Merce, 34
Curry, Tim, 141
Cynicism, 188

Dallas (television program), 132, 182, 272n42
Dance, 31–32, 34, 37
Dante, 24, 125
Darwin, Charles, 29, 31, 95, 228
Databases, 58, 59
Davis, Natalie Zemon, 116
DDT, 233
Dean, John, 185
Death, 38, 61, 62, 239; of children, 12; intentional, 92–93; sadness at, 158. *See also* Grief
Death of a Salesman (Miller), 39
Deaver, Michael, 185, 206
Decision making, 30, 99, 229; moral, 168, 241; and postmodernism, 238, power of, 95; rationality and, 77–80, 199, 202; and the stock market, 243; voluntary, 244
Declaration of Independence, the, 210
Deconstruction, 106–10, 113, 121, 124, 194; full-scale, undesirability of, 195, 196
Deferring, process of, 108, 109
Deleuze, Gilles, 218
Democracy, 5–6, 110; and the concept of the individual voter, 240; definition of, 107–8; and modernism, 47; and other forms of social organization, 107, 252–53; and the powers of reason and observation, 20, 31
Depression, 13, 15, 42, 94; personality tests for, 46, and sympathy, 166
Derrida, Jacques, 107, 109
Descartes, René, 20, 99, 160, 242
Desire, 27, 74–75, 97, 181, 190; interpretation of, 104, 105
Dewey, John, 39
Diaries, 22, 23–24
Dickens, Charles, 7
Dillinger, John, 39
Disney World, 2
Doesburg, Theo van, 35
Dollard, John, 41, 164
Dow Jones, 59
Drama, 149–50, 161, 178, 222, 224; and political protests, 186; of selfhood, 157
Dreams, 27
Drugs, 181, 183, 194, 228, 235, 236
Dubuffet, Jean, 34

East European nations, 200
Eating disorders, 13, 15, 181
Eco, Umberto, 225
Ecology, 132, 233–35, 237, 256, 270n24, 271n26
Edelman, Murray, 121
Education, 5–6, 33, 77–78, 103, 124; and authority, challenges to, 124, 125–26; Bloom on, 210; conflict regarding, 258; criticism of, and self-renewal, 199; family and, 236; and functional conceptions of careers, 183, 184–85; Montaigne on, 12; and personal history, 161; and postmodernism, 250; and the powers of reason and observation, 20; and power structures, 95, 96; and religion, 252. *See also* Teachers
Edwards Personality Preference Inventory (EPPI), 46
Ego, 40
Ehrenreich, Barbara, 235
Einstein, Albert, 39
Eldridge, Richard, 262n22
Electronic mail, 58–59, 60, 64
Eliot, T. S., 78, 103, 125, 147, 205
Emerson, Ralph Waldo, 125
Emotion, 7, 94, 110, 199, 208, 242; and "cultural performance," 165–66; and the "deep interior," 20, 25; and the essence of mind, 109; experience of, in different cultures, 9–10, 165; genetic basis for, 12; labeling of, 165; Lutz on, 8; and the metaphor of the machine, 40–41; power of, 13; and relatedness, 160, 164–66, 170; and romanticism, 20–21, 25, 164; and technology, 66–68; true, and social saturation, 148

Empiricism, 29, 31, 93
England. *See* Britain
Enlightenment, 20, 21, 23, 25, 99, 227, 267n15; and individualism, 239–40; return of, 29–30
Equality, 107
Erikson, Erik, 41, 133
Eros, 167
Ersatz being, 182–87, 212
Ersatz social movement, 185–86
Essence(s), 6, 7, 32–36, 38, 112; democracy as an existing, 107–8; doubt in, 207; emotions as natural, 165; in language, 108, 109; and modern art, 113; and modernism, 32–36, 146, 147; and object and subject, distinction between, 103, 106–7; and personality tests, 46–47; and postmodernism, 130, 139, 146, 150, 170; and psychology, 41
Ethics, 30, 96. *See also* Morality
Ethiopia, 186
Ethnicity, 178, 183, 200, 251–52
Ethnocentrism, 45
Ethnomethodology, 92–93
Euripides, 7
Evidence, 91
Evolutionary theory, 95, 246

Facts, 123; and fiction, 118, 138; study of, 91–92, 94
Fago, 165
Fall of Public Man, The (Sennett), 241
Family, 6, 8, 17, 42, 271n26; concerns of, vs. the concerns of the self, 239; and education, 236; and fractional relationships, 179–80; and the microwave relationship, 65–66; and the media, 224; and morality, 166; and patriarchy, 96; and personal histories, 163–64; and personality production, 179; and relatedness, 168; and romanticism, 27, 146; therapists, 126; and transportation technology, 211. *See also* Childhood; Child rearing
Fantasy, 64, 67, 69; and careers, 184; and celebrities, 143
Farrow, Mia, 136–37
Fascination, 218–20
Fascism, 31
Fashion, 154–55, 273n17, 273n18
Faulkner, William, 39
Federal Aviation Administration (FAA), 54
Feininger, Lyonel, 36
Femininity, 143–45, 146; and fashion, 154–55; and morality, 168–69, 170
Feminism, 38n, 96, 104–5, 168–69, 185, 195–96; Bloom on, 210; and gender, 145; and modernism, waning of, 208
Fertilizer, 234–35
Feyerabend, Paul, 90, 126, 128
Fiction, 116, 118, 138
Film. *See* Motion pictures
Fish, Stanley, 104
Fitzgerald, F. Scott, 147
Fletcher, Joseph, 206
Ford Foundation, 85
Foreign languages, 12
Foreign policy, 59

Form, and architecture, 113, 115
Foucault, Michel, 95, 106
France, 12, 50
Fraser, David, 127
Freedom, 74–75, 107, 208, 242
Freud, Sigmund, 27, 41–42, 262n23, 263n45; rationality in, 40; repression in, 40, 42
Friedrich, Casper David, 25
Friendships, 6, 62, 75, 76; and career advancement, 238; among children, 236; as "connections," 246; definition of, 174–75; and emphasis on individuality, 9; and fractional relationships, 181–82; genuine, 175; and the media, 224; and the pastiche personality, 150; romantic view of, 21–22, 27, 240; and sincerity, 219–20, 225
Fromm, Erich, 42
Frustration and Aggression (Dollard), 164
Future, 16, 36, 173, 199; acceleration of, 62; and modernism, 227; and postmodernism, 226–59; sense of, in literature, 129; wisdom for, and history, 109. *See also* Time

Gablick, Suzi, 130
Gadamer, Hans-Georg, 104, 197, 268n25
Galileo, 90, 91
Games, 200, 224, 235–36, 247; finite, 197–98; "serious," 17, 159, 197–98
Gandhi, Mahatma, 39
Garfinkel, Harold, 92
Gates, Henry Louis, Jr., 125
Gaulle, Charles de, 39, 206
Gaylin, Willart, 164
Geertz, Clifford, 8, 9, 113, 226
Gender, 143–45, 170, 178, 272n3; and morality, 168
Genetics, 12, 31, 144
Genius, 23–24, 27, 41, 123, 202, 227
Genre, 113, 157–58, 161–62
Gergen, Mary, 71
Germany, 45–46, 52
Ghosts, 71, 72, 77, 173
Gilligan, Carol, 168
Glass, Philip, 117
God, 20, 22, 106, 231, 256, 257; and the soul, 25–26
Goethe, Johann Wolfgang von, 22, 24
Goffman, Erving, 149, 185
Goodman, Sidney, 241

Government, 30, 208, 240; and modernism, 32; officials, 123; and patriarchy, 96; and satellites, 59. *See also* Politics
Graham, Martha, 34
Graves, Robert, 29
Great Depression, 52
Greeks, 12, 248
Greenberg, Clement, 34
Grief, 22, 24, 155, 158, 165, 217, 227
Grooms, Red, 191
Groups, 44, 242
Guattari, Felix, 218
Guerin, Maurice de, 26
Guilt, 77, 150, 151, 245

Habermas, Jürgen, 111, 124
Habits of the Heart (Bellah), 240
Hanson, Duane, 191, 192
Hanson, Norbert, 91–92
Harcourt Brace Jovanovich, 212
Hawksworth, Mary, 94
Hebdige, Dick, 134
Hebrides, 11
Heimel, Cynthia, 56
Heisenberg, Werner, 89
Hemingway, Ernest, 35–36, 39, 178
Heredity, 12, 31, 144
Hesse, Herman, 85
Heteroglossia, 247
Heterosexuality, 144, 146
Highways, 51, 234
Hill Street Blues (TV program), 132
Hinckley, John, 56
Hispanics, 86, 96
History, 10–13, 82, 145, 187; and architecture, 113; and cultural restoration, 206; "monumental," Nietzsche on, 23; personal, and relatedness, 160, 161–66; study of, 83; writing of, 108–9, 116, 122
Hitler, Adolf, 39, 202–3
Hobbes, Thomas, 20
Hochschild, Arlie, 148
Hollis, Martin, 74
Holocaust, 121, 194
Homeownership, 18–19
Homosexuality, 42, 144, 146, 186, 208
Hope, Bob, 39
Hormones, 96–97
Horney, Karen, 40, 42, 217
Housing, 237
Hudson, Rock, 143
Hull, Clark, 39
Humanization, 204–5

Human nature, 4, 19, 25–26, 38n, 40, 208; and mothers' love for their children, 12
Human rights. *See* Rights
Hume, David, 20, 133
Humphrey, Doris, 34

Id, 42
Ideology, 16, 29, 96, 98; and art history, 125; and bias, 112; individualistic, 240–41; and language, 228; written works as expressions of, 126
Ifaluk, 165
Illness, 74, 120, 122
Ilongot, 10
Image: A Guide to Pseudo-Events in America, The (Boorstin), 119–20
Imagination, 22–23, 84
Income, personal, 237
Independent, 2
India, 46, 52
Individuality, 8–9, 41–47, 72; historical perspective on, 11, 97–98; manufacture of, 41–44; and modernism, 231; and relational realities, 239–45; and single minds, idea of, 106; and smoking, 78. *See also* Self
Information services, 58
Inoculation theory, 45
Inspiration, 7, 15, 27, 41, 82, 103, 123, 227, 229; and the "deep interior," 24; and leadership, 202; and modernism, 228
Integrity, 118, 140–41, 245
Intensity, 66–68, 78
Intentions, 103–4, 105, 110, 140, 241; and modernism, 228; and morality, 167
Intimacy, 17, 63, 67, 217; committed, and freedom, 242; conflict regarding, 258; crisis in, 175–77, 181; sexual, 181, 240; and "true knowledge," 100
Intimate Strangers (Schickel), 56
Iran, 59
Irony, 134, 137, 138, 188
Isolation, 241, 243
Italy, 50

Jackson, Michael, 141
Jameson, Frederic, 205
Janowitz, Tama, 116
Japan, 50, 78
Jealousy, 135
Jencks, Charles, 130

Jesus, 56, 71, 118
Johnson, Philip, 114
Journalism. *See* News media
Joy, 19, 24
Joyce, Ed, 120–21
Joyce, James, 129, 263n45
Judicial system, 95, 123, 240, 243, 244
Justice, 77, 257

Kandinsky, Wassily, 34, 36
Kaplan, E. Ann, 133
Kauffman, Linda, 143
Keats, John, 21, 23
Keller, Catherine, 245
Kellner, Hansfried, 73
Kelly, George, 40–41, 264n52, 264n51
Kennedy, Edward, 185
Kennedy, John F., 185
Kessler, Suzanne, 144
King, Vincent, 33
Kingston, Maxine Hong, 252
Klee, Paul, 34
Kleptomania, 13
Klinger, Eric, 71
Knowledge, 95–103; conception of, revolution regarding, 89–90; conscious, 21; and demagoguery, 95–98; and *liget*, 10; and modernism, 86–87, 91–92, 99, 111–12; "problems of," 101–2; "reliable," 8; and the true self, 39. *See also* Objectivity; Reason; Truth
Kohlberg, Lawrence, 168
Kohut, Heinz, 40
Kosinski, Jerzy, 242
Kozinn, Allan, 112
Kristeva, Julia, 196
Kuhn, Thomas, 90, 91, 92, 267n7
Kundera, Milan, 111, 129, 132, 278n1

Laing, R. D., 89
Language, 12, 94, 124, 128, 257; of architecture, 114–15; bounds of, 137; and deconstructionism, 106–10 (see also Deconstruction); and the expansion of postmodern discourse, 230, 250; and "freeing the signifiers," 157–58, 259; games, 102, 105; and heteroglossia, 247; and ideology, 228; loss of truth in, 186–87; of morality, 247–48; public, and inner states, 105; and relatedness, 157, 160–70, 227; of self-con-

struction, 157; and understanding, 81–82
Lasch, Christopher, 204, 240
Last Year at Marienbad (film), 129
Latour, Bruno, 93, 128
Laval, Pierre, 39
Law, 96, 103, 124, 257, 258; legal procedures, 5; legal studies, 111, 124
Lawson, Hilary, 134
Leadership, 46, 216; nostalgia for, 201–6; and the relational self, 158; and romanticism, 225, 227; and "superior knowers," 250–51
Learned Helplessness (Seligman), 42
Learning, "knowing how" as a form of, 70–71, 80
Le Corbusier, 31–32, 37, 115–16
Léger, Fernand, 36, 37
L'Enclose, Ninon de, 21
Lendl, Ivan, 166
Lennon, John, 56
Lethaby, W. R., 31
Letterman, David, 56, 136
Library of Congress, 58
Lichtenstein, Roy, 191
Lifton, Robert Jay, 226, 248
Liget, 10
Lightfoot, Sara L., 69
Literary studies, 81, 96, 263n45; "critique of the canon" in, 85; and deconstruction, 106–110, 113 (see also Deconstruction); and modernism, 31, 106–7. *See also* Language; specific authors
Live Aid concert (1986), 186
Localism, 252
Locke, John, 20
Logic, 29, 30, 189
Logocentrism, 107
London Times, 120
Lonely Crowd (Riesman), 44
Long Day's Journey into Night (O'Neill), 39
Lorenz, Konrad, 164
Louis, Joe, 39
Love, 4–5, 8, 10, 75–76, 165–66, 199; biological bases for, Schachter on, 165; and the construction of self, 146; as dangerous, 21; and the friendly-lover relationship, 65, 67, 68; and language, 227, 229; and modernism, 175–76; and motherhood, 12–14; and postmodern consciousness, 122; proof of, 220; and the relational self, 158; and romanticism, 20–22, 27, 65, 175–76; as a standard for life decisions, 207; value of, 77. *See also* Courtship; Emotion; Romance
Loyalty, 19, 146

Luckmann, Thomas, 119
Luhmann, Niklas, 66
Lutz, Catherine, 8, 165
Lying, 169
Lyons, John, 11, 261n11
Lyotard, Jean-François, 87–88, 189, 251

Ma'ari, Sami, 155
McClelland, David, 46
McDougall, Duncan, 38
McFarlane, Richard, 185
McGinniss, Joe, 151
McGuire, William, 45
Machine, metaphor of, 16, 30, 36–38, 42–44, 118, 123–24, 140, 149, 227; and careers, 184; and emotion, 40–41; and the family, 179–80; and sincerity, lack of, 217
MacIntyre, Alasdair, 166, 211, 253
McKenna, Wendy, 144
Mal du siècle (sickness of the century), 24
Malevich, Kazimir, 36
Man, Paul de, 32, 161
Managers, 64
Manet, Édouard, 34
Maps, 106–7, 187
March, J. G., 43
Marinetti, Filippo, 36
Markus, Hazel, 72
Marriage, 6, 18–19, 57, 66; arranged, 78; and commitment, 174 (see also Commitment); and ersatz being, 183; and friendship, bonds of, comparison of, 175; and "geographic propinquity," 177; hostility and, 250; and personality tests, 47; and romanticism, 27, 240, and telephones, 64; for "true love," 65, 78. *See also* Courtship; Intimacy; Love; Romance
Martin, Emily, 96–97
Marxism, 105, 261n11
Masculinity, 10, 143–45, 146, 155, 170
Mason, Bobbie Ann, 174
Mass media. *See* Media; Motion pictures; News media; Radio; Television
Mass production, 28, 50–51
Mathematics, 30
Mauss, Marcel, 139
Meaning, 103, 105, 129, 157; and individualism, 243; in language, and relatedness, 167; maze of, and mazing grace, 256
Media, 55–56, 119, 148; and politics, 121, 122, 151, 158, 203–6; and sincerity, 221–22, 224; and social movements, 186. *See*

Postmodernism, 7, 15–17; and architecture, 113–16, 118, 130, 138, 191, 251; and art, 111, 113, 130–32, 138; and decision making, 238; discourse of, and language, 230, 250; and education, 250; emergence of, 47, 111–38; and essences, 130, 139, 146, 150, 170; and the future, 226–59; and inner resources, 207–8; life and, a collage of, 171–98; and love, 122; and morality, 230, 253; and motion pictures, 120, 122; and music, 138; and narrative form, 132; and the news media, 111, 138; and politics, 121, 122, 123, 131, 138; and the populated self, 49, 69, 80; and rationality, 126–34; and self as relationship, 139–69, 172, 173; and television, 122, 132–33, 136; and the validity of romantic and modern realities, 19. *See also* Pluralism

Power structures, 259; distribution of, and claims to truth, 95; and education, 95, 96; and gender, 145; and the presidency, 158

Pre-Raphaelites, 25

Pregression, 231–39

Presidency, 151, 158, 244; and the nostalgia for leadership, 202, 205

Pretense, use of the term, 187

Prime Times and Bad Times (Joyce), 120–21

Prince, Bart, 114

Principia Ethica (Moore), 208

Principles of Behavior (Hull), 39

Printing equipment, 58, 60

Progress, 17, 30–32, 90, 181, 229, 231–39

Progressive regression, 233–39

Pronouns, 110

Propaganda, 45, 120

Protean lifestyle, 248

Proust, Marcel, 205, 263n45

Psychiatry, 126; and personal histories, 163–64; and problems of knowledge, 101–2

Psychology, 13, 30, 81, 83; behaviorist theory in, 246; and child rearing, 180; and the deterioration of authority, 126; and disciplinary contraints, 112–13; ego, 40; "environmentalist," 42, 43–44; and essences, 112; and the image of the machine, 40; and moral behavior, theory of, 167–68; and the pastiche personality, 151–52; reliance upon, 227; Sampson on, 98; scientific, 38; specialties within the field of, 87; and the true self, 39–40. *See also* Psychotherapy

Psychopathology, 13

Psychotherapy, 41, 95, 251; amenability to, and personality tests, 46–47; and the relational self, 158. *See also* Psychology

Ptolemy, 90

Publishing industry, 52–53, 54

Puritanism, 21

Purple Rose of Cairo, The (film), 136

Purposive Behavior in Animals and Men (Tolman), 39

Race, 145, 251–52

Radio, 51, 60; and satellites, 59; and self-multiplication, 55; and social movements, 221

Railroad, 50, 61

Ransom, John C., 31

Rationality, 156, 199; and decision making, 77–80, 199, 202; and the foundations for knowledge, 89; and the meanings placed on cultural events, 244; and morality, 168; and postmodernism, 126–34; in "recession," 77–80. *See also* Reason

Rauschenberg, Robert, 130–31

Reagan, Ronald, 56, 125

Realism, 73

Reality, 189; breakdown of, and MTV, 133; and myth, 25; social construction of, 16, 119–22

Realpolitik, 28

Reason, 5, 7, 10, 94, 242; "agents" of, human beings as, 19, 38–39, 111–12, 140, 197; capacity for, and childhood, 11; and the "deep interior," 20, 22, 123; distorted, Freud on, 27; and emotion, 164; and the essence of mind, 6, 7, 109; growing disregard of, 16–17; infinite regress of, 207; and modernism, 6, 31, 32, 36, 38–39, 41, 82, 99, 111–12, 128, 130, 202, 208, 229, 230, 240; and morality, 25, 208; and music, 25; and nature, 23; and romanticism, 20, 22, 23–24, 25, 29, 246; and the true self, 40; and valued traditions, 203. *See also* Rationality

Reckoning, 226–59

Reflexivity, 134, 135–36, 137–38, 196, 272n47

Regionalism, 251

Reid, Thomas, 133

Relationships. *See* Courtship; Family; Friendship; Intimacy; Love; Marriage; Romance

Religion, 6, 81, 145, 227, 236, 238; and education, 252; and individuality, 11; and patriarchy, 96; and romanticism, 25–26. *See also* Bible; Buddhism; Christianity; Religious figures; Spirituality

Religious figures, 56, 71–72

Renoir, Pierre Auguste, 34

Repression, 13, 40, 42, 164

Résumés, 161, 184–85

Retrenchment, 200, 201–16, 218

Return of Martin Guerre, The (film), 116

Revolution, 109

Rhetorical study, 108–9

Ricoeur, Paul, 246

Riesman, David, 44, 151, 242

Rights, 8, 200, 202, 240, 258

Riley, Terry, 117

Robbe-Grillet, Alain, 129

Rocking Around the Clock (Kaplan), 133

Rogers, Carl, 41, 42

Rogers, Will, 39

Rohe, Mies van der, 33

Role playing, 150

Romance: and collage communities, 212–13; and the construction of self, 146; and ersatz being, 182, 183; and the media, 224. *See also* Courtship; Love

Romanticism, 6–8, 15–16, 18–47, 111, 118, 156, 173, 226–30, 254; and authentic communication, 203; and authority, 123, 124, 126; and careers, 183; and education, 126; and inner resources, 207–10; and love, 20–22, 27, 85, 175–76, and morality, 22, 25, 27, 42, 67, 82, 123, 208–9, 228, 229, 257; and the populated self, 69, 80; and the presence of the absent, 24; and the reality of the deep interior, 20–27, 38–39, 123, 172, 208, 217, 227, 229 (see also Self, interior of); and social upheaval, 208, 210; and totalizing discourse, 245–52; traditions of speech deriving from, 187; waning of, 28, 146, 174, 194, 202, 226–27

Roosevelt, Franklin D., 39

Roosevelt, Theodore, 39

Rorty, Richard, 102, 193, 278n1

Rosaldo, Michelle, 10

Rosenblatt, Paul, 72

Rousseau, Jean-Jacques, 125

Rubens, Peter Paul, 130

Ruskin, John, 37

Russell, Bertrand, 30

Russia. *See* Soviet Union

Ryder, Robert, 123

Sadomasochism, 13

Salant, Walter, 120

Sampson, Edward, 98

Sansom, William, 149

Satellites, 59, 60

Satire, 193, 194

Schachter, Stanley, 165

Schaeffer, Rebecca, 56

Schickel, Richard, 56

Schiller, Friedrich, 21–22, 23

Schiller, Herbert I., 49

Schlemmer, Oskar, 36

Schneider, Maria, 178

Scholastic Aptitude Test (SAT), 46, 47

Schönberg, Arnold, 31

Schopenhauer, Arthur, 27

Schwartz, Barry, 246

Schweitzer, Albert, 39

Science, 16, 32–33, 43, 84, 87, 111; and architecture, 37; and challenges to authority, 123, 124; and critical scrutiny from peers, 123–24; and the Enlightenment, 29–30 (see also Enlightenment); and modernism, 32, 41, 128–29, 228; natural, 30, 96–97; and patriarchy, 96; worldview of, 38. *See also* Biology; Physics

Self, 3–4, 8–9, 13–14, 154; construction of, 145–60, 196, 207; criteria for, 77, 148–49, 150; -esteem, 13, 46, 72, 236; and fractional relationships, 178–82, 219, 225; and the pastiche personality, 147, 150–55, 156, 170; populated, 48–80, 82–85, 176, 177, 182; as process, 154; reconstruction of, as relationship, 139, 140, 146–69; relational, 147, 156–60, 172, 173–74, 239–45, 229; and sense of continuity, 109, 133; and substance and style, boundary between, 155; "substitutions" of, 141–42; as a strategic manipulator, 17, 147, 149–50, 156. *See also* Individuality; Personality; Self, interior of; Self, other and; Self, true

Self, interior of: and modernism, 228; and the relational self, emergence of, 156; and reason, 20, 22, 123; and romanticism, 20–27, 38–39, 123, 172, 208, 217, 227, 229

Self, other and, 42, 174, 254, 257; and commitment and intimacy, crisis in, 176–77, 181; and fragments of the other, 172–73

Self, true, 38–41, 82, 89, 146, 150–51; and authentic communication, 203–4, 205; disappearance of, and fractional relationships, 178; and intimacy and commitment, 177; and sincerity, 217, 218, 219. *See also* Truth

Seligman, Martin, 42
Selling of the President 1968, The (McGinniss), 151
Sennett, Richard, 241
Sensory awareness, 24
Seurat, Georges, 34
Sexism, 168, 193, 210
Sexuality, 27, 144–45, 176, 207, 240; and addiction, 15; and fractional relationships, 181
Shadowfax, 118
Shadow realities, 72
Shakespeare, William, 7, 58, 103, 104, 125
Sham, use of the term, 187
Shelley, Percy Bysshe, 20, 21, 25
Sherman, Cindy, 152
Sherman, Tom, 88
Shotter, John, 155
Signac, Paul, 34
Signifiers, 257, 259
Simmel, Georg, 18
Simon, Herbert, 43
Simulation, 225
Sincerity, 199–225, 240; half-life of, 216 25; and modernism, 228; and romanticism, 230
Skepticism, 73
Skinner, B. F., 39
Slater, Philip E., 182, 212
Sloterdijk, Peter, 187
Smallpox, 156
Smith, Alex, 221
Smoking, 78
Snyder, Mark, 151
Socialization, 69, 167, 227–28
Social movements, 185–86, 210, 218, 221–22
Sontag, Susan, 120
Sophrosyne, concept of, 248
Soul, 4, 24, 172, 176, 217, 227; and God, 15–26; immortality of, 22, 26; and love, 21, 27; McDougall's experiment regarding, 38; and the metaphor of the machine, 37, 38; and morality, 25; and romanticism, 6, 20, 21, 22, 24, 25, 38; truths of, 210
Soviet Union, 52, 144, 155, 200, 224, 252; and phone systems, 60; publishing industry in, 52; railroad in, 50
"Space race," 237
Spence, Donald, 163
Spinoza, Baruch, 20
Spirituality, 23, 27, 87, 100, 112, 118, 146; multiple forms of, 249; and self-renewal, 199, 200. *See also* Religion

Spontaneity, 77, 224
Sports, 57, 144, 196–97, 204, 215, 235–36; and individualism, 240
Stanford-Binet intelligence test, 46
Stereotypes, 126, 222
Stockhausen, Karlheinz, 34
Stock market, 243–44
Stoppard, Tom, 135
Storytelling, 17, 109, 129
Strategic manipulation, 17, 147, 149–50, 156
Stravinsky, Igor, 31
Stress, 13, 46
Strong Vocational Interest Test, 46
Style, 154–55
Subcultures, 221, 222
Subjectivity, 89, 99–110
Sufferings of Young Werther, The (Goethe), 22
Suicide, 22, 24, 92–93, 164, 228
Suleiman, Susan, 103
Sullivan, Harry S., 40
Sullivan, Louis, 33
Sun Also Rises, The (Hemingway), 35–36
Superficiality, 150, 151, 154–55, 230
Superiority, 15, 188, 189
Superstition, 29
Supreme Court, 103, 105, 186; and challenges to authority, 124
Surveillance, informal, 66–67
Sweden, 50
Symbolism, 25

Tavris, Carol, 144
Taylor, Frederick, 43
Taylor, Mark, 256
Teachers, 2, 75, 76, 183, 250. *See also* Education
Technology, 16–17, 29, 49–60, 69, 85–87, 172–75, 228; and the abortion issue, 143; and "bending the life-forms," 63–66; and the emotional level of relationships, 66–68; and fractional relationships, 178–79; high-tech, 49, 53–61; as inescapable, 200, 207; low-tech, 49–50; and multiphrenia, 73–74; and political leadership, 203; and progress, 232; and social movements, 185–86, 221. *See also* specific forms
"Tekonym," 9

Telegraph, 58
Telephone, 3, 16, 51; digital, 60; and relationships, 64; and satellites, 59; teleconference services, 58, 59
Television, 52, 54–57, 60, 63–64; channels, speed of flipping, 173; and communities, 215; and the family, 65; and linear plots, breakdown of, 132; and multidramas, 132; music (MTV), 111, 132–33; and postmodernism, 122, 132–33, 136; and the relational self, 158–60; romance on, depictions of, 182; and satellites, 59; and self-reflexivity, 136; and social movements, 221; UHF channels, 239
Terrorism, 186, 221
Tests, 46–47, 90
Textuality, 108
Thailand, 222–23
Theater, 135–36
Theology, 30, 106, 156
Thurow, Lester, 57
Tiananmen Square, 185, 223, 224
Time, 1–2, 74, 161; and distance, and relationships, 62, sense of, in literature, 129. *See also* Future; History; Past
Tolman, Edward, 39
Totalitarianism, 107, 108, 252–53
Tourism, 2, 120, 222
Tracy, David, 259
Transnational organizations, 254
Transsexualism, 181, 144
Tribalism, 251–52
Trilling, Lionel, 199
Trust, 6, 47, 154, 228
Truth, 8, 13, 38–41, 187–89, 228, 246; belief in, as a mainstay of Western culture, 199; claims to, and communities, 134; as a construction of the moment, 16; crisis regarding, in academia, 81–110; and fiction, 116–17; and lying, 169; and metaphors, 223; modernist conception of a single, 239; and multiple voices, 16, 17, 111, 229–30; and mystery stories, 39; object of, 32–33; and objectivity, 81–110, 111–12; and pluralism, 207; and positivism, 36; and psychiatry, 164; and the quest for an essence, 32–33; and reality, social construction of, 119–22; and reason, 20; and relatedness, 246, 249; and self-reflection, ironies of, 134, 137, 138; of the soul, 210; and totalizing discourses, 252. *See also* Self, true
Turner, J. M. W., 24
Tyler, Stephen, 189–90, 194, 195

Übermensch, 23
Ulysses (Joyce), 129
Unconscious, 27, 167, 207
USA Today, 2, 127
U.S. News and World Report, 57
Utopia, 36, 232

Valéry, Paul, 36
Value, 15, 20, 45, 74–77, 86, 202, 208–11; and bias, 112; and claims to truth, 134; and individualism, 97–98; moral, 27; and postmodernism, 230; and romanticism, 208, 210, 227; and social groups, 119; traditional sense of, 206, 207, 210; written works as expressions of, 126
Velázquez, Diego, 130
Venturi, Robert, 115, 116
Verdi, Giuseppe, 25, 254
Videocassette recorders (VCRs), 52, 55–57
Videotape, 57, 60, 74, 181
Vietnam war, 208
Voltaire, 20

Wagner, Jane, 245
Wagner, Richard, 25, 34, 254
Walter, Regine, 159
Warhol, Andy, 119
Watkins, Mary, 68, 71
Watson, J. B., 42–43
Wayne, John, 143
Wechsler intelligence test, 46
Wells, H. G., 30
Wells, Patricia, 117
White, Hayden, 109, 161
Whitman, Walt, 71
Who Framed Roger Rabbit? (film), 141
Wigley, Mark, 113
Williams, Tennessee, 39
Willis, Bruce, 136
Wilson, Robert, 117
Wisdom, 86, 96, 124
Wittgenstein, Ludwig, 5, 102, 242, 258
Women: body of, 96–97; experience of, and art, 132
Women's studies, 81, 85, 86
Woolgar, Stephen, 93
Wordsworth, William, 20, 262n22
Work addiction, 15
World Health Organization, 256

Permissions

We are grateful to the following for the permission to print their artwork in this book: Lee Bell, for the cartoon on p. 135; Gunter Krammer, Tom Sherman, Josef Astor, Alan Weintraub, Lawrence S. Williams, and Steven Goldblatt, for their photographs; and Regine Walter, for the painting on p. 159. Material from *United States* by Laurie Anderson reprinted by permission of HarperCollins Publishers, Inc. Figures from *Advances in Experimental Social Psychology*, vol. 21, reprinted by permission of the Academic Press. Figure from *Patterns of Discovery* by Norwood Russell Hanson reprinted by permission of Cambridge University Press. Cartoon by Glenn Baxter from *The Impending Gleam* reprinted by permission of Jonathan Cape, Ltd. Cartoon by Michael Leunig from *The Penguin Leunig* reprinted by permission of Penguin Books Australia, Ltd. Cartoon on p. 79 © 1987 by Mark Alan Stamaty, reprinted by permission. Cartoon on p. 209 copyright © 1990 by the New York Times Company, reprinted by permission. *Playboy* cover illustration copyright © 1988 *Playboy*, used by permission. *The Razorback Bunch* by Robert Rauschenberg reprinted by permission of Universal Limited Art Editions. The following works are reprinted with the permission of the Philadelphia Museum of Art: Sidney Goodman, *Figures in a Landscape*, purchased through the Adele Haas Turner and Beatrice Pastorius Turner Fund; Gilbert and George photograph, the gift of Mr. and Mrs. David N. Pincus; Wilhelm Amberg, *Contemplation*, from the Wilstach Collection; Theo van Doesburg, *Composition*, from the A. E. Gallatin Collection; and Cindy Sherman photograph, purchased through the Alice Newton Osborn Fund. Cindy Sherman photograph "b" reprinted by permission of the Whitney Museum of American Art. Fernand Léger, *Three Women*, reprinted by permission of the Museum of Modern Art. Duane Hanson, *Security Guard*, reprinted by permission of ACA Galleries, New York.